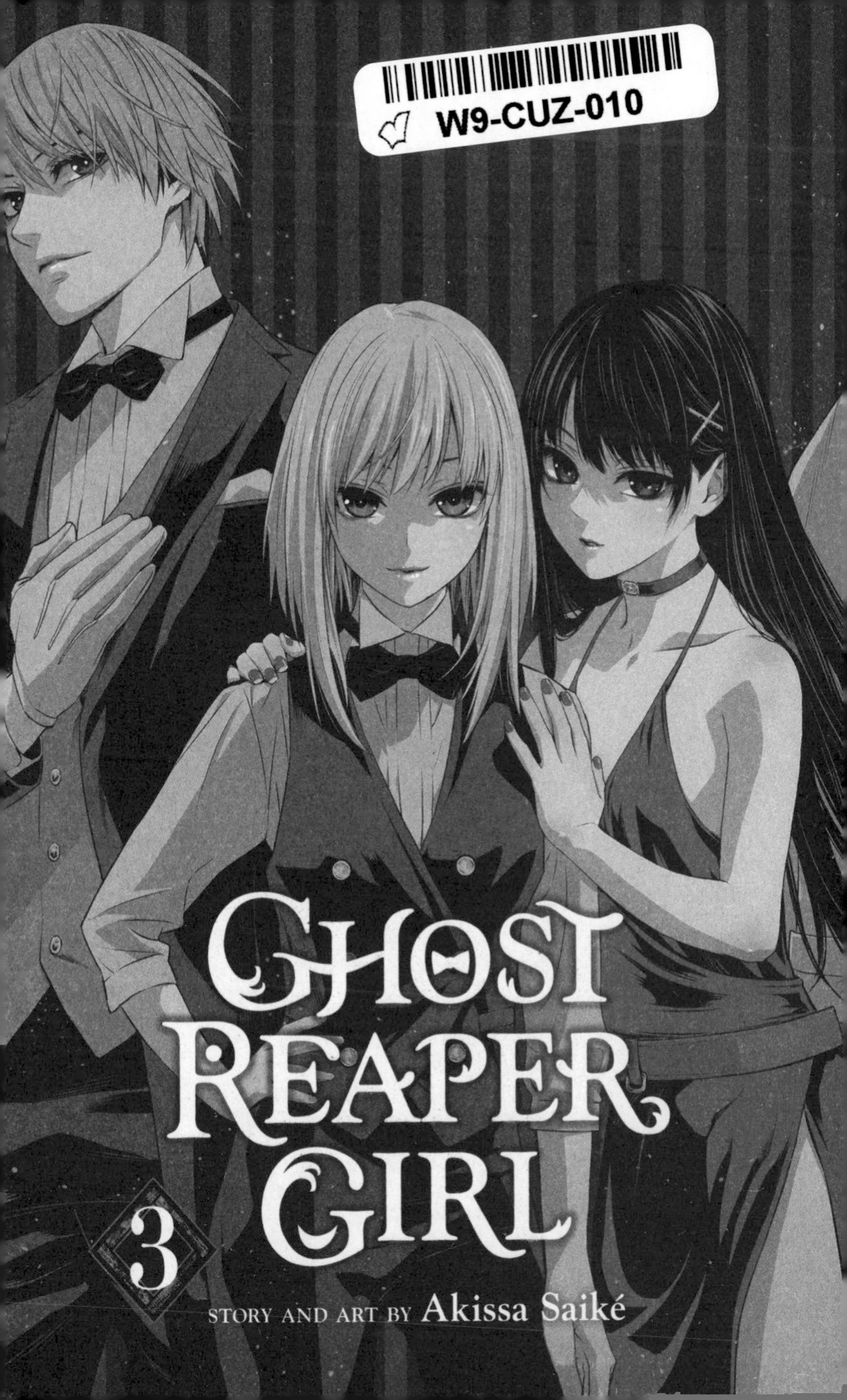

W9-CUZ-010
GHOST
REAPER
GIRL
3
STORY AND ART BY Akissa Saiké

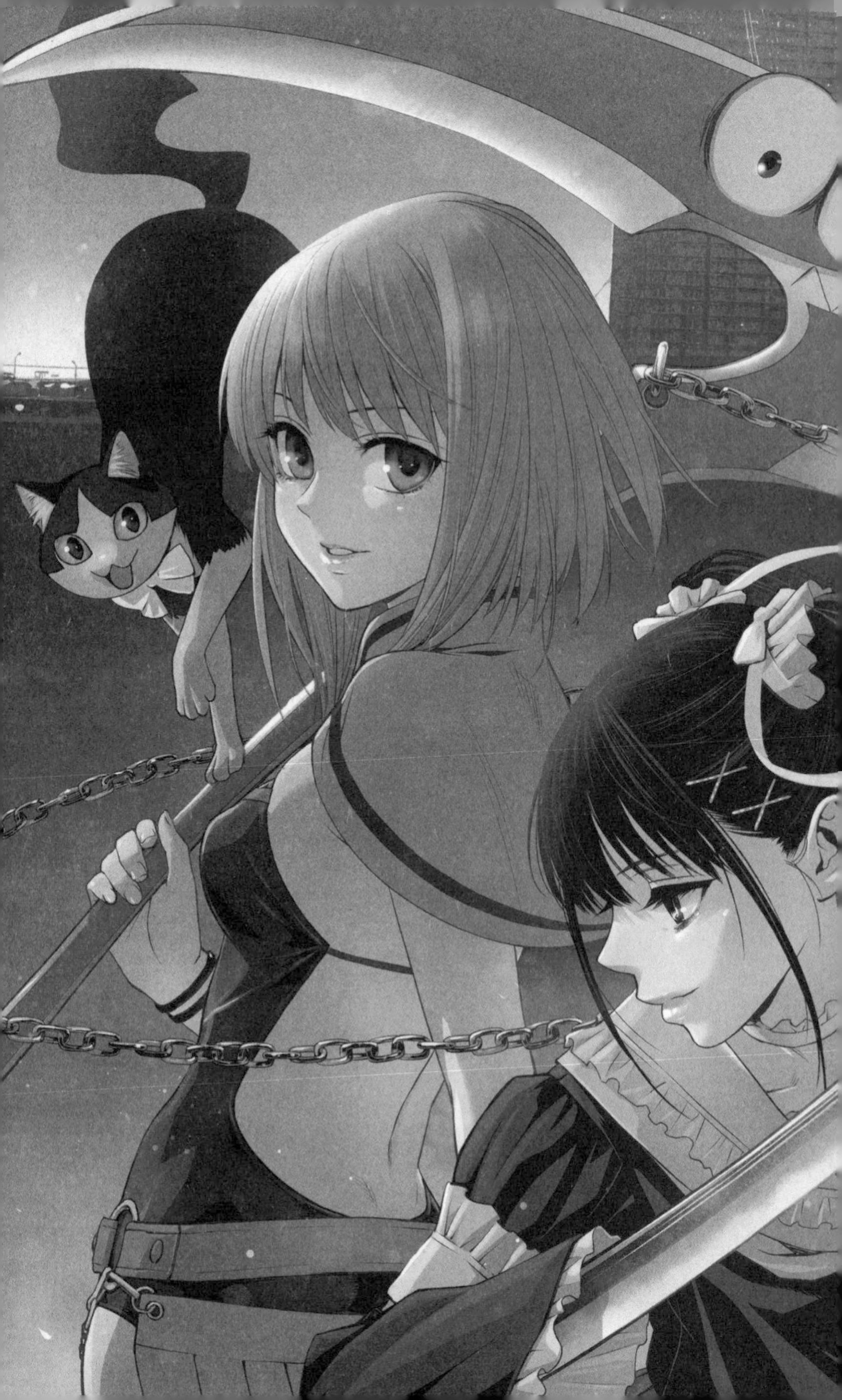

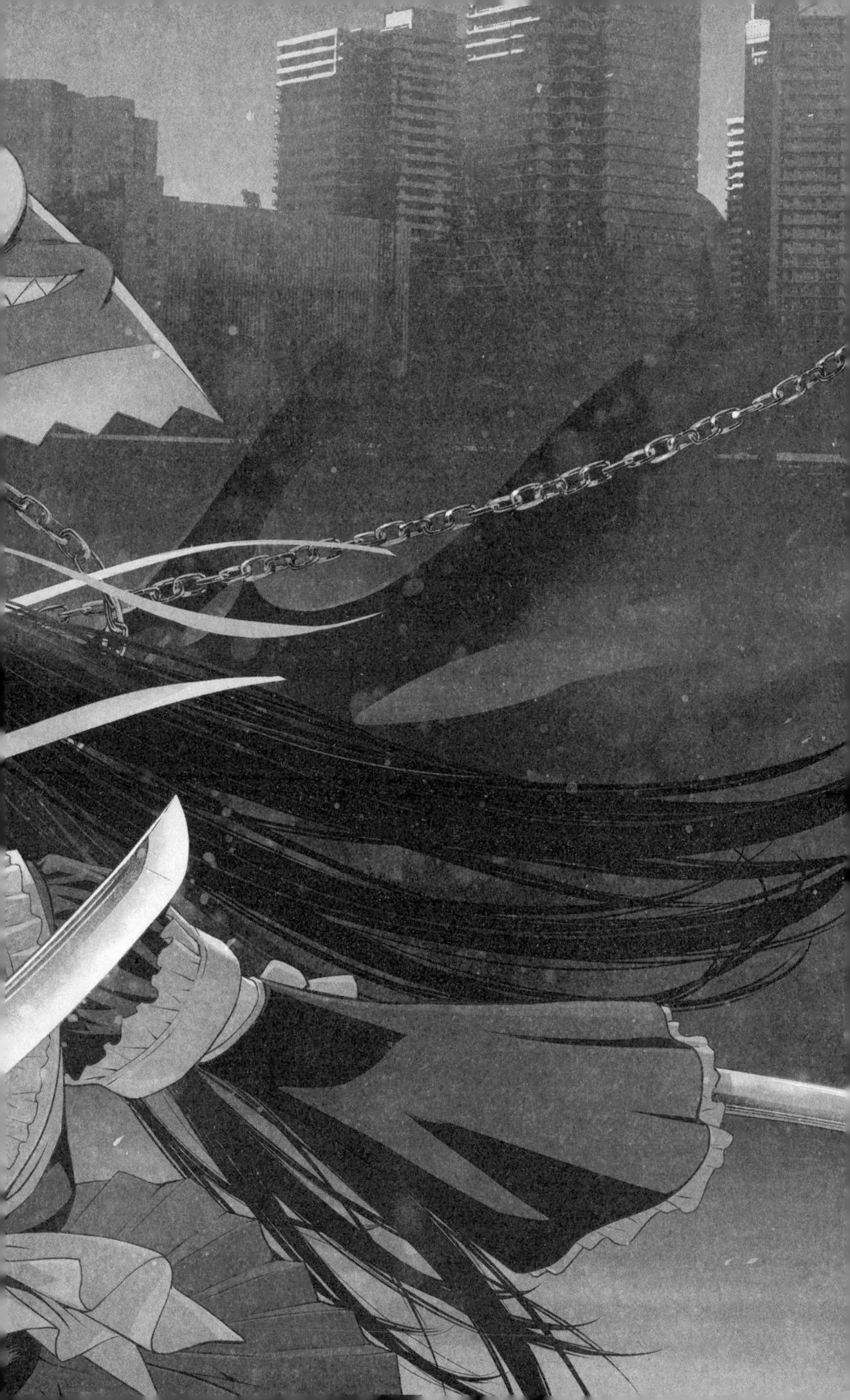

GHOST REAPER GIRL

Volume 3
SHONEN JUMP Edition

STORY AND ART BY **Akissa Saiké**

GRAPHIC NOVEL TRANSLATION **Amanda Haley**
TOUCH-UP ART & LETTERING **Annaliese "Ace" Christman**
DESIGN **Yukiko Whitley**
EDITOR **Alexis Kirsch**

Published by VIZ Media, LLC
P.O. Box 77010
San Francisco, CA 94107

10 9 8 7 6 5 4 3 2 1
First printing, December 2022

viz.com

GHOST REAPER GIRL

3

CONTENTS

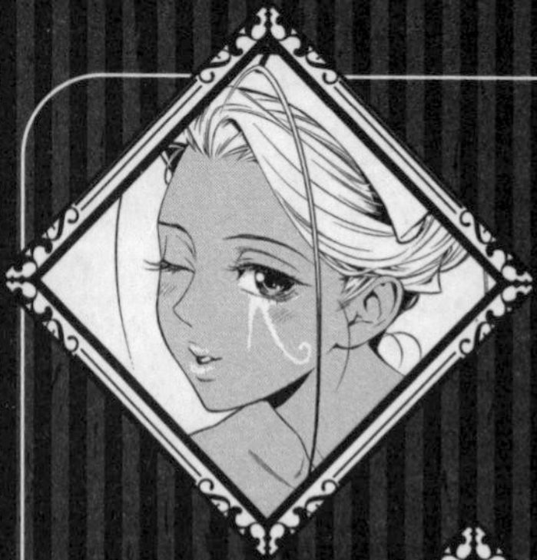

Nyarlathotep

Director of Arkham Bullet's Far East Branch. It seems she's planning something behind all the tough exterminations she's been assigning to Chloé...

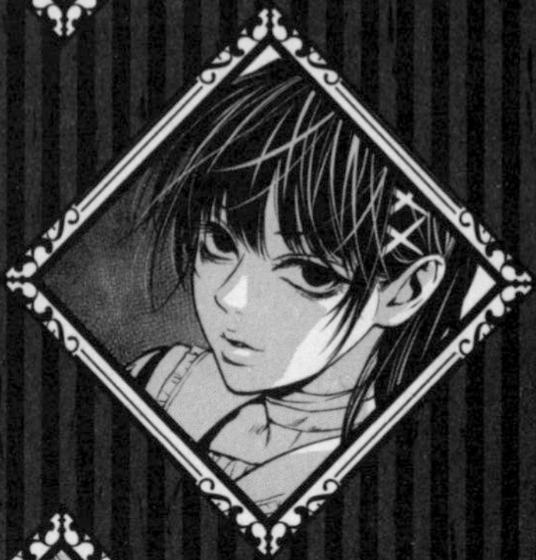

Shoggoth

A living weapon created by Doctor West called "the Killing Doll." She cuts up enemies with two razor-sharp swords! Since meeting Chloé, she's begun to develop emotions.

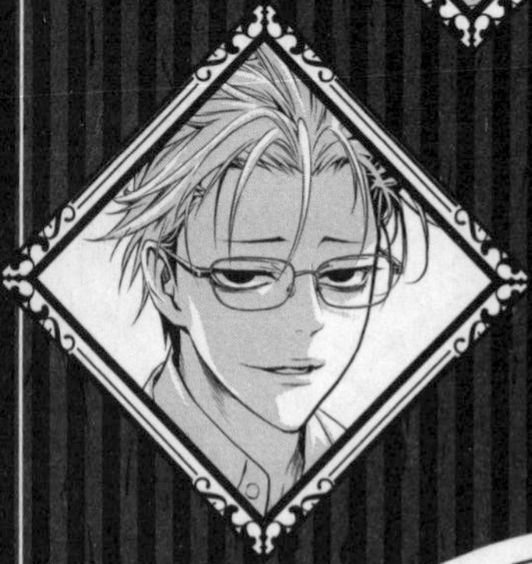

Doctor West

An Arkham executive and a researcher specializing in dead bodies. He can reanimate and control human corpses. Shoggoth's supportive parental figure.

STORY

When evil spirits escape from their jail in Hades, they return to the real world and plunge it into chaos... Unknown actress Chloé, joined by her new familiars Kai and Noel, has gained the power to fight evil spirits as a ghost reaper for Arkham Bullet! On their first mission, Chloé and the boys are attacked by Doctor West, a researcher of dead bodies, and Shoggoth, the Killing Doll. Despite getting off to a rocky start, Chloé and Shoggoth grow close after fighting an even more powerful evil spirit together. Now Chloé's busy taking missions to level up her skills as she makes new allies. What's next for our intrepid heroine?

CHARACTERS

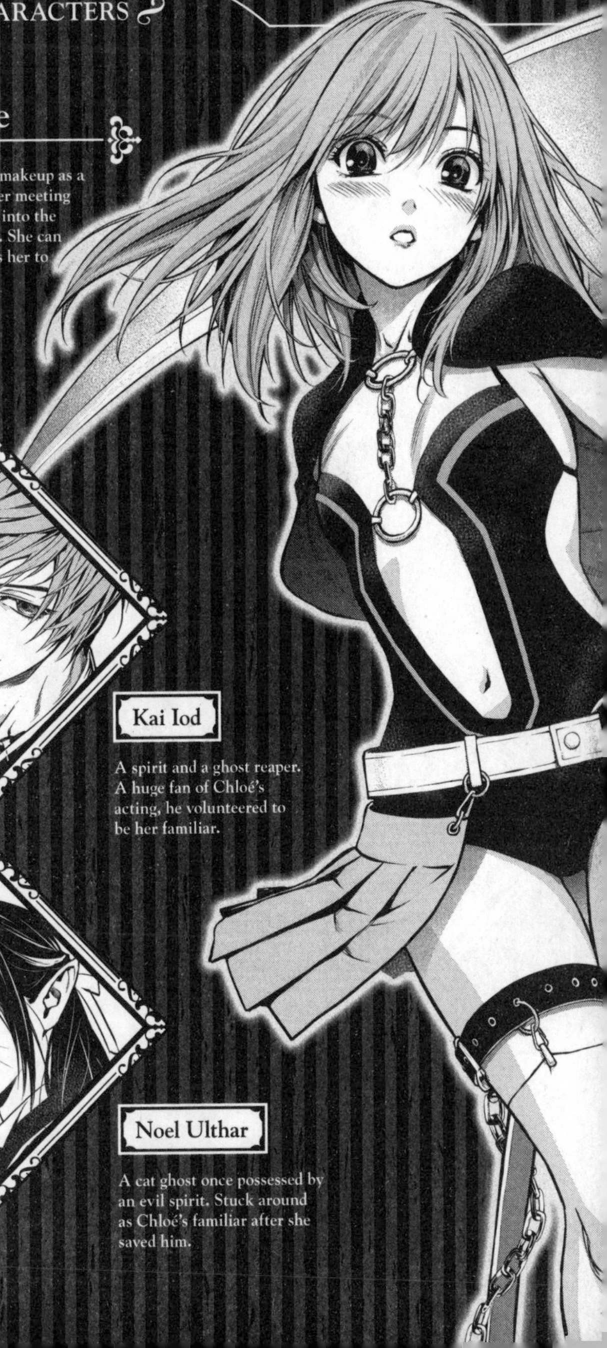

Chloé Love

After her rare genetic makeup as a spirit medium led to her meeting Kai, Chloé was thrust into the world of ghost reaping. She can let Kai or Noel possess her to transform and fight!

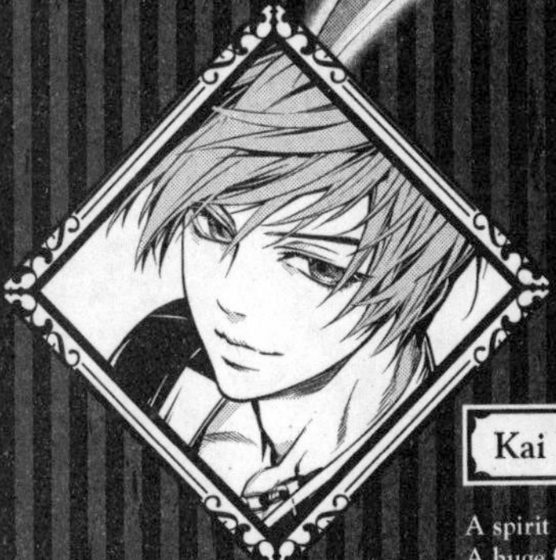

Kai Iod

A spirit and a ghost reaper. A huge fan of Chloé's acting, he volunteered to be her familiar.

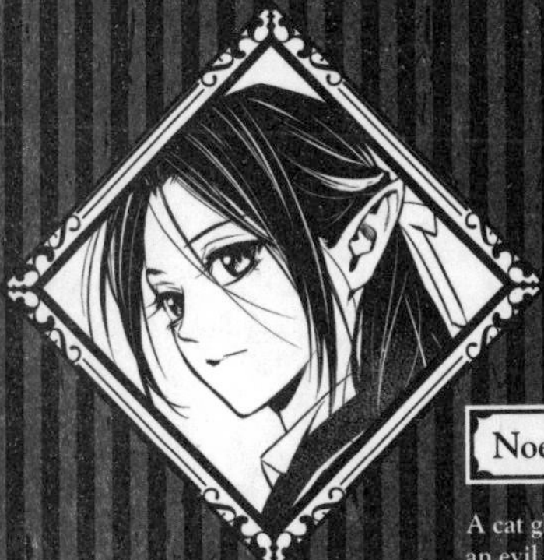

Noel Ulthar

A cat ghost once possessed by an evil spirit. Stuck around as Chloé's familiar after she saved him.

GHOST REAPER GIRL

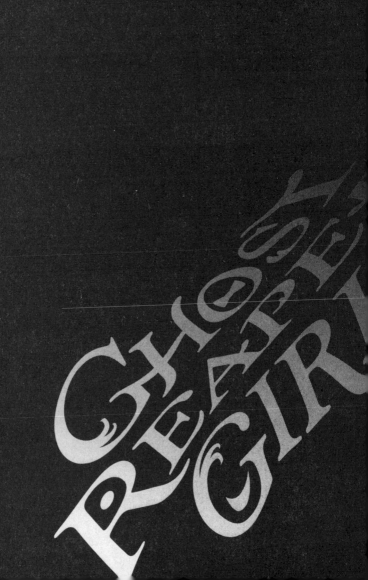

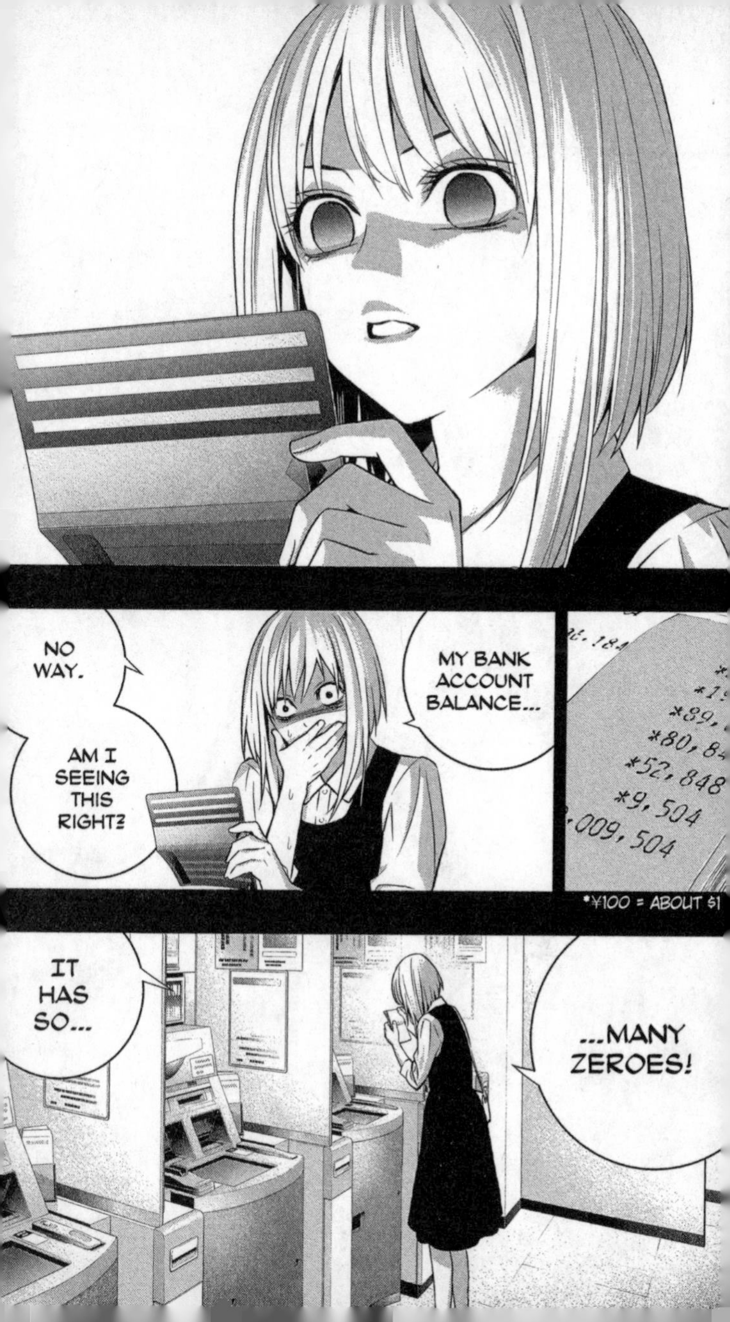
NO WAY.
MY BANK ACCOUNT BALANCE...
AM I SEEING THIS RIGHT?
*52,848
*9,504
*¥100 = ABOUT $1
IT HAS SO...
...MANY ZEROES!

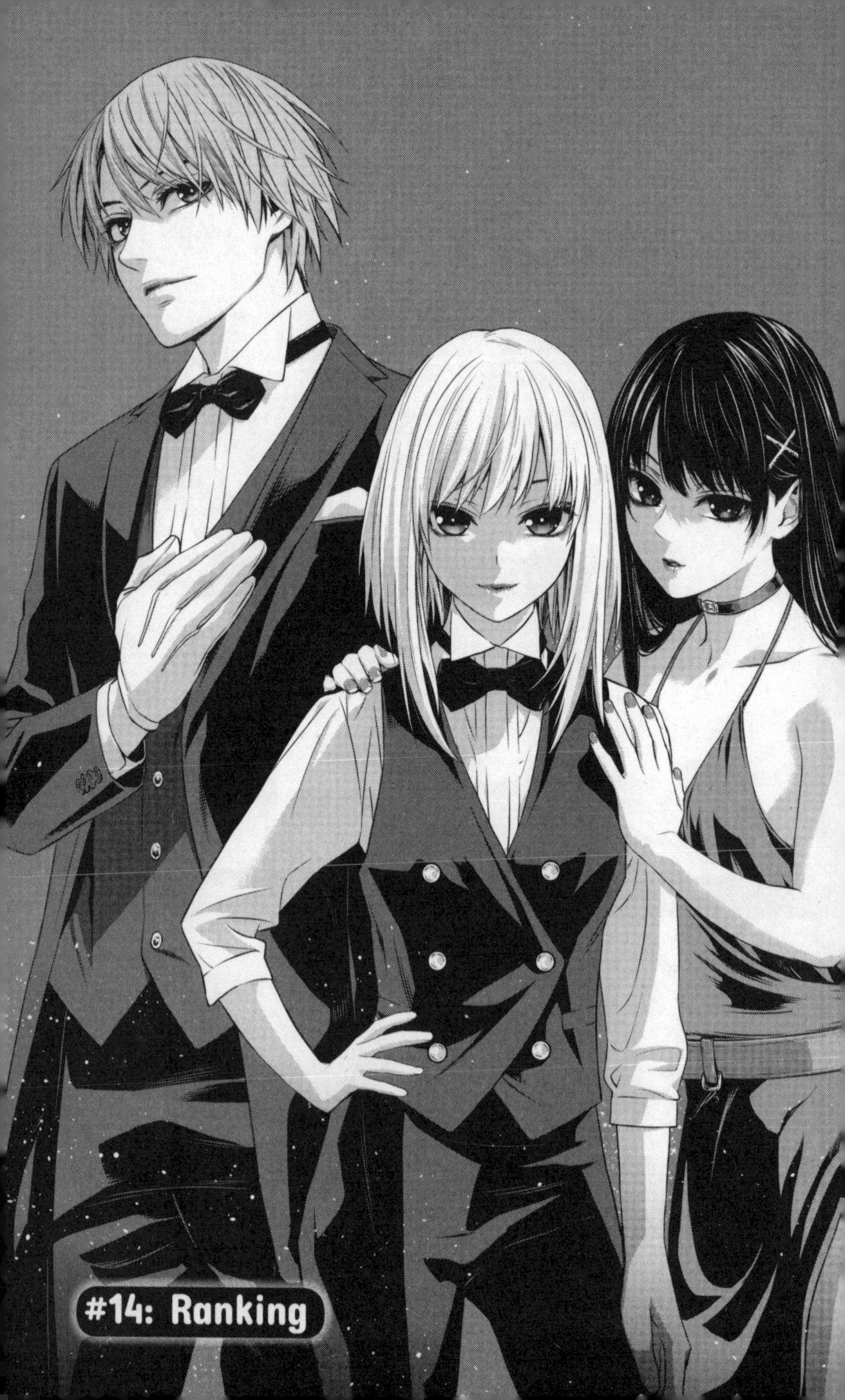
#14: Ranking

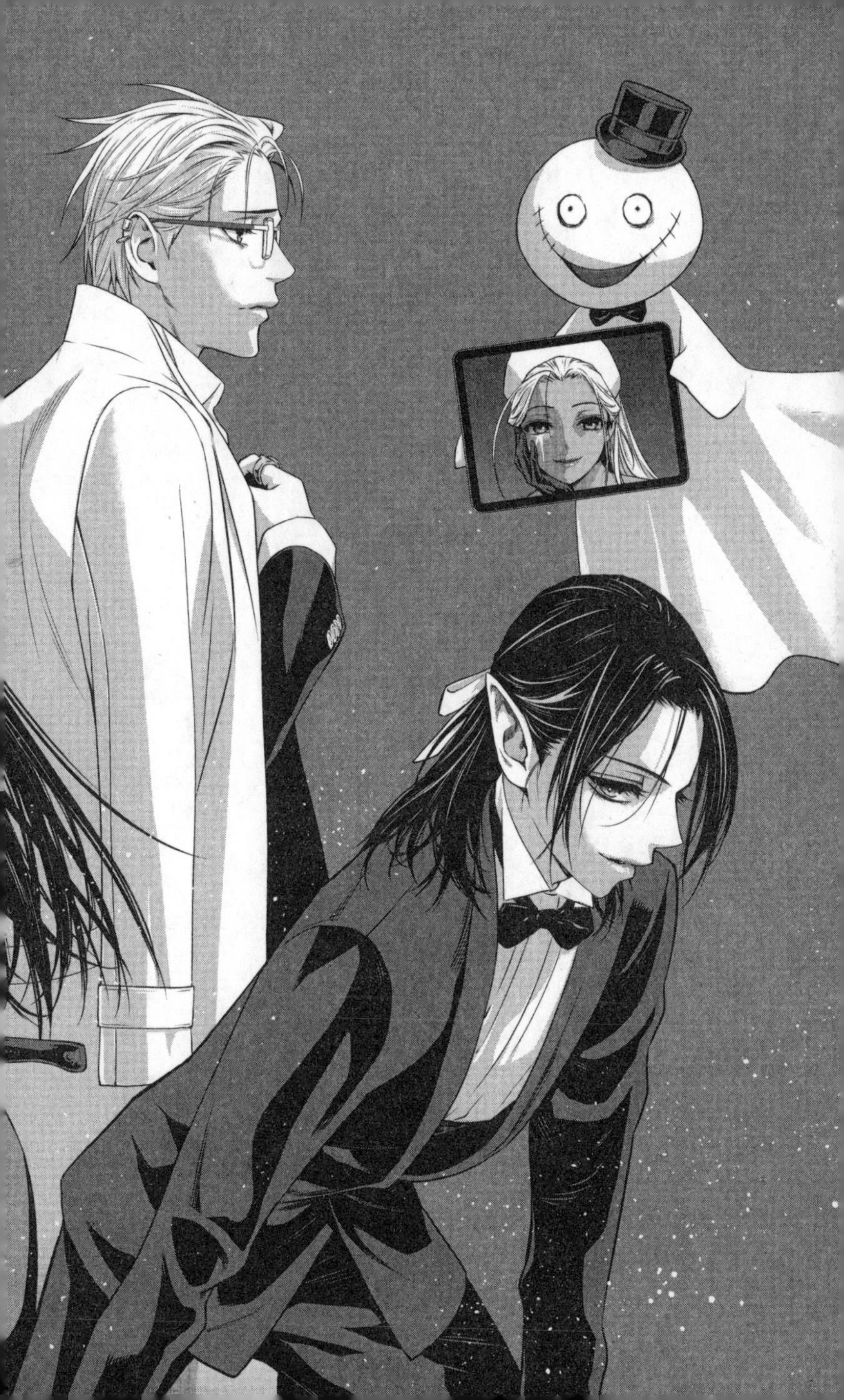

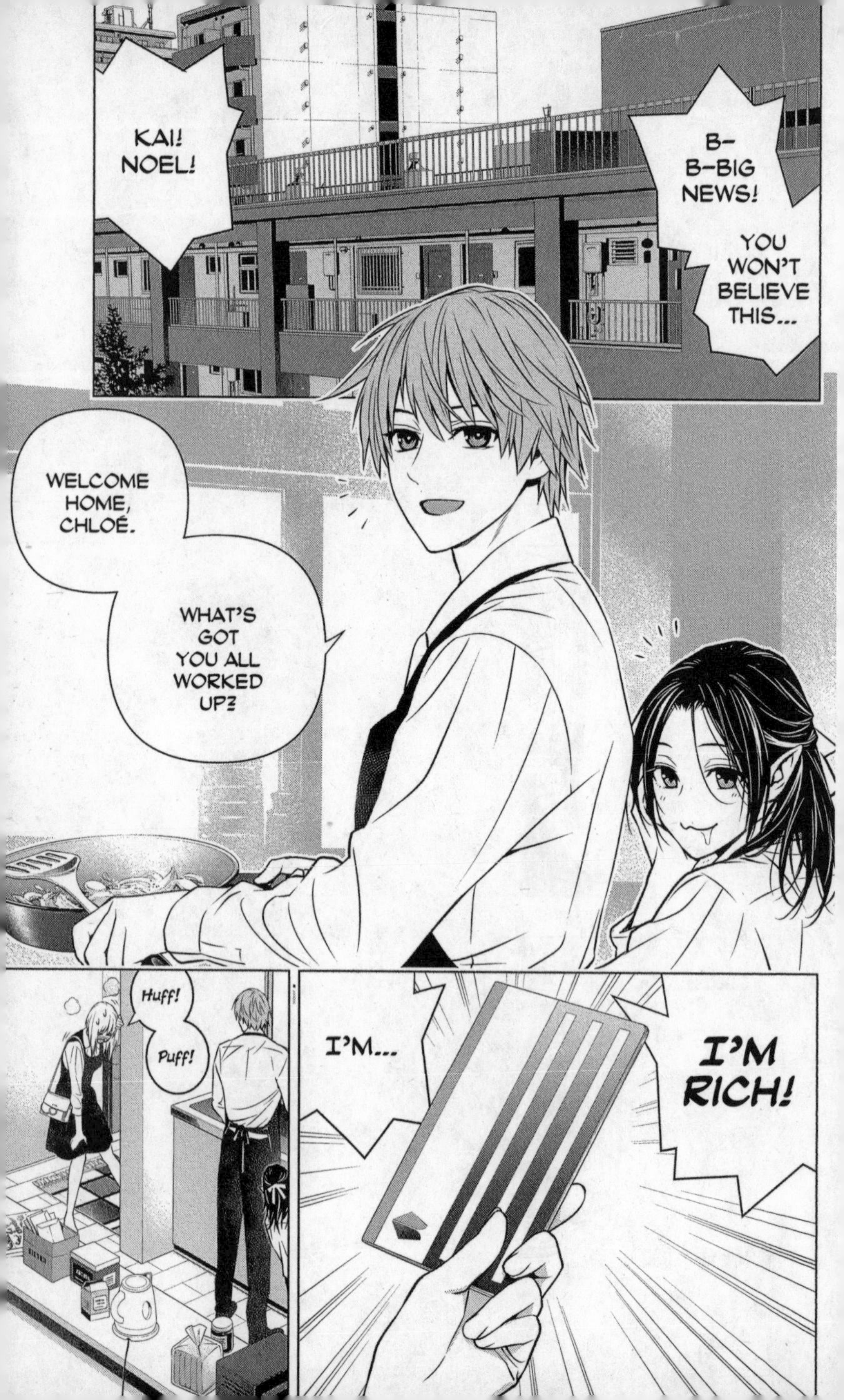
KAI! NOEL!
B– B–BIG NEWS!
YOU WON'T BELIEVE THIS...
WELCOME HOME, CHLOÉ.
WHAT'S GOT YOU ALL WORKED UP?
Huff!
Puff!
I'M...
I'M RICH!

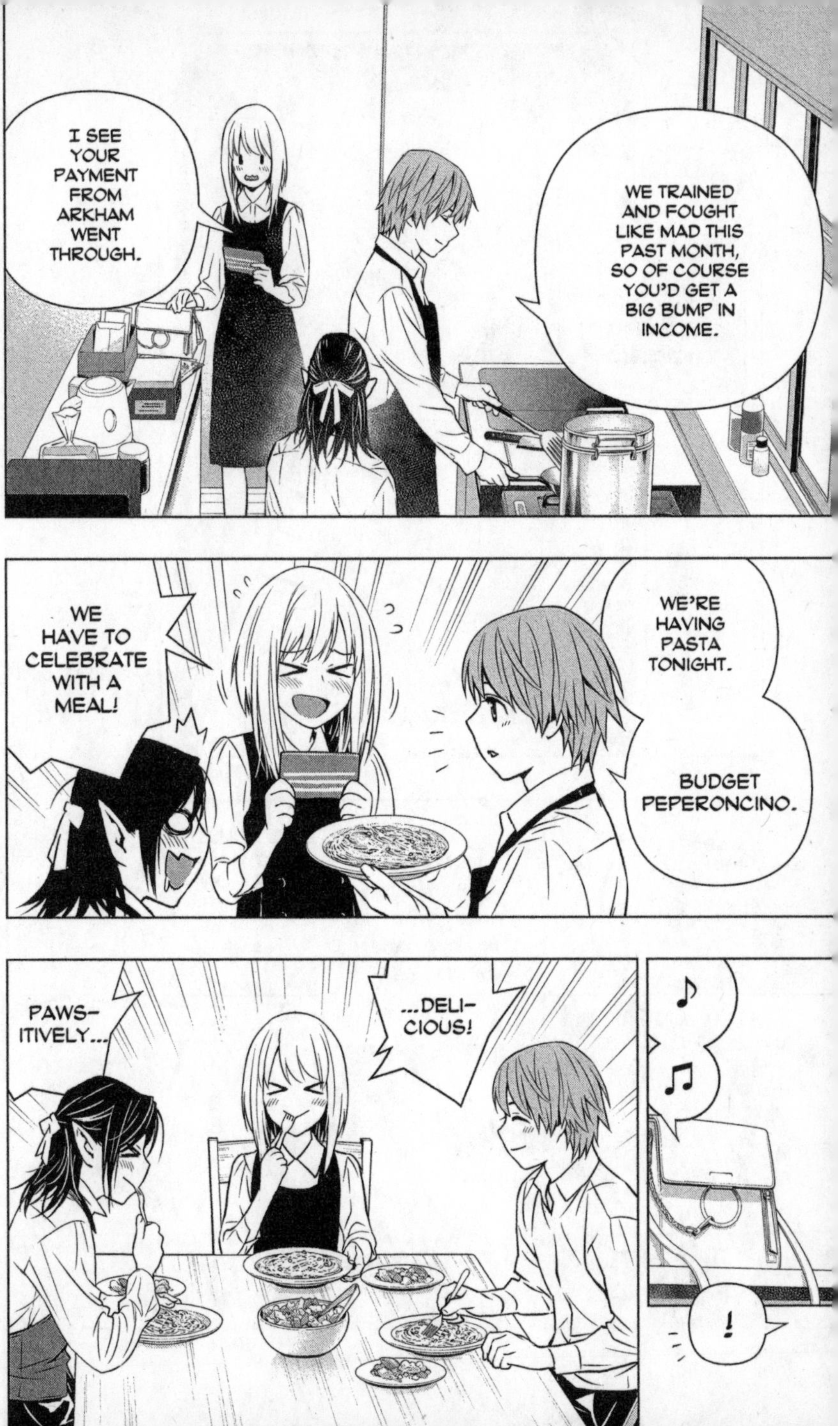
I SEE YOUR PAYMENT FROM ARKHAM WENT THROUGH.
WE TRAINED AND FOUGHT LIKE MAD THIS PAST MONTH, SO OF COURSE YOU'D GET A BIG BUMP IN INCOME.
WE HAVE TO CELEBRATE WITH A MEAL!
WE'RE HAVING PASTA TONIGHT.
BUDGET PEPERONCINO.
PAWS-ITIVELY...
...DELI-CIOUS!
♪ ♫
!

Why hello, Chloé.
I trust you received your compensation?
DIRECTOR!
I WAS SHOCKED! YOU REALLY MEANT IT WHEN YOU SAID I COULD MAKE A KILLING EXTERMINATING EVIL SPIRITS.
Nee hee hee. Keep it up and you'll be buying a house by next year.
A HOUSE?!
I COULD OWN MY VERY OWN DREAM HOME? ♡
YOU'RE DROOLING.

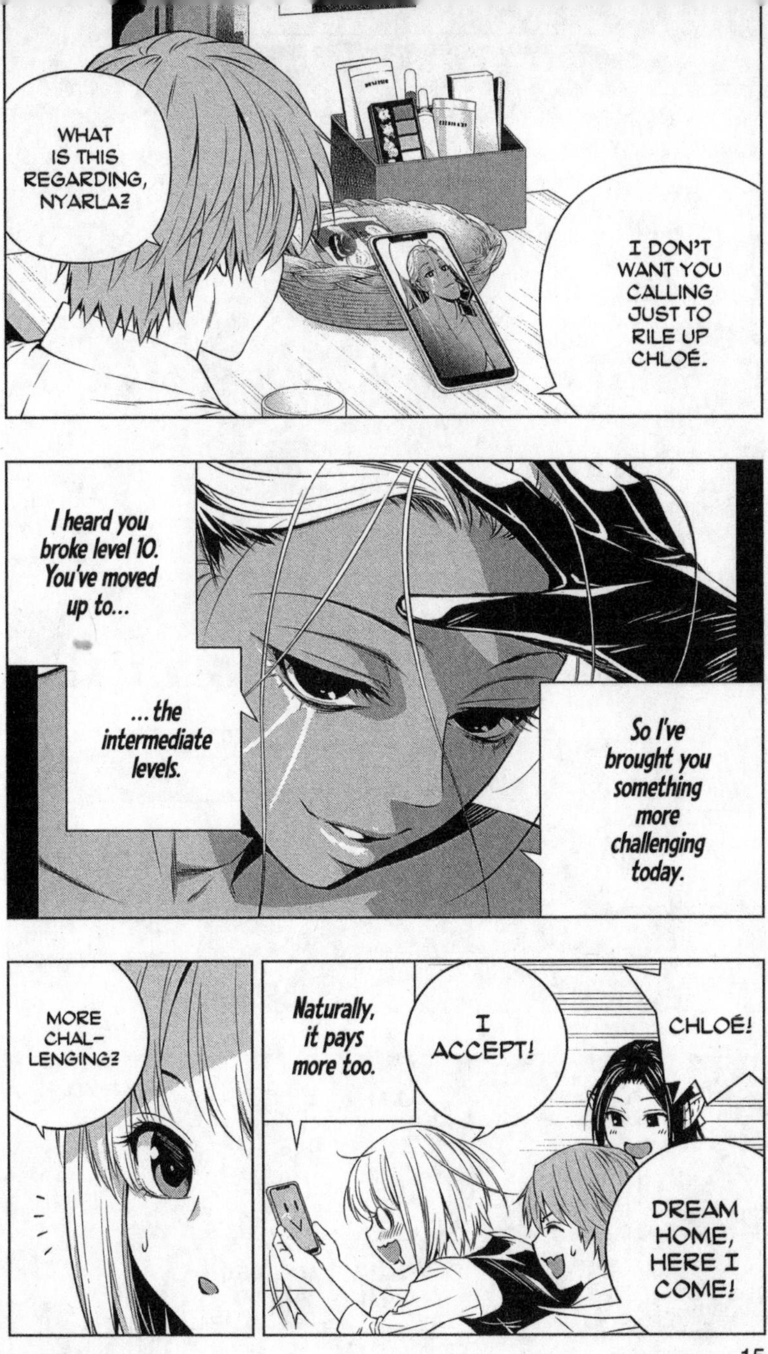
WHAT IS THIS REGARDING, NYARLA?
I DON'T WANT YOU CALLING JUST TO RILE UP CHLOÉ.
I heard you broke level 10. You've moved up to...
...the intermediate levels.
So I've brought you something more challenging today.
MORE CHAL-LENGING?
Naturally, it pays more too.
I ACCEPT!
CHLOÉ!
DREAM HOME, HERE I COME!

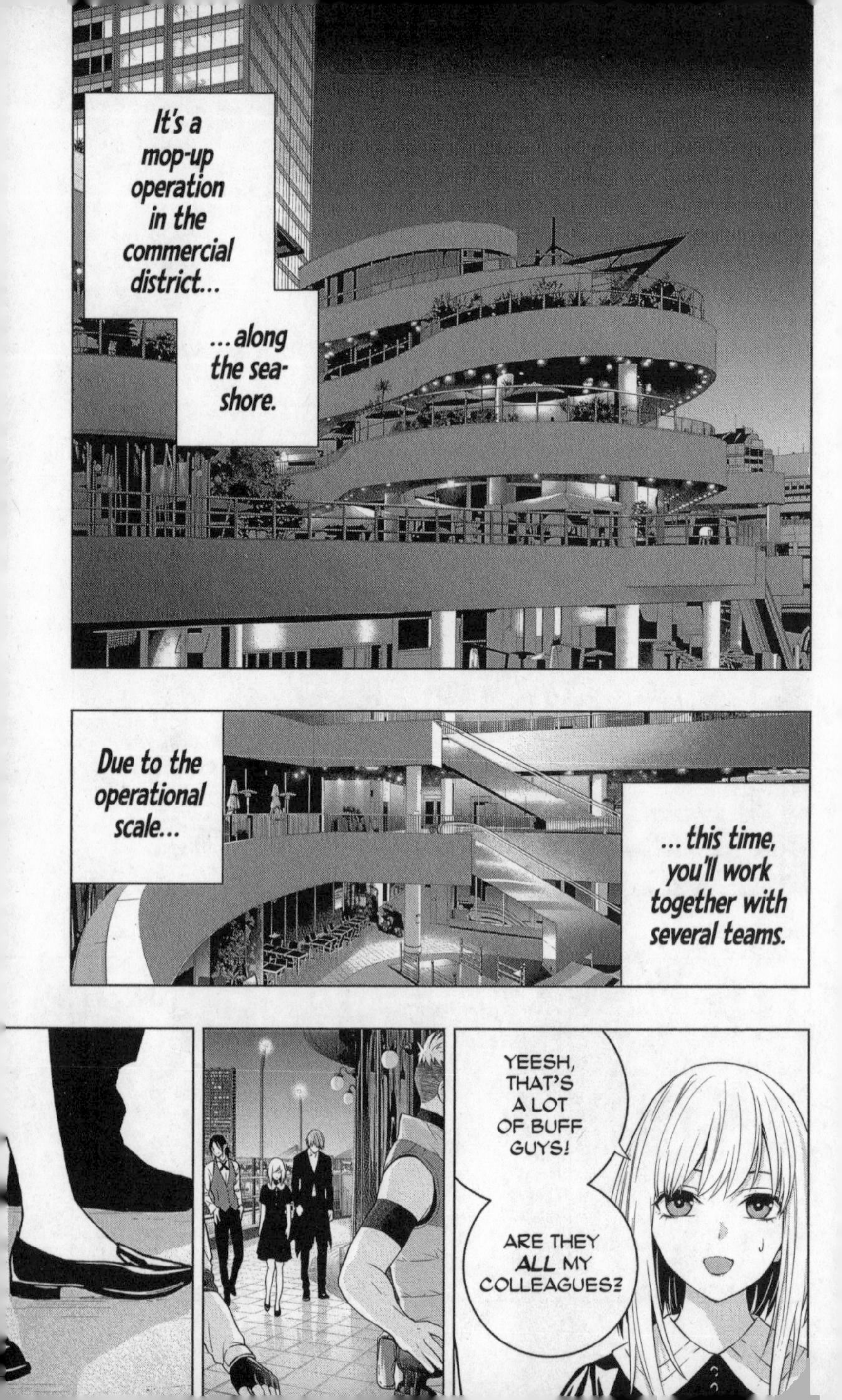

It's a mop-up operation in the commercial district...
...along the sea-shore.
Due to the operational scale...
...this time, you'll work together with several teams.
YEESH, THAT'S A LOT OF BUFF GUYS!
ARE THEY ALL MY COLLEAGUES?

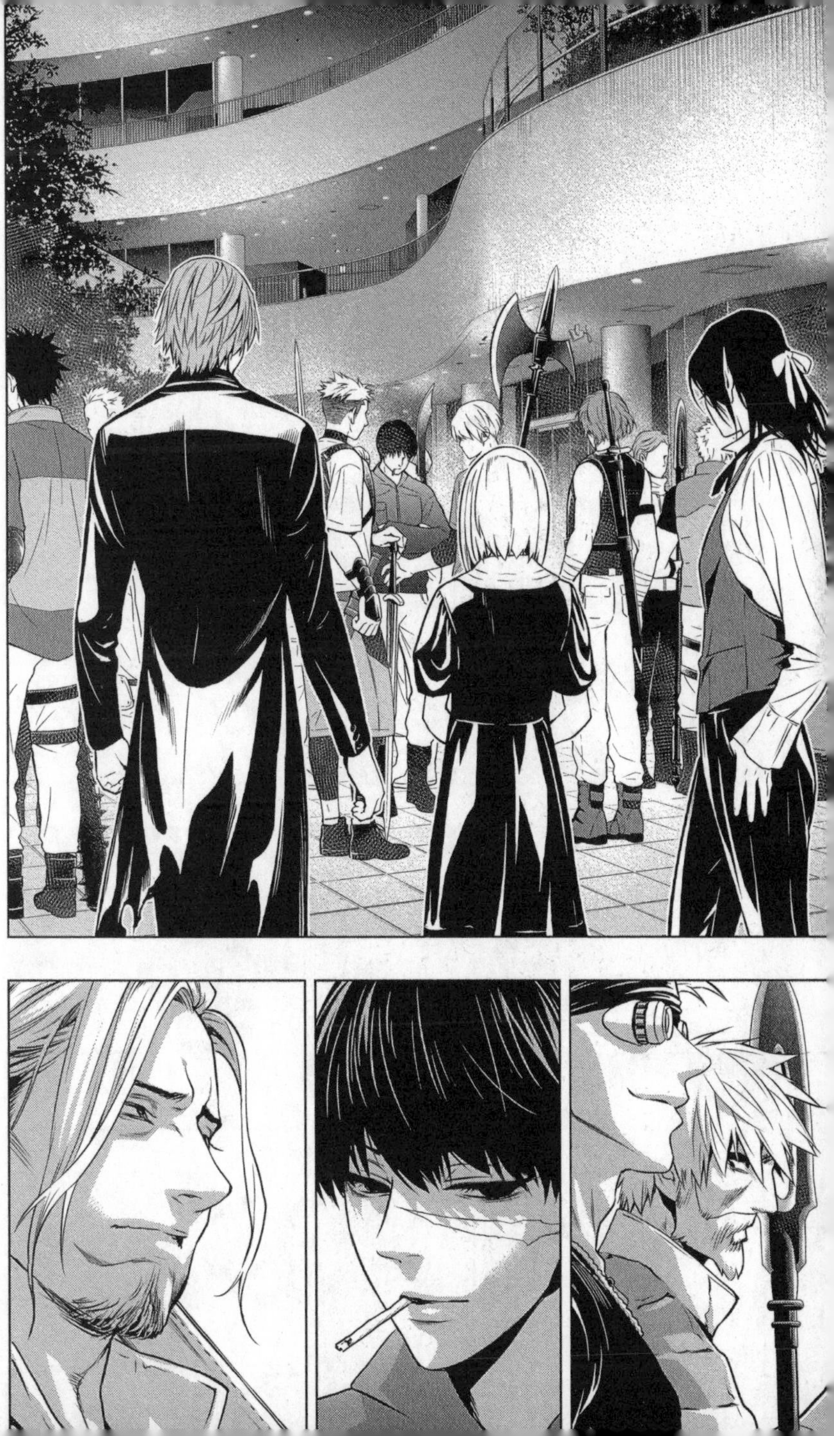

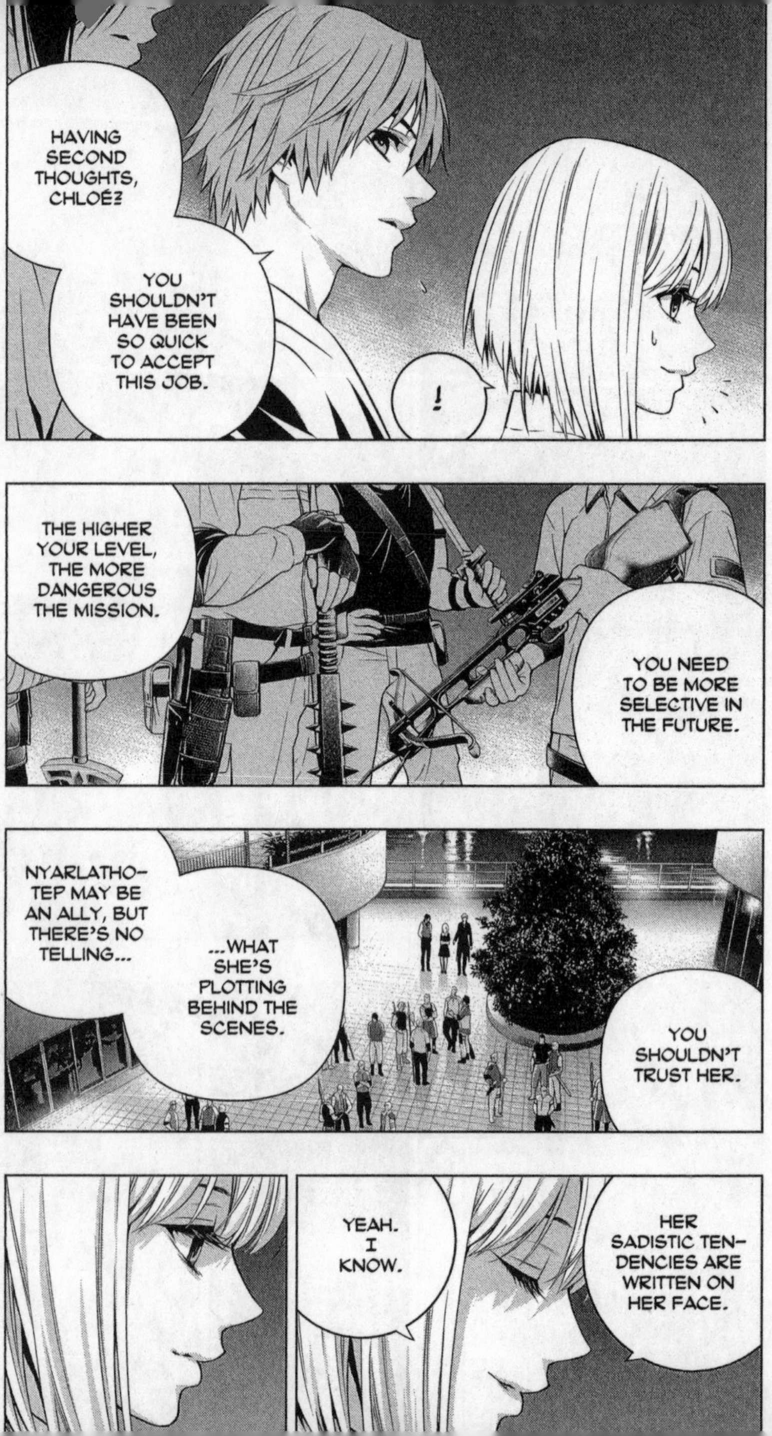
HAVING SECOND THOUGHTS, CHLOÉ?
YOU SHOULDN'T HAVE BEEN SO QUICK TO ACCEPT THIS JOB.
!
THE HIGHER YOUR LEVEL, THE MORE DANGEROUS THE MISSION.
YOU NEED TO BE MORE SELECTIVE IN THE FUTURE.
NYARLATHO-TEP MAY BE AN ALLY, BUT THERE'S NO TELLING...
...WHAT SHE'S PLOTTING BEHIND THE SCENES.
YOU SHOULDN'T TRUST HER.
YEAH. I KNOW.
HER SADISTIC TEN-DENCIES ARE WRITTEN ON HER FACE.

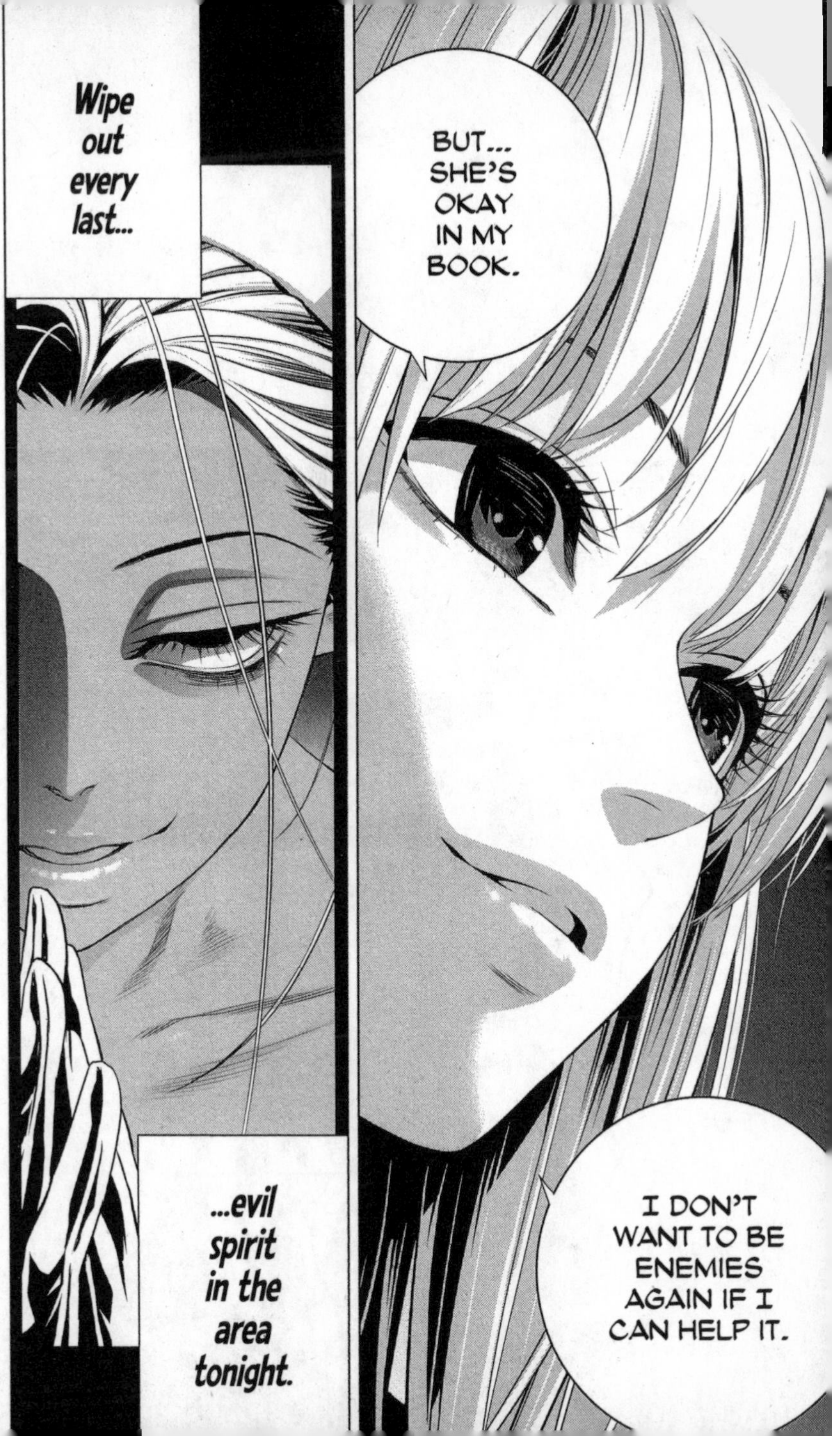
Wipe out every last...
...evil spirit in the area tonight.
BUT... SHE'S OKAY IN MY BOOK.
I DON'T WANT TO BE ENEMIES AGAIN IF I CAN HELP IT.

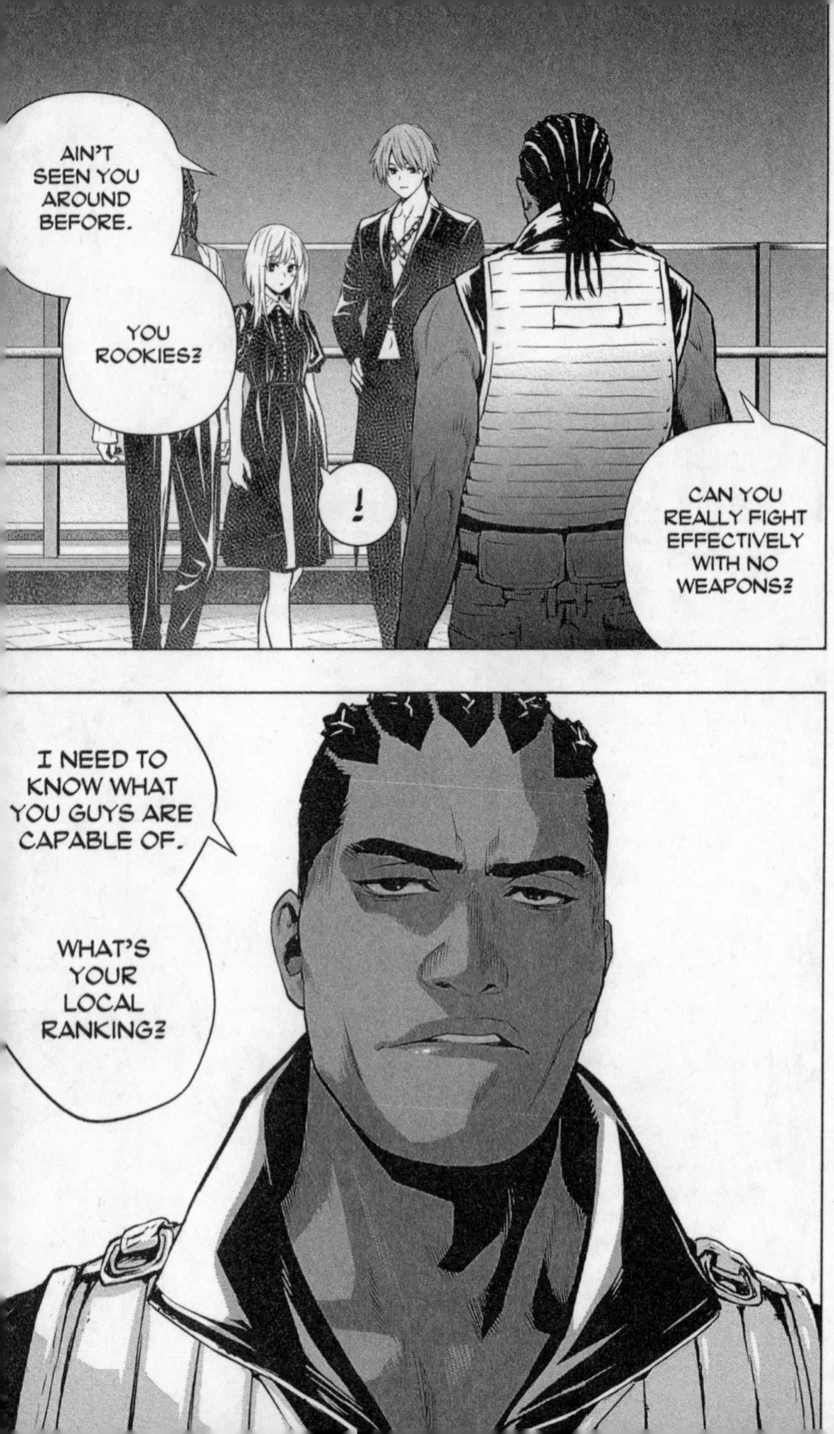
AIN'T SEEN YOU AROUND BEFORE.
YOU ROOKIES?
!
CAN YOU REALLY FIGHT EFFECTIVELY WITH NO WEAPONS?
I NEED TO KNOW WHAT YOU GUYS ARE CAPABLE OF.
WHAT'S YOUR LOCAL RANKING?

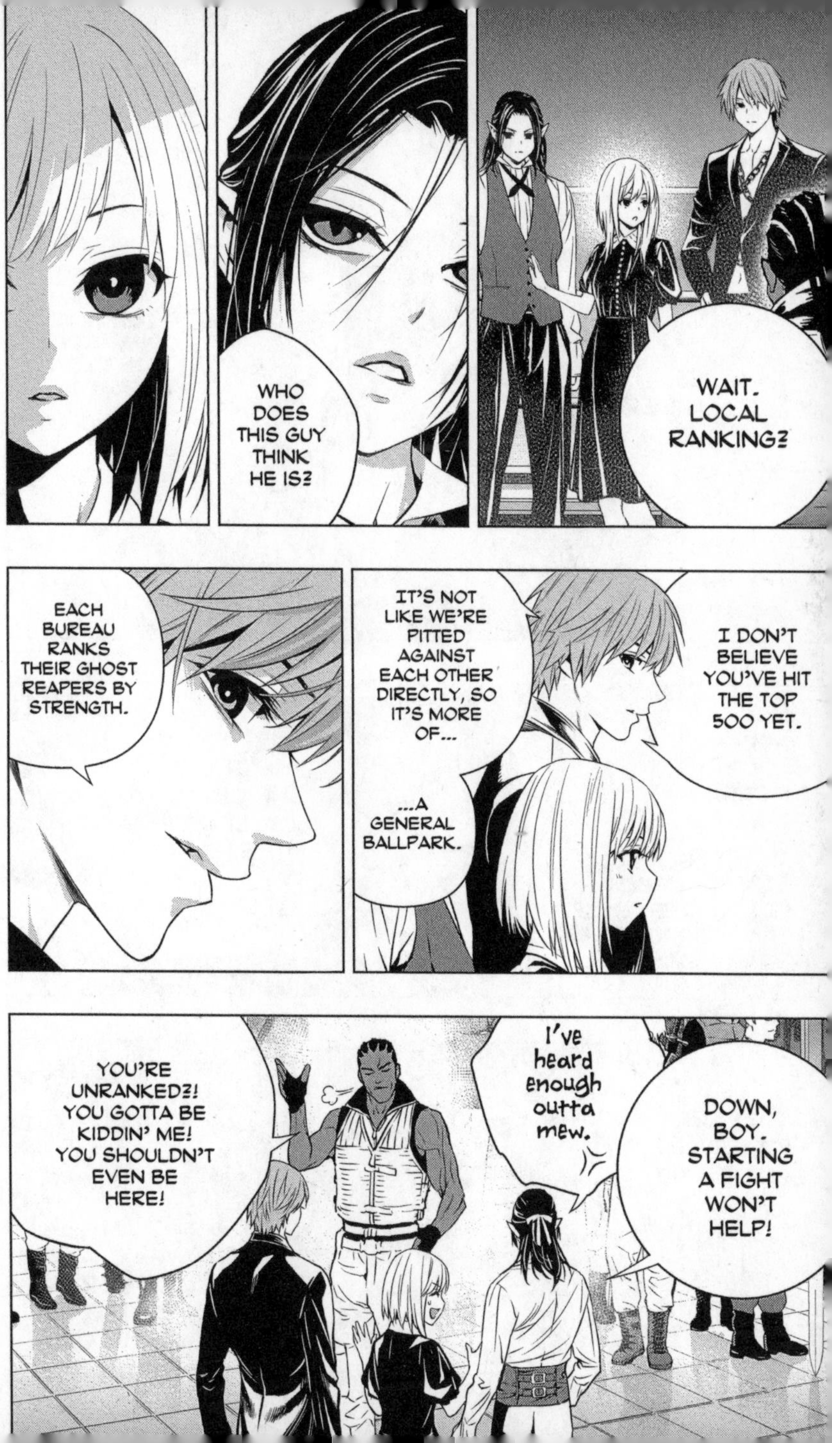
WHO DOES THIS GUY THINK HE IS?
WAIT. LOCAL RANKING?
EACH BUREAU RANKS THEIR GHOST REAPERS BY STRENGTH.
IT'S NOT LIKE WE'RE PITTED AGAINST EACH OTHER DIRECTLY, SO IT'S MORE OF...
...A GENERAL BALLPARK.
I DON'T BELIEVE YOU'VE HIT THE TOP 500 YET.
YOU'RE UNRANKED?! YOU GOTTA BE KIDDIN' ME! YOU SHOULDN'T EVEN BE HERE!
I've heard enough outta mew.
DOWN, BOY. STARTING A FIGHT WON'T HELP!

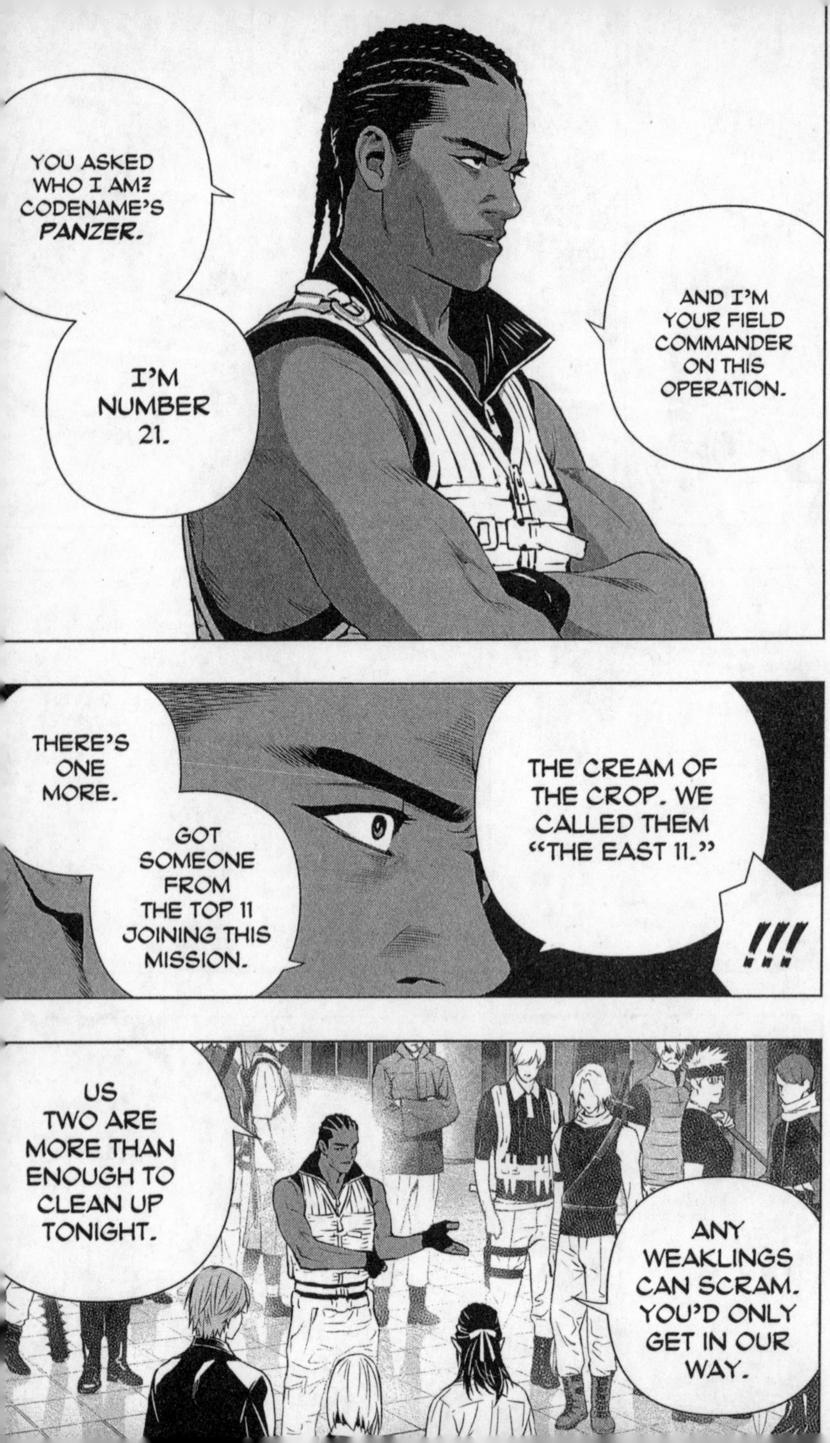
YOU ASKED WHO I AM? CODENAME'S PANZER.
I'M NUMBER 21.
AND I'M YOUR FIELD COMMANDER ON THIS OPERATION.
THERE'S ONE MORE.
GOT SOMEONE FROM THE TOP 11 JOINING THIS MISSION.
THE CREAM OF THE CROP. WE CALLED THEM "THE EAST 11."
!!!
US TWO ARE MORE THAN ENOUGH TO CLEAN UP TONIGHT.
ANY WEAKLINGS CAN SCRAM. YOU'D ONLY GET IN OUR WAY.

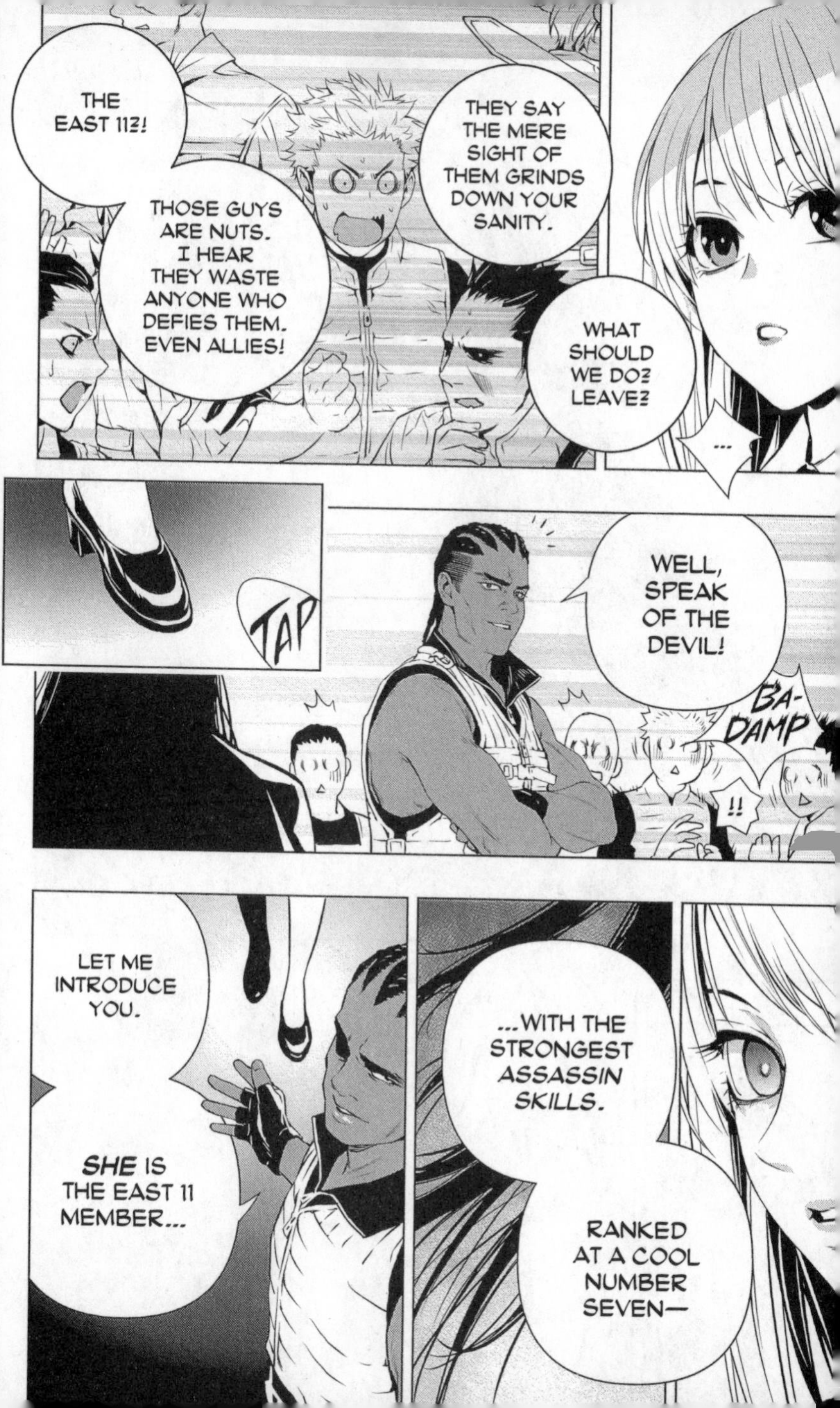
THE EAST 11?!
THOSE GUYS ARE NUTS. I HEAR THEY WASTE ANYONE WHO DEFIES THEM. EVEN ALLIES!
THEY SAY THE MERE SIGHT OF THEM GRINDS DOWN YOUR SANITY.
WHAT SHOULD WE DO? LEAVE?
...
TAP
WELL, SPEAK OF THE DEVIL!
BA-DAMP
!!
LET ME INTRODUCE YOU.
SHE IS THE EAST 11 MEMBER...
...WITH THE STRONGEST *ASSASSIN* SKILLS.
RANKED AT A COOL NUMBER SEVEN—

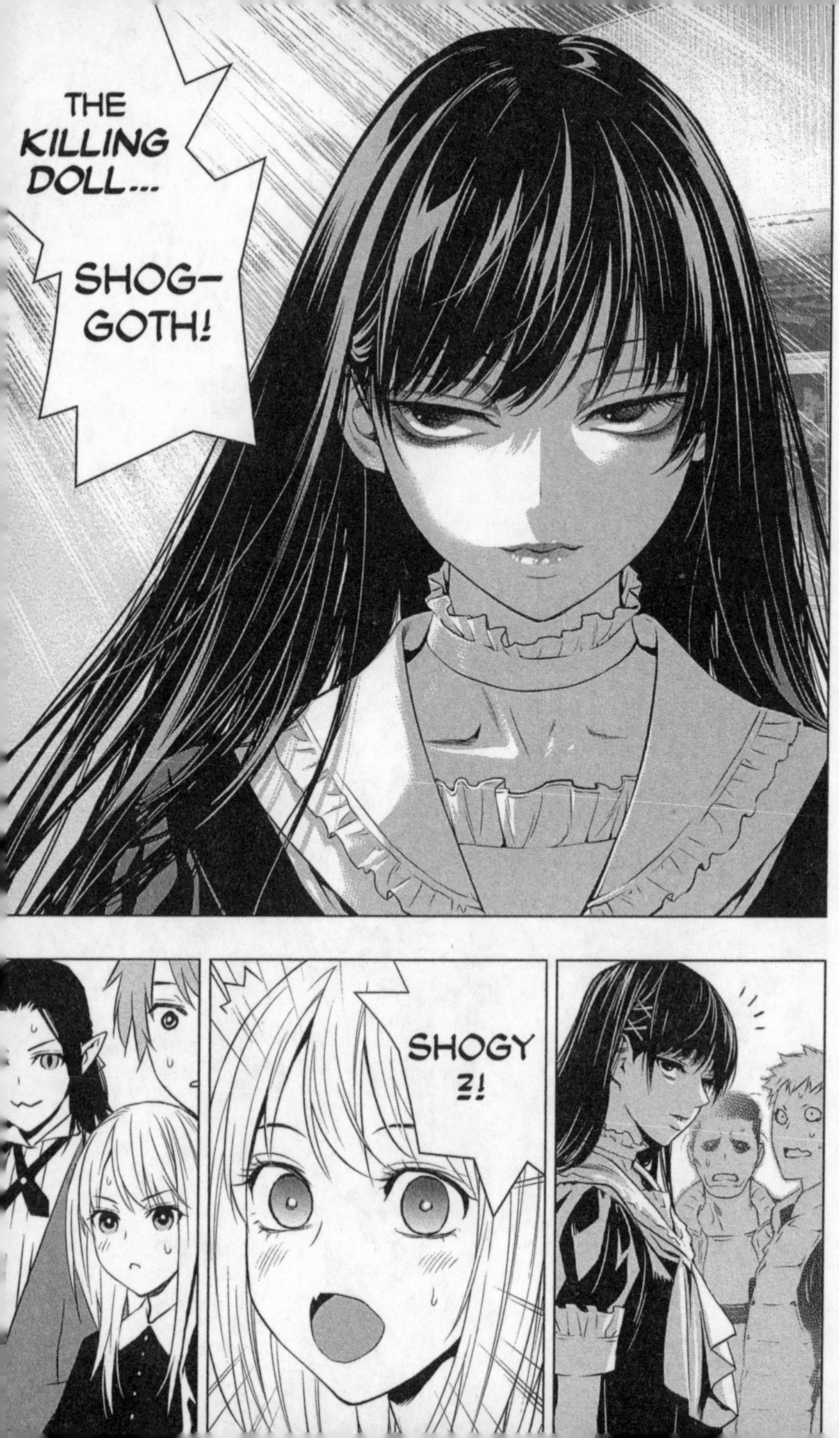
THE KILLING DOLL...
SHOG-GOTH!
SHOGY Z!

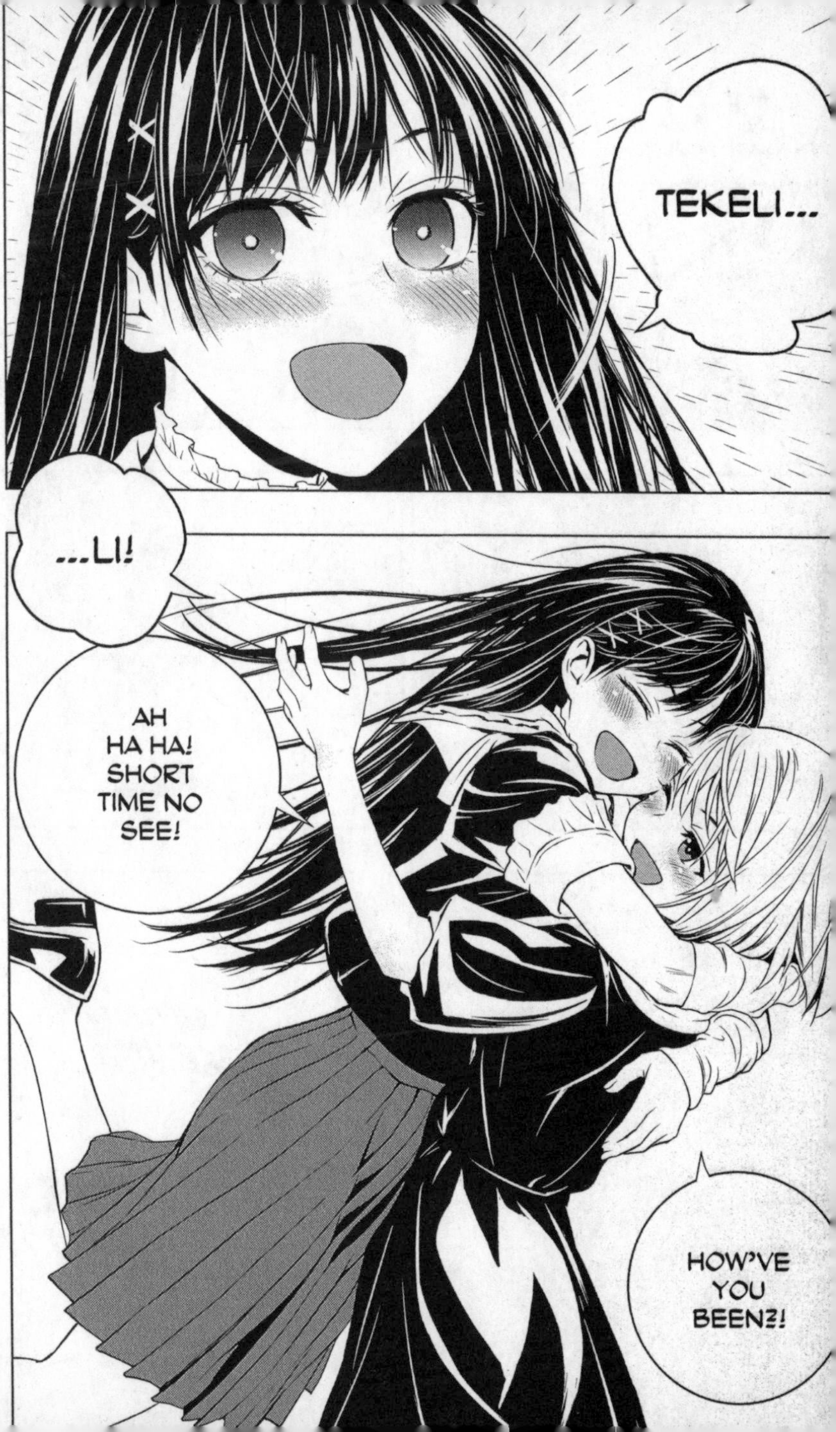
TEKELI...
...LI!
AH HA HA! SHORT TIME NO SEE!
HOW'VE YOU BEEN?!

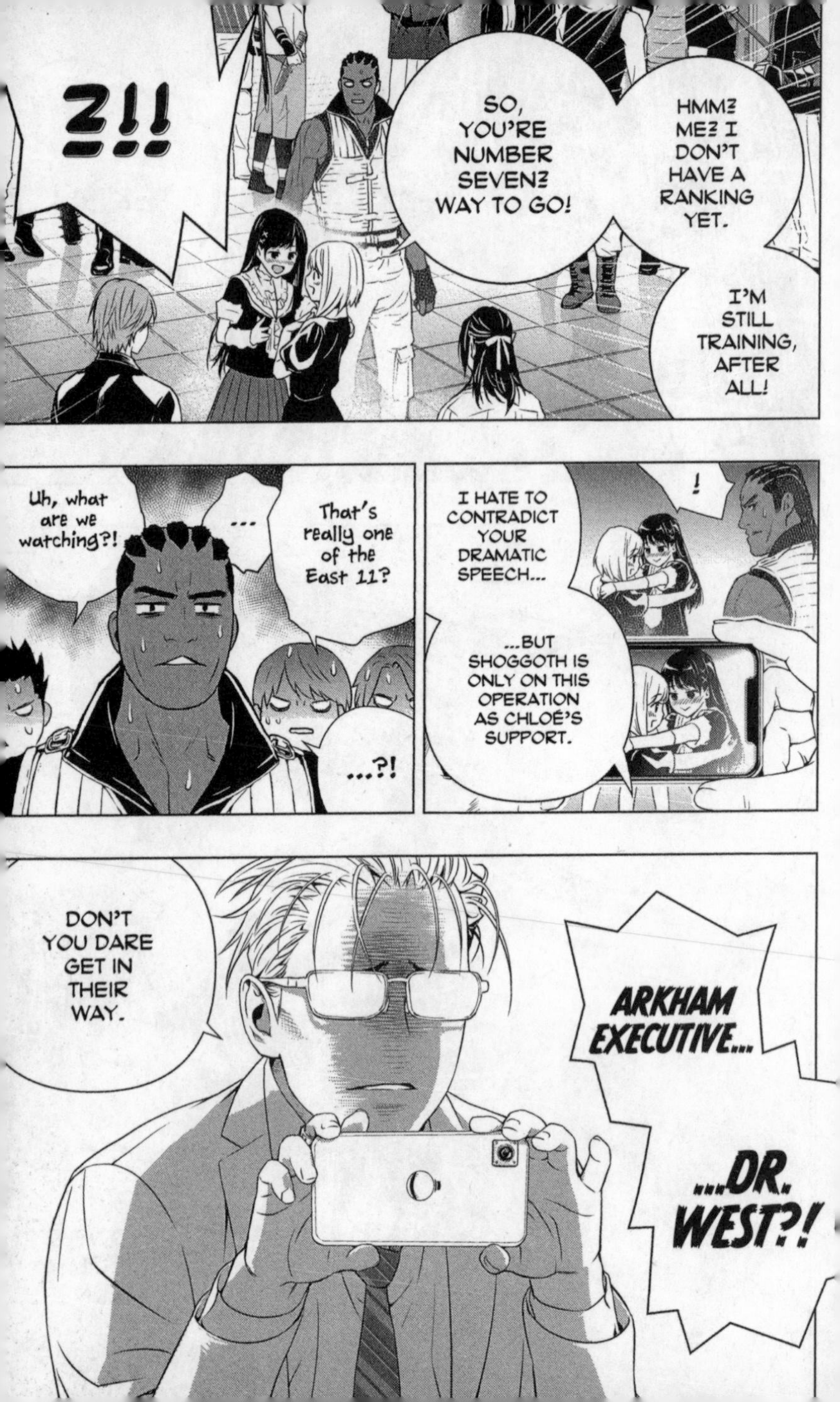
?!!
SO, YOU'RE NUMBER SEVEN? WAY TO GO!
HMM? ME? I DON'T HAVE A RANKING YET.
I'M STILL TRAINING, AFTER ALL!
Uh, what are we watching?!
...
That's really one of the East 11?
...?!
I HATE TO CONTRADICT YOUR DRAMATIC SPEECH...
!
...BUT SHOGGOTH IS ONLY ON THIS OPERATION AS CHLOÉ'S SUPPORT.
DON'T YOU DARE GET IN THEIR WAY.
ARKHAM EXECUTIVE...
...DR. WEST?!

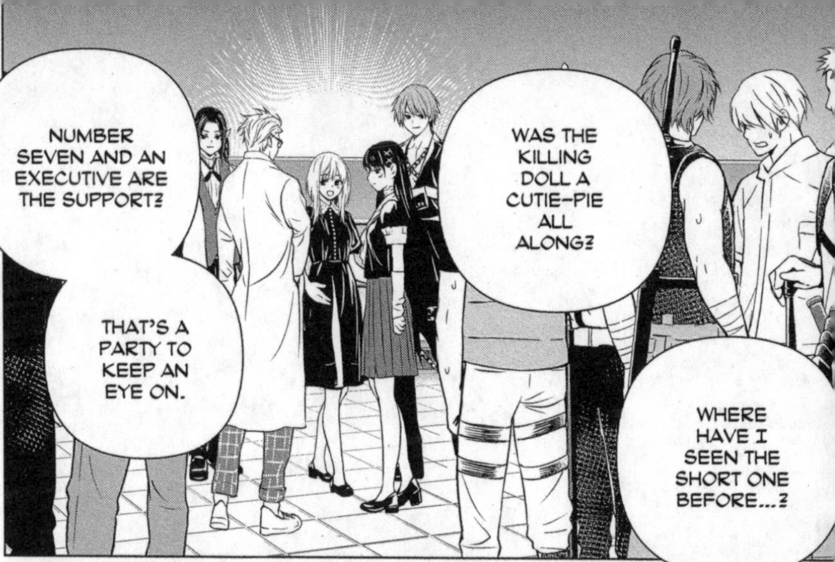
NUMBER SEVEN AND AN EXECUTIVE ARE THE SUPPORT?
THAT'S A PARTY TO KEEP AN EYE ON.
WAS THE KILLING DOLL A CUTIE-PIE ALL ALONG?
WHERE HAVE I SEEN THE SHORT ONE BEFORE...?

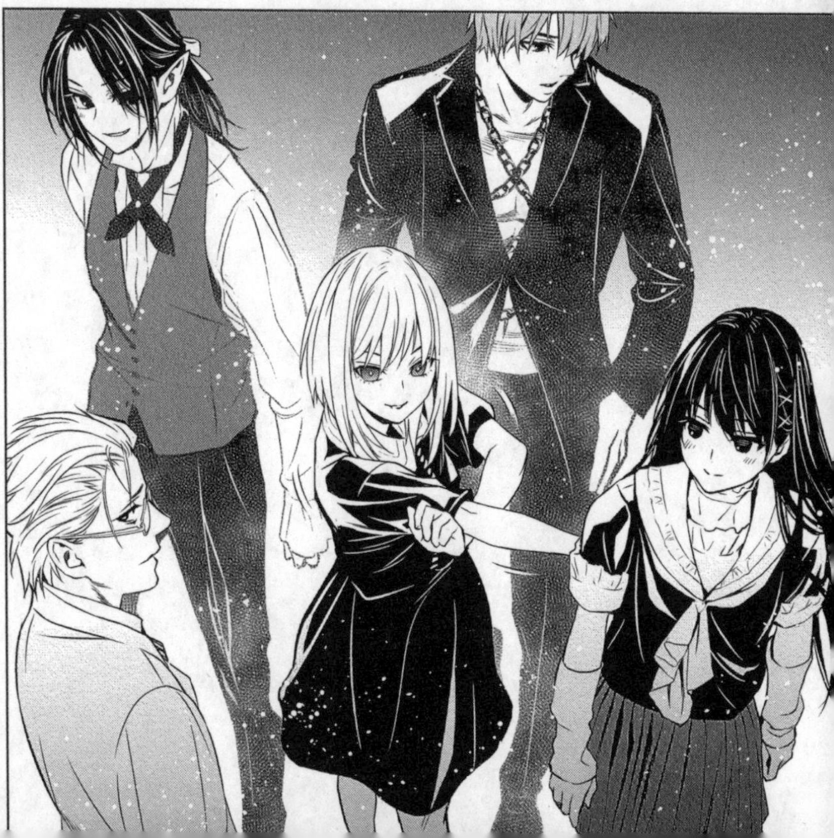

15:NEST

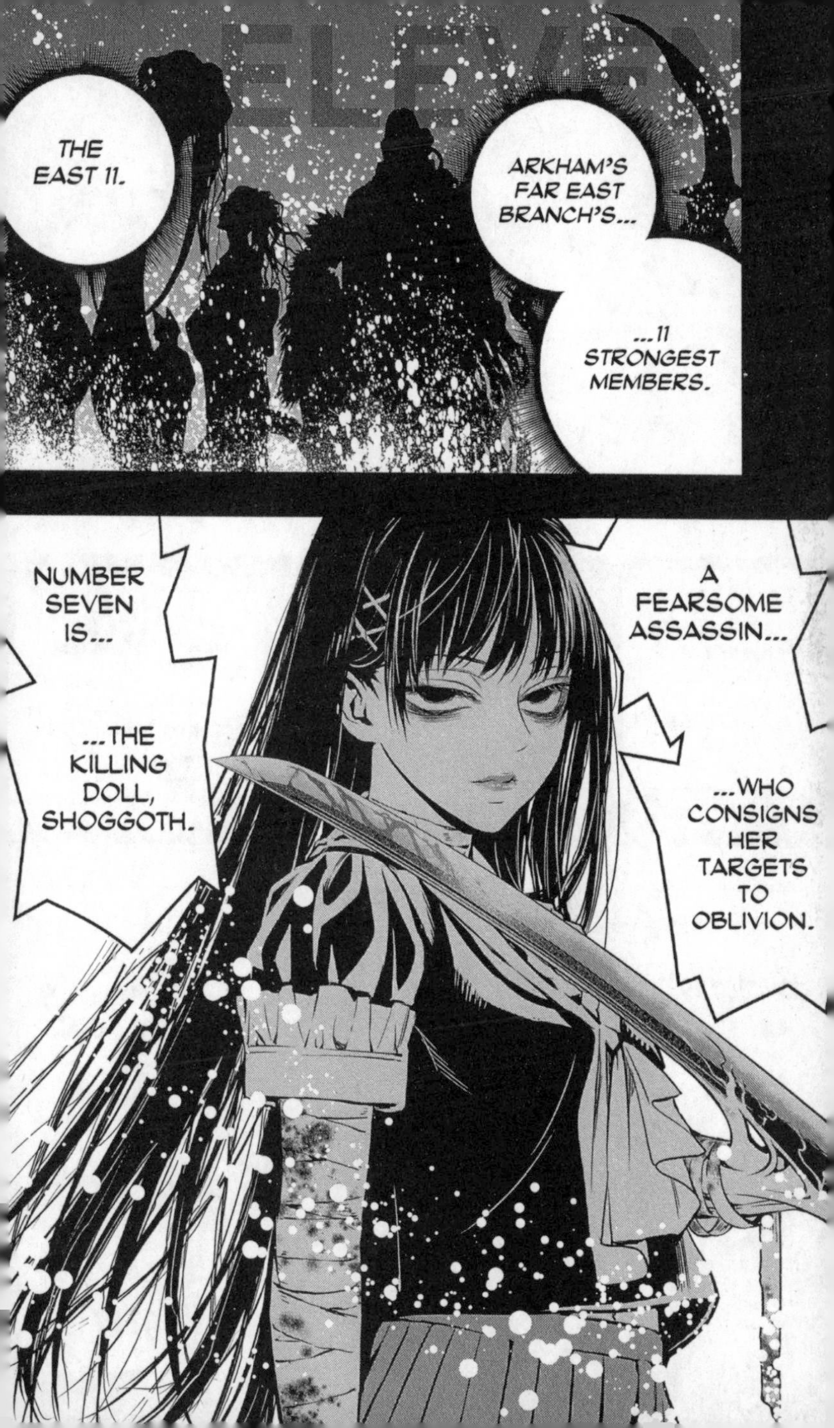
THE EAST 11.
ARKHAM'S FAR EAST BRANCH'S...
...11 STRONGEST MEMBERS.
NUMBER SEVEN IS...
...THE KILLING DOLL, SHOGGOTH.
A FEARSOME ASSASSIN...
...WHO CONSIGNS HER TARGETS TO OBLIVION.

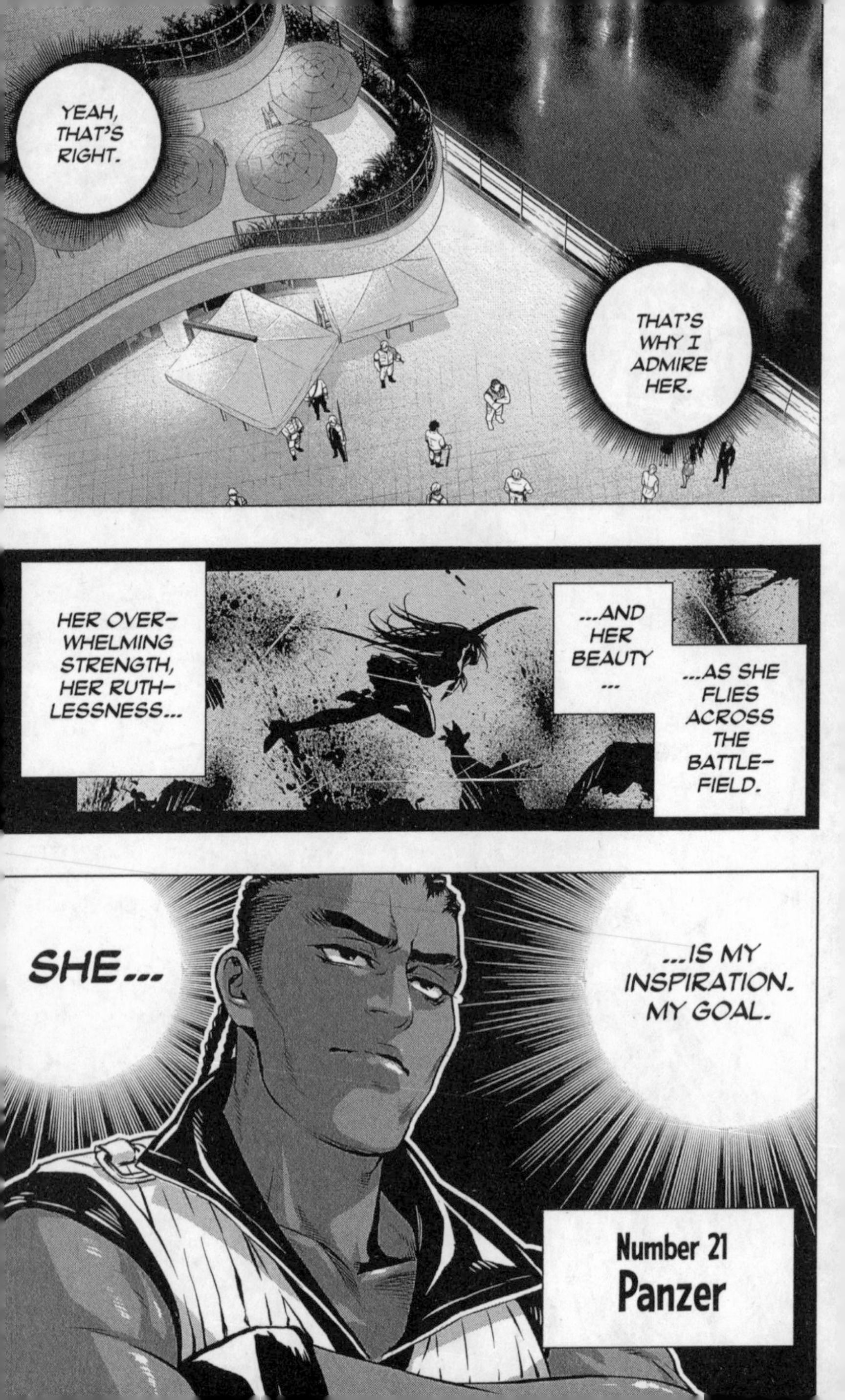
YEAH, THAT'S RIGHT.
THAT'S WHY I ADMIRE HER.
HER OVER-WHELMING STRENGTH, HER RUTH-LESSNESS...
...AND HER BEAUTY...
...AS SHE FLIES ACROSS THE BATTLE-FIELD.
SHE...
...IS MY INSPIRATION. MY GOAL.
Number 21
Panzer

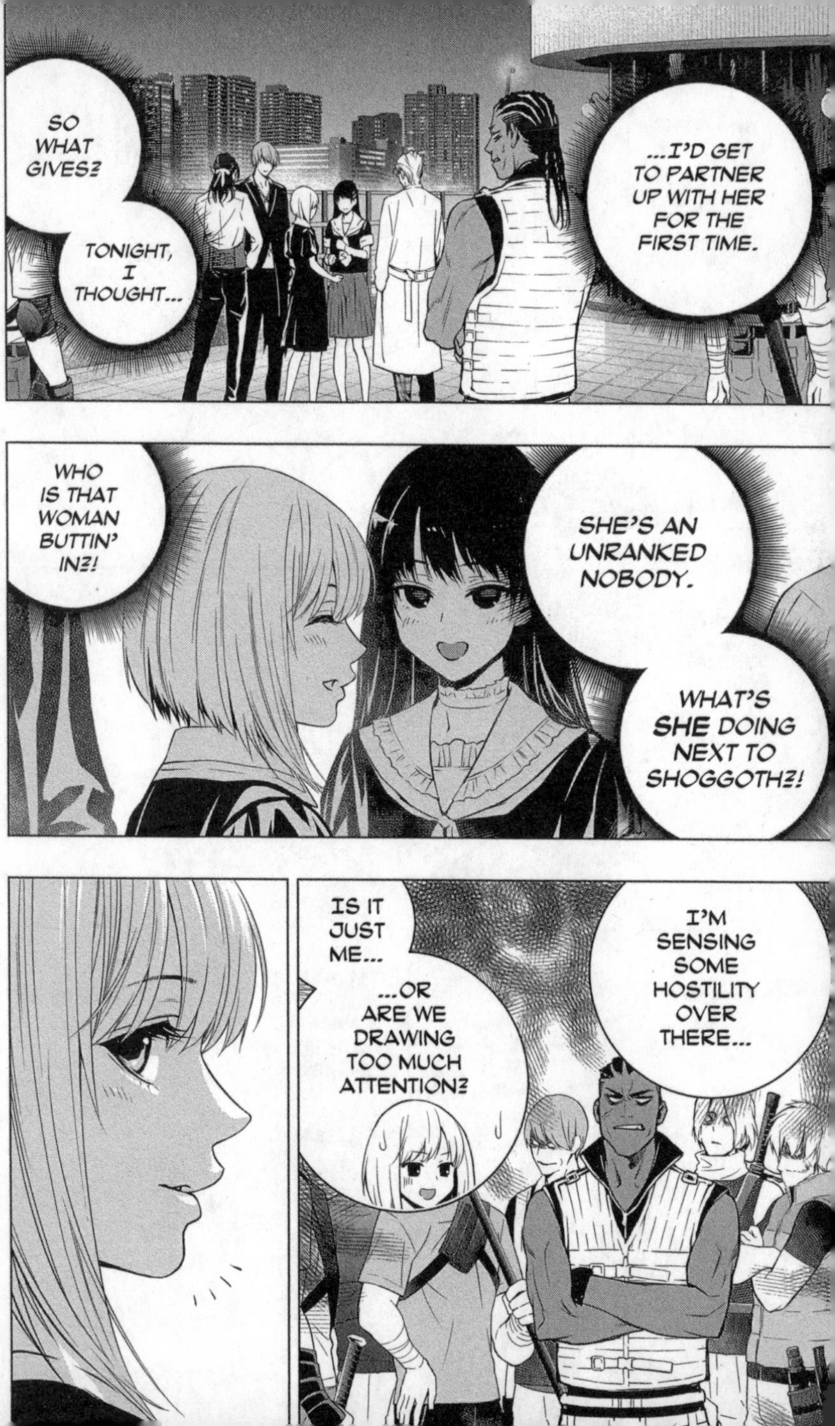
SO WHAT GIVES?
TONIGHT, I THOUGHT...
...I'D GET TO PARTNER UP WITH HER FOR THE FIRST TIME.
WHO IS THAT WOMAN BUTTIN' IN?!
SHE'S AN UNRANKED NOBODY.
WHAT'S SHE DOING NEXT TO SHOGGOTH?!
IS IT JUST ME...
...OR ARE WE DRAWING TOO MUCH ATTENTION?
I'M SENSING SOME HOSTILITY OVER THERE...

THEY'RE JEALOUS OF YOU.

AFTER ALL...

...YOU TOOK MY ADORABLE SHOGGOTH...

...AND MADE HER YOURS.

DON'T JOKE LIKE THAT, WEST.

PEOPLE WILL...

...GET THE WRONG IDEA.

THE DOTING PARENT SHTICK AGAIN.

TEKELI-LI. ♡

GEEZ. YOU COULD DENY IT TOO, SHOGY!

DON'T WORRY ABOUT WHAT OTHERS THINK OF YOU.

YEAH, EXACTLY!

KAI! NOEL!

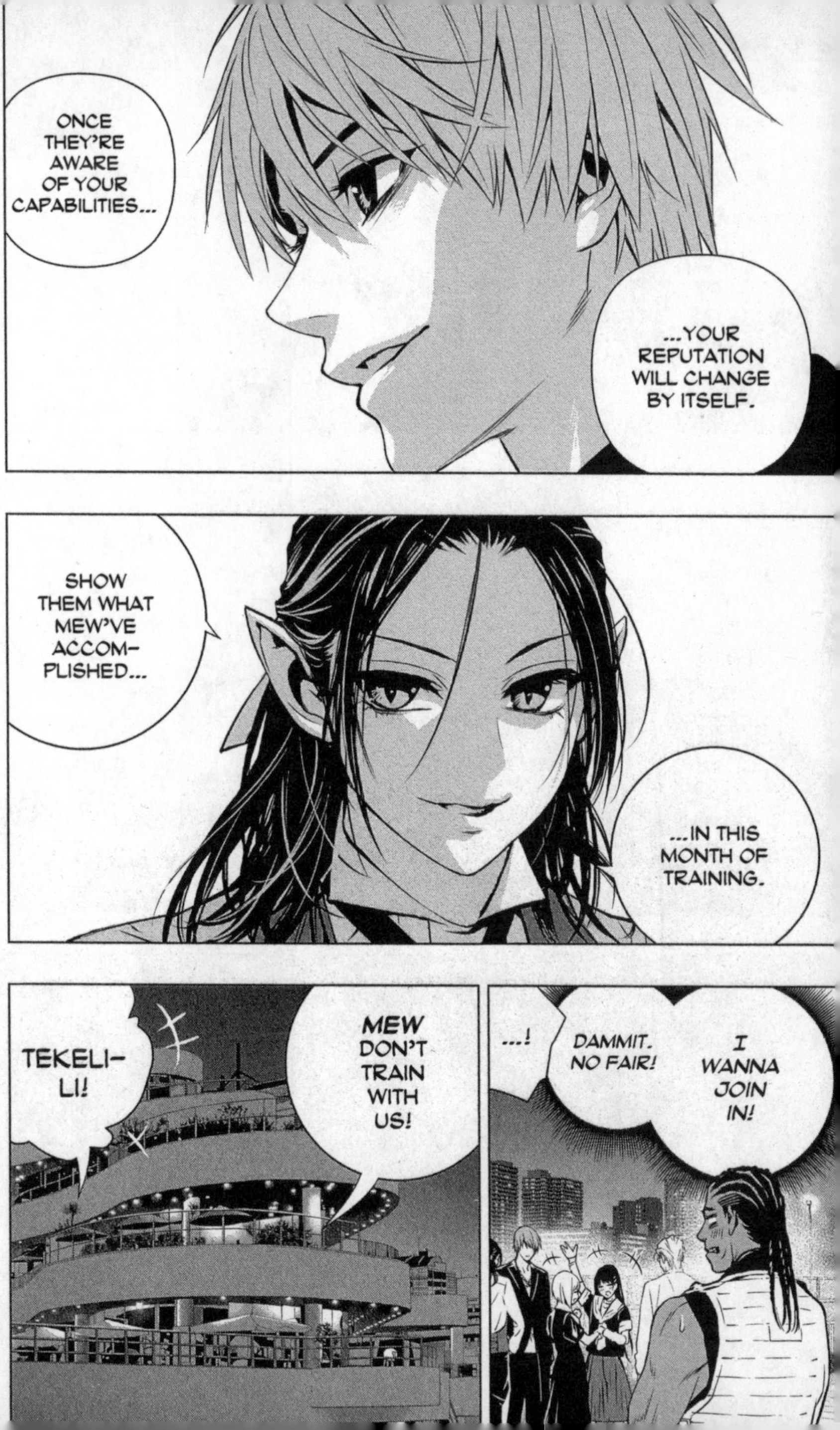
ONCE THEY'RE AWARE OF YOUR CAPABILITIES...
...YOUR REPUTATION WILL CHANGE BY ITSELF.
SHOW THEM WHAT MEW'VE ACCOMPLISHED...
...IN THIS MONTH OF TRAINING.
TEKELI-LI!
MEW DON'T TRAIN WITH US!
...!
DAMMIT. NO FAIR!
I WANNA JOIN IN!

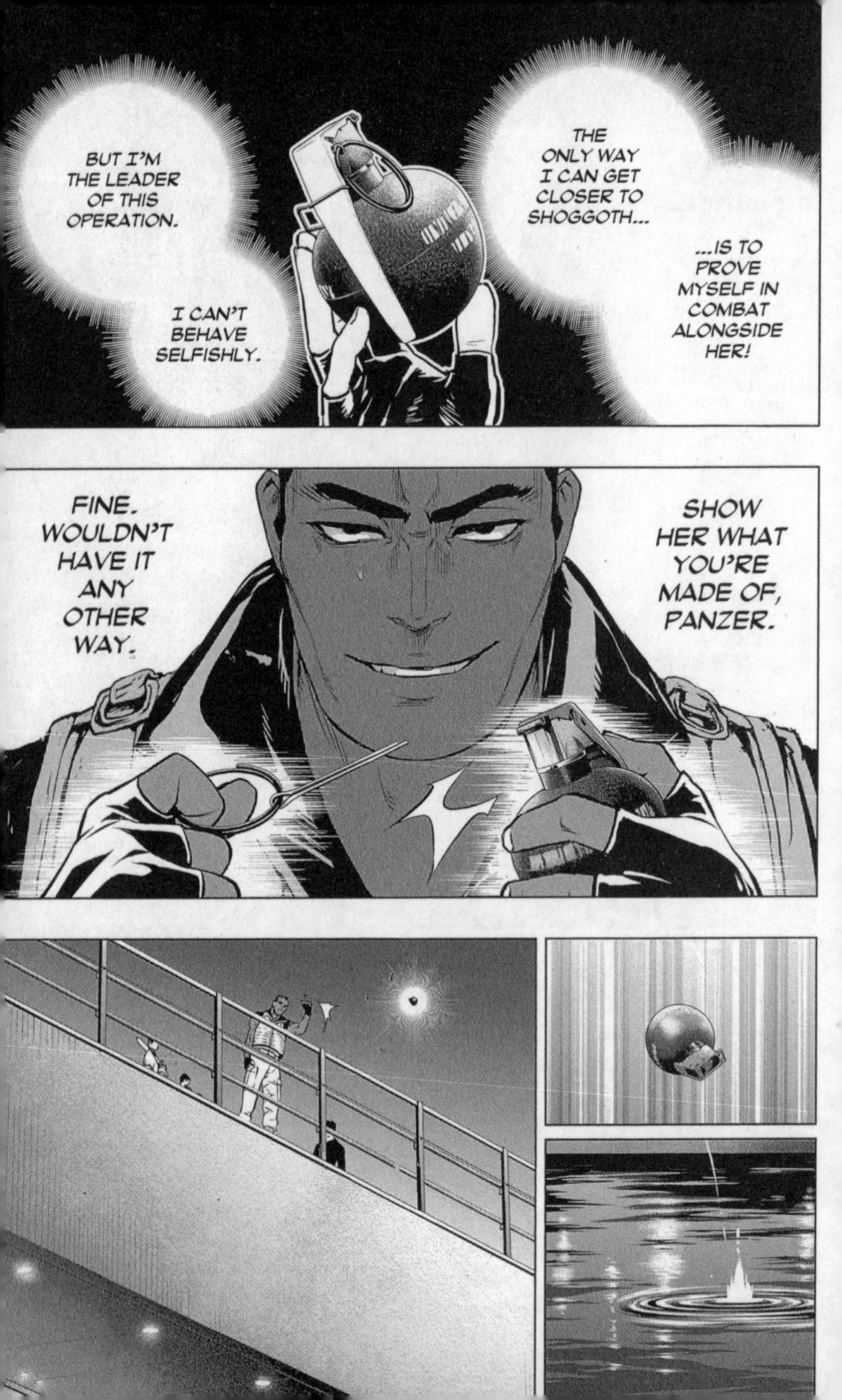
BUT I'M THE LEADER OF THIS OPERATION.
I CAN'T BEHAVE SELFISHLY.
THE ONLY WAY I CAN GET CLOSER TO SHOGGOTH...
...IS TO PROVE MYSELF IN COMBAT ALONGSIDE HER!
FINE. WOULDN'T HAVE IT ANY OTHER WAY.
SHOW HER WHAT YOU'RE MADE OF, PANZER.

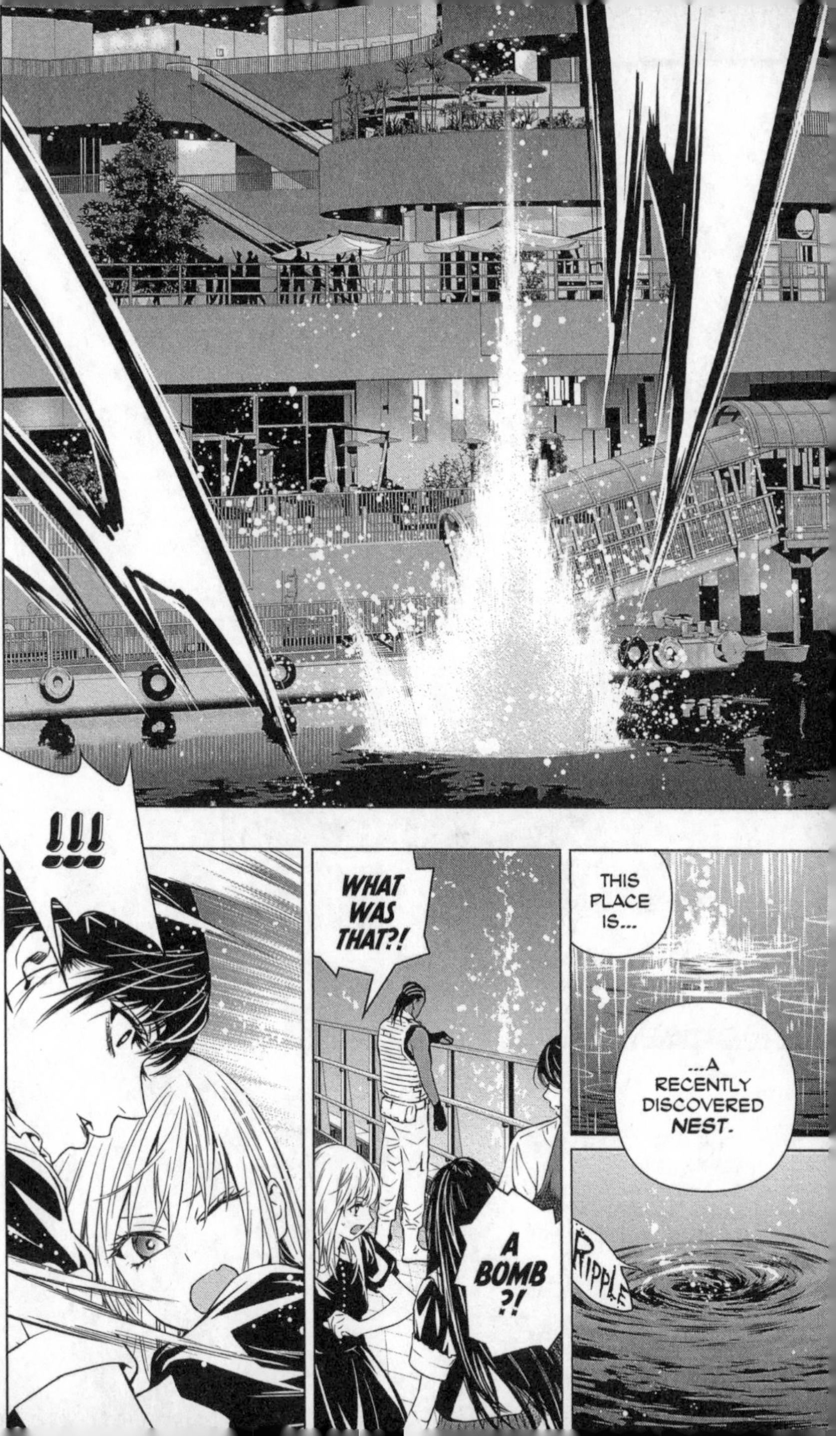
!!!
WHAT WAS THAT?!
A BOMB ?!
THIS PLACE IS...
...A RECENTLY DISCOVERED NEST.
RIPPLE

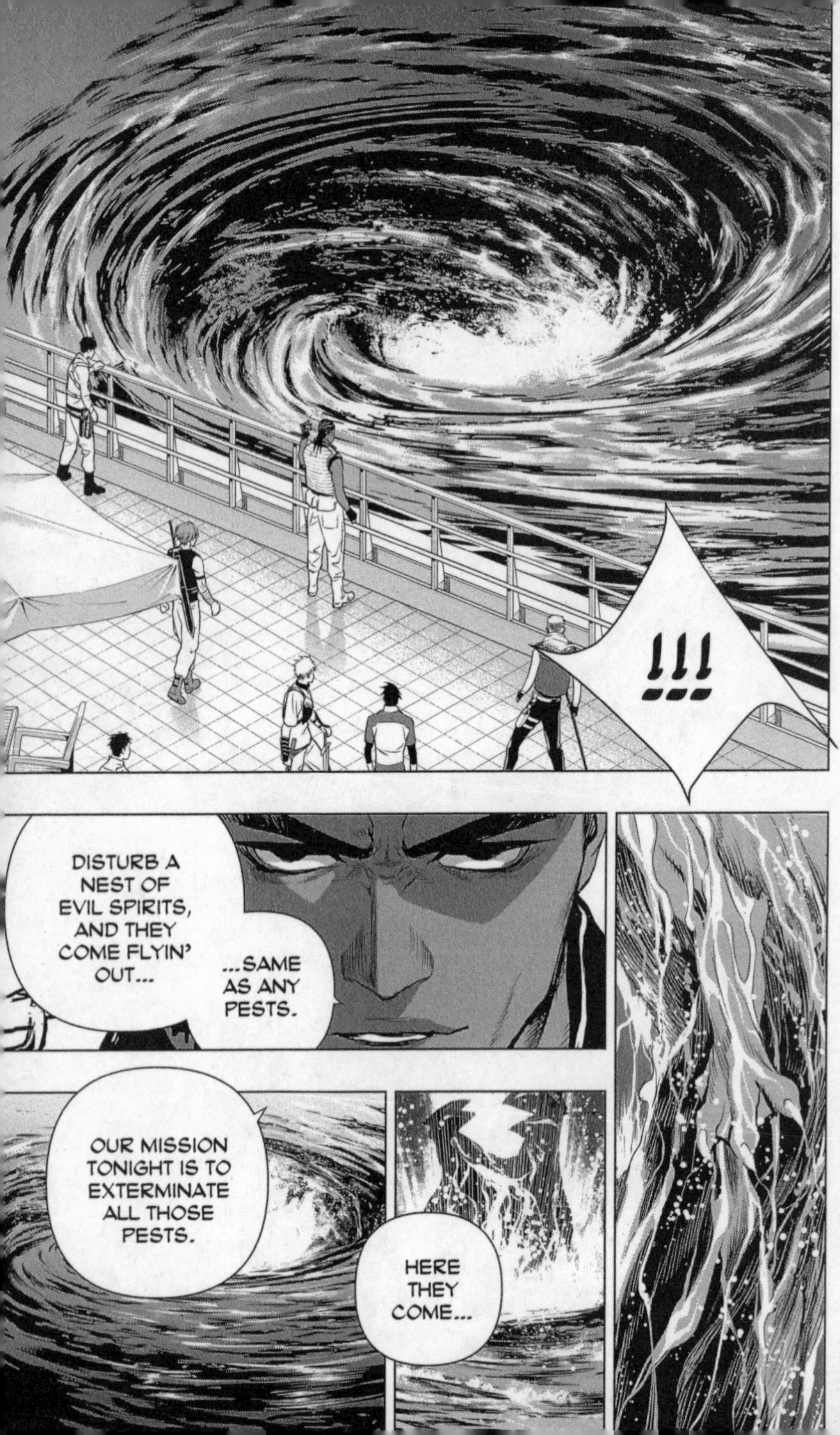
!!!
DISTURB A NEST OF EVIL SPIRITS, AND THEY COME FLYIN' OUT...
...SAME AS ANY PESTS.
OUR MISSION TONIGHT IS TO EXTERMINATE ALL THOSE PESTS.
HERE THEY COME...

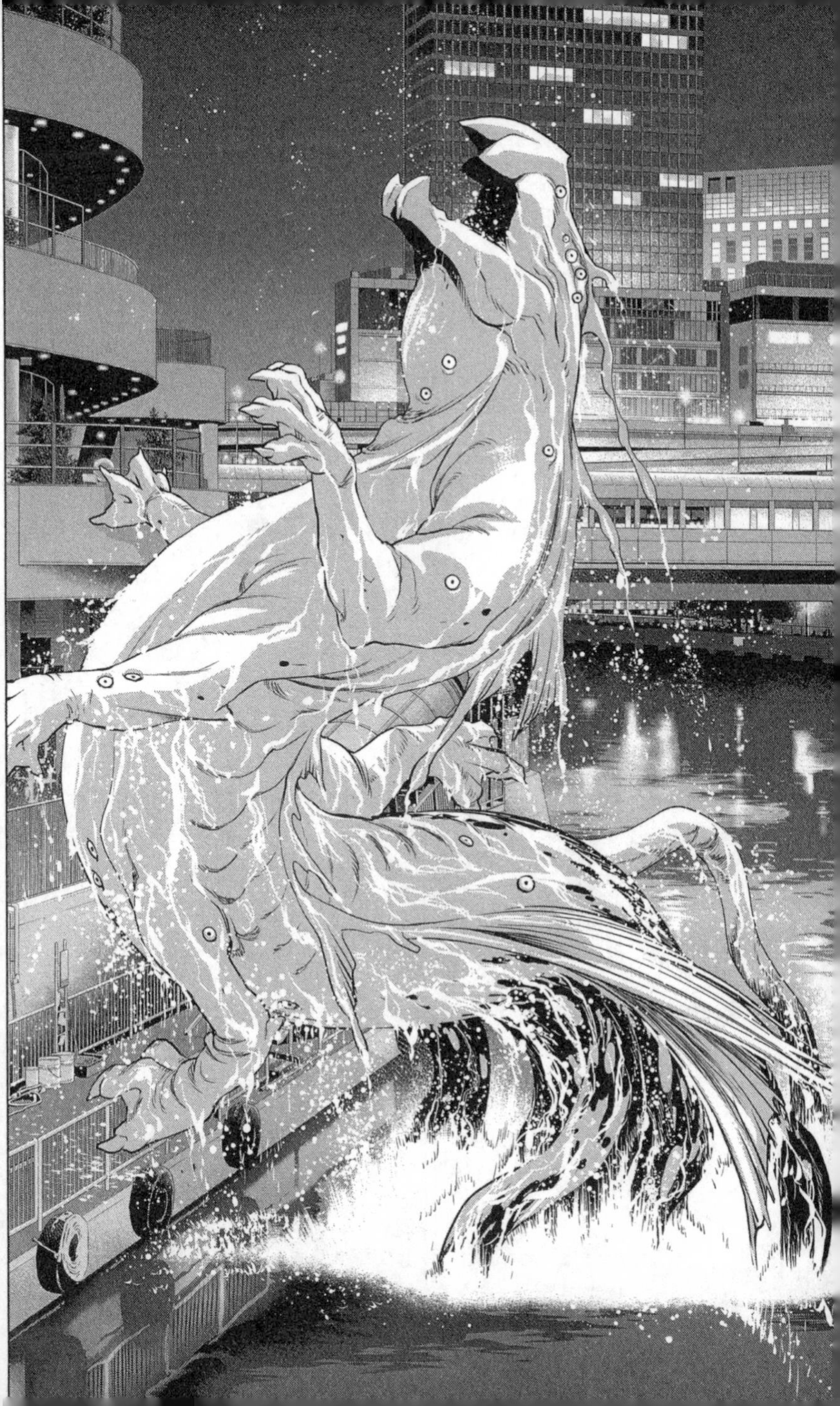

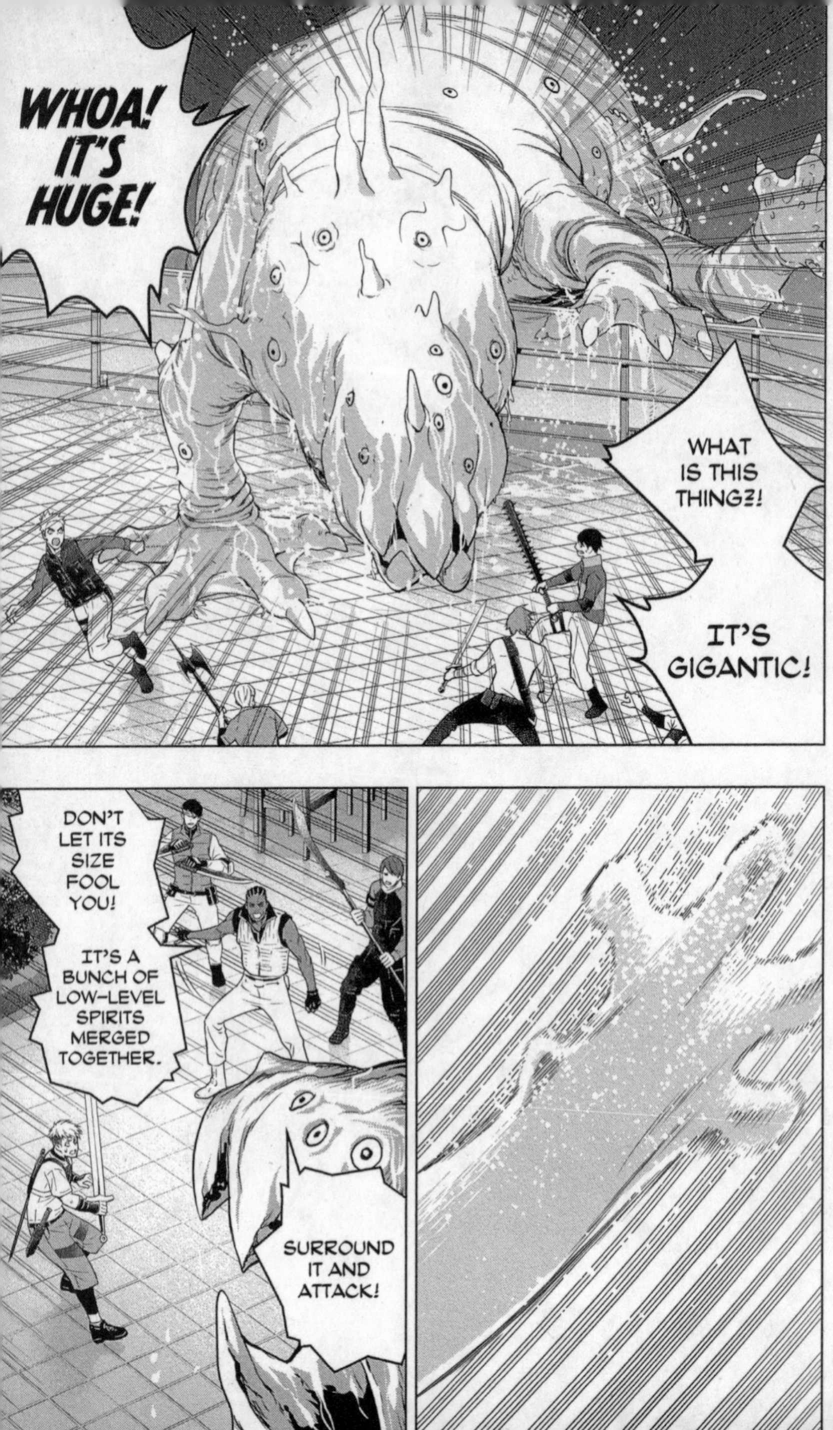
WHOA! IT'S HUGE!
WHAT IS THIS THING?!
IT'S GIGANTIC!
DON'T LET ITS SIZE FOOL YOU!
IT'S A BUNCH OF LOW-LEVEL SPIRITS MERGED TOGETHER.
SURROUND IT AND ATTACK!

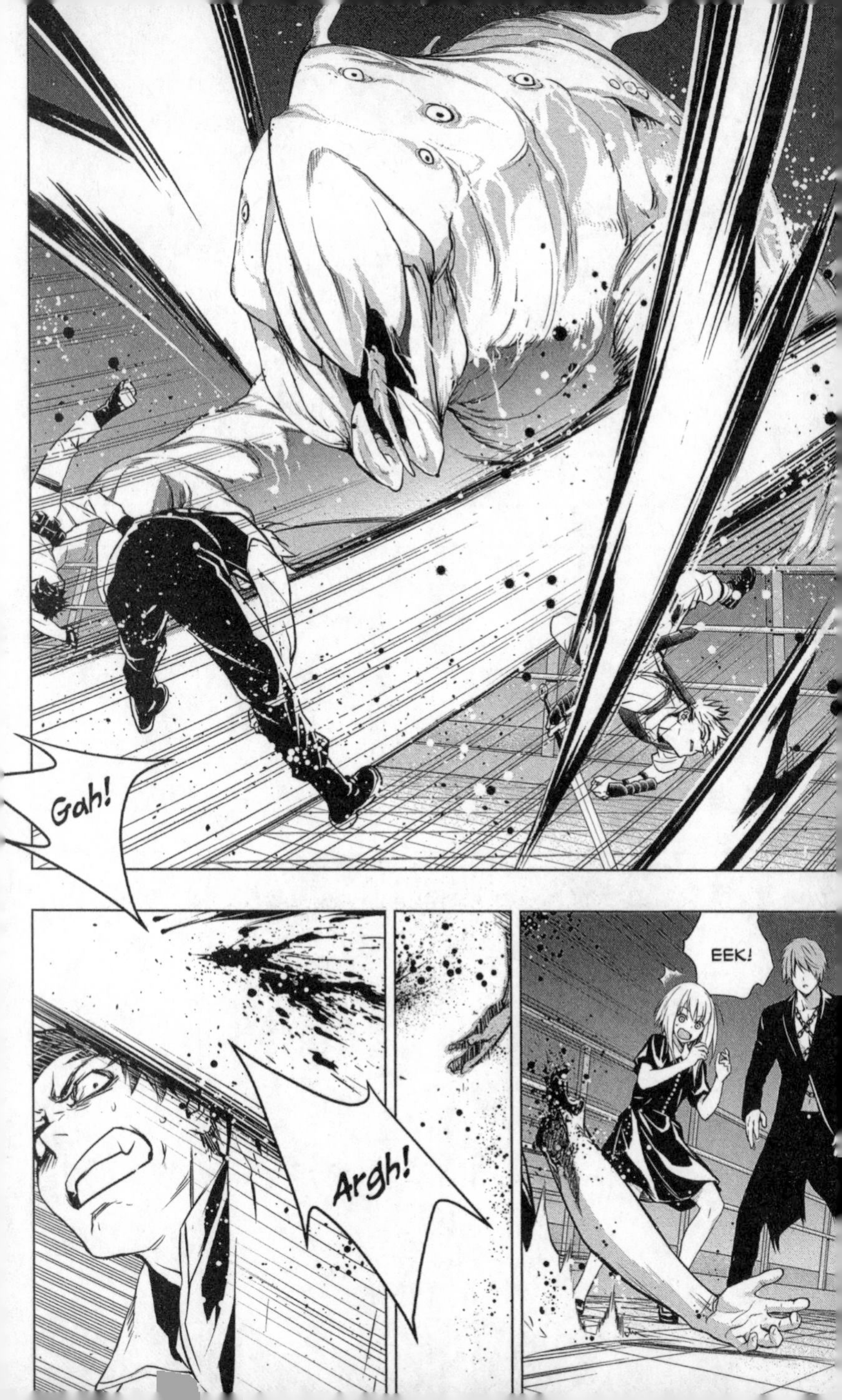
Gah!
Argh!
EEK!

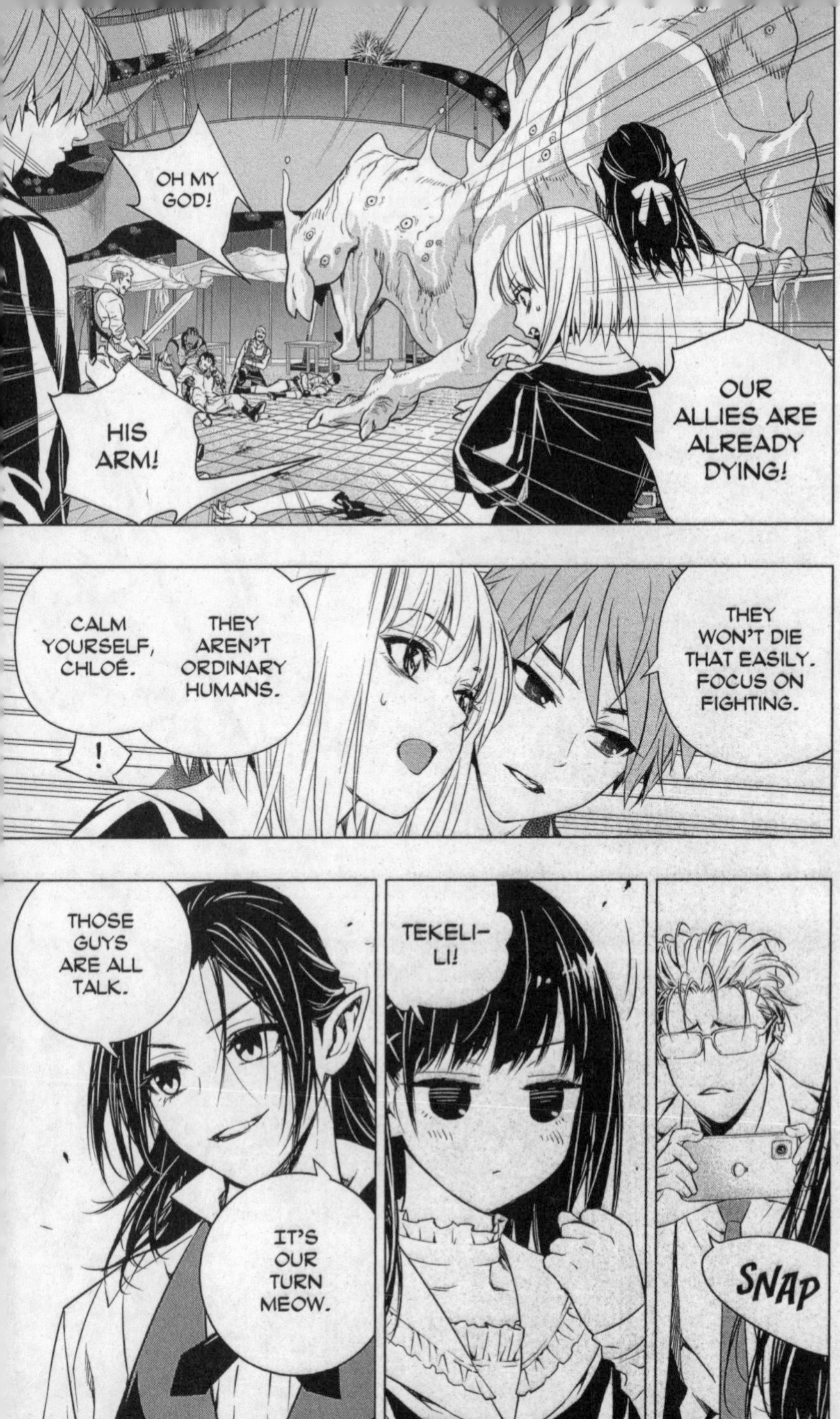
OH MY GOD!
HIS ARM!
OUR ALLIES ARE ALREADY DYING!
CALM YOURSELF, CHLOÉ.
THEY AREN'T ORDINARY HUMANS.
!
THEY WON'T DIE THAT EASILY. FOCUS ON FIGHTING.
THOSE GUYS ARE ALL TALK.
IT'S OUR TURN MEOW.
TEKELI-LI!
SNAP

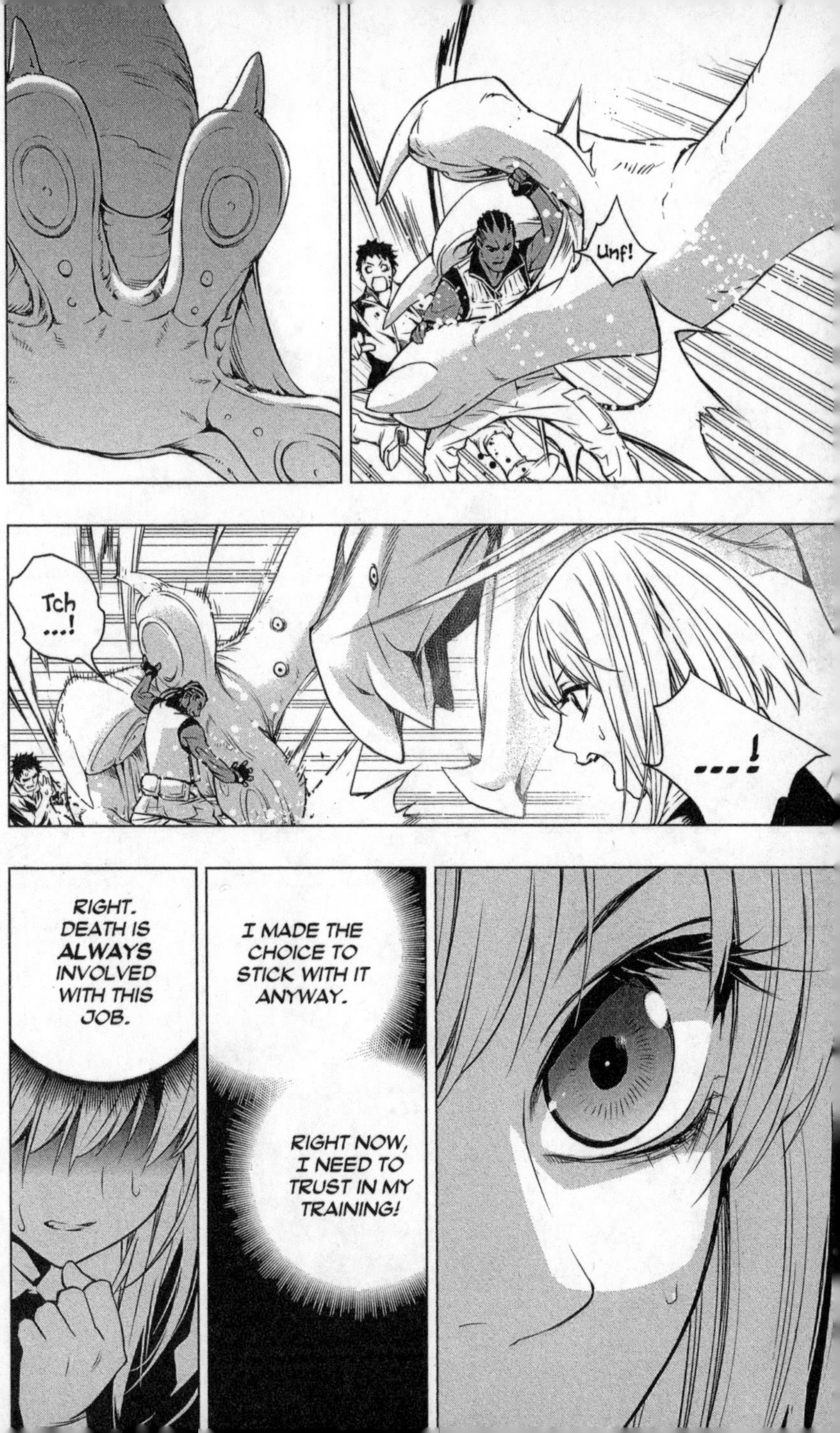
Unf!
Tch ...!
...!
RIGHT. DEATH IS ALWAYS INVOLVED WITH THIS JOB.
I MADE THE CHOICE TO STICK WITH IT ANYWAY.
RIGHT NOW, I NEED TO TRUST IN MY TRAINING!

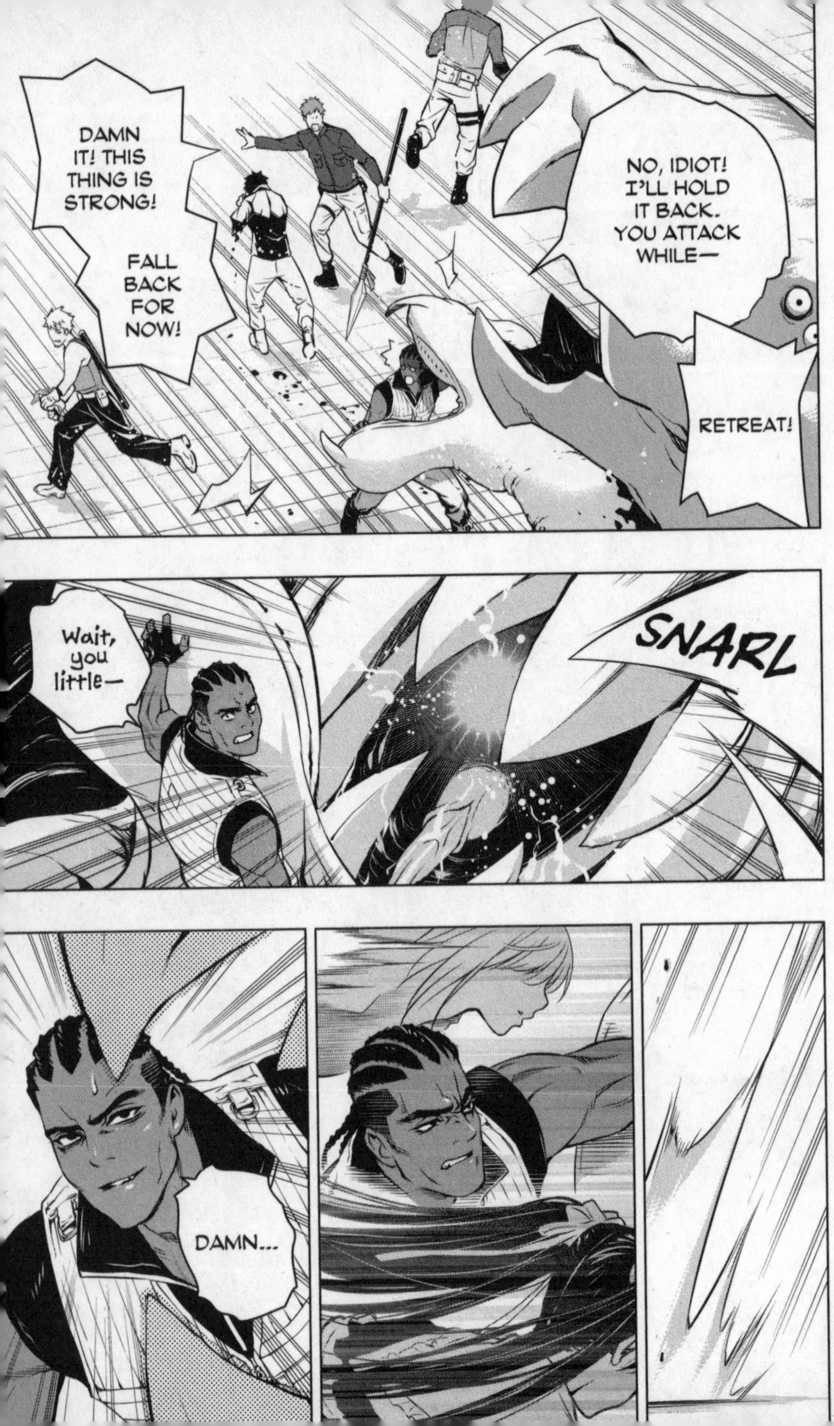
DAMN IT! THIS THING IS STRONG!
FALL BACK FOR NOW!
NO, IDIOT! I'LL HOLD IT BACK. YOU ATTACK WHILE—
RETREAT!
Wait, you little—
SNARL
DAMN...

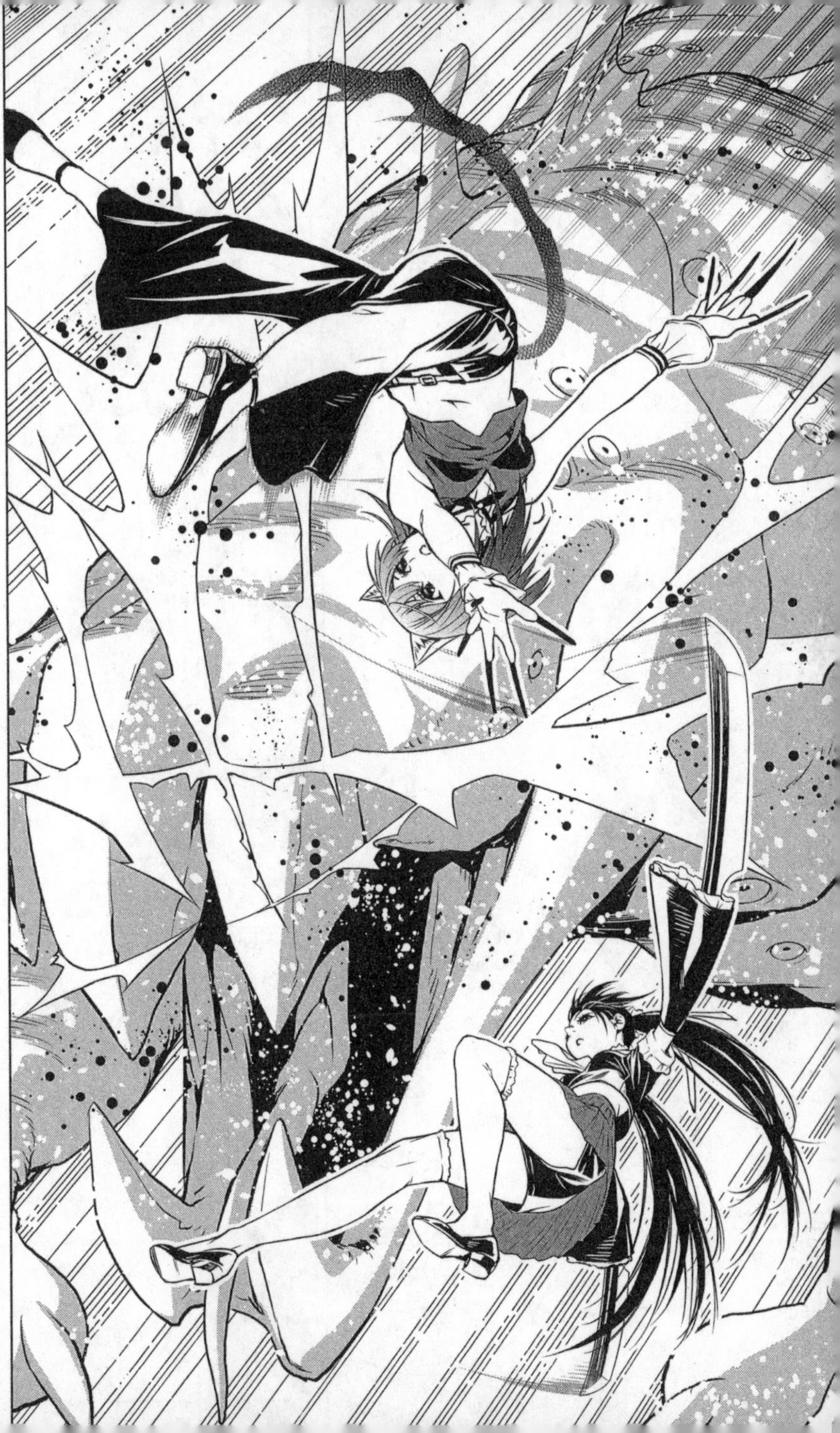

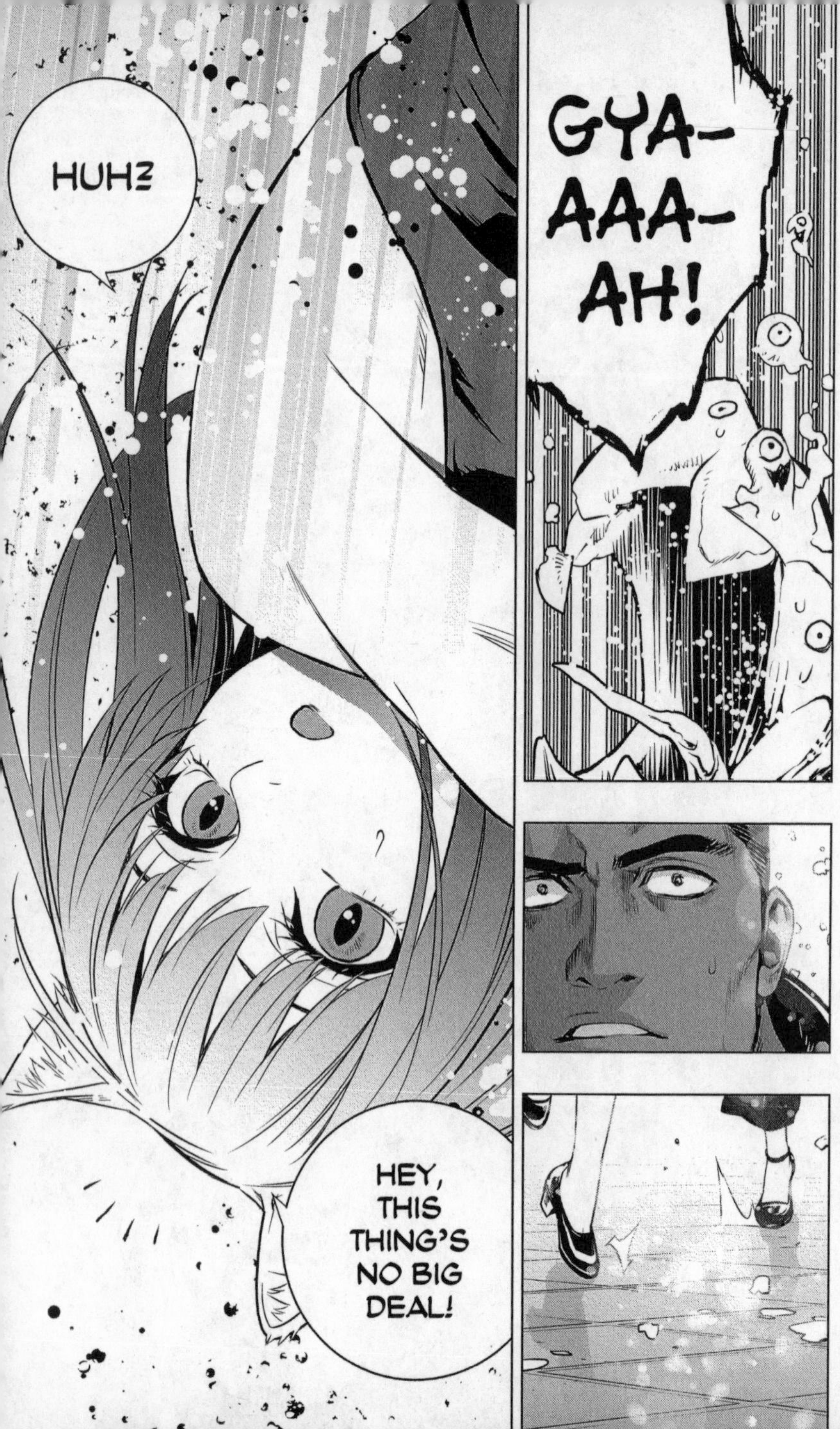
HUH?
HEY, THIS THING'S NO BIG DEAL!
GYA-AAA-AH!

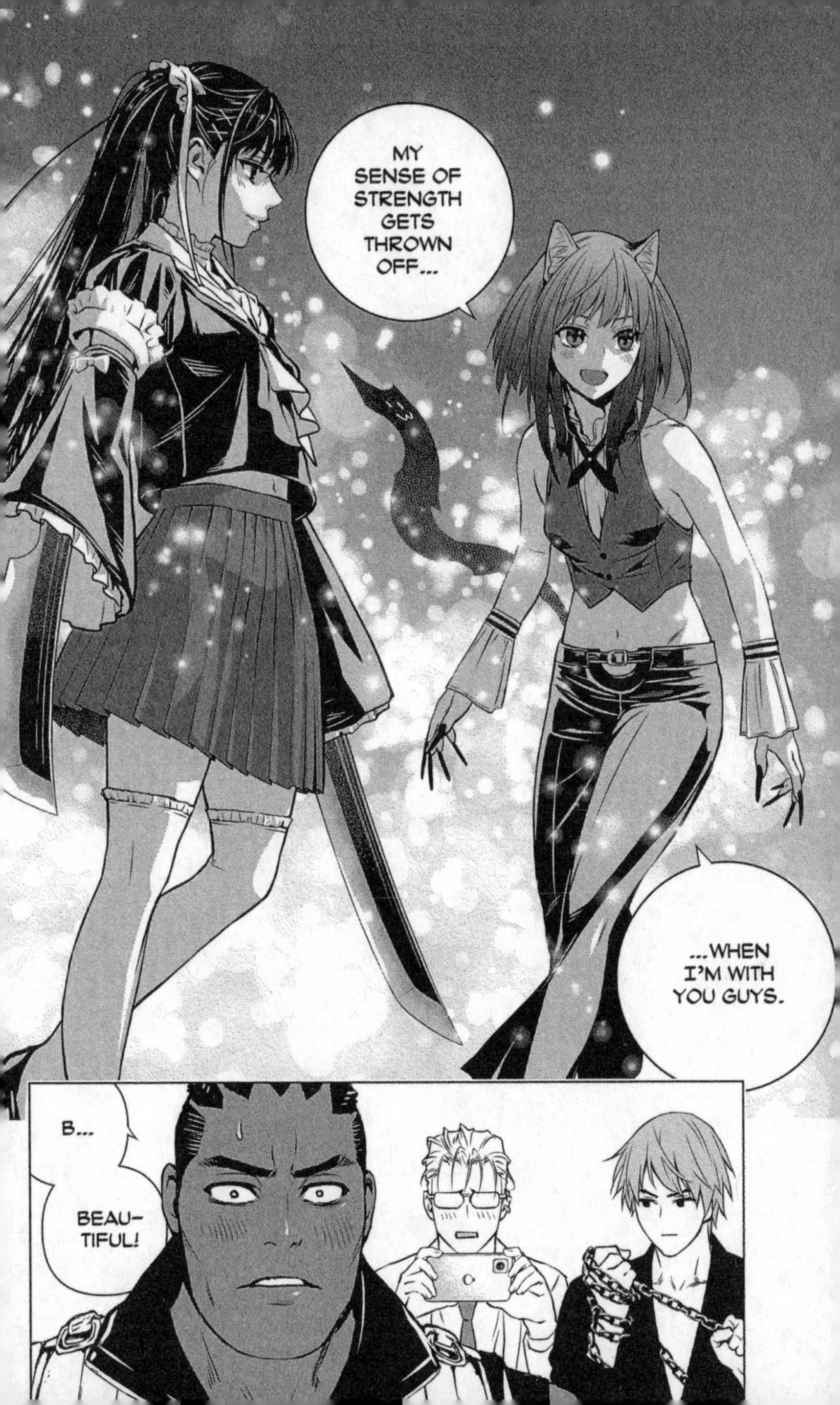
MY SENSE OF STRENGTH GETS THROWN OFF...
...WHEN I'M WITH YOU GUYS.
B...
BEAU-TIFUL!

16: BATTLEFIELD

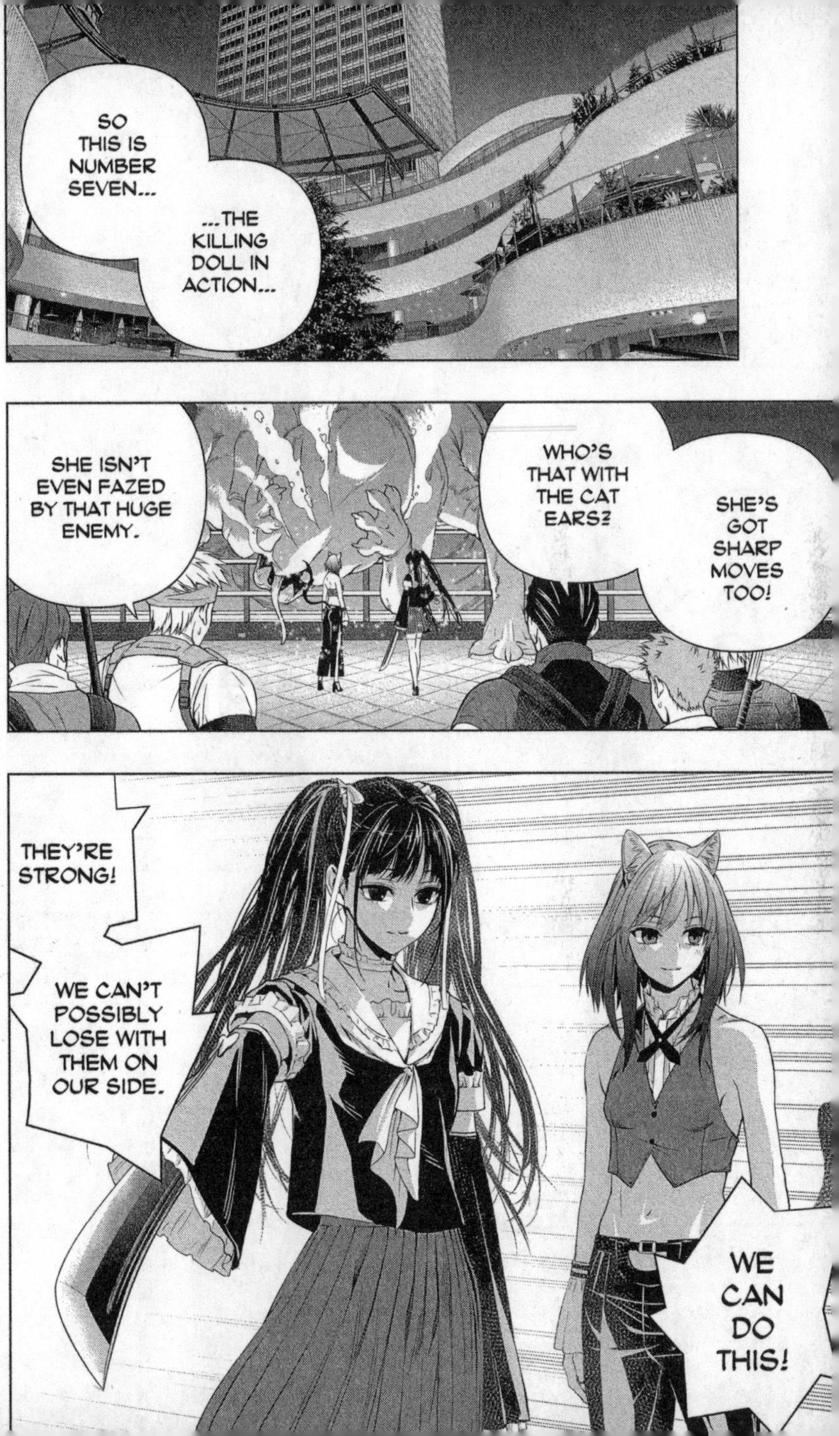
SO THIS IS NUMBER SEVEN...
...THE KILLING DOLL IN ACTION...
SHE ISN'T EVEN FAZED BY THAT HUGE ENEMY.
WHO'S THAT WITH THE CAT EARS?
SHE'S GOT SHARP MOVES TOO!
THEY'RE STRONG!
WE CAN'T POSSIBLY LOSE WITH THEM ON OUR SIDE.
WE CAN DO THIS!

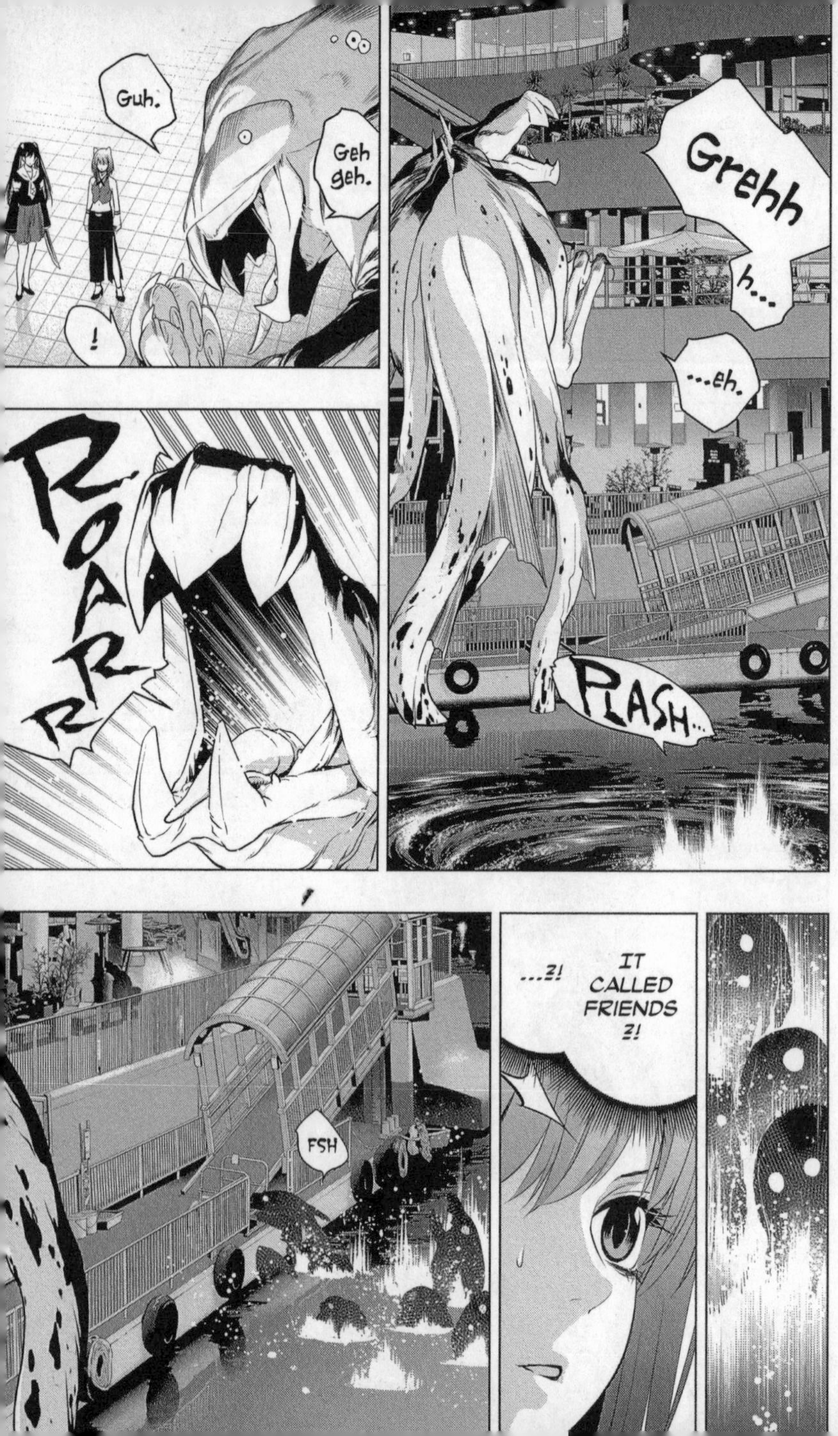
Guh.
Geh geh.
!
ROARR
Grehh h...
...eh.
PLASH...
FSH
...?!
IT CALLED FRIENDS?!

RAAH!

HNF!

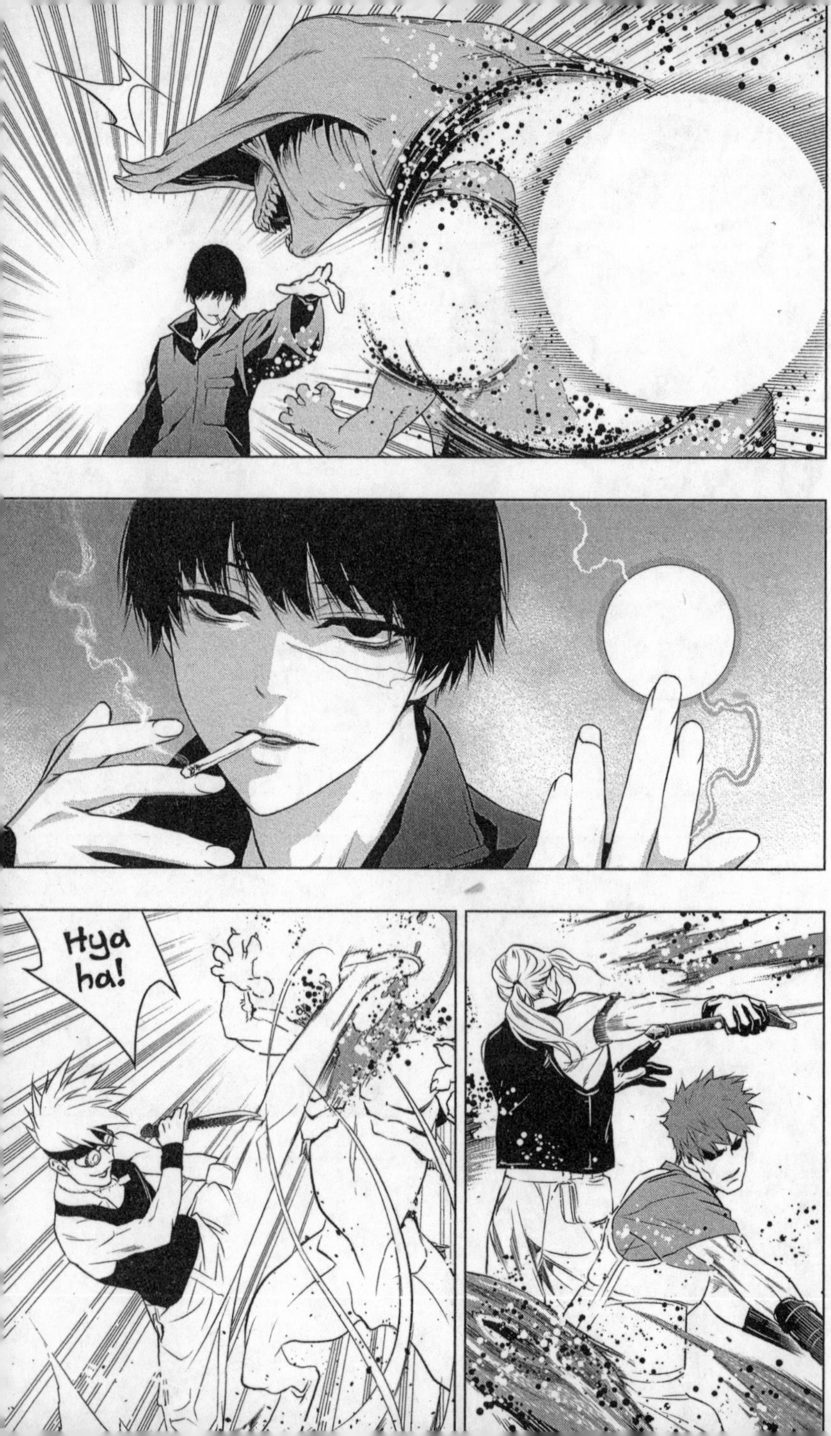
Hya ha!

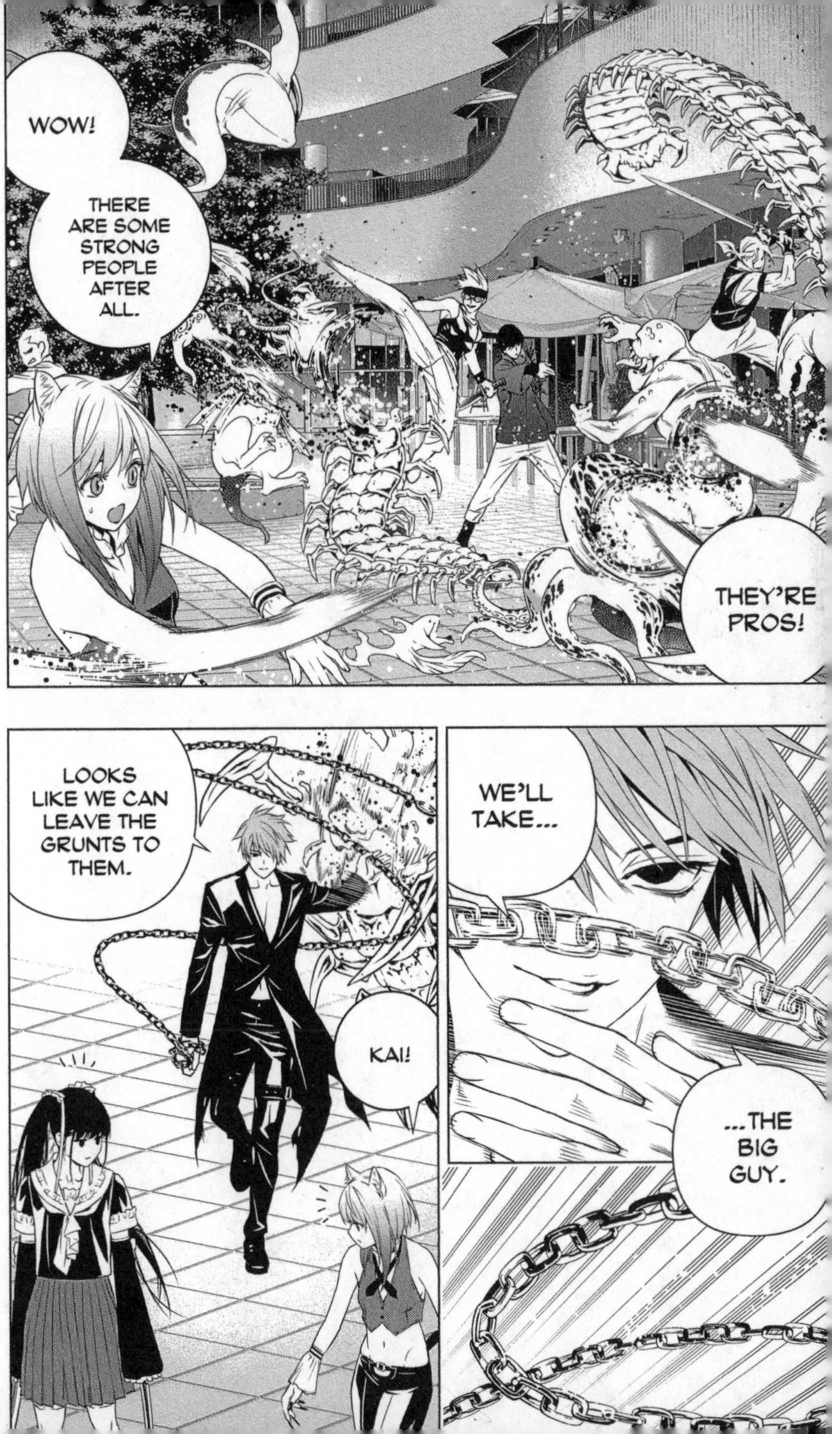
WOW!
THERE ARE SOME STRONG PEOPLE AFTER ALL.
THEY'RE PROS!
LOOKS LIKE WE CAN LEAVE THE GRUNTS TO THEM.
KAI!
WE'LL TAKE...
...THE BIG GUY.

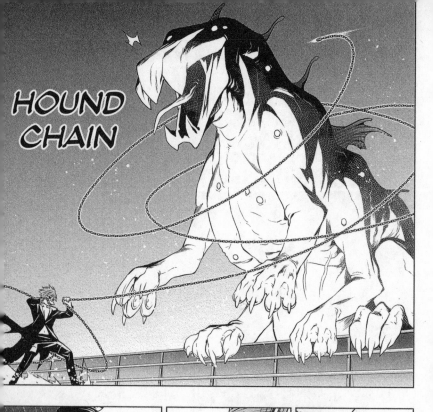

HOUND CHAIN

Greh!

I BOUND IT!

NOW!

TEKELI...

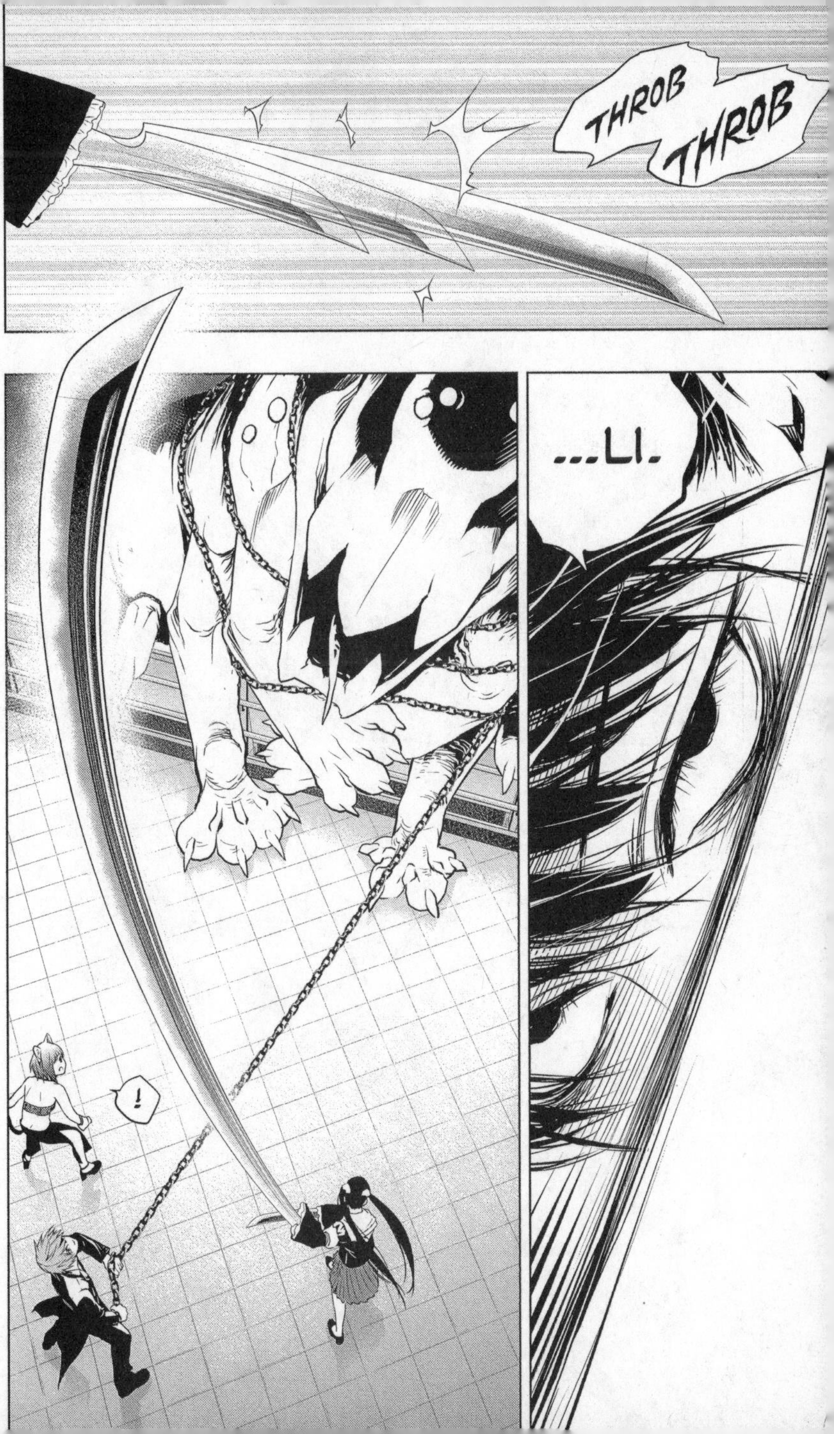
THROB THROB
...LI.
!

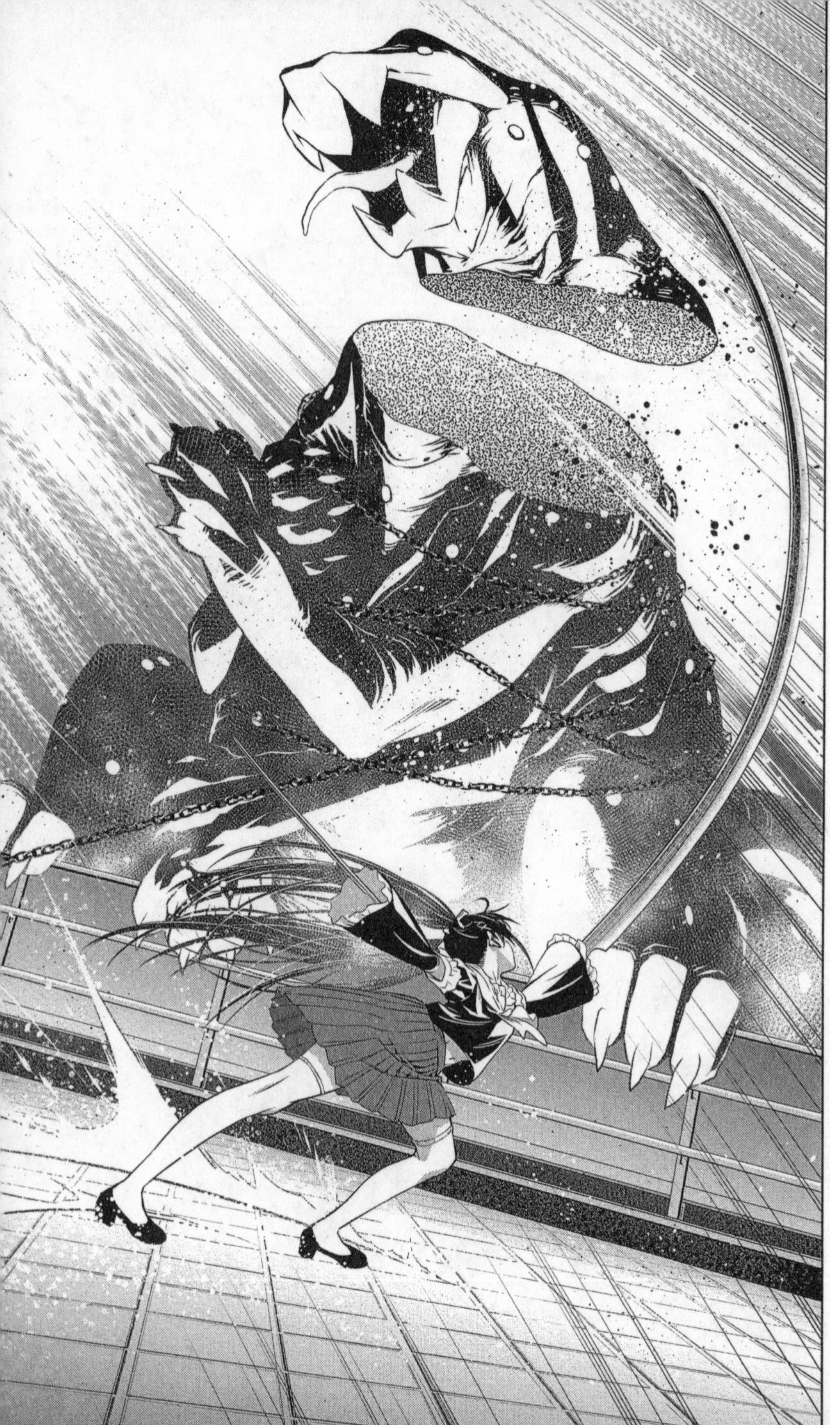

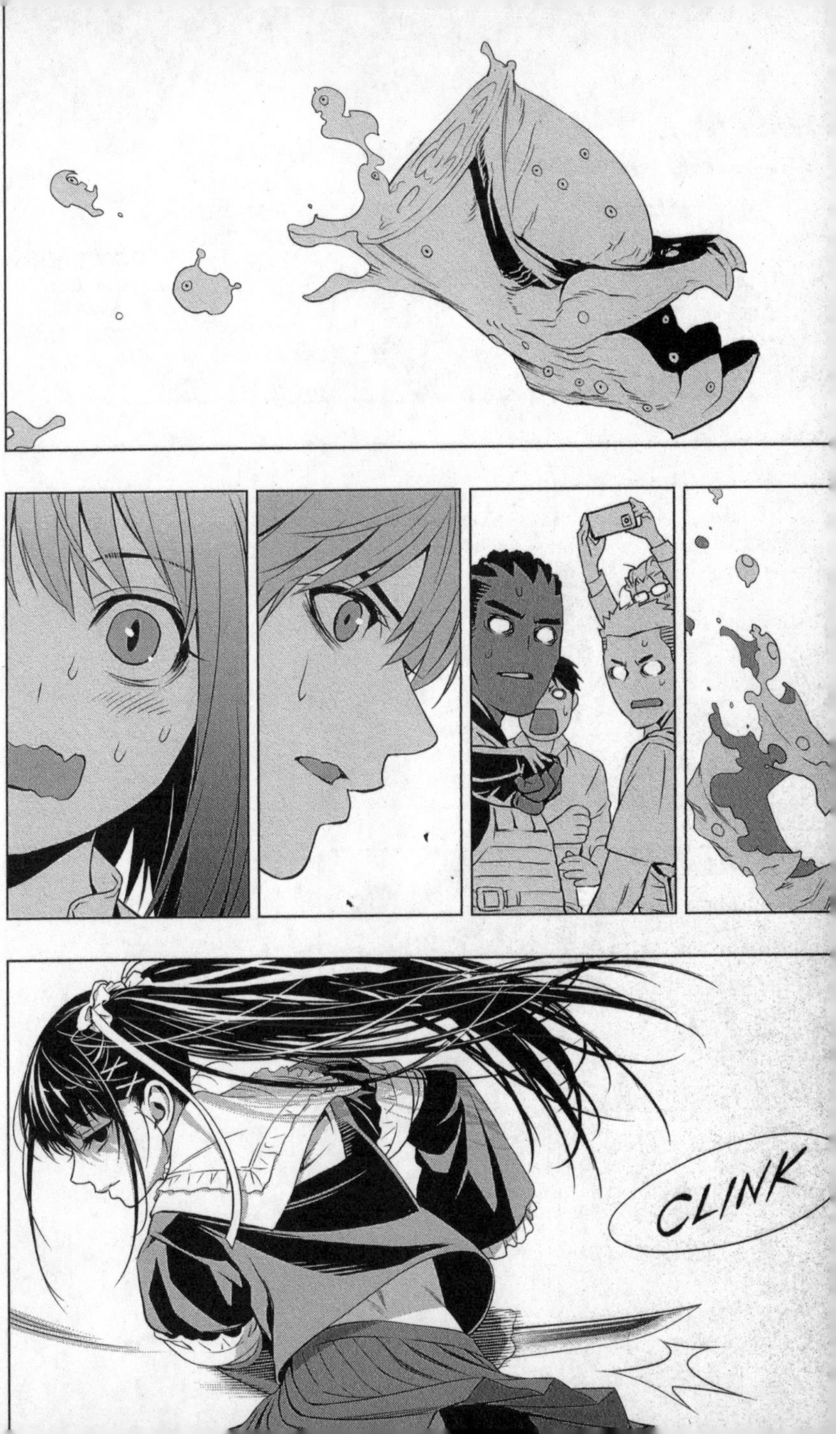
CLINK

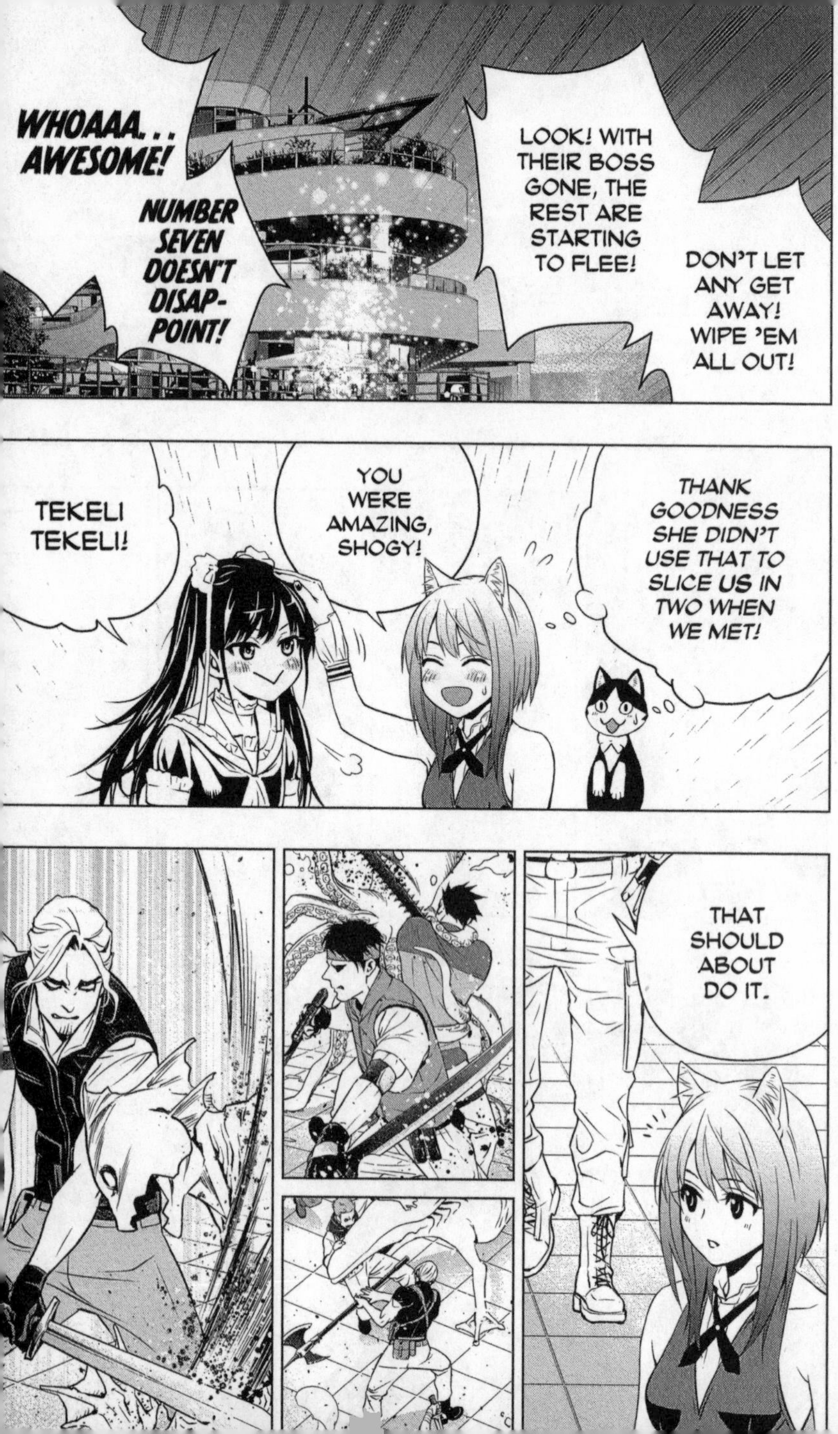
WHOAAA... AWESOME!
NUMBER SEVEN DOESN'T DISAP-POINT!
LOOK! WITH THEIR BOSS GONE, THE REST ARE STARTING TO FLEE!
DON'T LET ANY GET AWAY! WIPE 'EM ALL OUT!
TEKELI TEKELI!
YOU WERE AMAZING, SHOGY!
THANK GOODNESS SHE DIDN'T USE THAT TO SLICE US IN TWO WHEN WE MET!
THAT SHOULD ABOUT DO IT.

AHEM...

YOU'RE PRETTY STRONG.

SORRY FOR BEIN' SO RUDE TO YOU GUYS AT FIRST.

MISTER...

...PANTS?

I think?

IT'S *PANZER.*

BUT IF THAT'S EASIER FOR YOU TO REMEMBER, THAT'S FINE BY ME TOO.

IT IS?

LET ME BUY YOU A DRINK SOMETIME TO MAKE THINGS RIGHT.

IF YOU WANT, UH...

...MASTER SHOGGOTH COULD JOIN US—

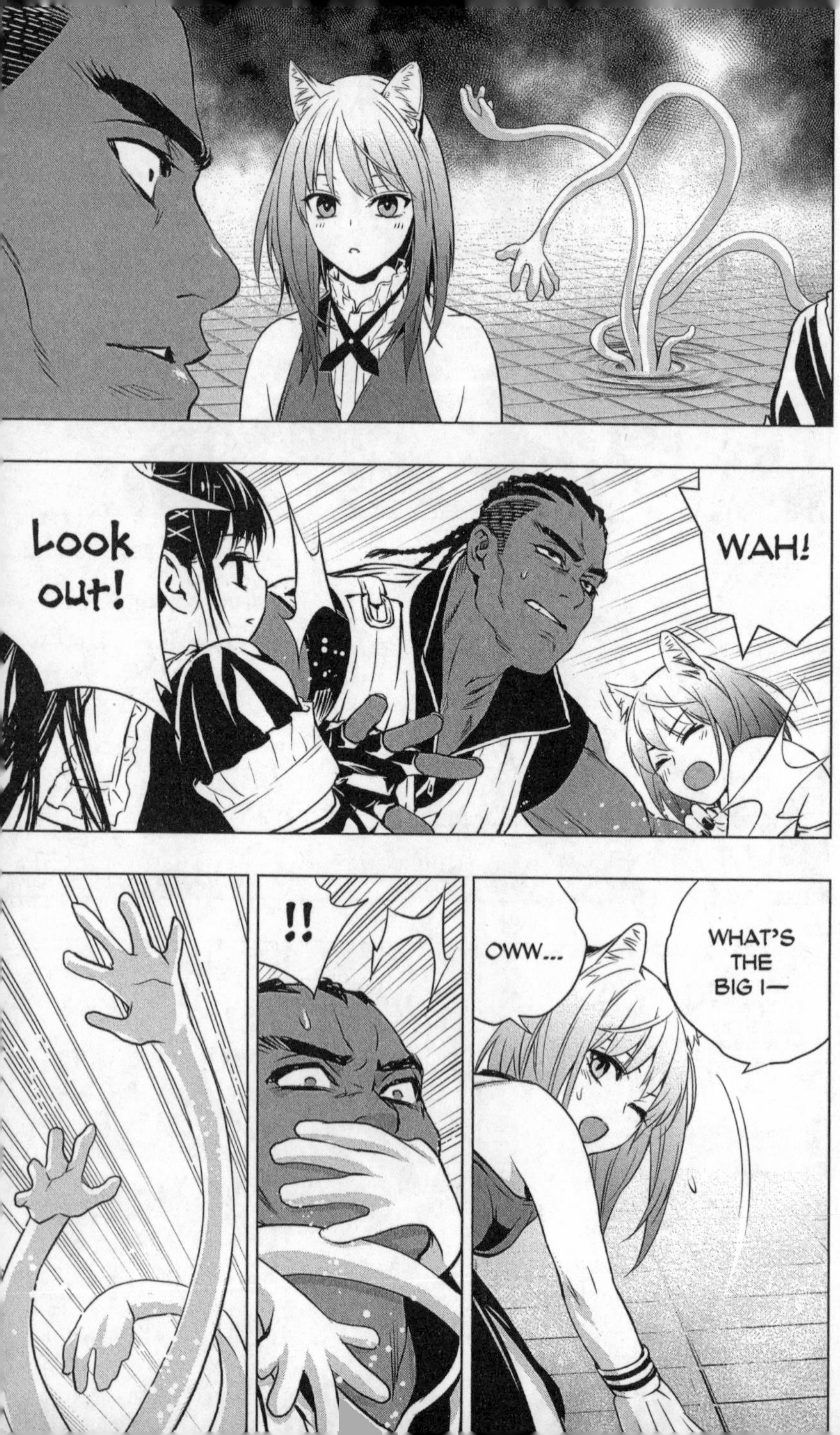
Look out!
WAH!
!!
OWW...
WHAT'S THE BIG I—

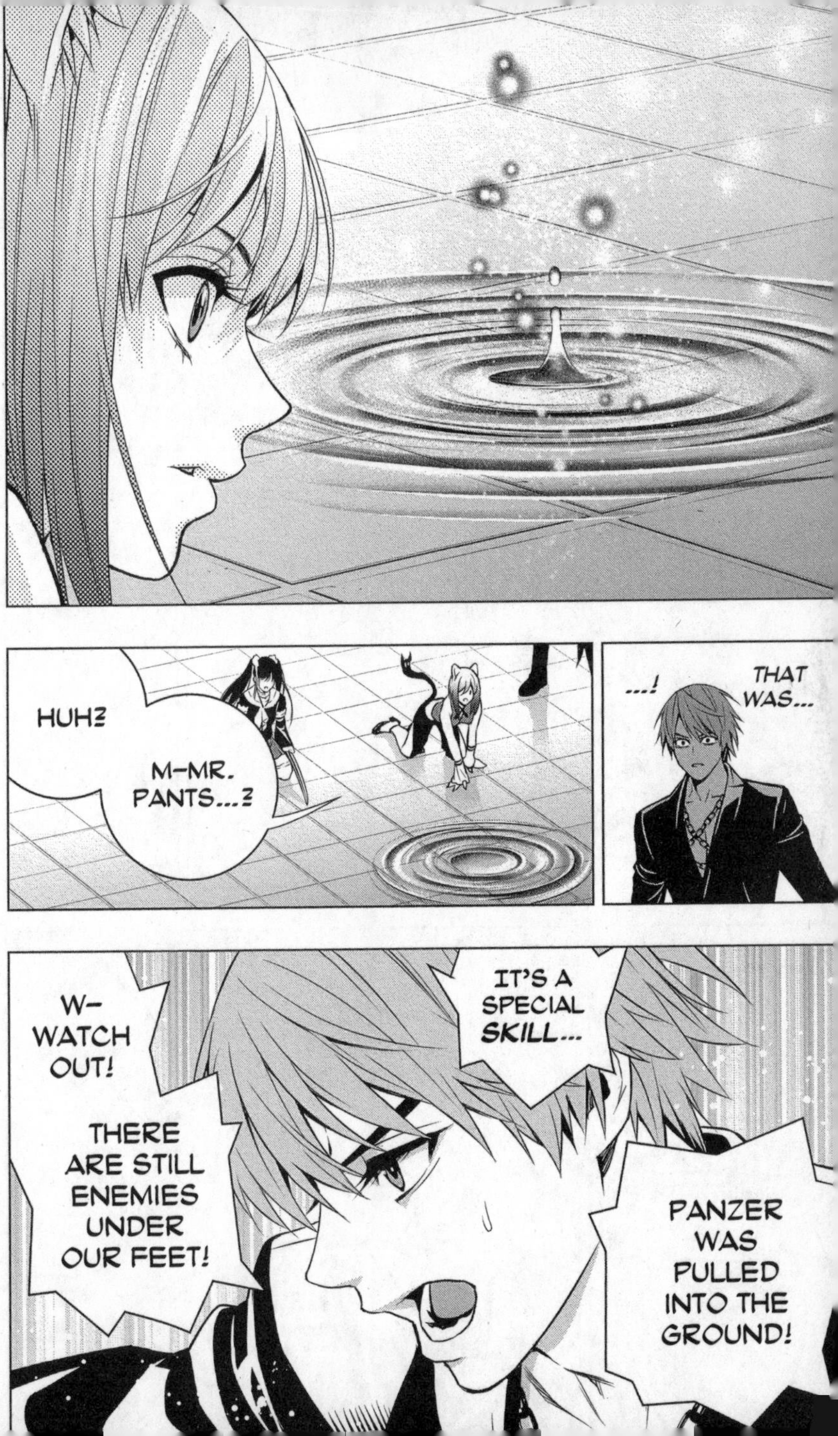
HUH?
M-MR. PANTS...?
...!
THAT WAS...
W-WATCH OUT!
THERE ARE STILL ENEMIES UNDER OUR FEET!
IT'S A SPECIAL SKILL...
PANZER WAS PULLED INTO THE GROUND!

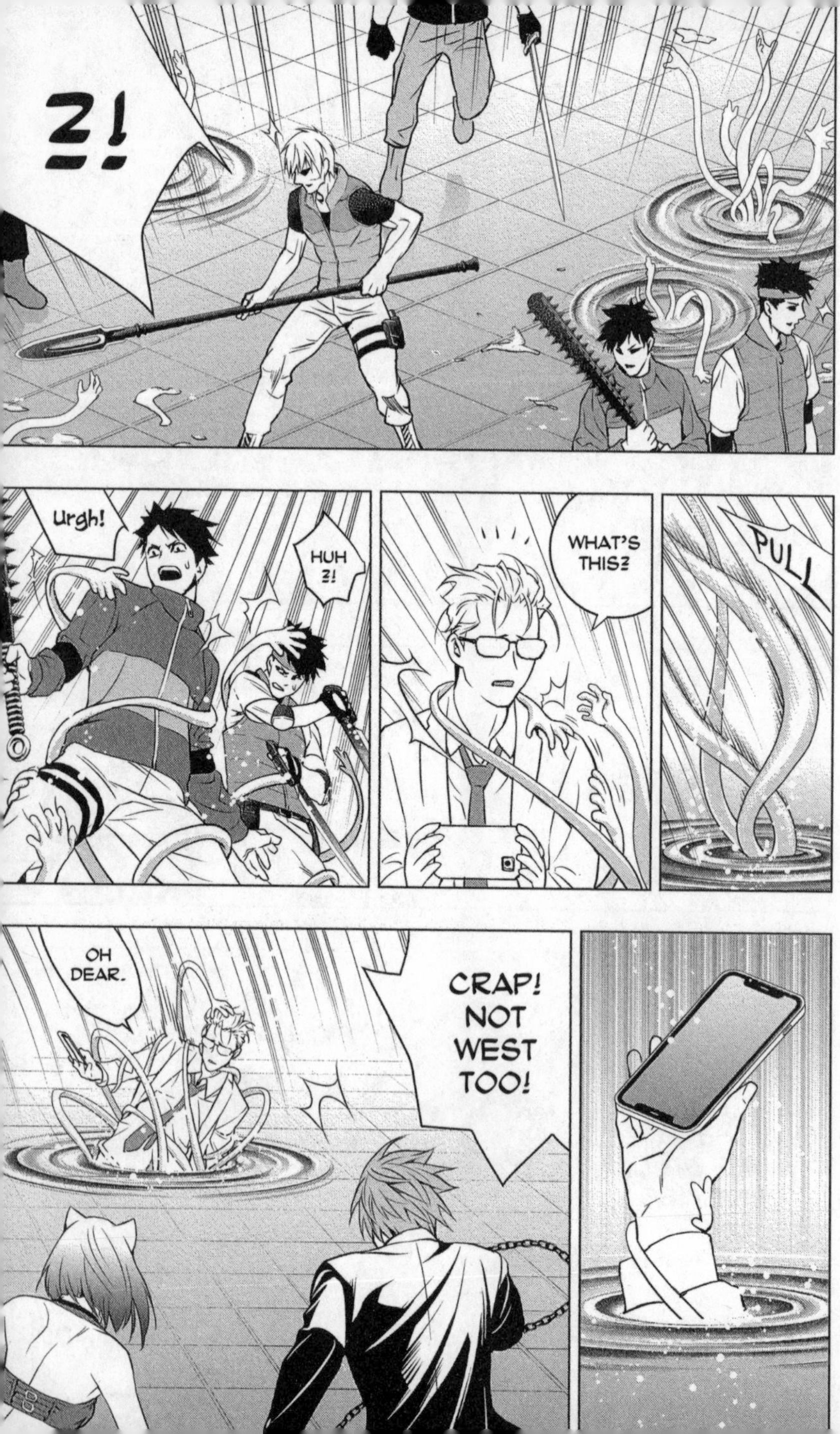
Z!
Urgh!
HUH ?!
WHAT'S THIS?
PULL
OH DEAR.
CRAP! NOT WEST TOO!

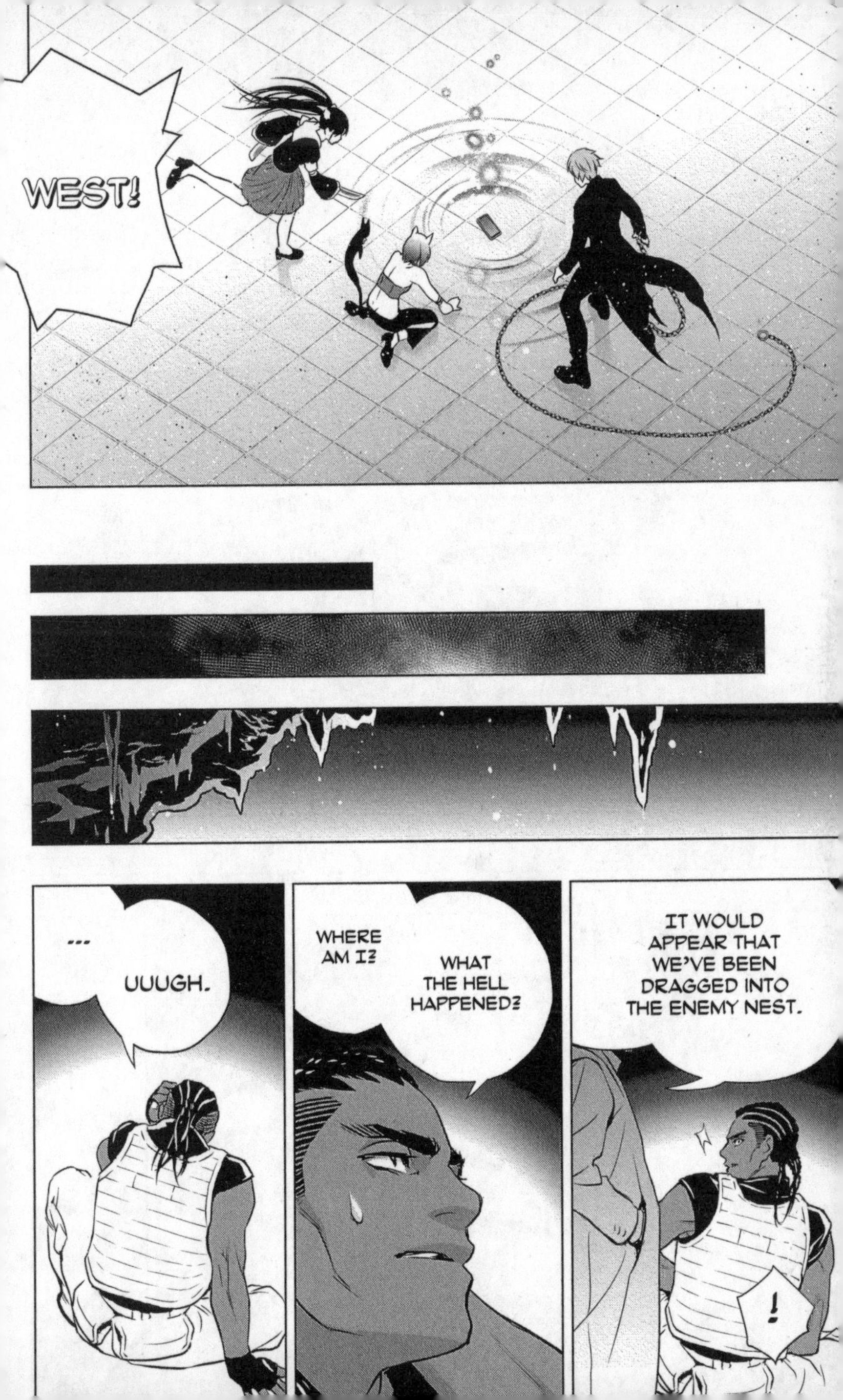
WEST!
...
UUUGH.
WHERE AM I?
WHAT THE HELL HAPPENED?
IT WOULD APPEAR THAT WE'VE BEEN DRAGGED INTO THE ENEMY NEST.
!

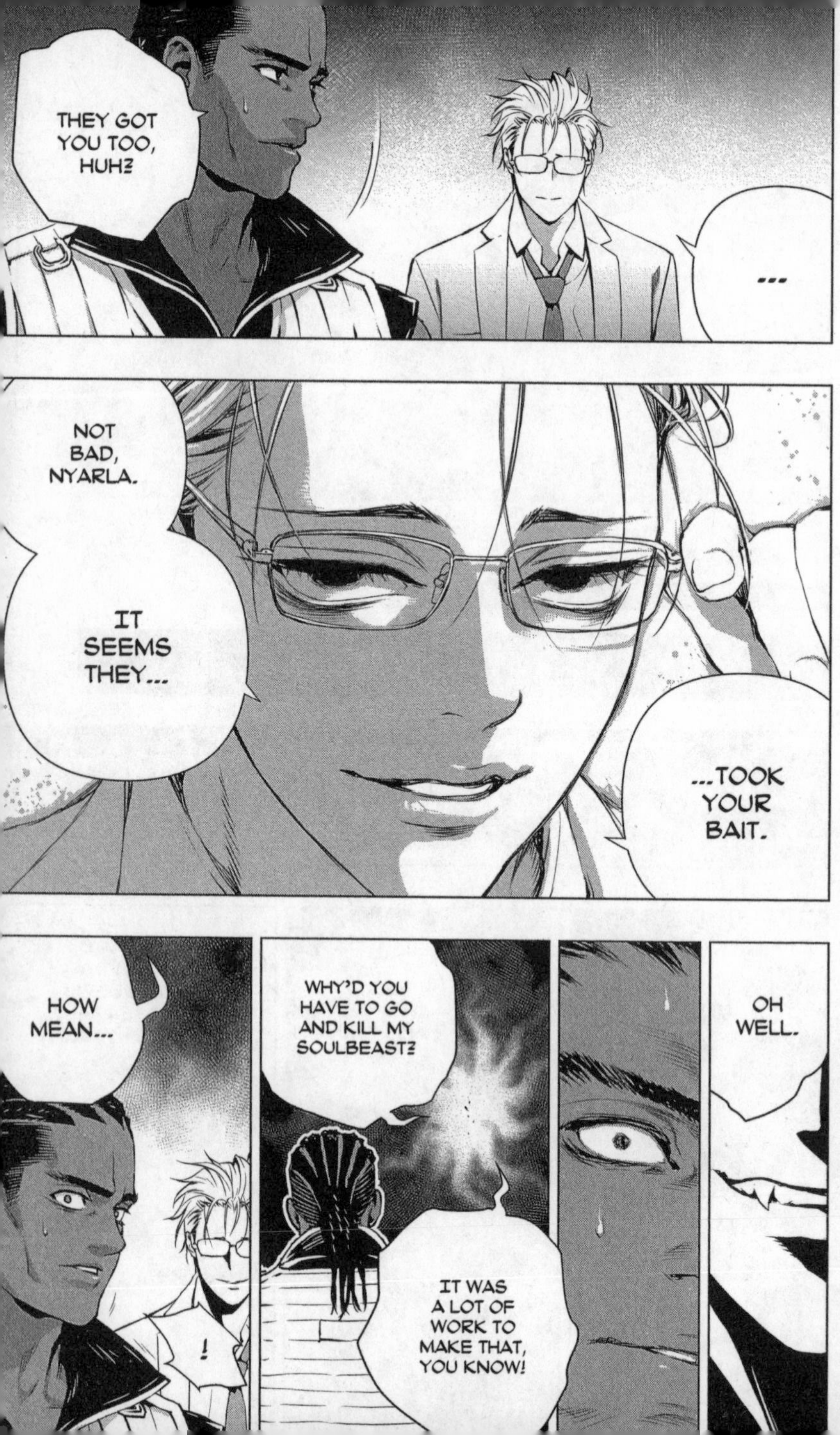
THEY GOT YOU TOO, HUH?
...
NOT BAD, NYARLA.
IT SEEMS THEY...
...TOOK YOUR BAIT.
HOW MEAN...
!
WHY'D YOU HAVE TO GO AND KILL MY SOULBEAST?
IT WAS A LOT OF WORK TO MAKE THAT, YOU KNOW!
OH WELL.

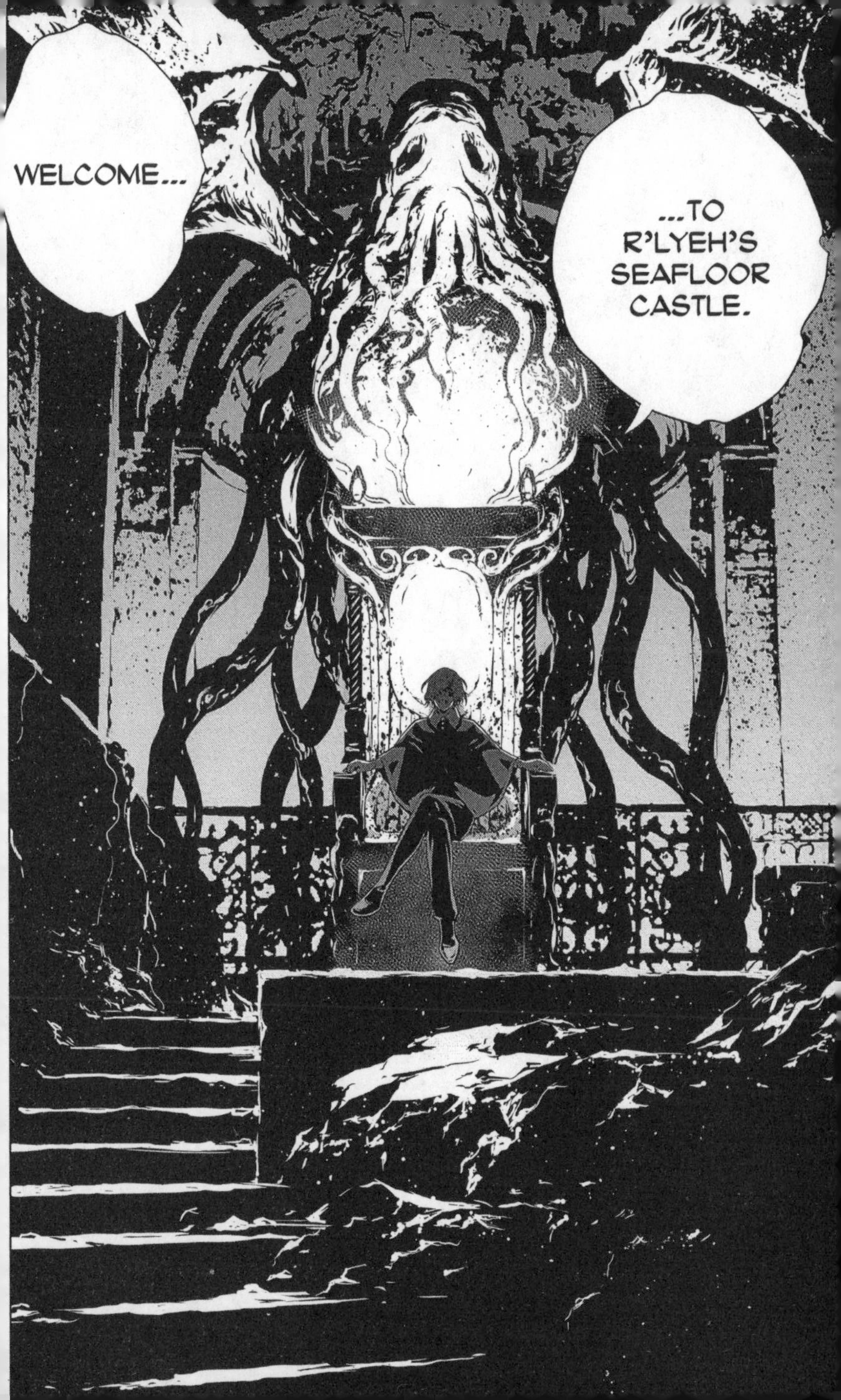
WELCOME...
...TO R'LYEH'S SEAFLOOR CASTLE.

17: CALL OF "C"

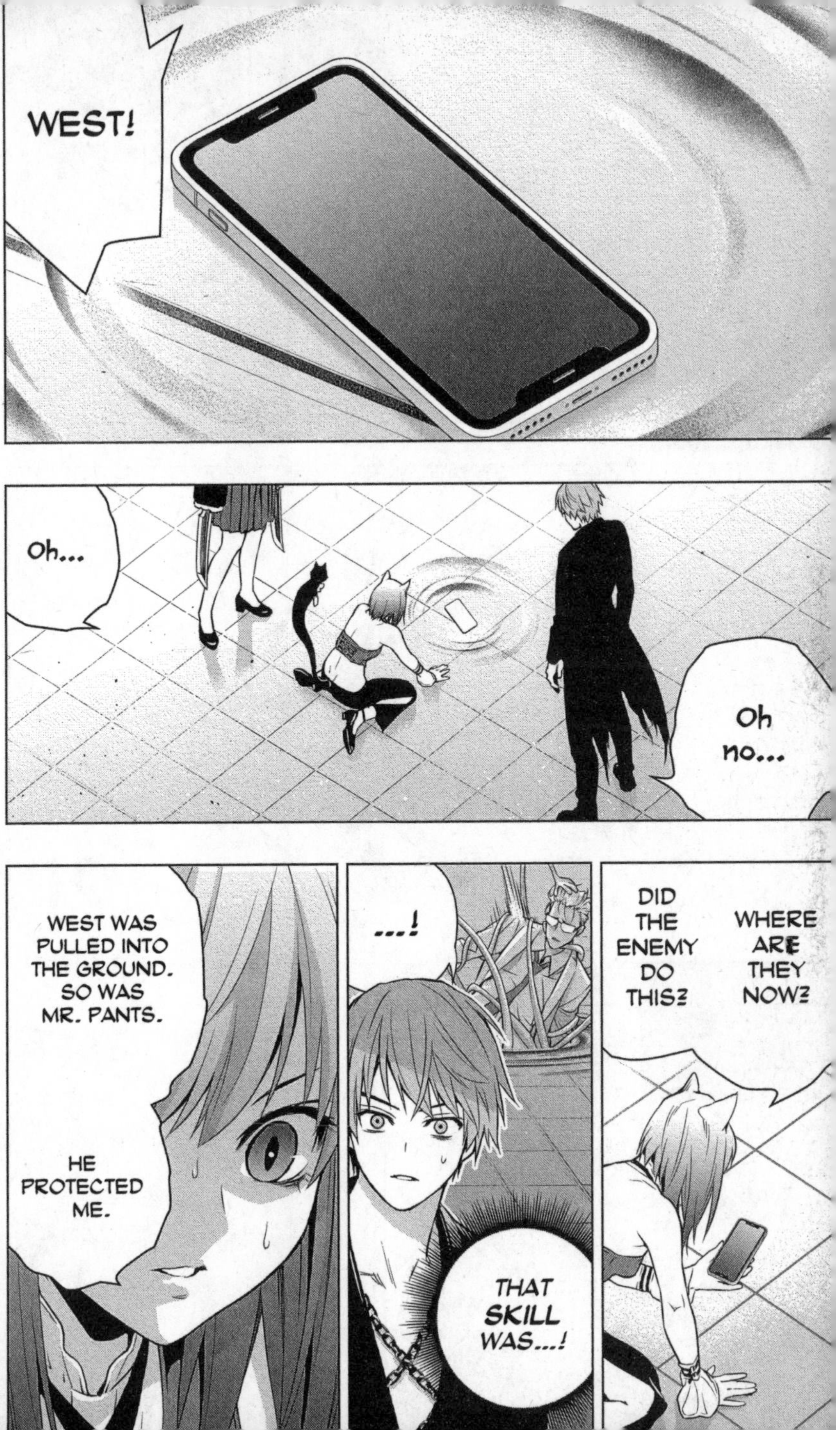
WEST!
Oh...
Oh no...
WEST WAS PULLED INTO THE GROUND. SO WAS MR. PANTS.
HE PROTECTED ME.
...!
THAT SKILL WAS...!
DID THE ENEMY DO THIS?
WHERE ARE THEY NOW?

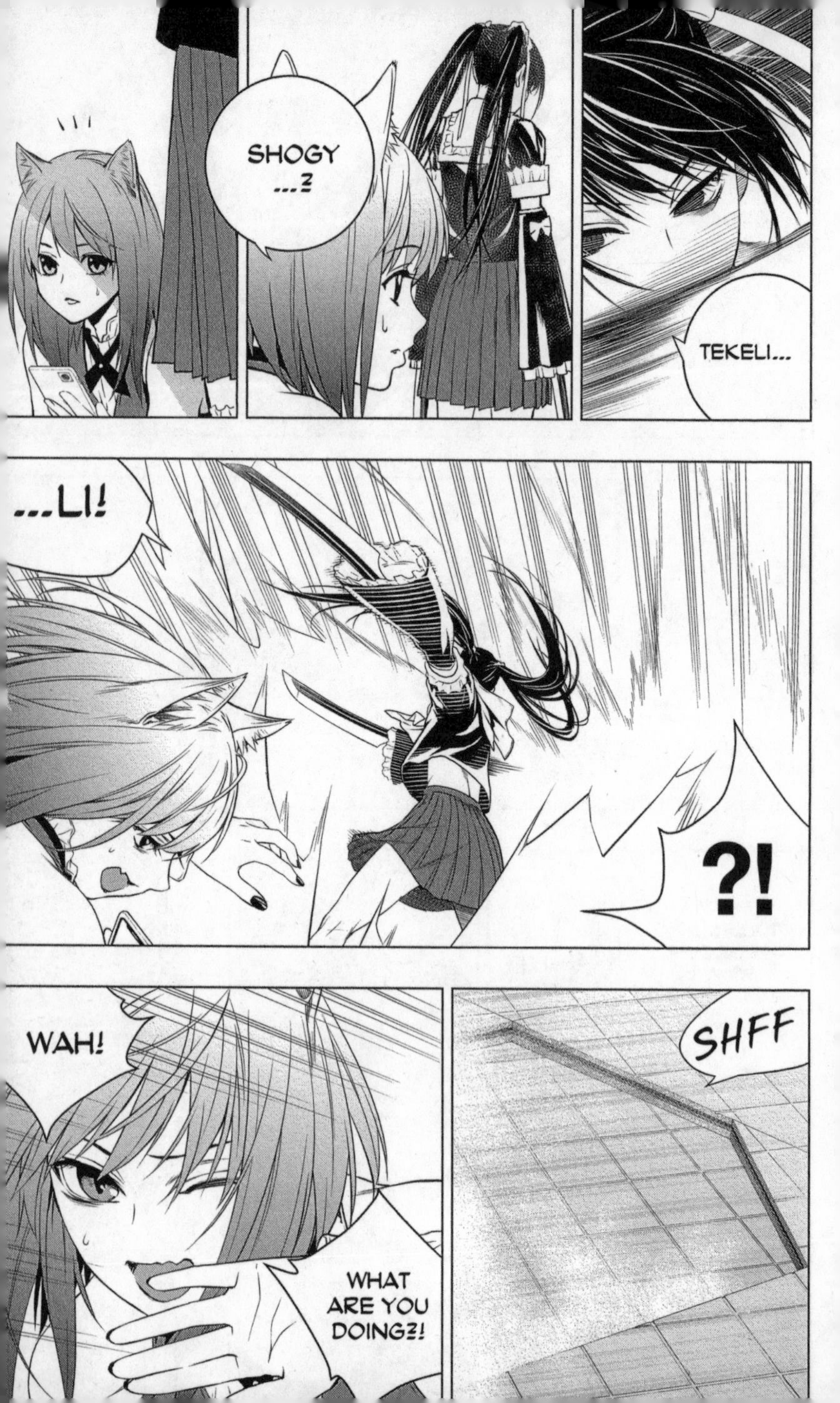
SHOGY ...?
TEKELI...
...LI!
?!
WAH!
WHAT ARE YOU DOING?!
SHFF

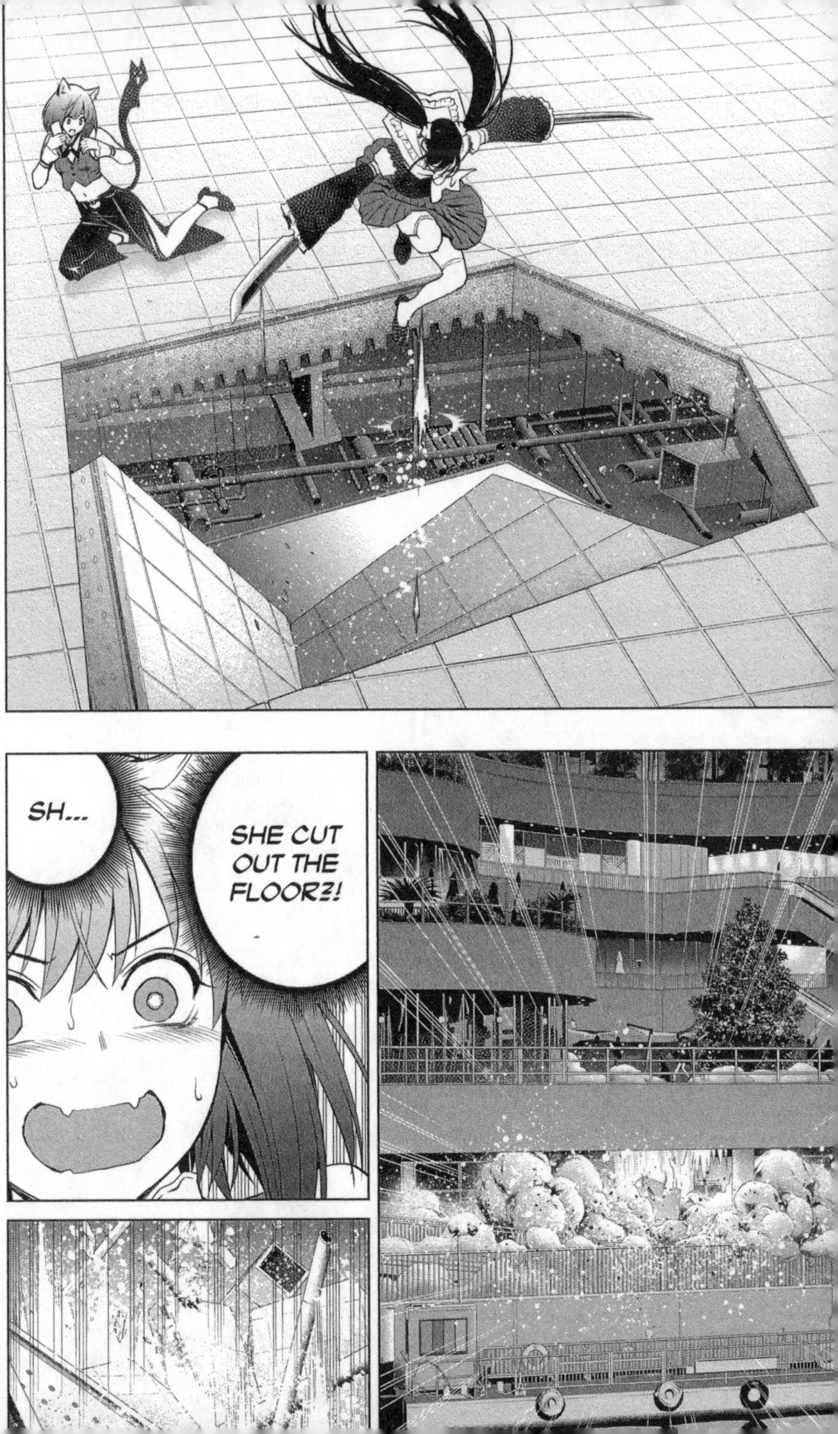
SH...
SHE CUT OUT THE FLOOR?!

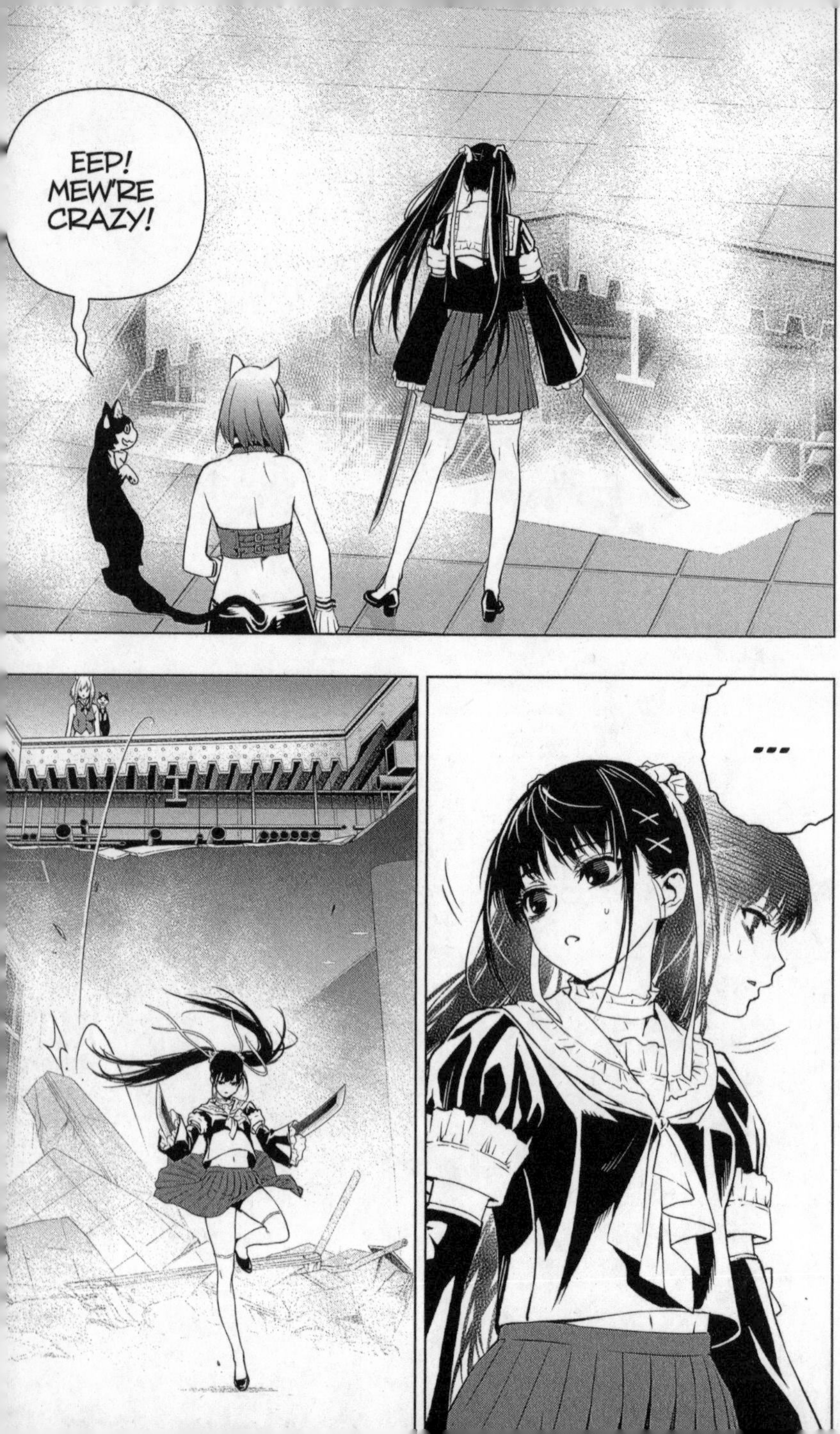
EEP! MEW'RE CRAZY!
...

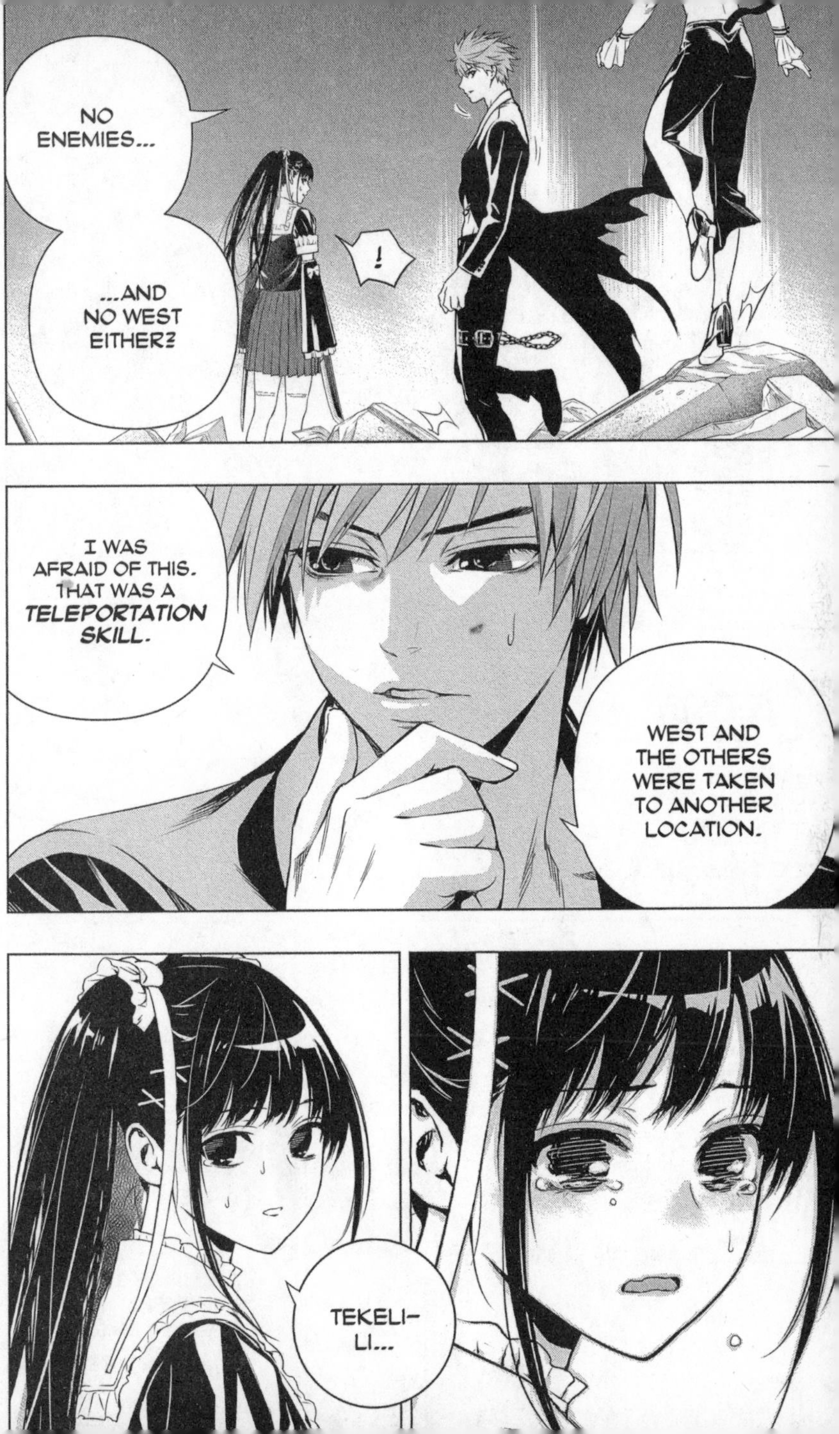
NO ENEMIES...
...AND NO WEST EITHER?
!
I WAS AFRAID OF THIS. THAT WAS A *TELEPORTATION SKILL*.
WEST AND THE OTHERS WERE TAKEN TO ANOTHER LOCATION.
TEKELI-LI...

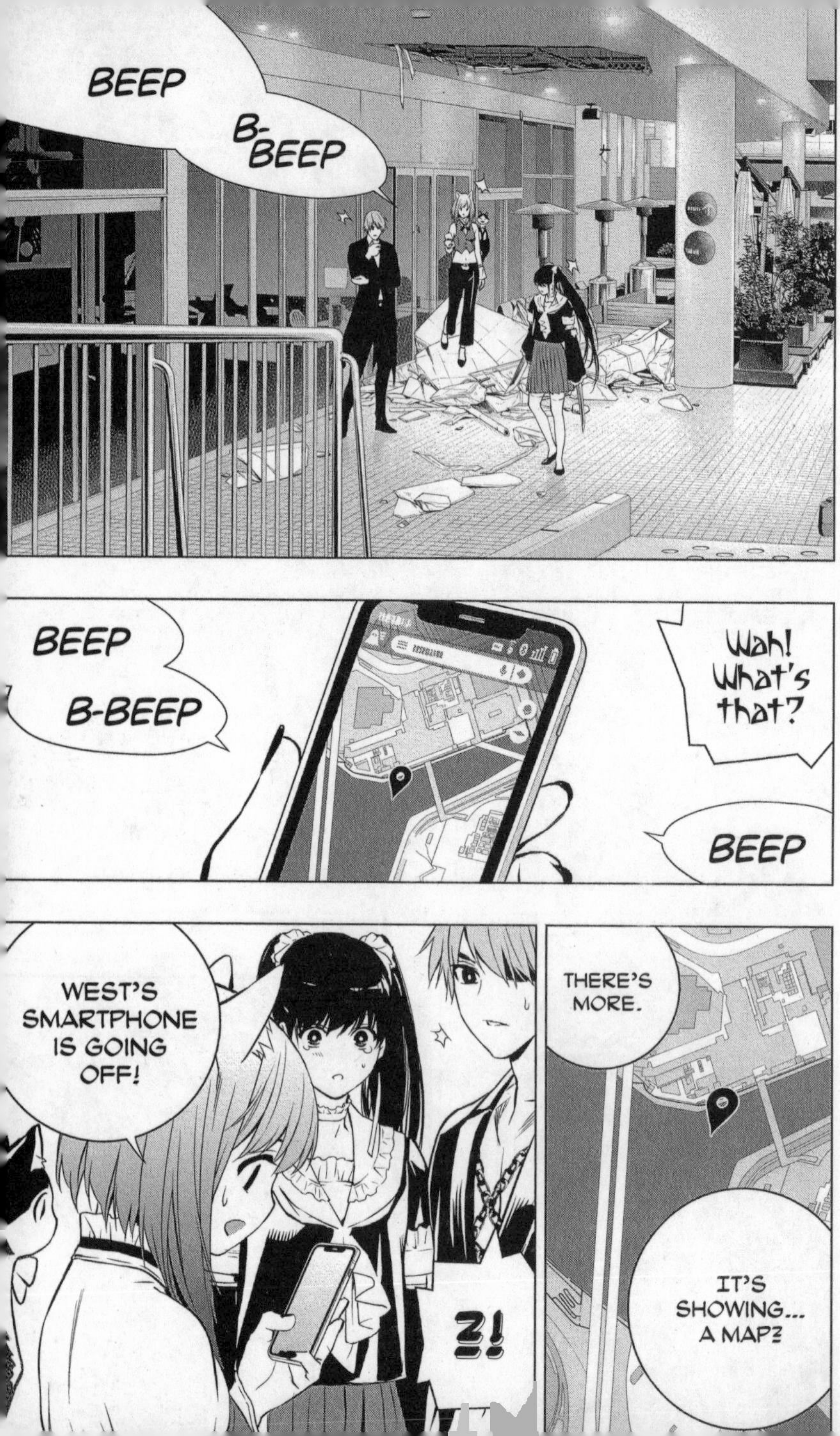
BEEP
B-BEEP
BEEP
B-BEEP
Wah! What's that?
BEEP
WEST'S SMARTPHONE IS GOING OFF!
Z!
THERE'S MORE.
IT'S SHOWING... A MAP?

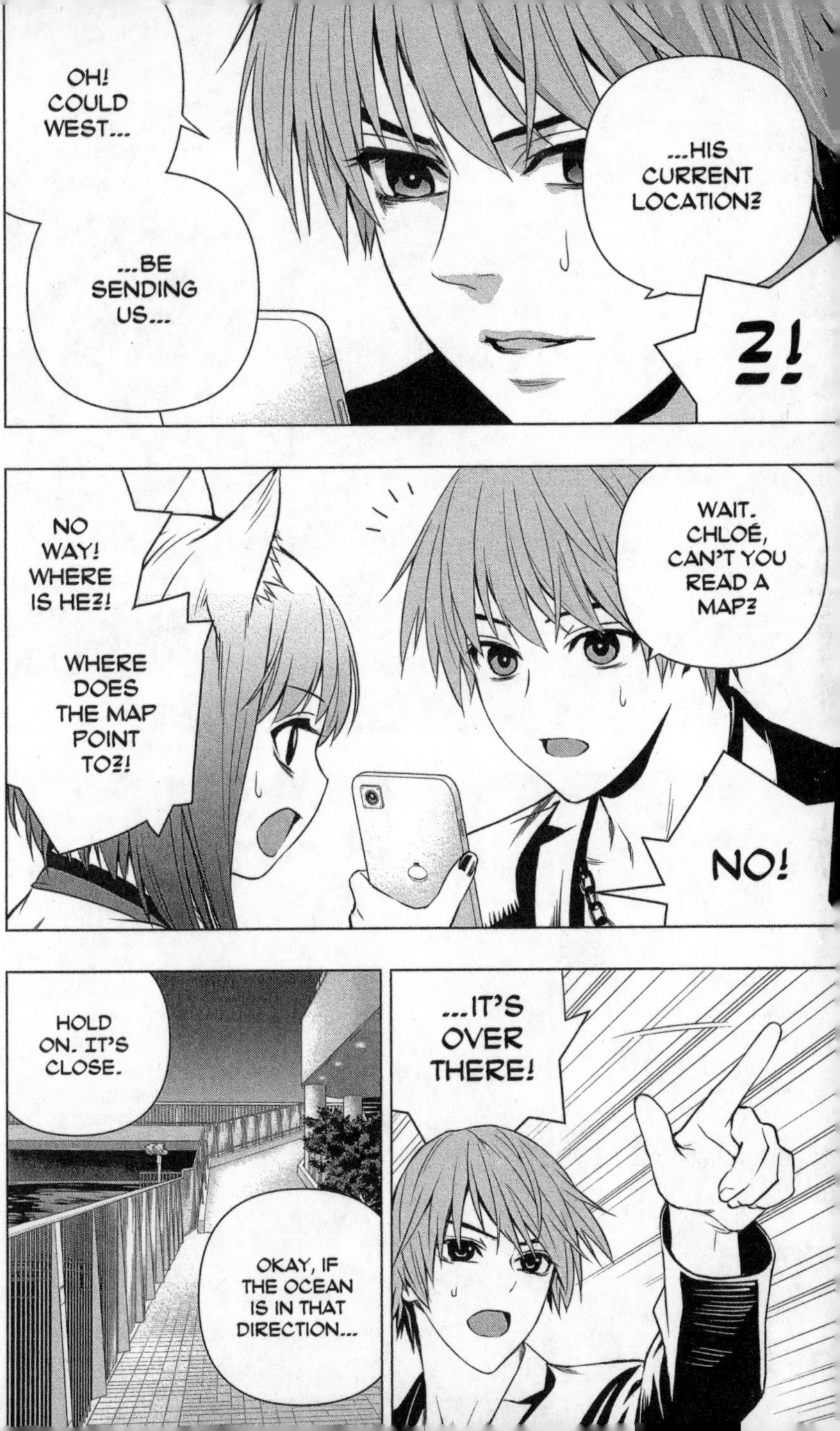
OH! COULD WEST...
...BE SENDING US...
...HIS CURRENT LOCATION?
?!
NO WAY! WHERE IS HE?!
WHERE DOES THE MAP POINT TO?!
WAIT. CHLOÉ, CAN'T YOU READ A MAP?
NO!
HOLD ON. IT'S CLOSE.
OKAY, IF THE OCEAN IS IN THAT DIRECTION...
...IT'S OVER THERE!

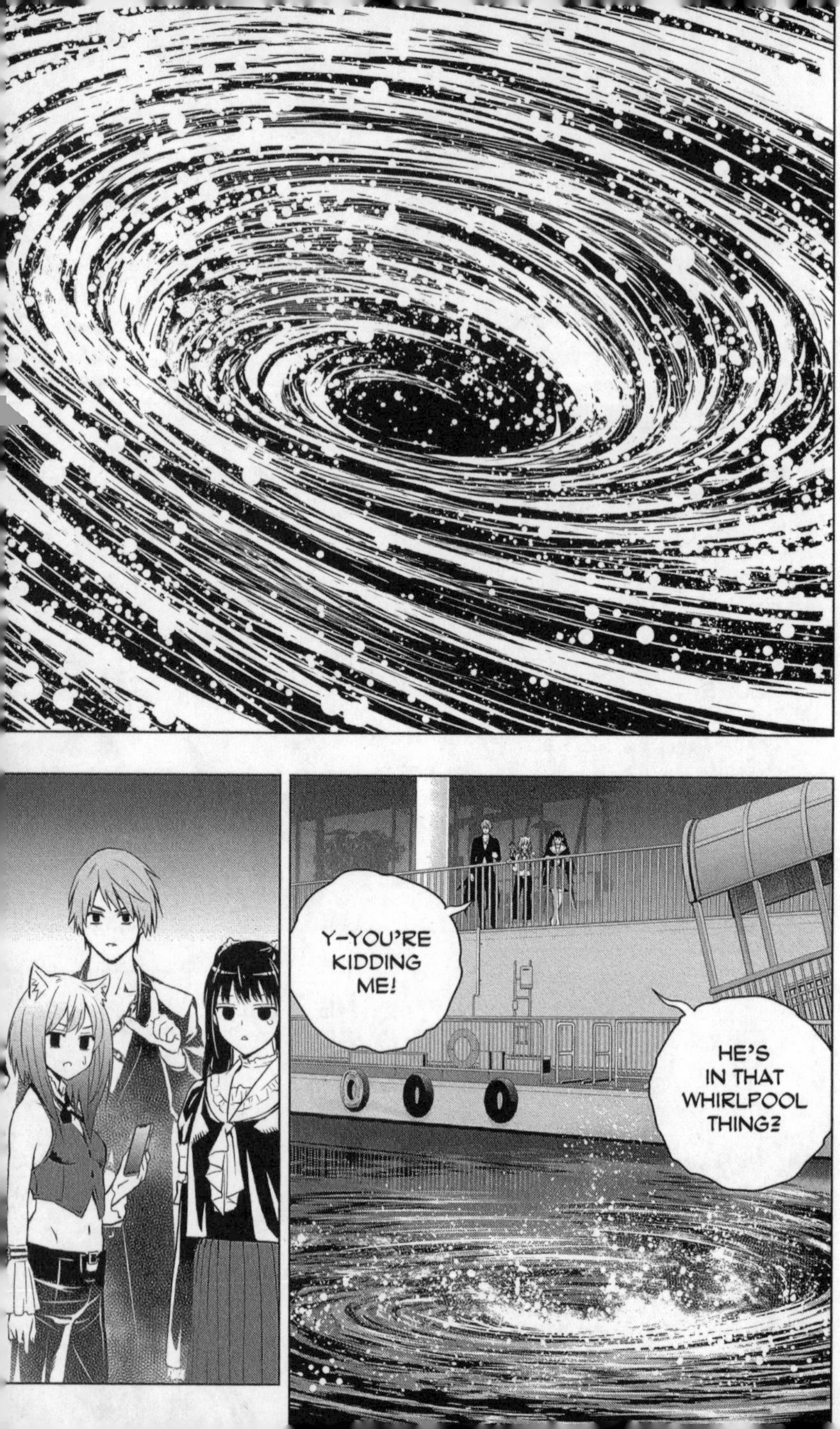
Y-YOU'RE KIDDING ME!
HE'S IN THAT WHIRLPOOL THING?

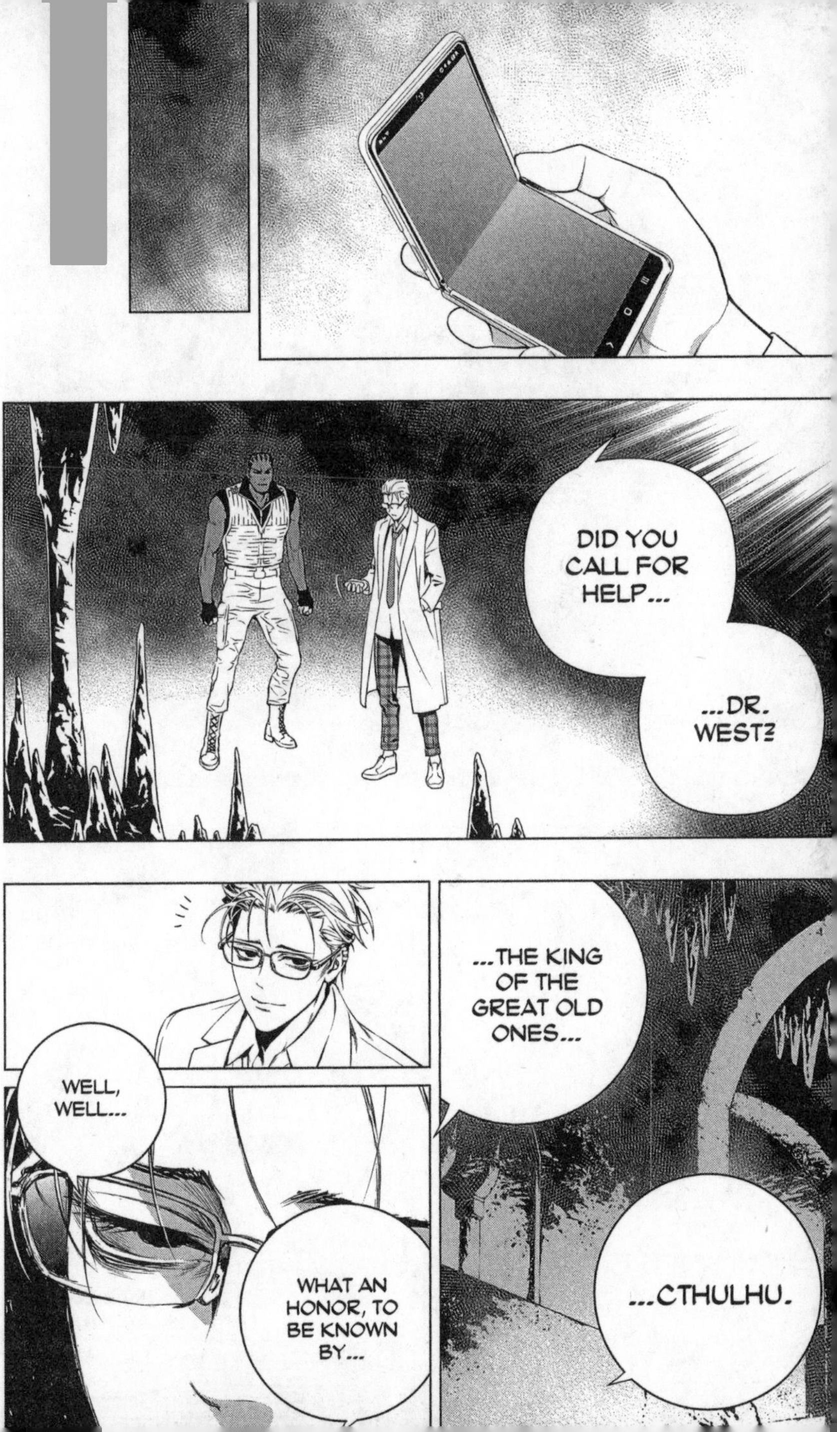
DID YOU CALL FOR HELP...
...DR. WEST?
WELL, WELL...
WHAT AN HONOR, TO BE KNOWN BY...
...THE KING OF THE GREAT OLD ONES...
...CTHULHU.

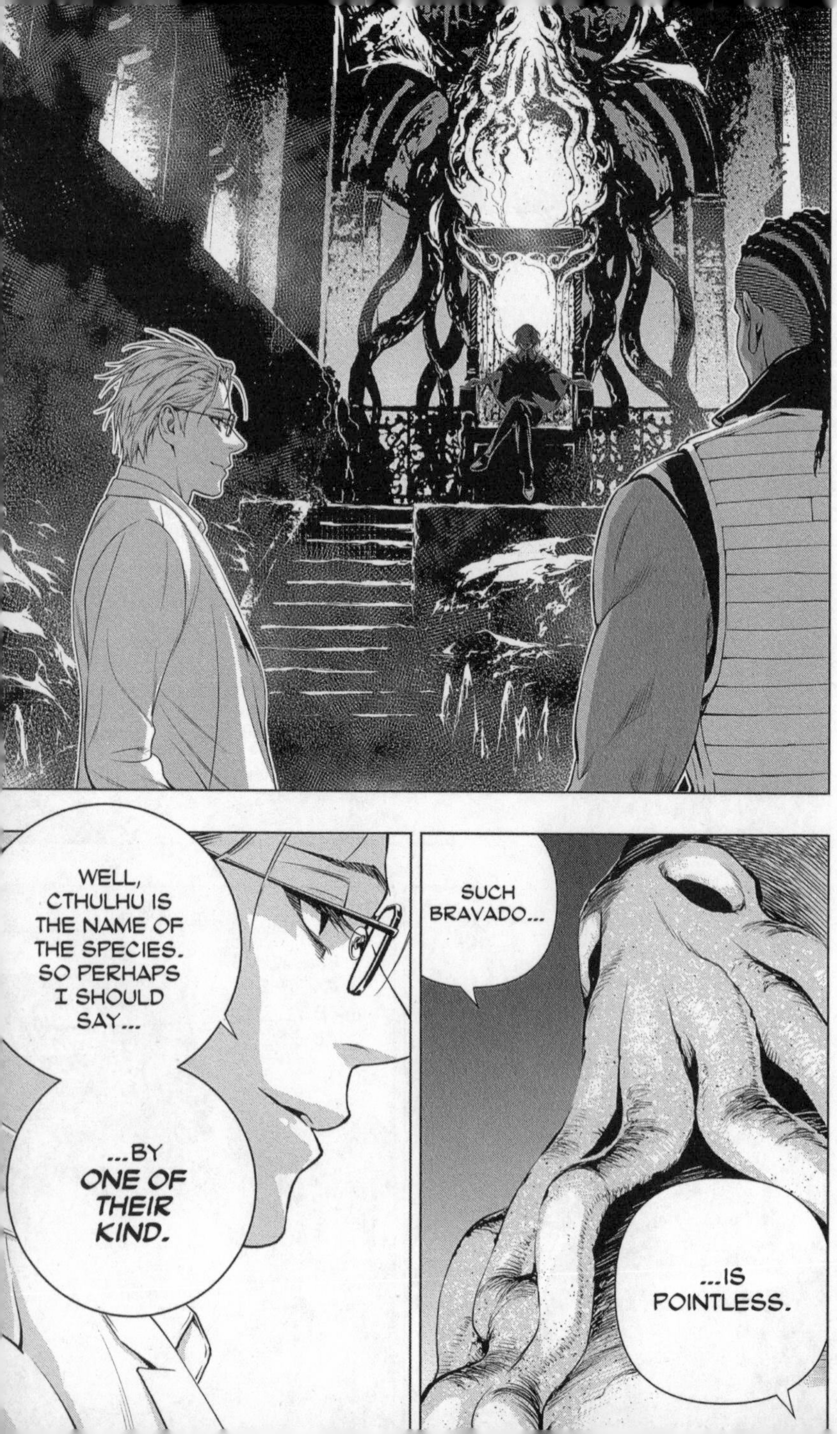
WELL, CTHULHU IS THE NAME OF THE SPECIES. SO PERHAPS I SHOULD SAY...
...BY **ONE OF THEIR KIND.**
SUCH BRAVADO...
...IS POINTLESS.

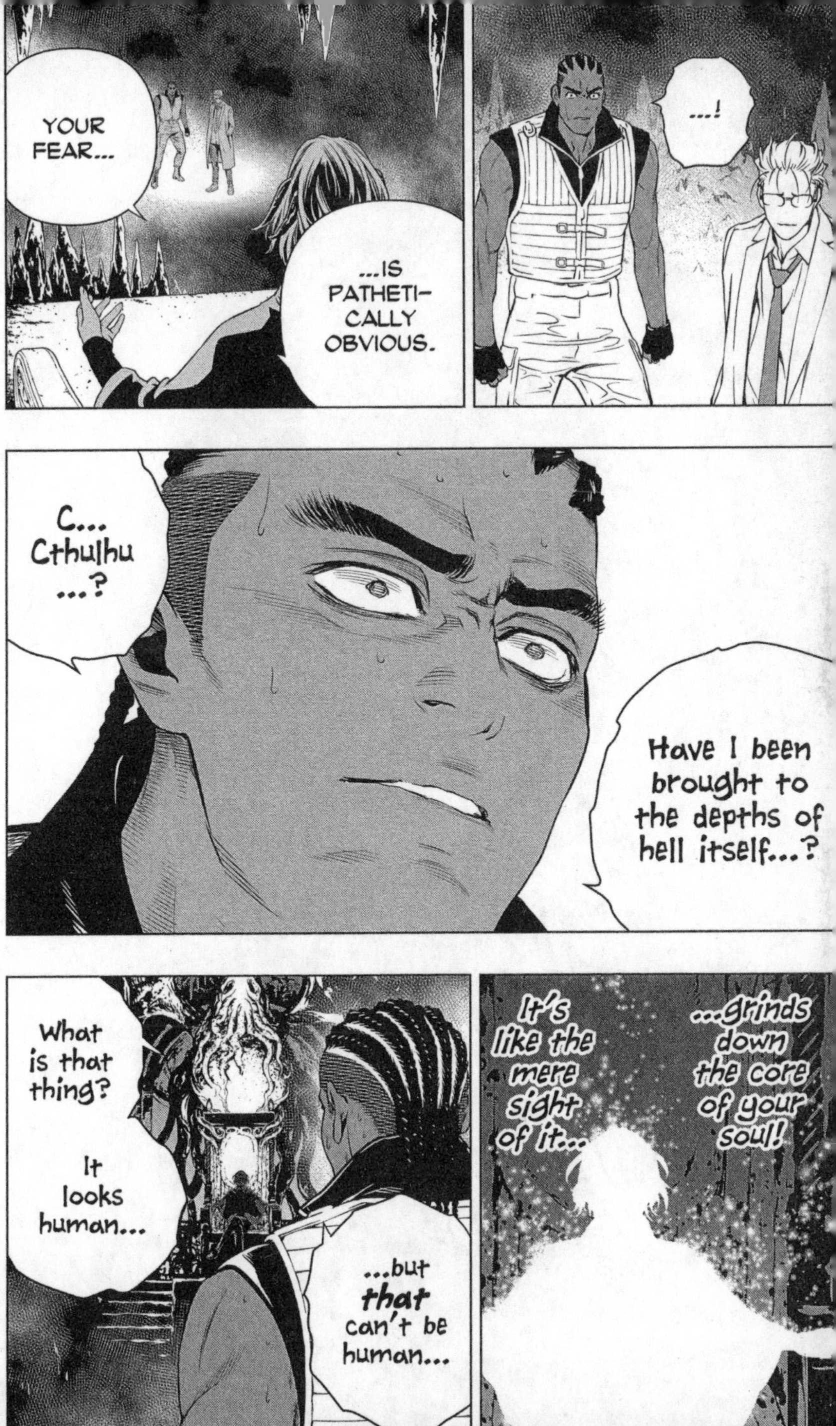
YOUR FEAR...
...IS PATHETI- CALLY OBVIOUS.
...!
C... Cthulhu ...?
Have I been brought to the depths of hell itself...?
What is that thing?
It looks human...
...but *that* can't be human...
It's like the mere sight of it...
...grinds down the core of your soul!

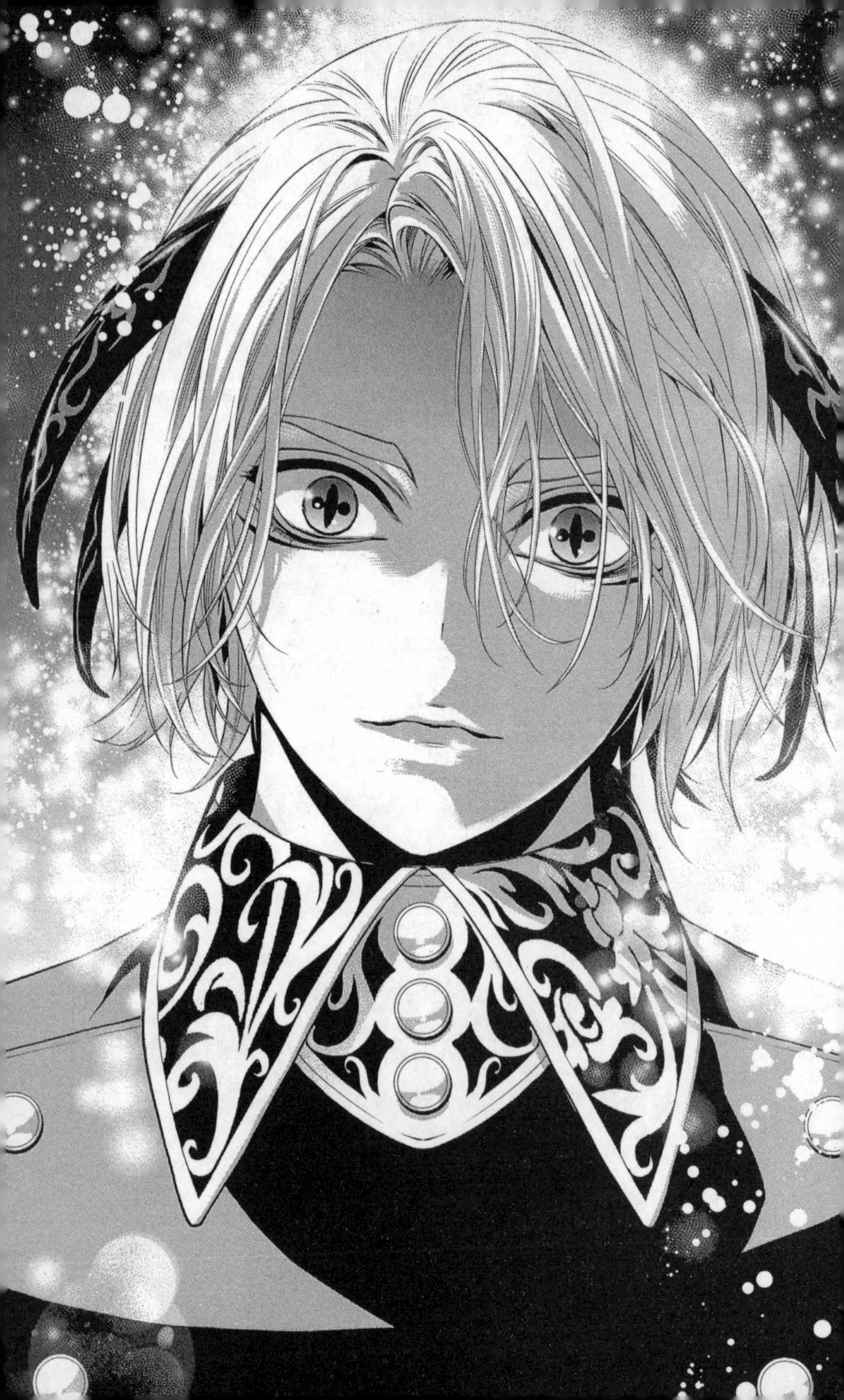

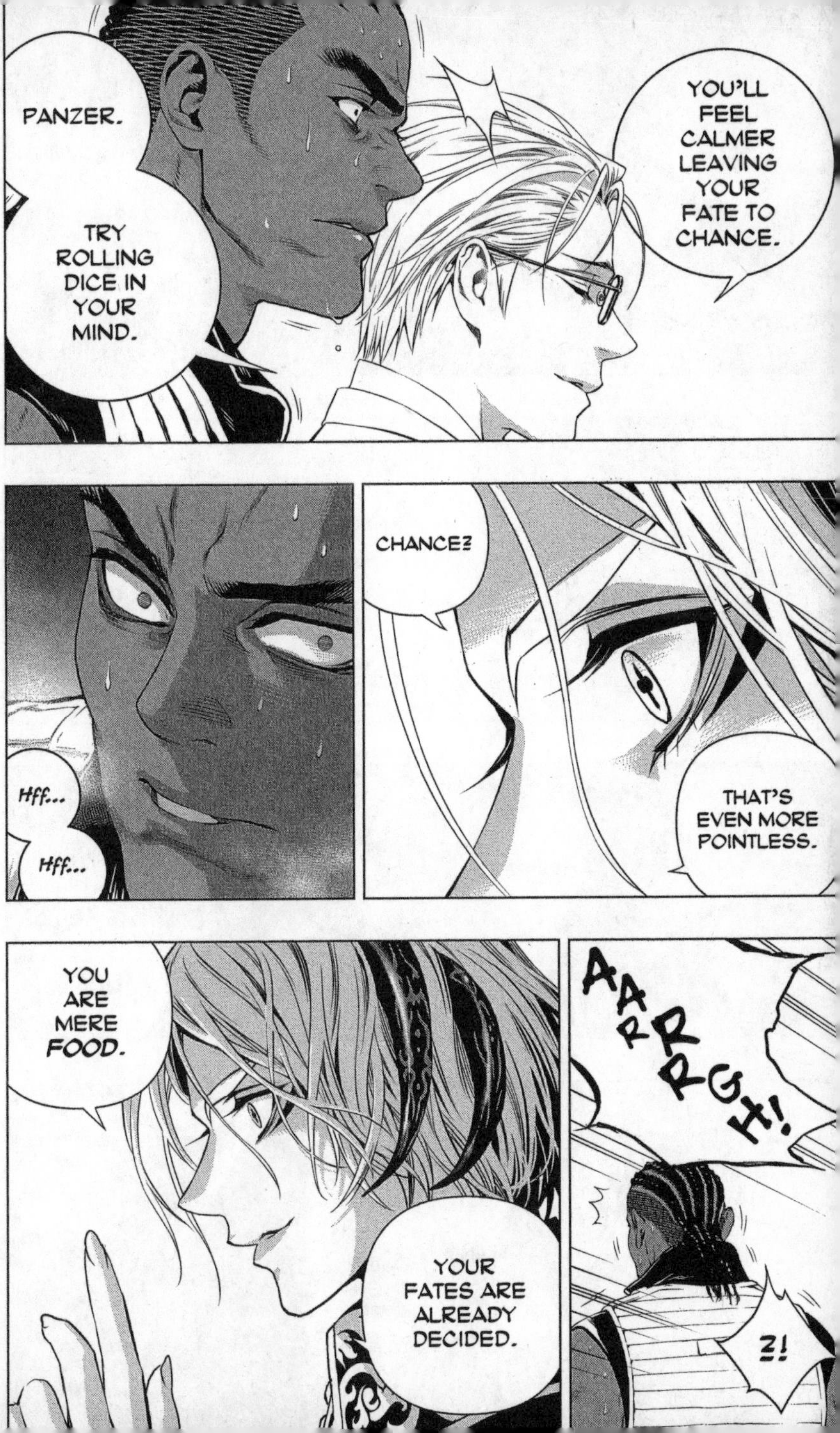
PANZER.
TRY ROLLING DICE IN YOUR MIND.
YOU'LL FEEL CALMER LEAVING YOUR FATE TO CHANCE.
Hff...
Hff...
CHANCE?
THAT'S EVEN MORE POINTLESS.
YOU ARE MERE FOOD.
YOUR FATES ARE ALREADY DECIDED.
AARRRGH!
?!

H... Help!

Somebody help me...

WHO'S ...

... THERE?!

TSK.

IS THAT THE OTHERS WHO WERE BROUGHT HERE WITH US?

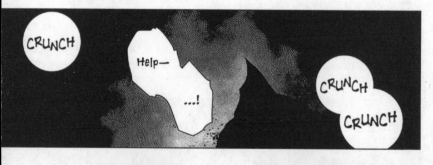

CRUNCH

Help— ...!

CRUNCH

CRUNCH

H–HEY, DO YOU HEAR THAT?

SOME-THING'S THERE.

CRUNCH

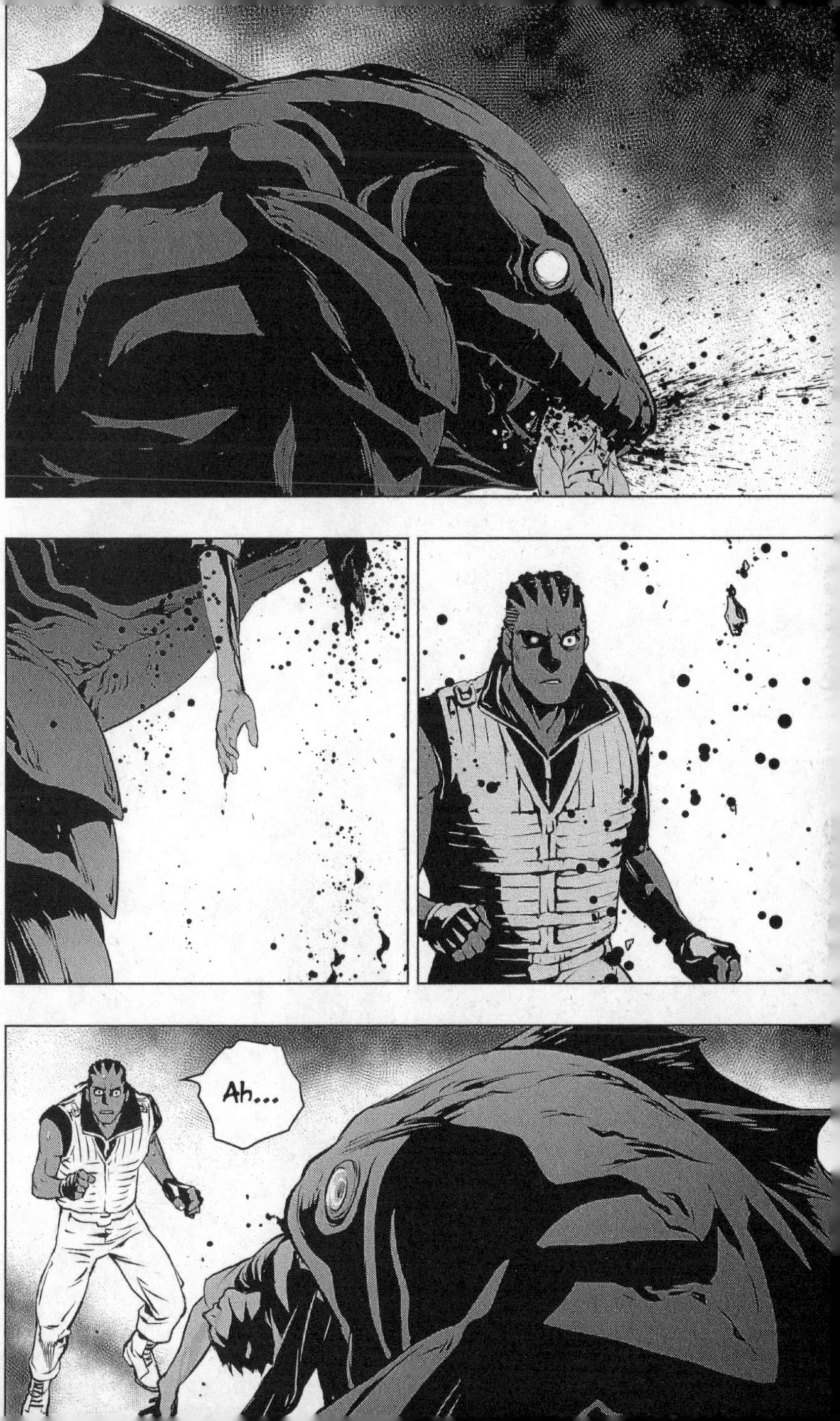
Ah...

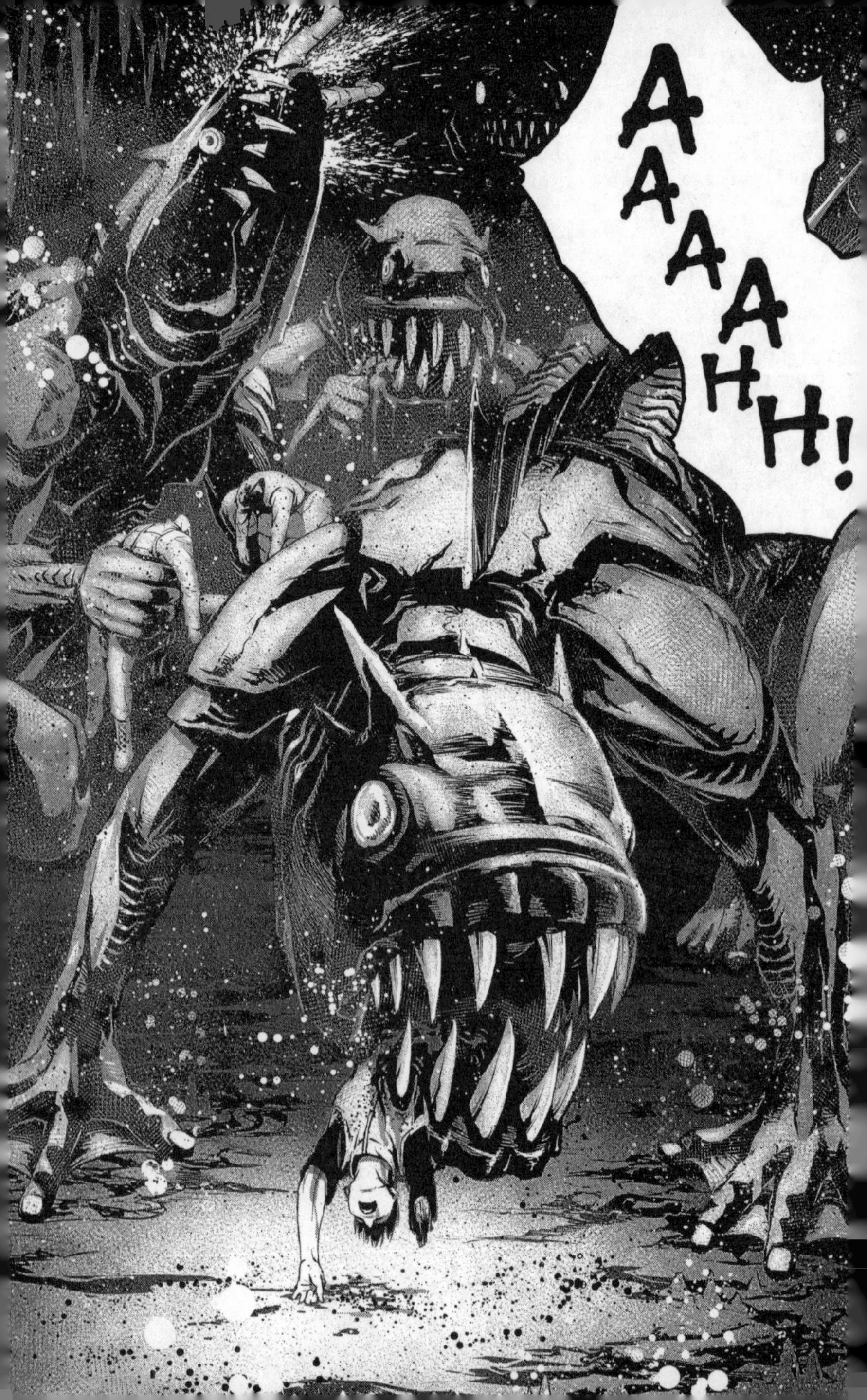
AAAAAHH!

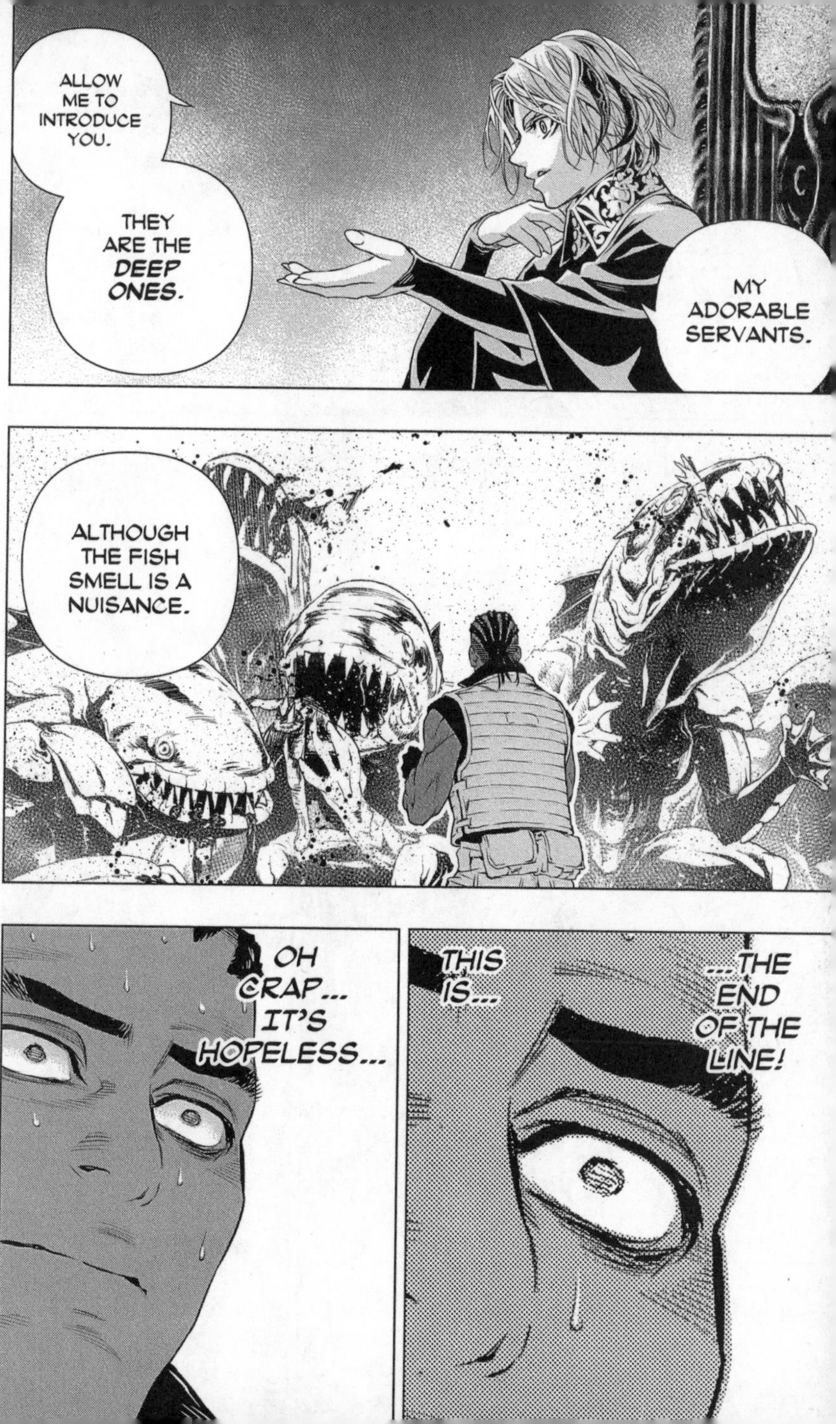
ALLOW ME TO INTRODUCE YOU.
THEY ARE THE *DEEP ONES*.
MY ADORABLE SERVANTS.
ALTHOUGH THE FISH SMELL IS A NUISANCE.
OH CRAP... IT'S HOPELESS...
THIS IS...
...THE END OF THE LINE!

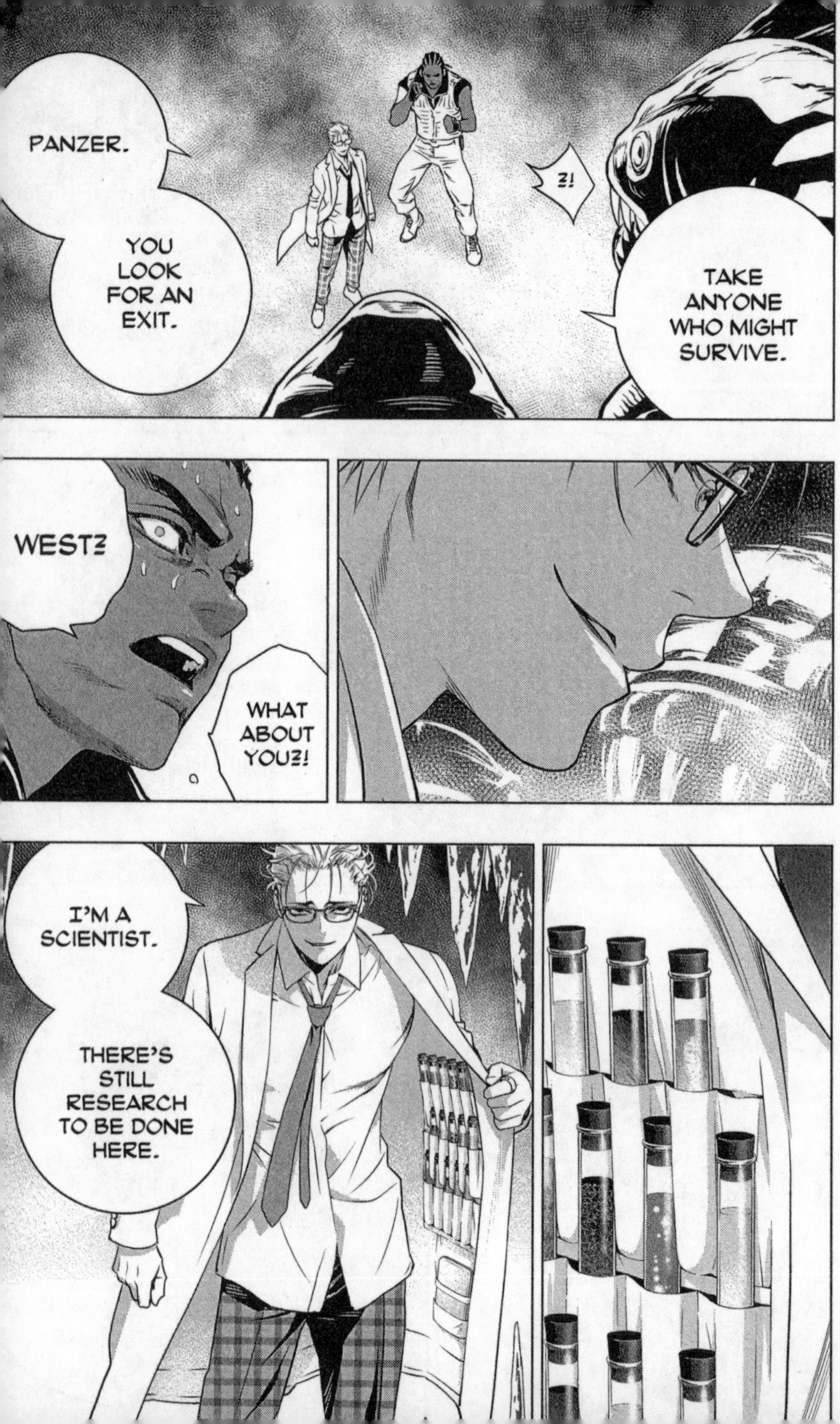
PANZER.
YOU LOOK FOR AN EXIT.
?!
TAKE ANYONE WHO MIGHT SURVIVE.
WEST?
WHAT ABOUT YOU?!
I'M A SCIENTIST.
THERE'S STILL RESEARCH TO BE DONE HERE.

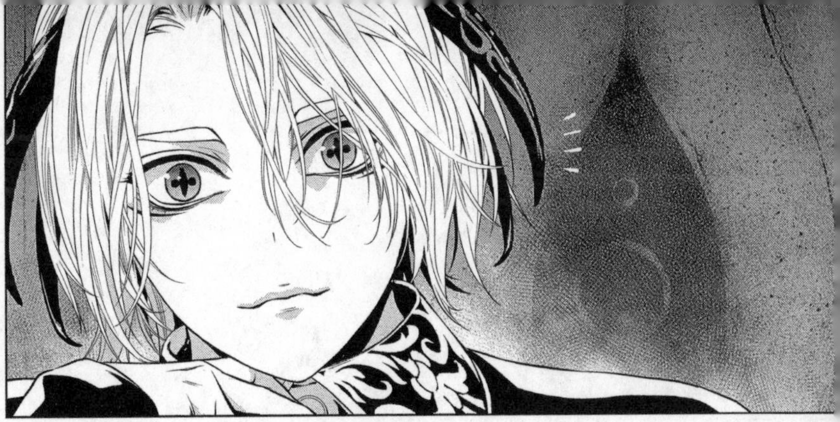

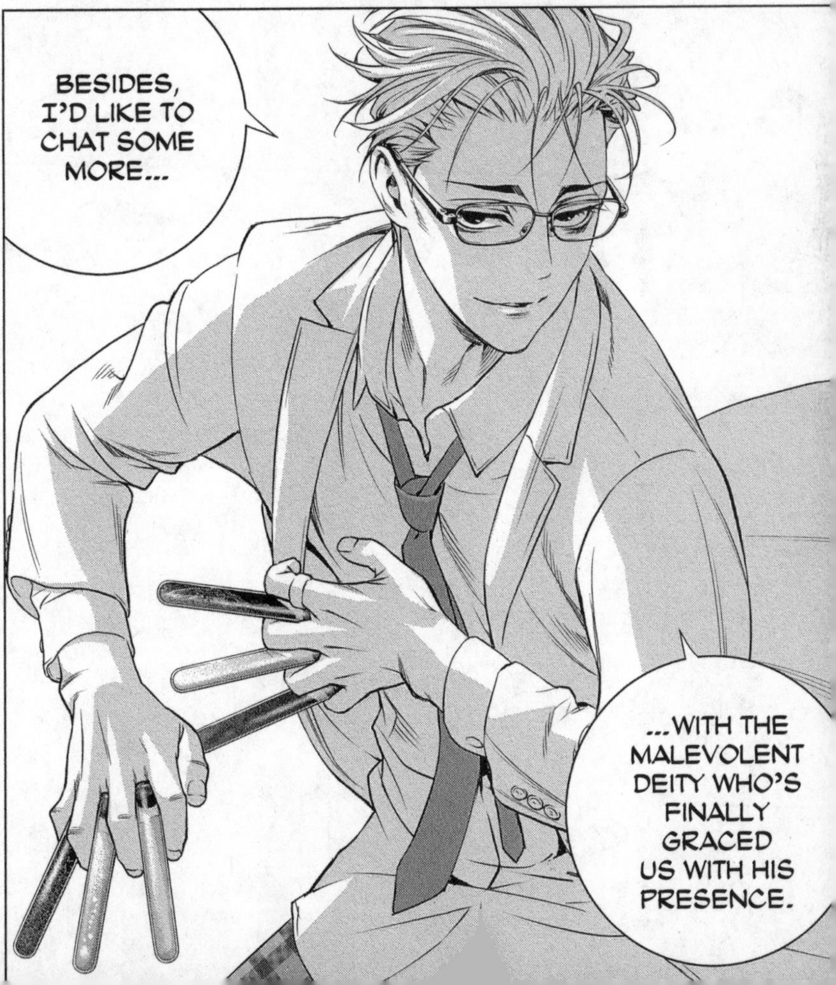
BESIDES, I'D LIKE TO CHAT SOME MORE...
...WITH THE MALEVOLENT DEITY WHO'S FINALLY GRACED US WITH HIS PRESENCE.

18: RE-ANIMATOR

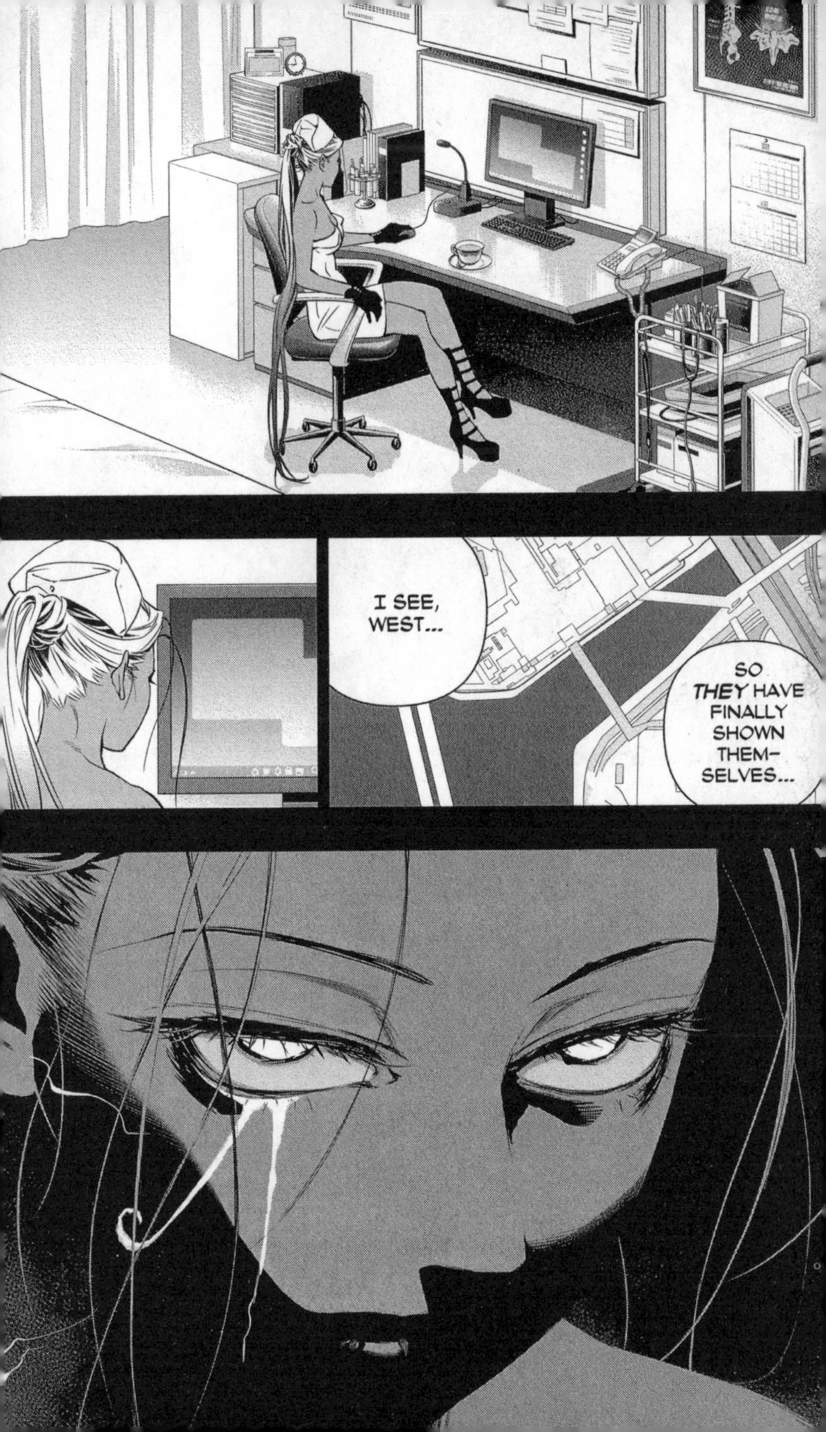
I SEE, WEST...
SO THEY HAVE FINALLY SHOWN THEM-SELVES...

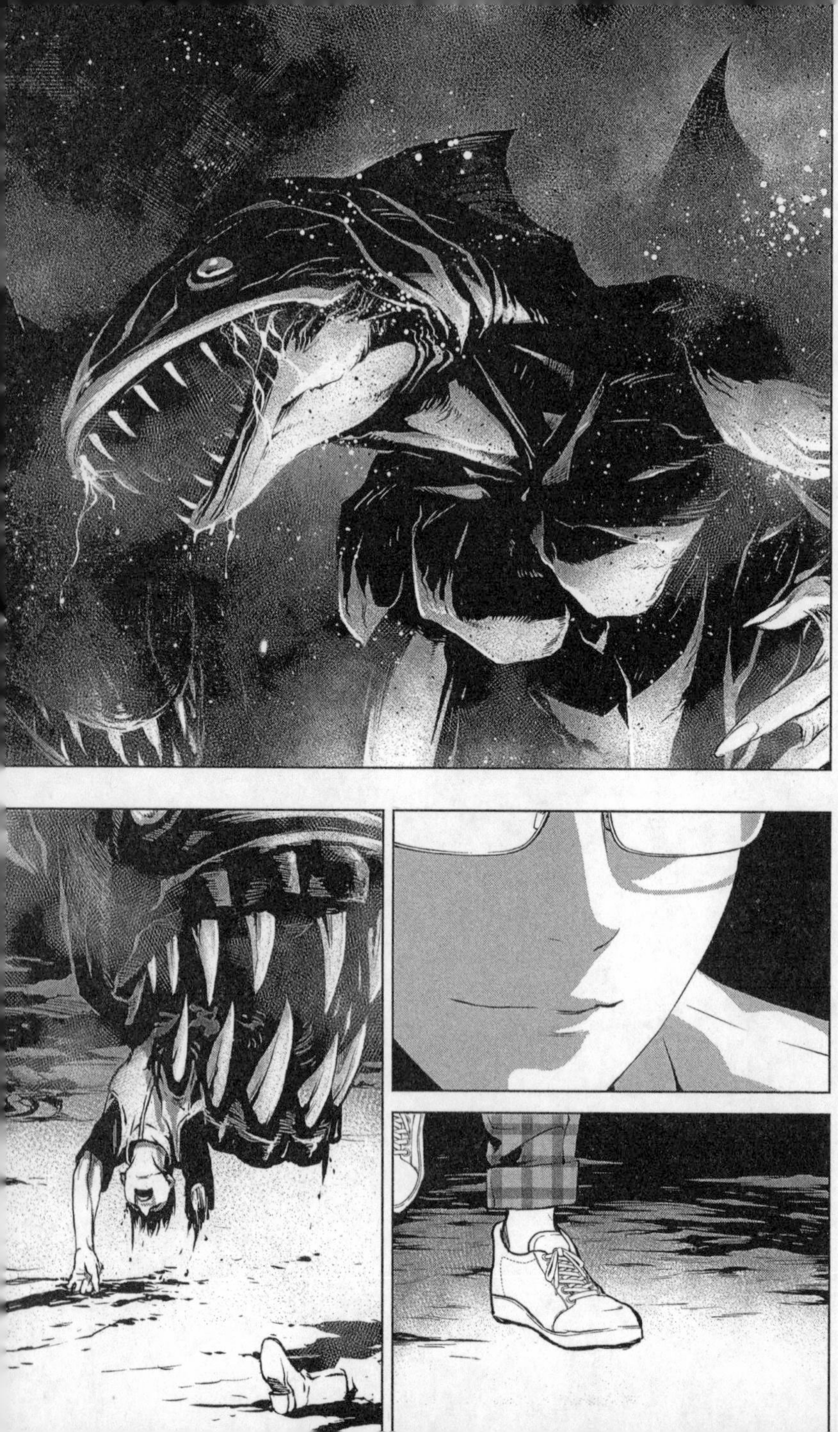

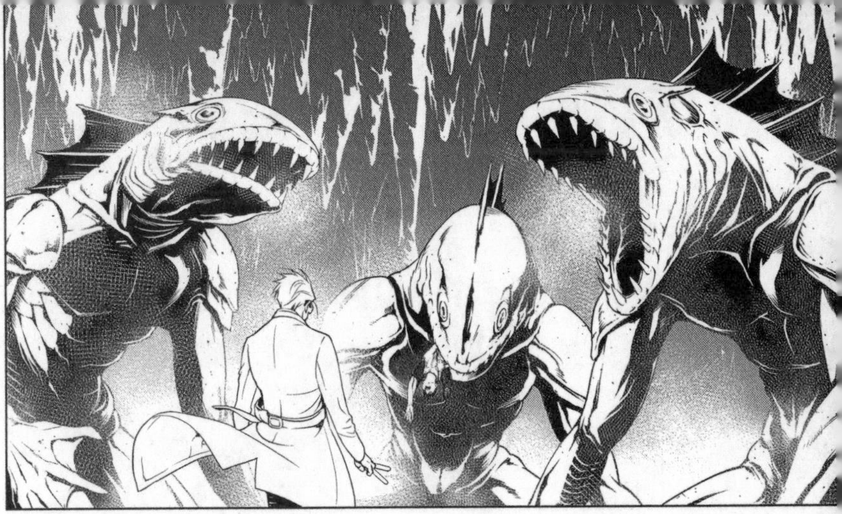
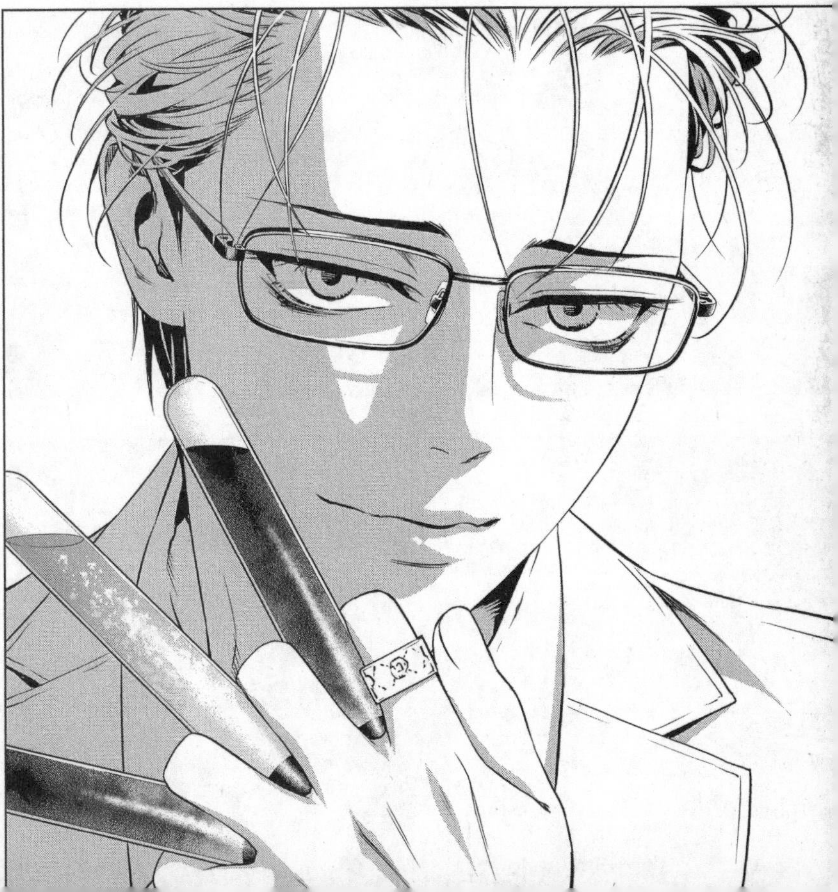

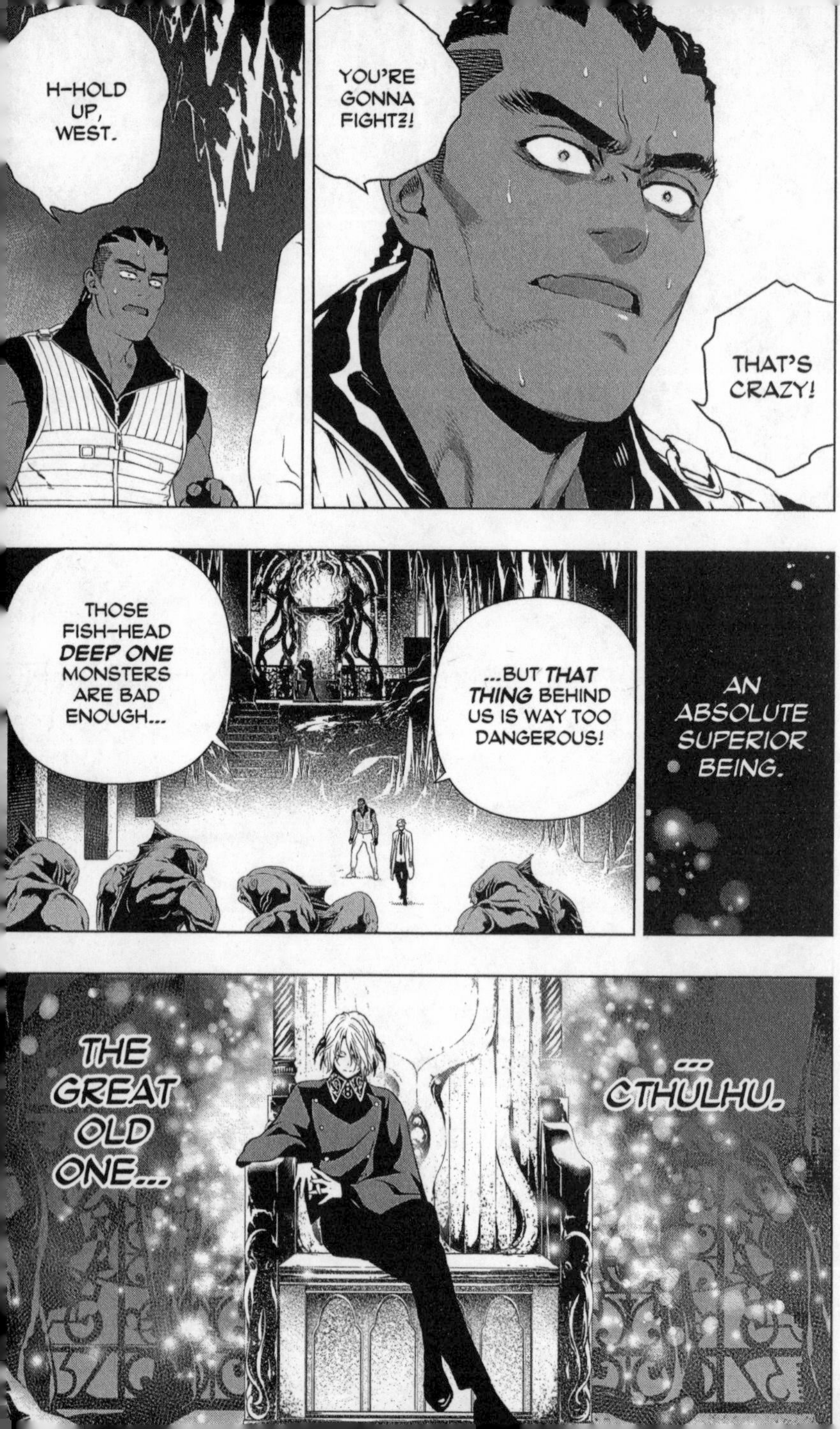
H-HOLD UP, WEST.
YOU'RE GONNA FIGHT?!
THAT'S CRAZY!
THOSE FISH-HEAD *DEEP ONE* MONSTERS ARE BAD ENOUGH...
...BUT *THAT THING* BEHIND US IS WAY TOO DANGEROUS!
AN ABSOLUTE SUPERIOR BEING.
THE GREAT OLD ONE...
...CTHULHU.

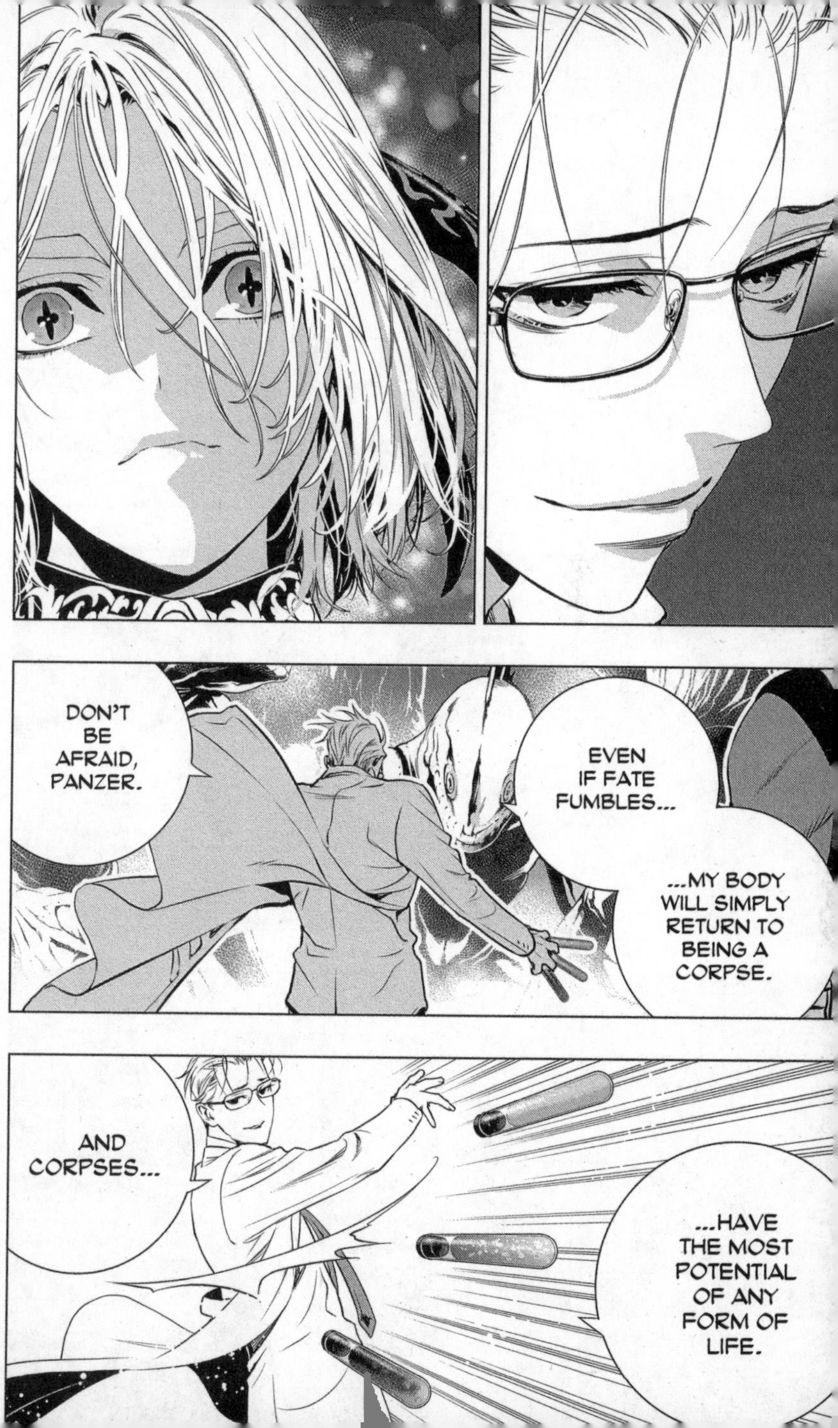
DON'T BE AFRAID, PANZER.
EVEN IF FATE FUMBLES...
...MY BODY WILL SIMPLY RETURN TO BEING A CORPSE.
AND CORPSES...
...HAVE THE MOST POTENTIAL OF ANY FORM OF LIFE.

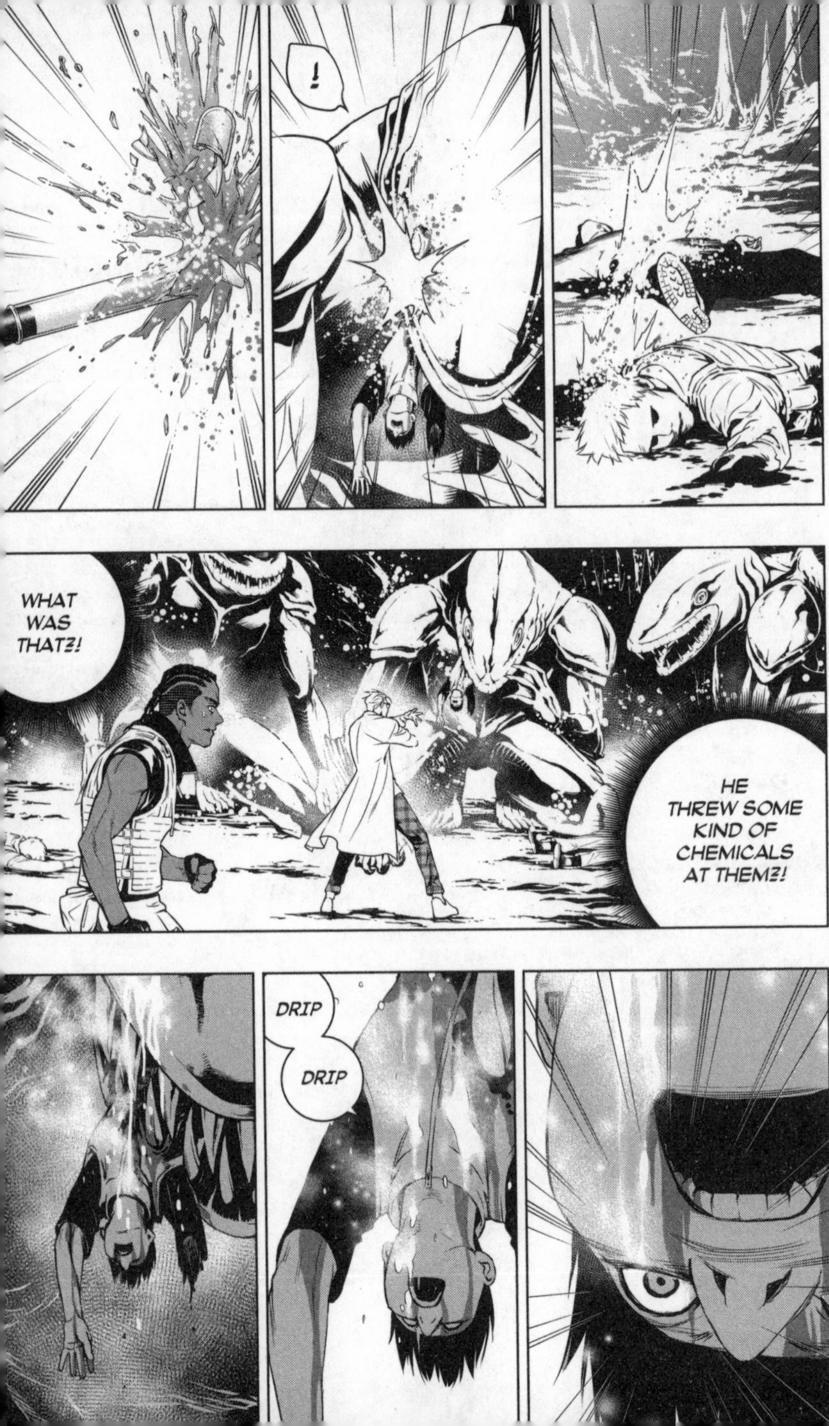
!
WHAT WAS THAT?!
HE THREW SOME KIND OF CHEMICALS AT THEM?!
DRIP
DRIP

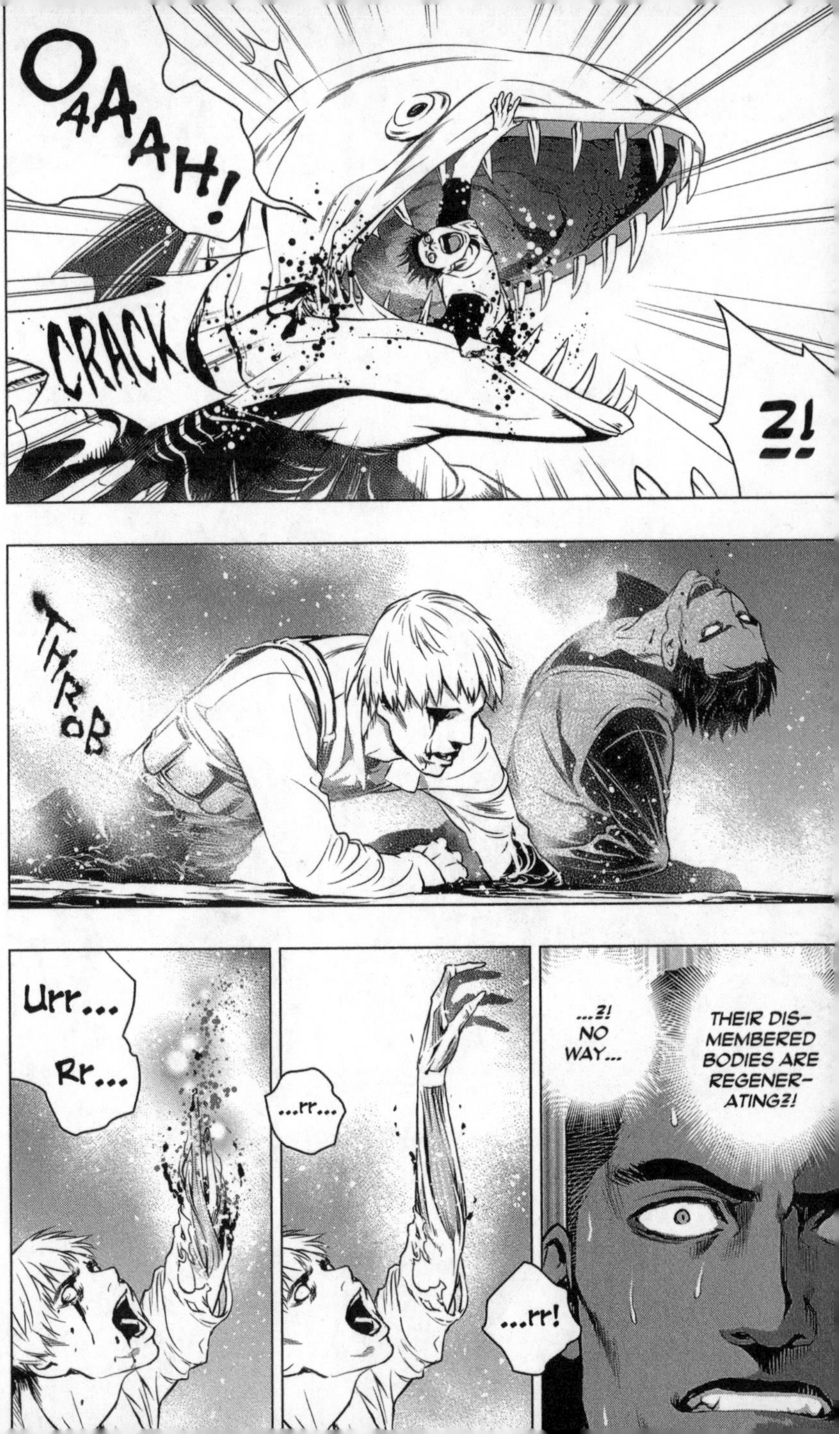
OAAAH!
CRACK
?!
THROB
Urr...
Rr...
...rr...
...?! NO WAY...
THEIR DIS-MEMBERED BODIES ARE REGENER-ATING?!
...rr!

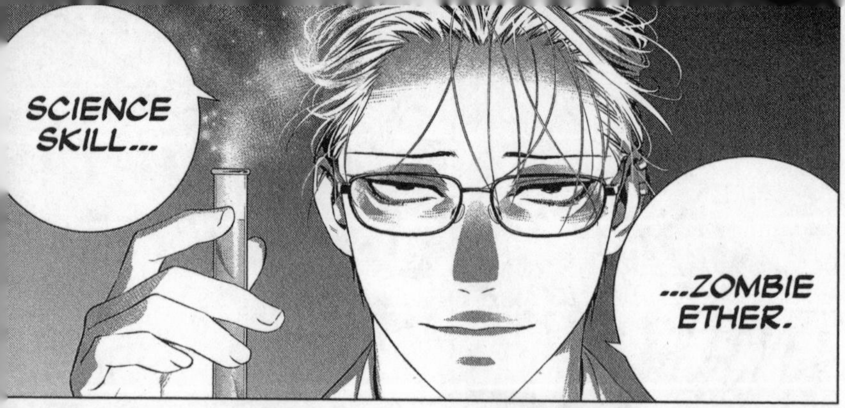
SCIENCE SKILL...
...ZOMBIE ETHER.
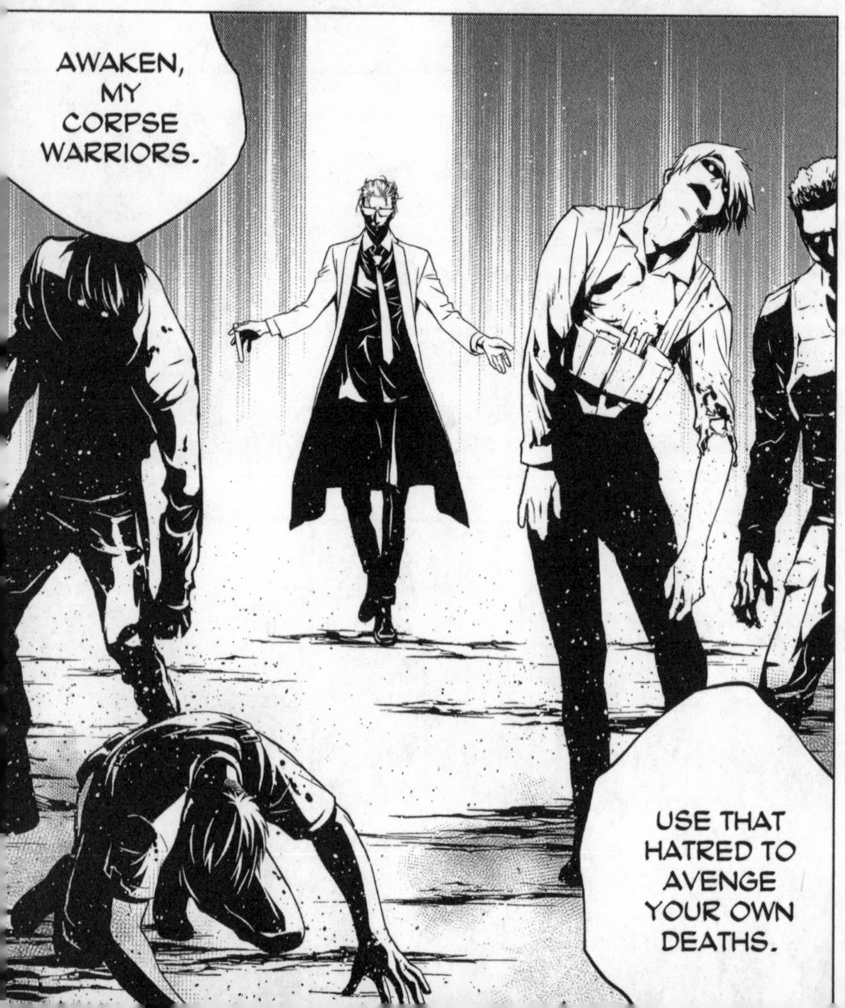
AWAKEN, MY CORPSE WARRIORS.
USE THAT HATRED TO AVENGE YOUR OWN DEATHS.

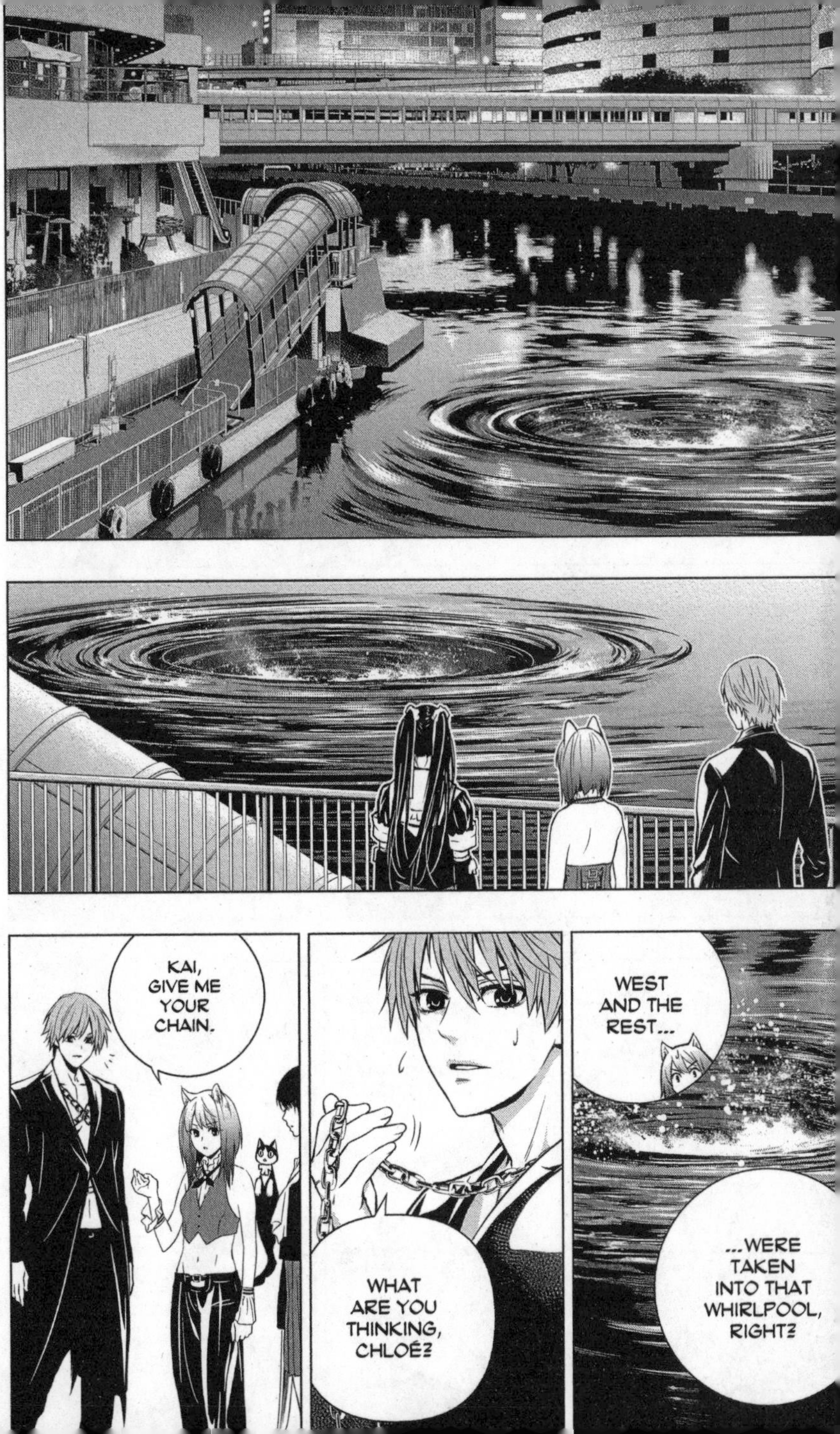
KAI, GIVE ME YOUR CHAIN.
WHAT ARE YOU THINKING, CHLOÉ?
WEST AND THE REST...
...WERE TAKEN INTO THAT WHIRLPOOL, RIGHT?

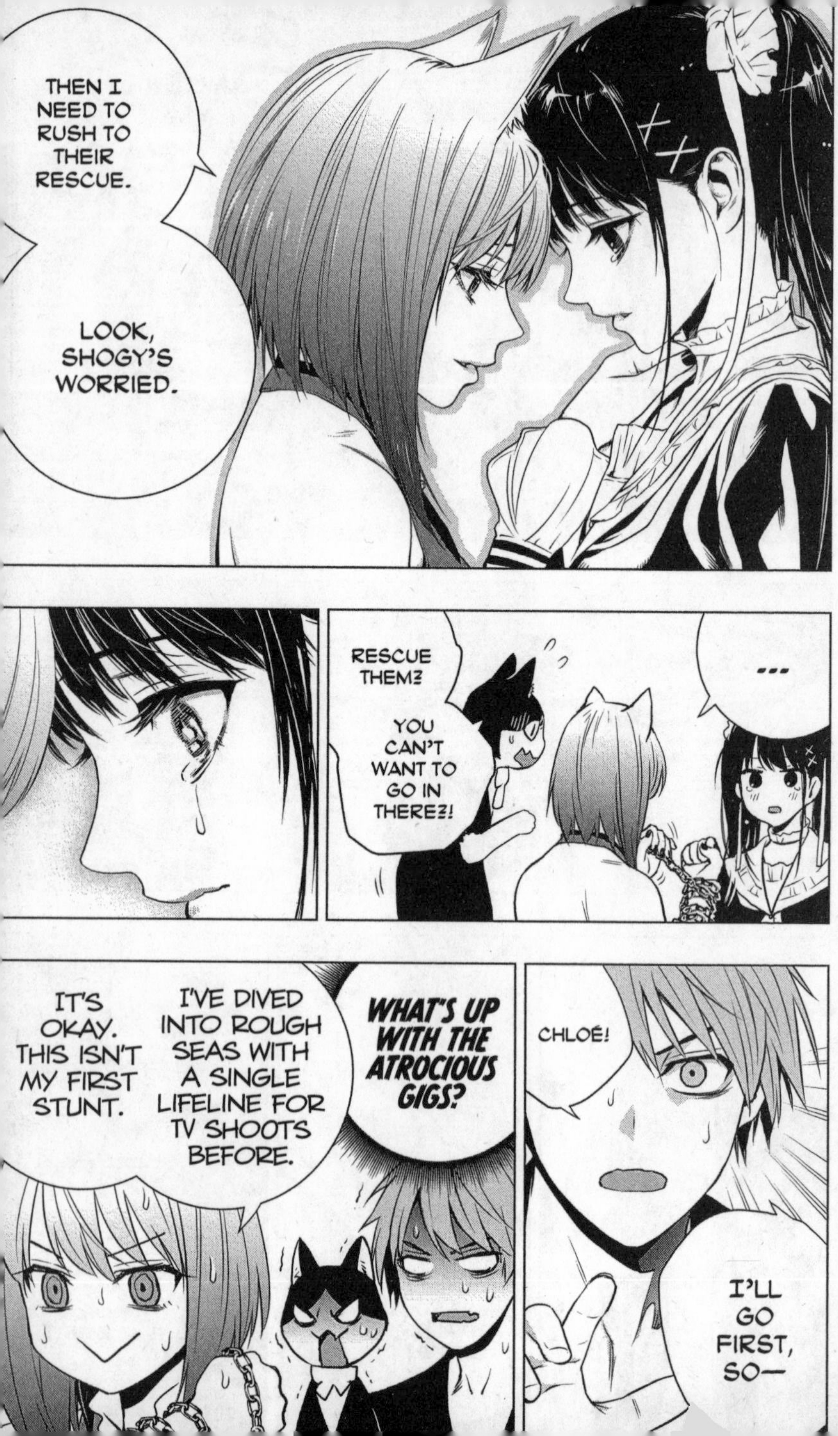
THEN I NEED TO RUSH TO THEIR RESCUE.
LOOK, SHOGY'S WORRIED.
RESCUE THEM?
YOU CAN'T WANT TO GO IN THERE?!
...
IT'S OKAY. THIS ISN'T MY FIRST STUNT.
I'VE DIVED INTO ROUGH SEAS WITH A SINGLE LIFELINE FOR TV SHOOTS BEFORE.
WHAT'S UP WITH THE ATROCIOUS GIGS?
CHLOÉ!
I'LL GO FIRST, SO—

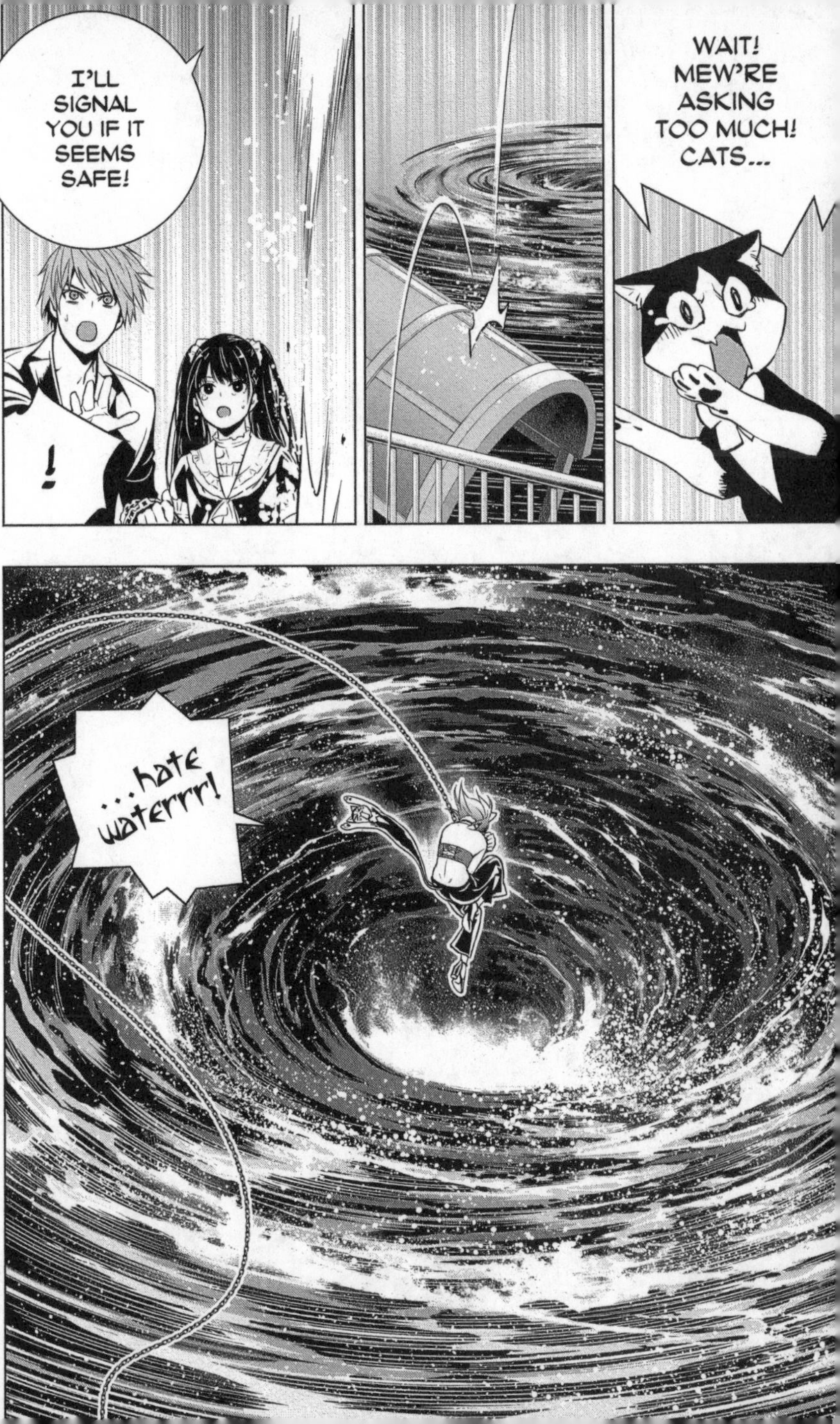
I'LL SIGNAL YOU IF IT SEEMS SAFE!
!
WAIT! MEW'RE ASKING TOO MUCH! CATS...
...hate waterrr!

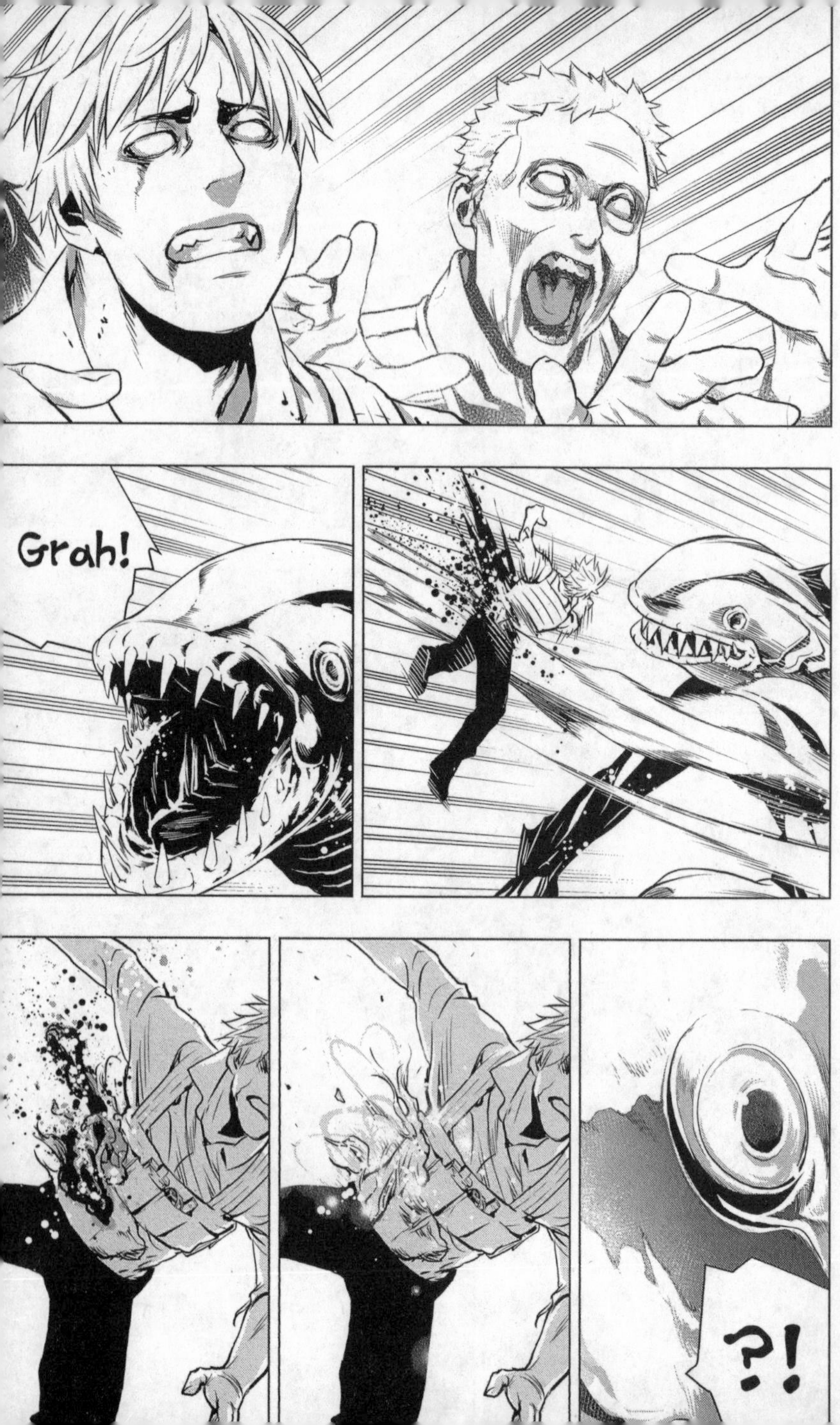
Grah!
?!

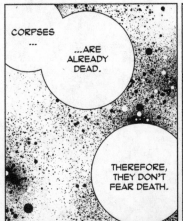

Gya-argh!

AMAZING!

THEY'RE SHRUGGING OFF ANY DAMAGE AND KILLING MONSTER AFTER MONSTER.

CORPSES ...

...ARE ALREADY DEAD.

THEREFORE, THEY DON'T FEAR DEATH.

MY SKILL...

...BUFFS THEM WITH SUPER-REGENERATION AND A BERSERK STATE.

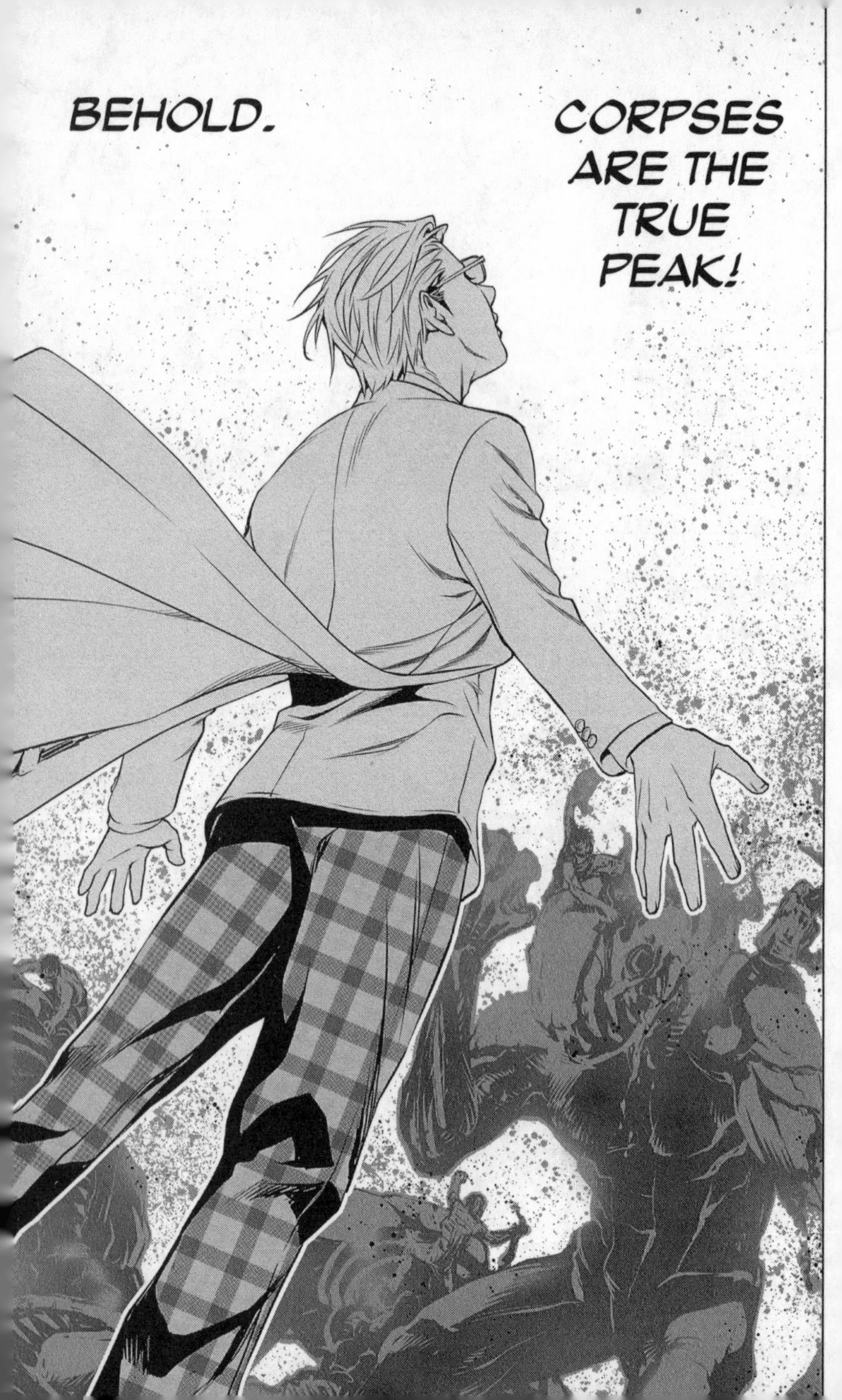
CORPSES ARE THE TRUE PEAK!
BEHOLD.

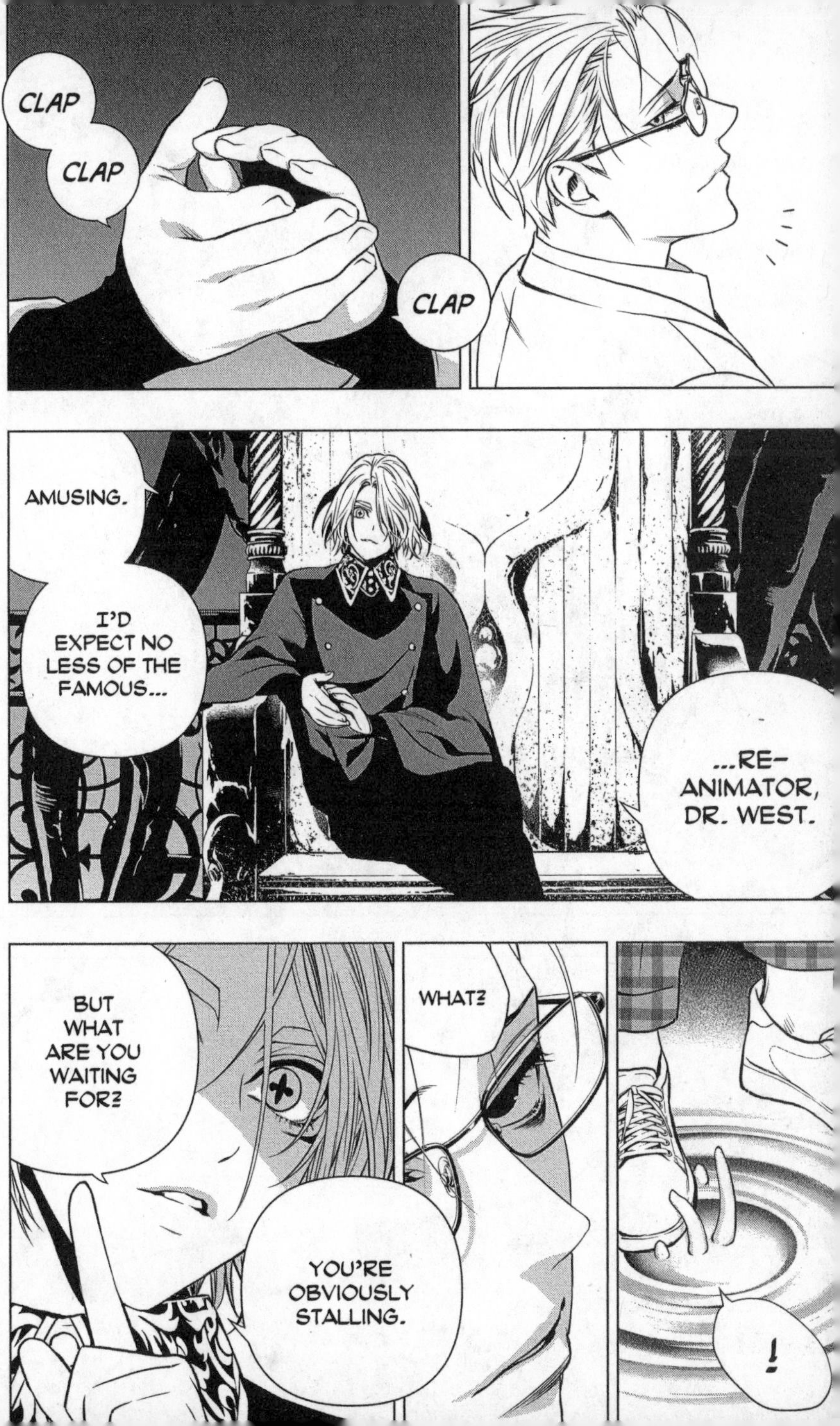
CLAP
CLAP
CLAP
AMUSING.
I'D EXPECT NO LESS OF THE FAMOUS...
...RE-ANIMATOR, DR. WEST.
BUT WHAT ARE YOU WAITING FOR?
YOU'RE OBVIOUSLY STALLING.
WHAT?
!

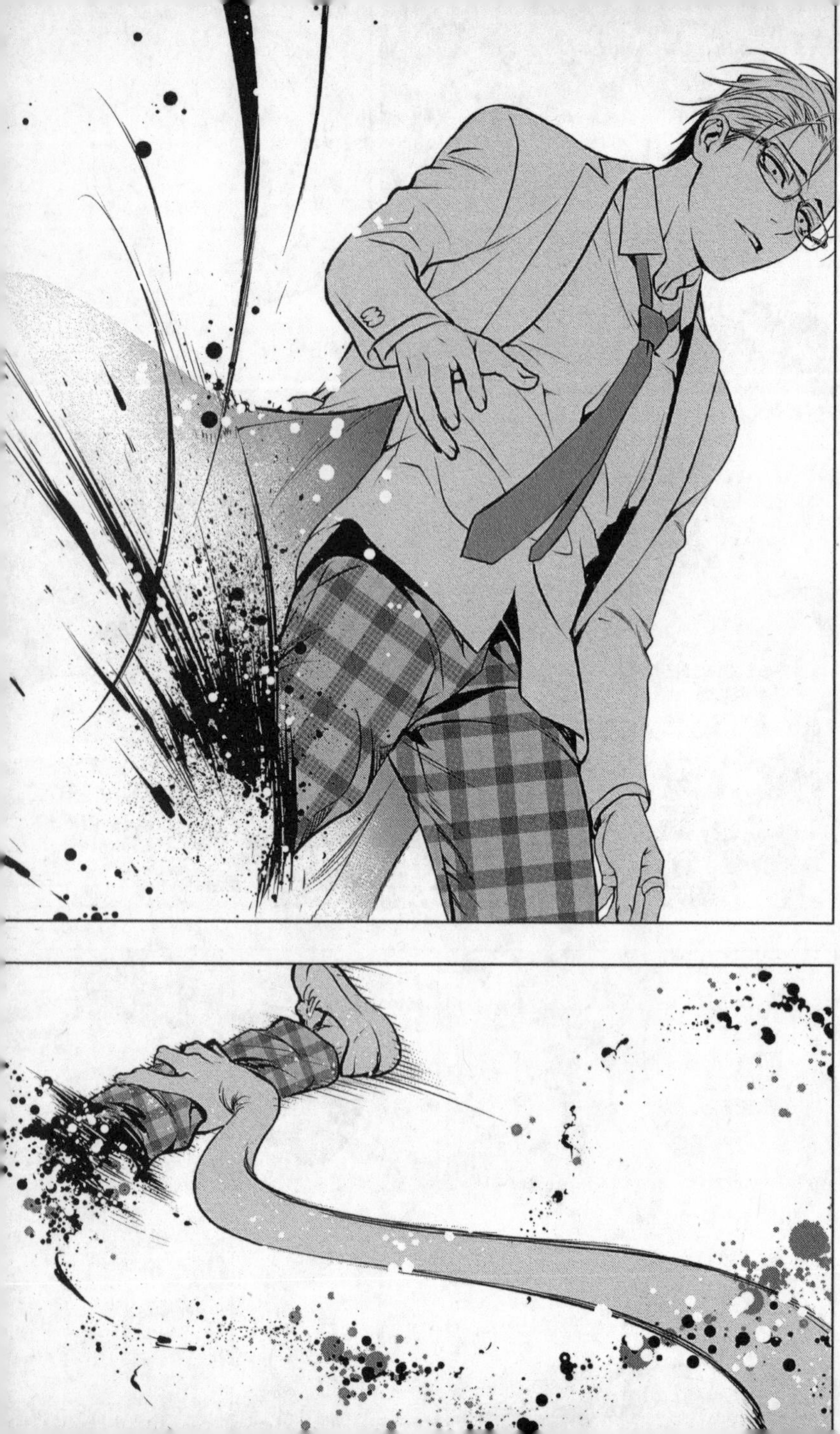

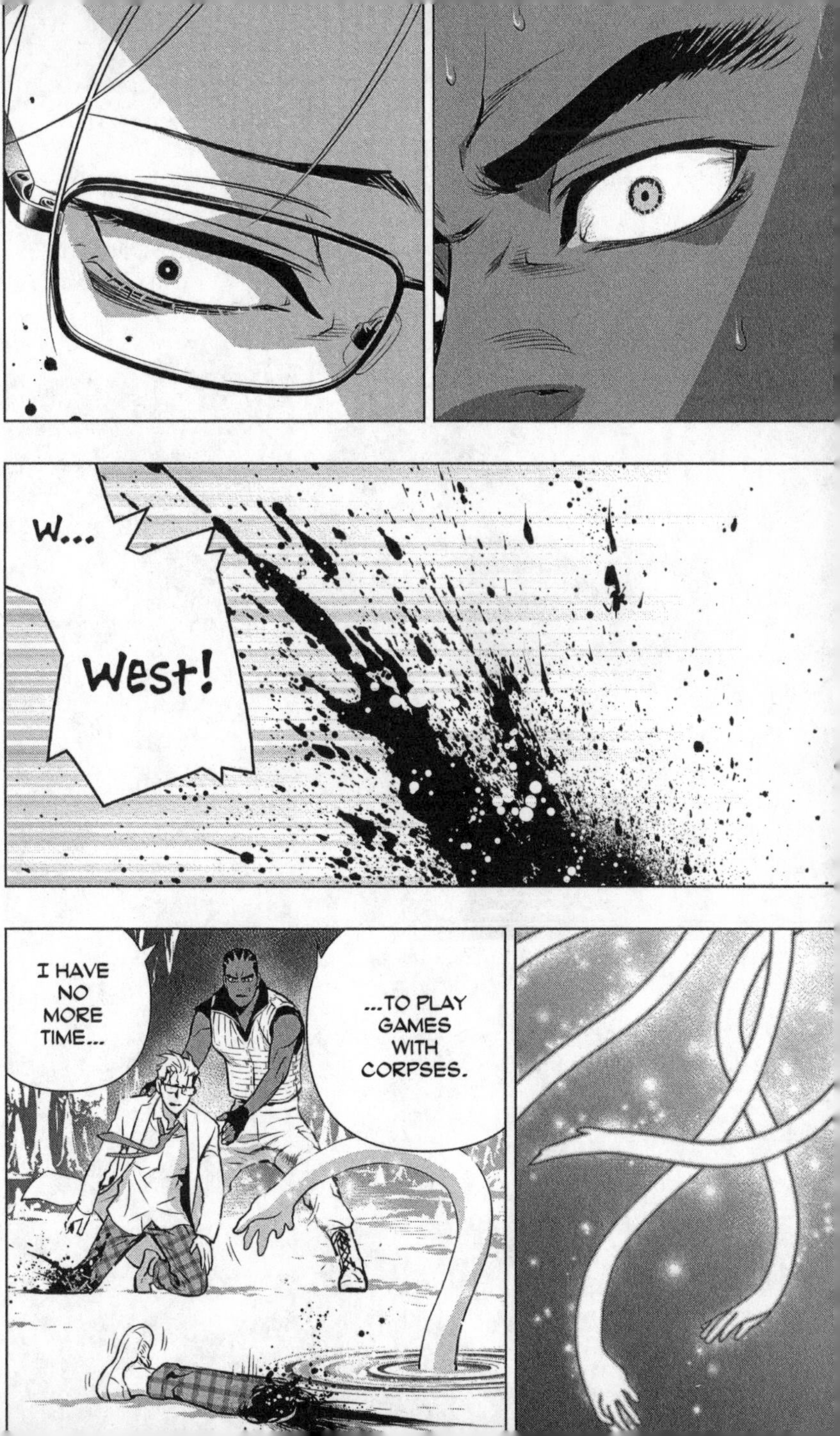
W...
West!
I HAVE NO MORE TIME...
...TO PLAY GAMES WITH CORPSES.

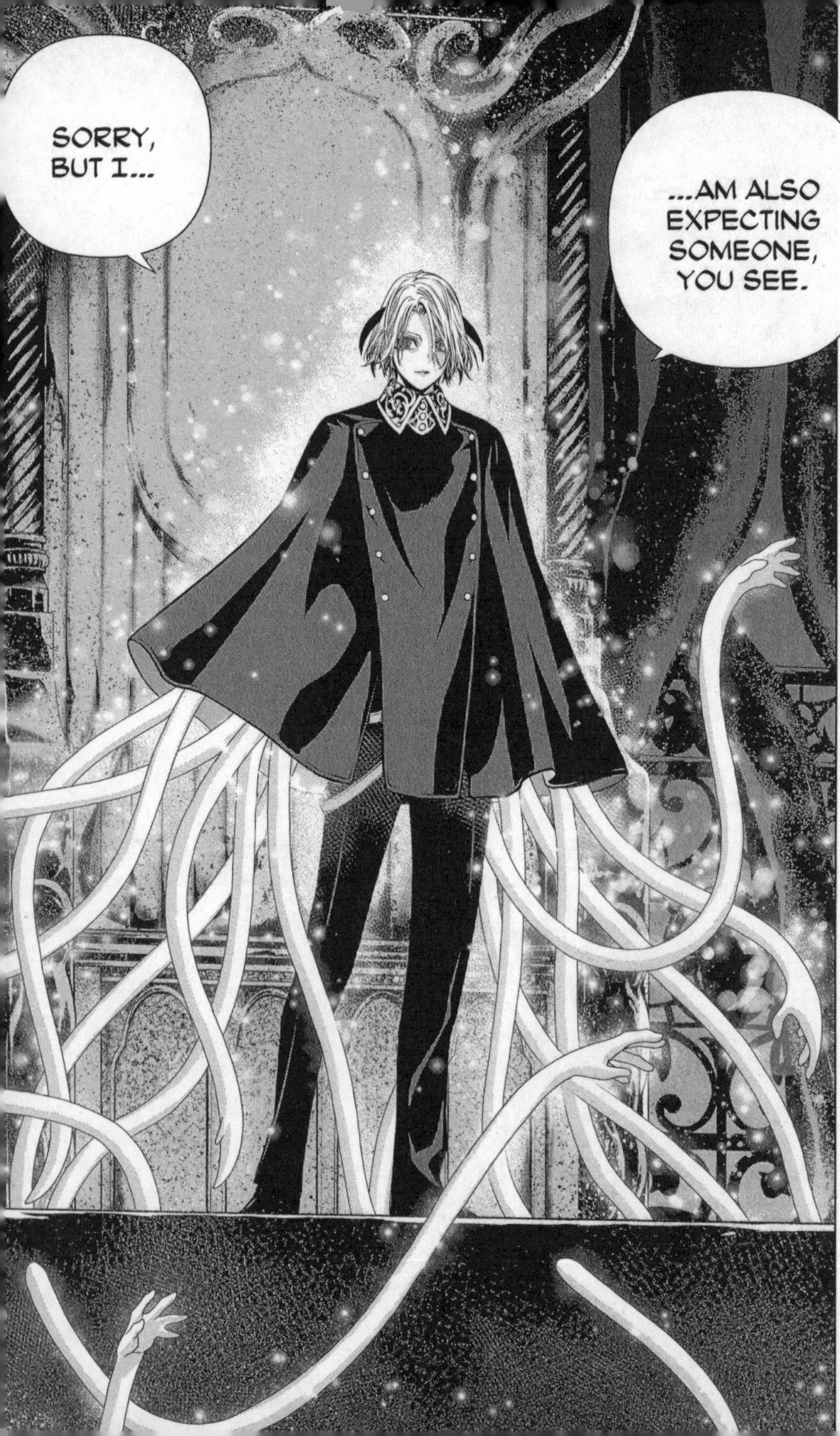
SORRY, BUT I...
...AM ALSO EXPECTING SOMEONE, YOU SEE.

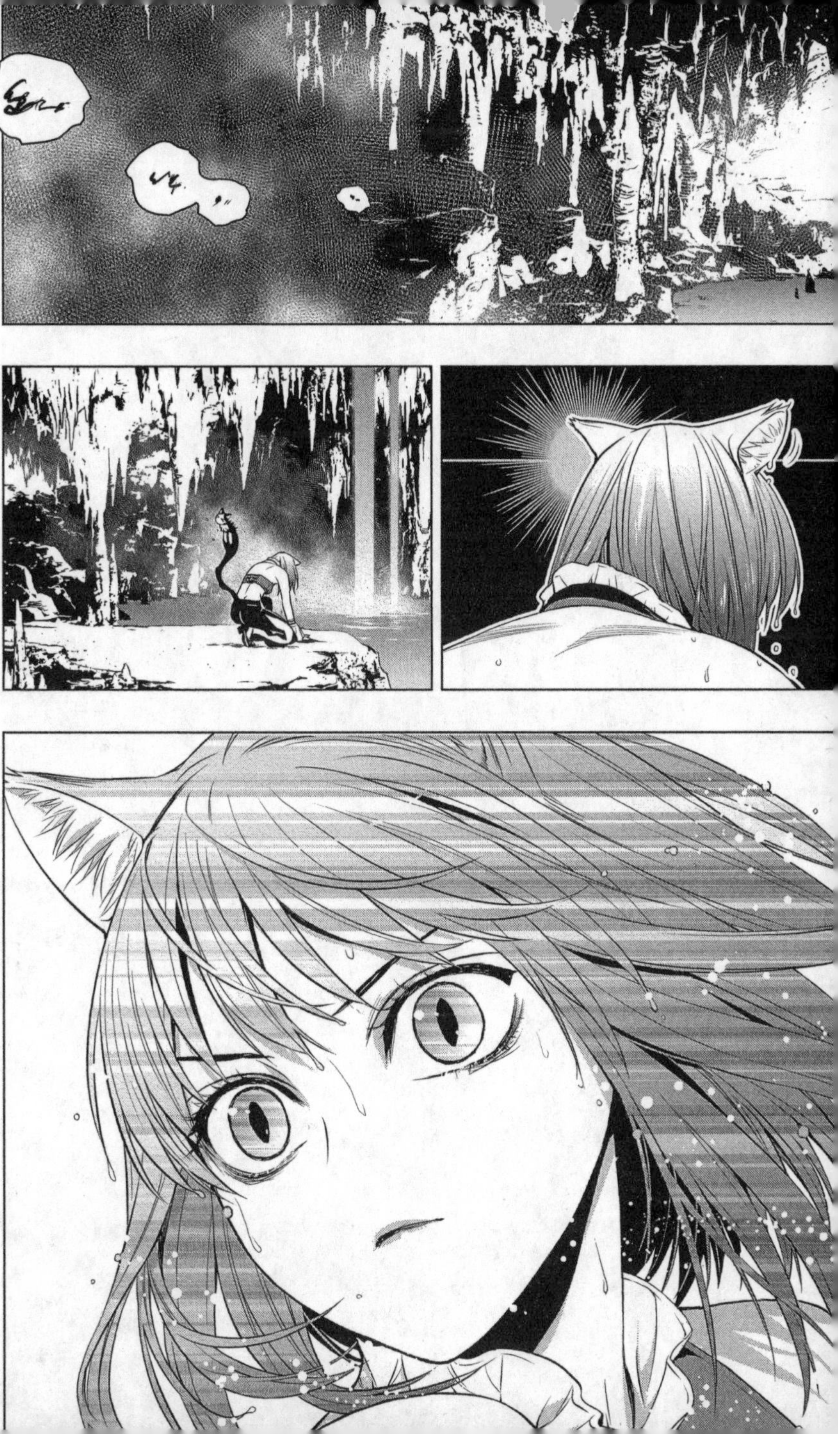

19: SEA-GOD

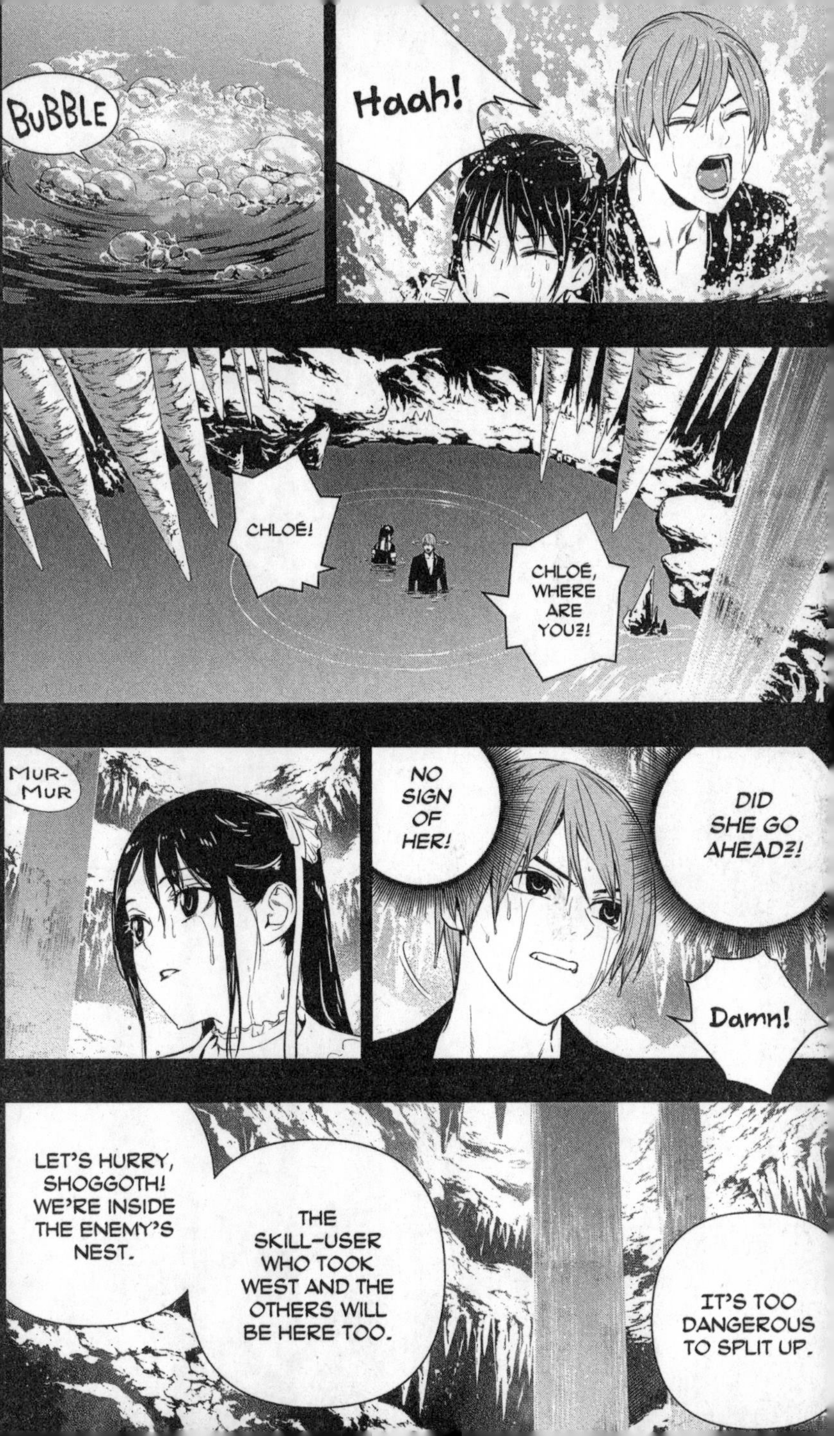
BUBBLE
Haah!
CHLOÉ!
CHLOÉ, WHERE ARE YOU?!
MUR-MUR
NO SIGN OF HER!
DID SHE GO AHEAD?!
Damn!
LET'S HURRY, SHOGGOTH! WE'RE INSIDE THE ENEMY'S NEST.
THE SKILL-USER WHO TOOK WEST AND THE OTHERS WILL BE HERE TOO.
IT'S TOO DANGEROUS TO SPLIT UP.

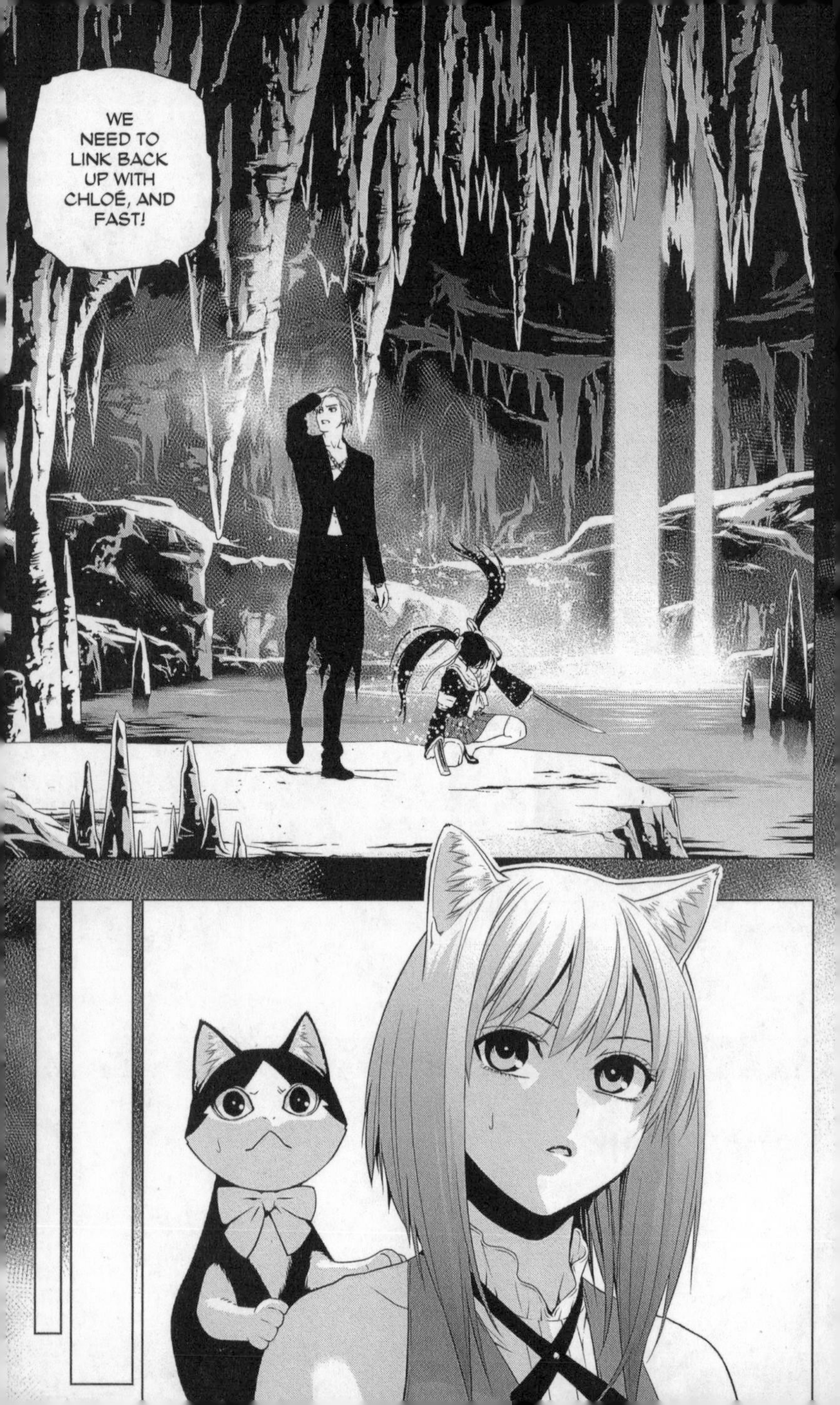
WE NEED TO LINK BACK UP WITH CHLOÉ, AND FAST!

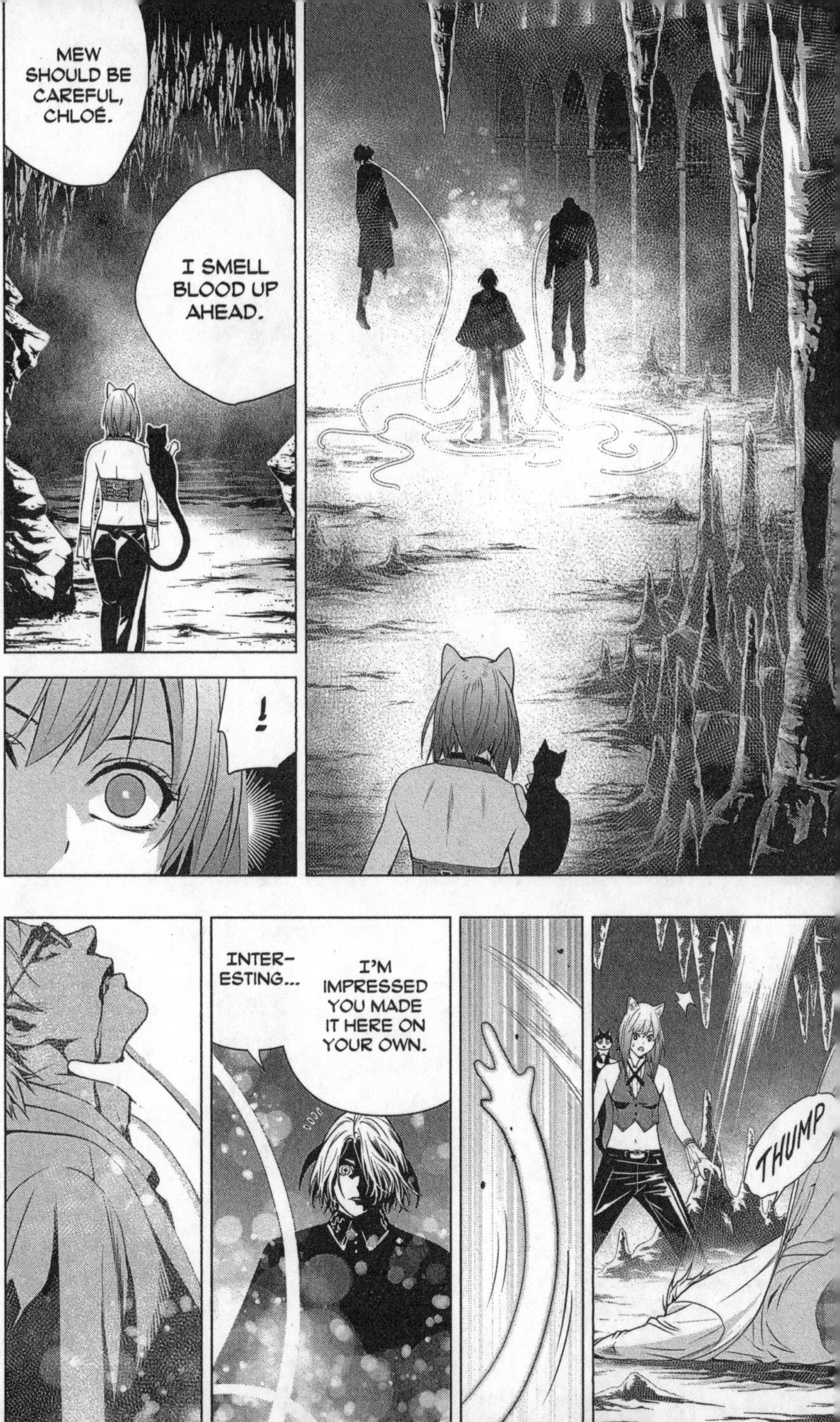
MEW SHOULD BE CAREFUL, CHLOÉ.
I SMELL BLOOD UP AHEAD.
!
INTER-ESTING...
I'M IMPRESSED YOU MADE IT HERE ON YOUR OWN.
THUMP

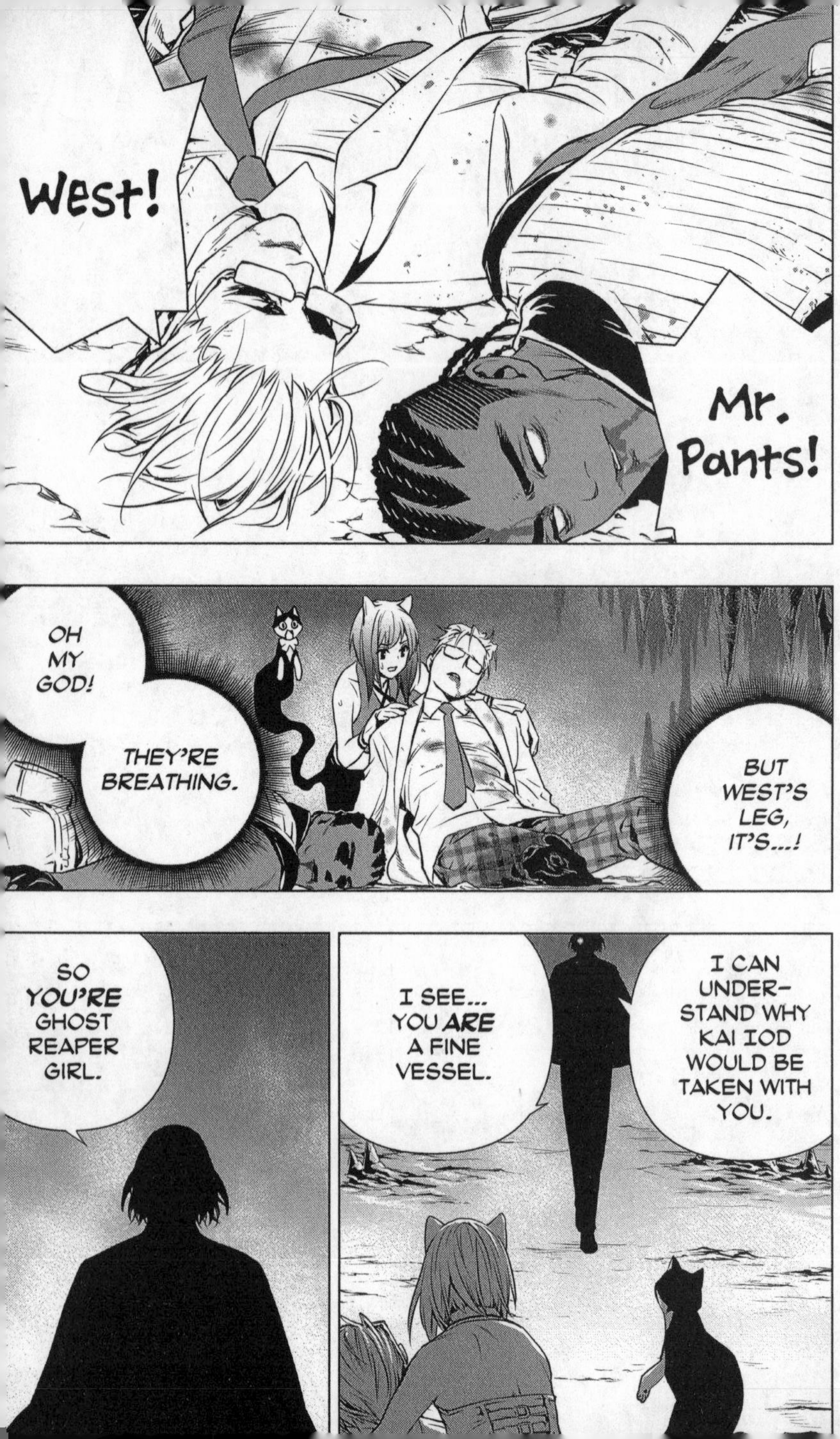
West!
Mr. Pants!
OH MY GOD!
THEY'RE BREATHING.
BUT WEST'S LEG, IT'S...!
SO *YOU'RE* GHOST REAPER GIRL.
I SEE... YOU *ARE* A FINE VESSEL.
I CAN UNDER-STAND WHY KAI IOD WOULD BE TAKEN WITH YOU.

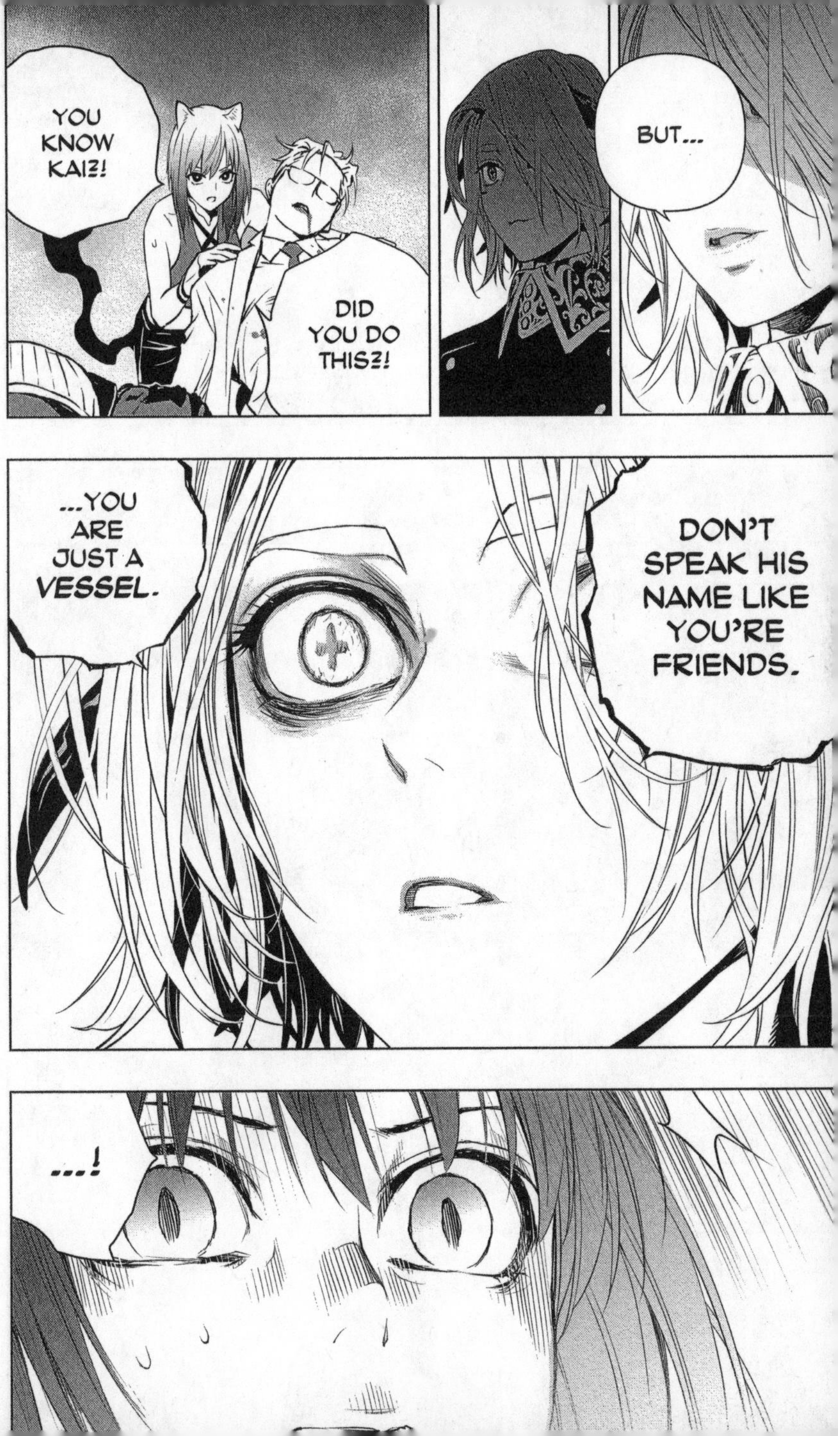
YOU KNOW KAI?!
DID YOU DO THIS?!
BUT...
...YOU ARE JUST A VESSEL.
DON'T SPEAK HIS NAME LIKE YOU'RE FRIENDS.
...!

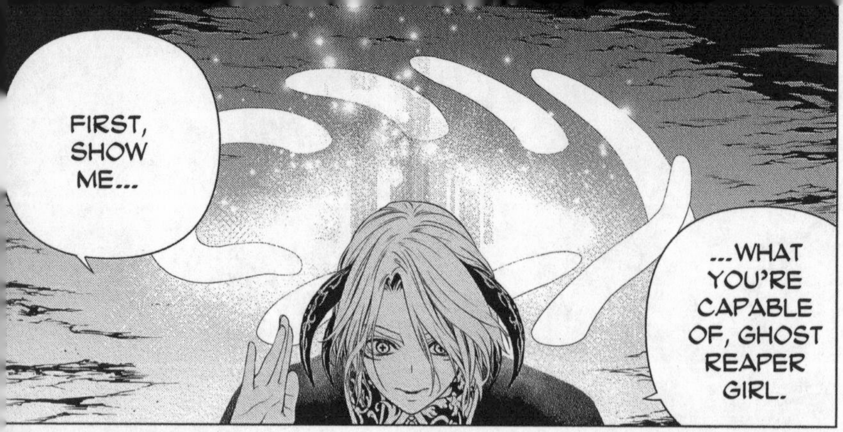
FIRST, SHOW ME...
...WHAT YOU'RE CAPABLE OF, GHOST REAPER GIRL.

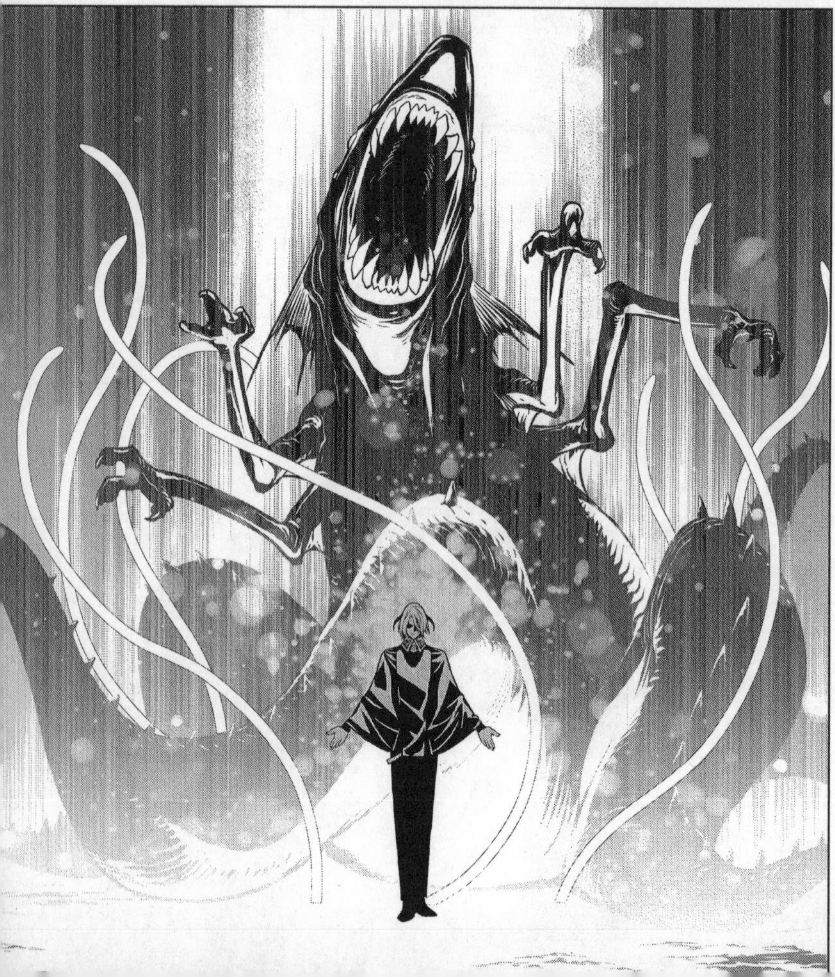

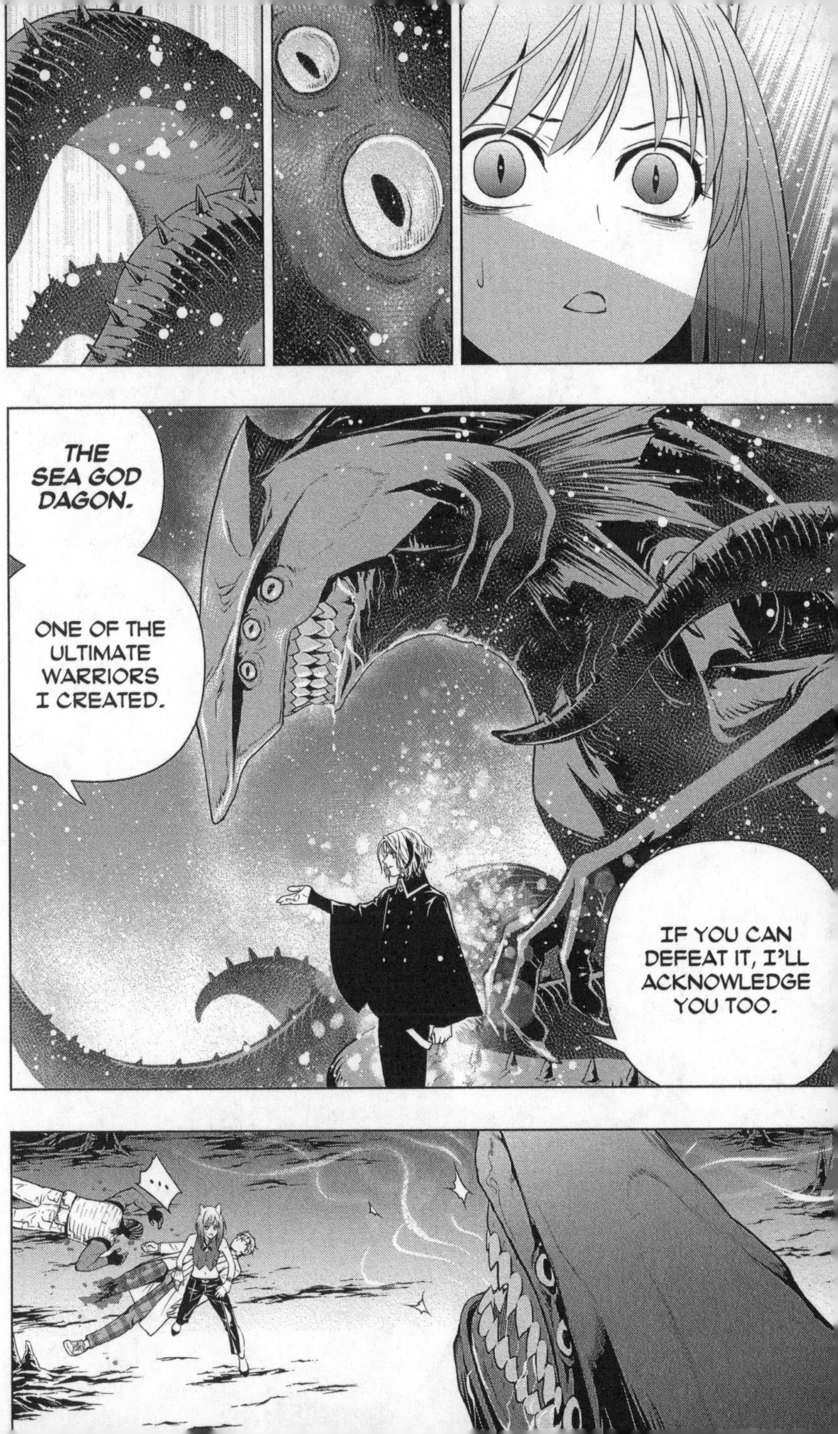
THE SEA GOD DAGON.
ONE OF THE ULTIMATE WARRIORS I CREATED.
IF YOU CAN DEFEAT IT, I'LL ACKNOWLEDGE YOU TOO.
...

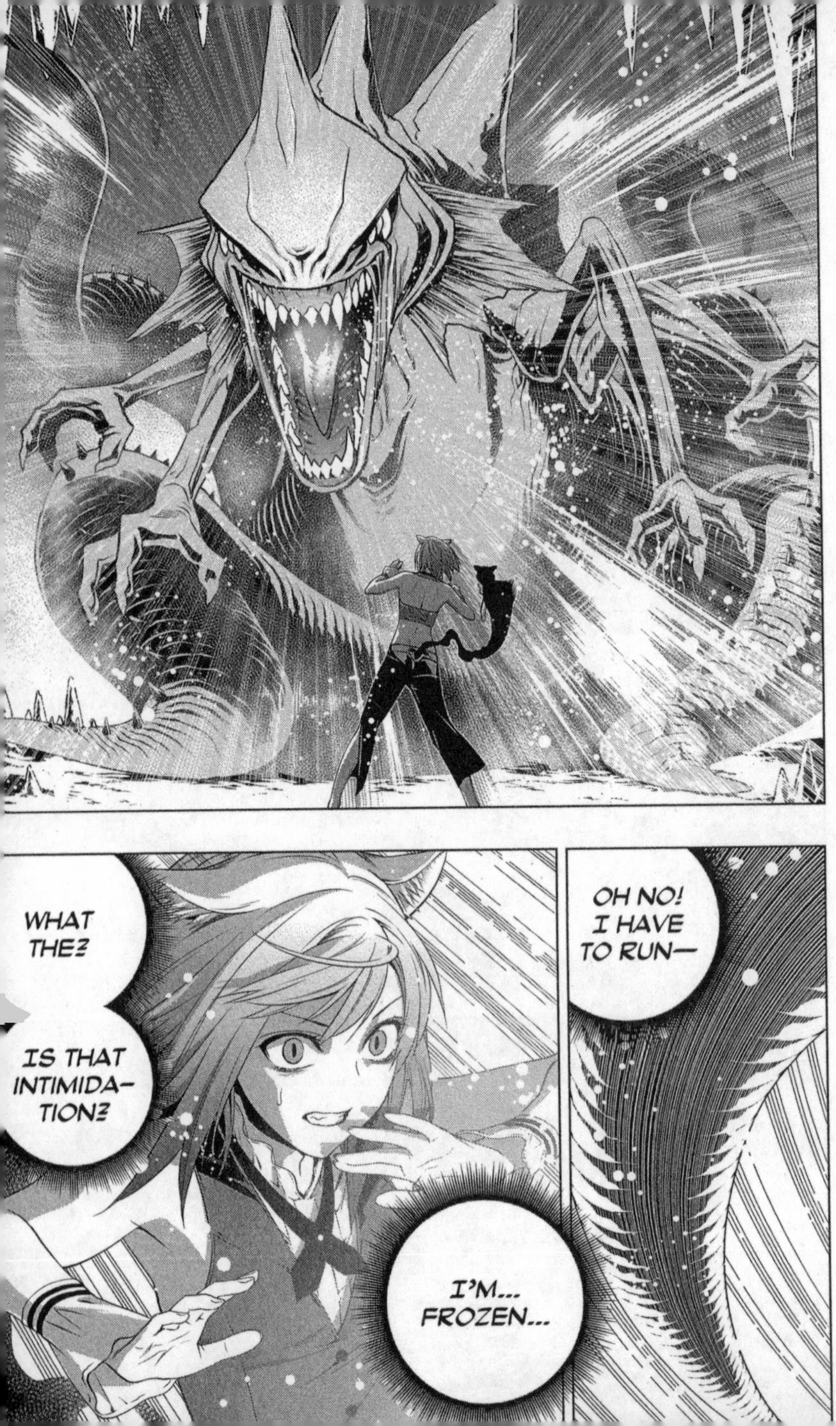
WHAT THE?
IS THAT INTIMIDATION?
I'M... FROZEN...
OH NO! I HAVE TO RUN—

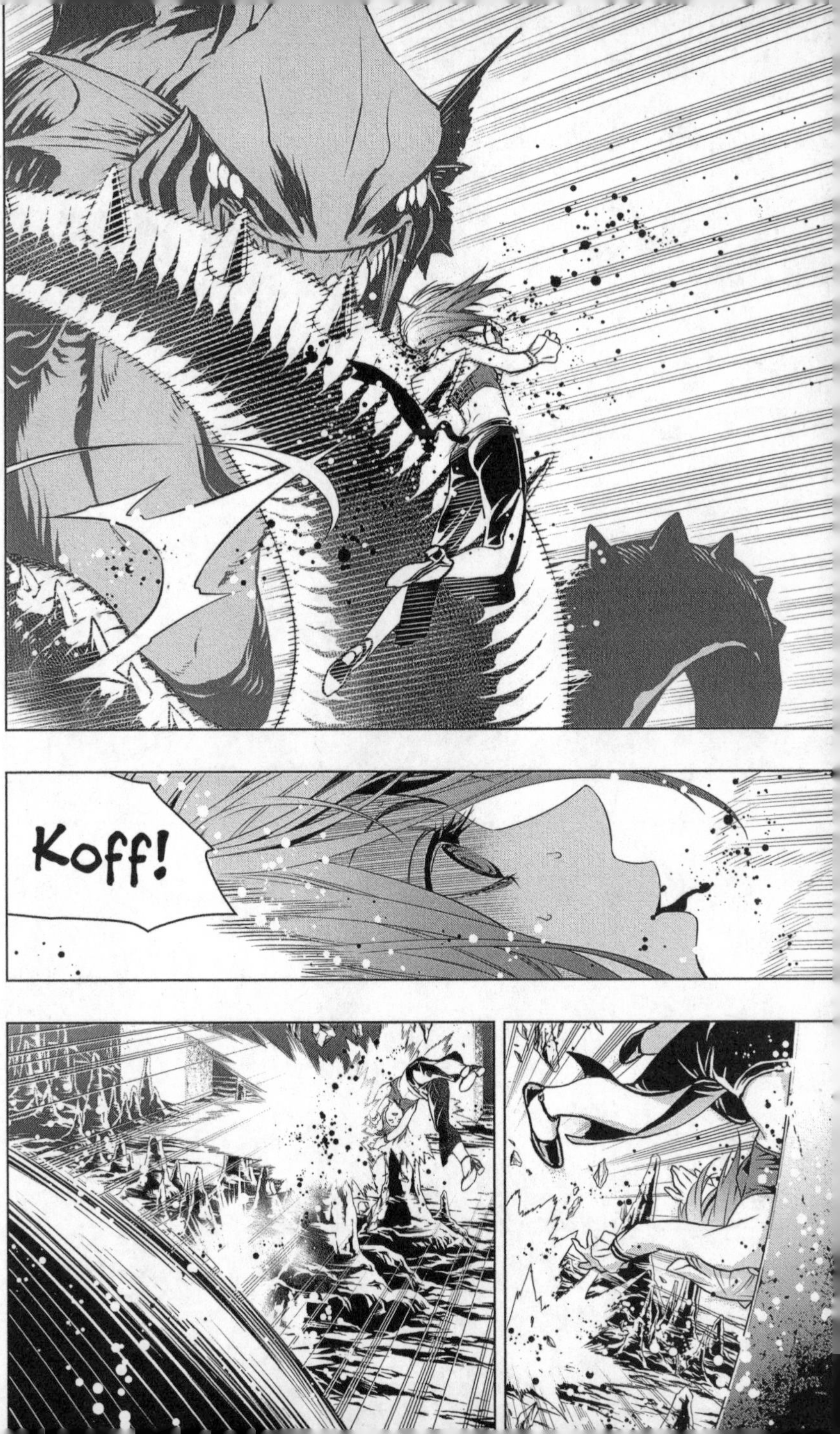
Koff!

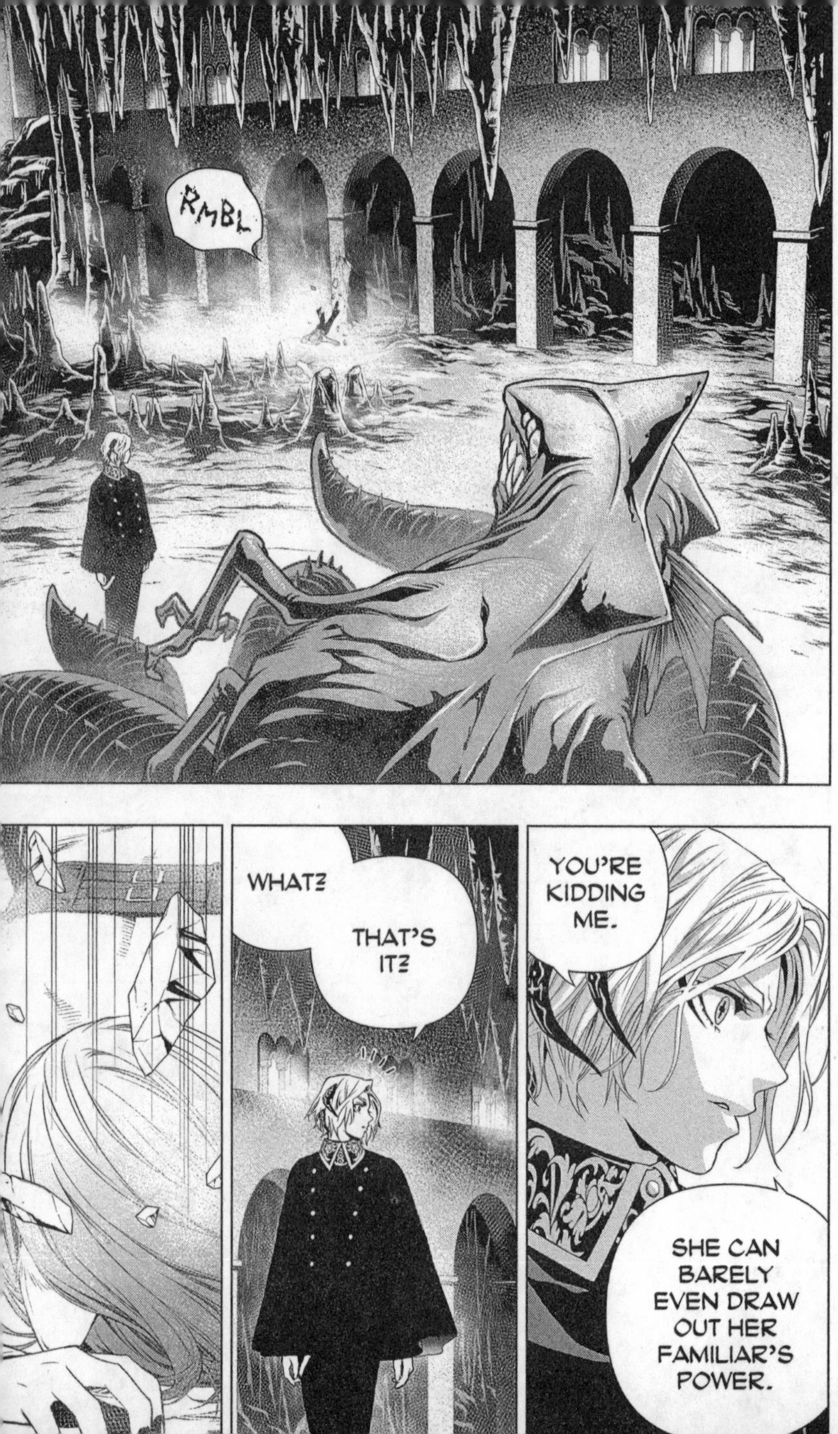
RMBL
WHAT?
THAT'S IT?
YOU'RE KIDDING ME.
SHE CAN BARELY EVEN DRAW OUT HER FAMILIAR'S POWER.

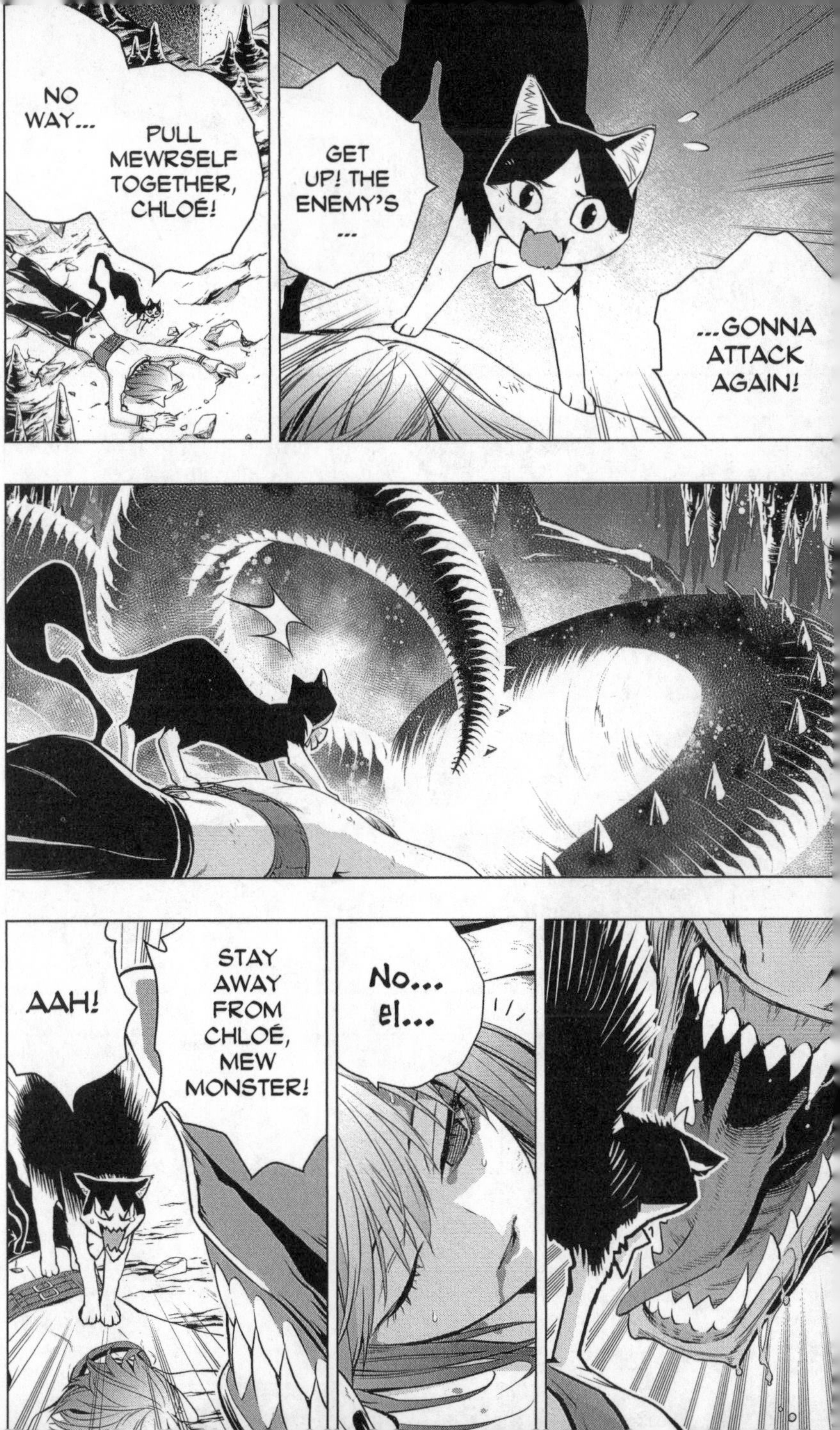
NO WAY...
PULL MEWRSELF TOGETHER, CHLOÉ!
GET UP! THE ENEMY'S ...
...GONNA ATTACK AGAIN!
AAH!
STAY AWAY FROM CHLOÉ, MEW MONSTER!
No... el...

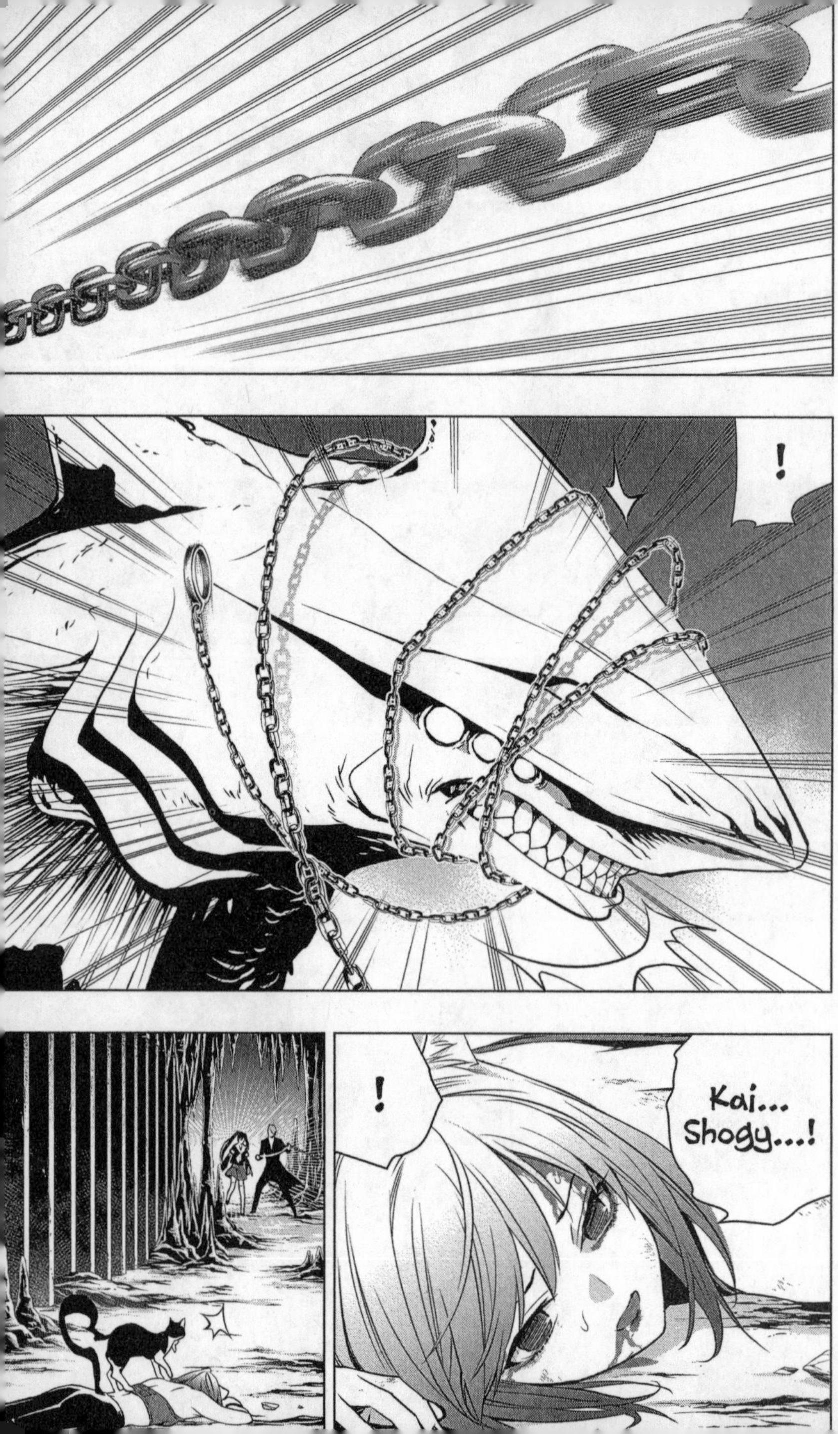
!
!
Kai... Shogy...!

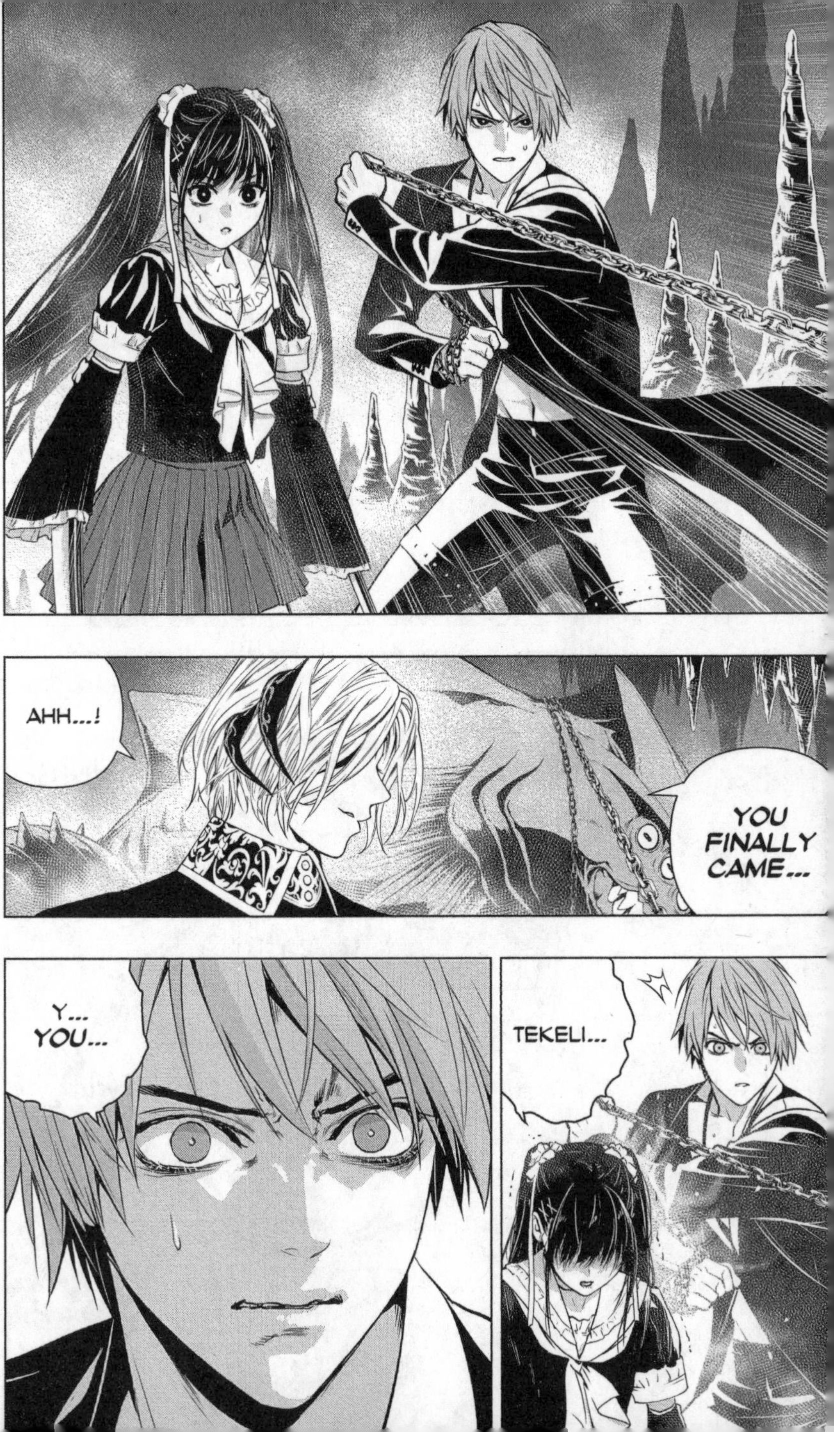
AHH...!
YOU FINALLY CAME...
Y... YOU...
TEKELI...

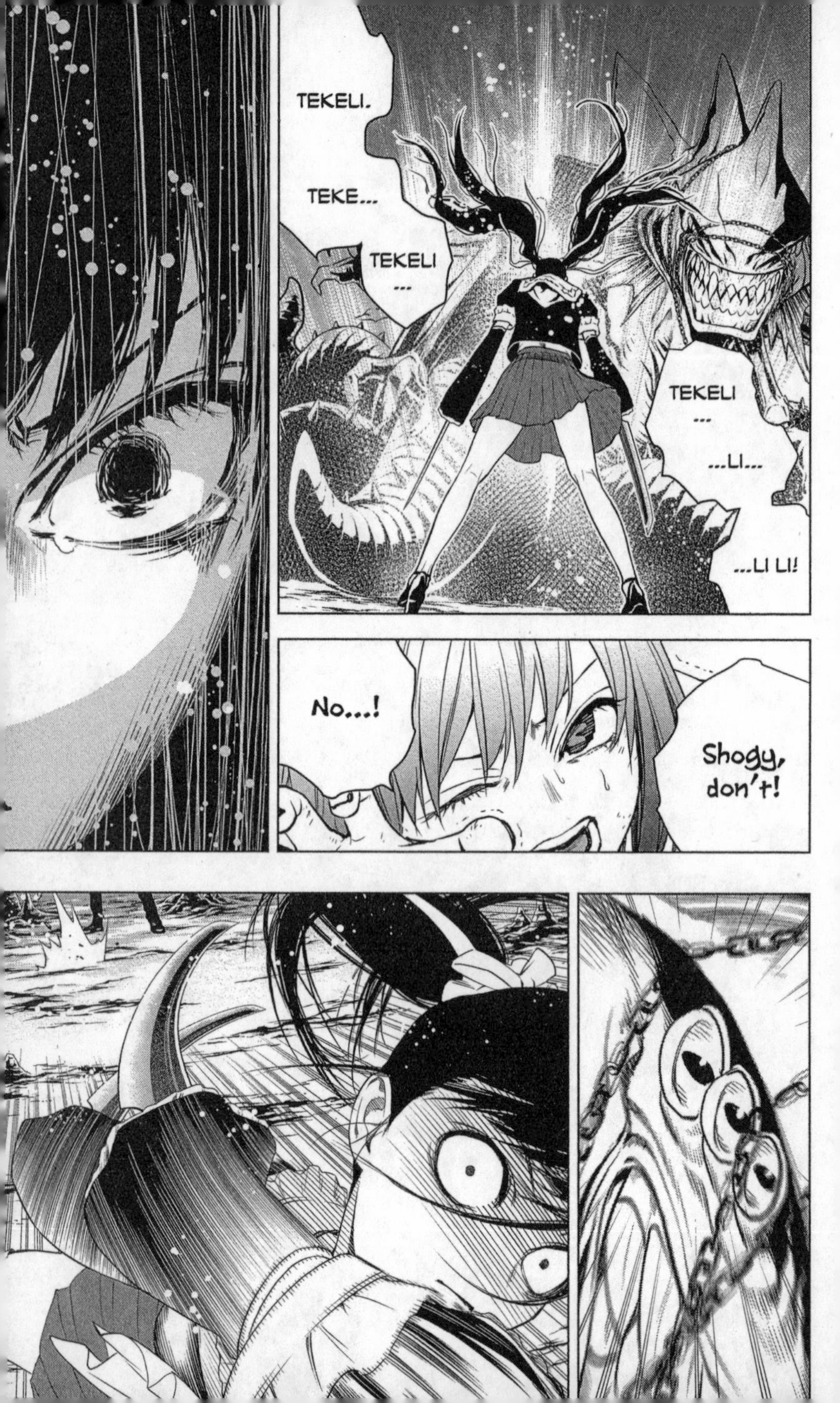

TEKELI.
TEKE...
TEKELI
...
TEKELI
...
...LI...
...LI LI!
No...!
Shogy, don't!

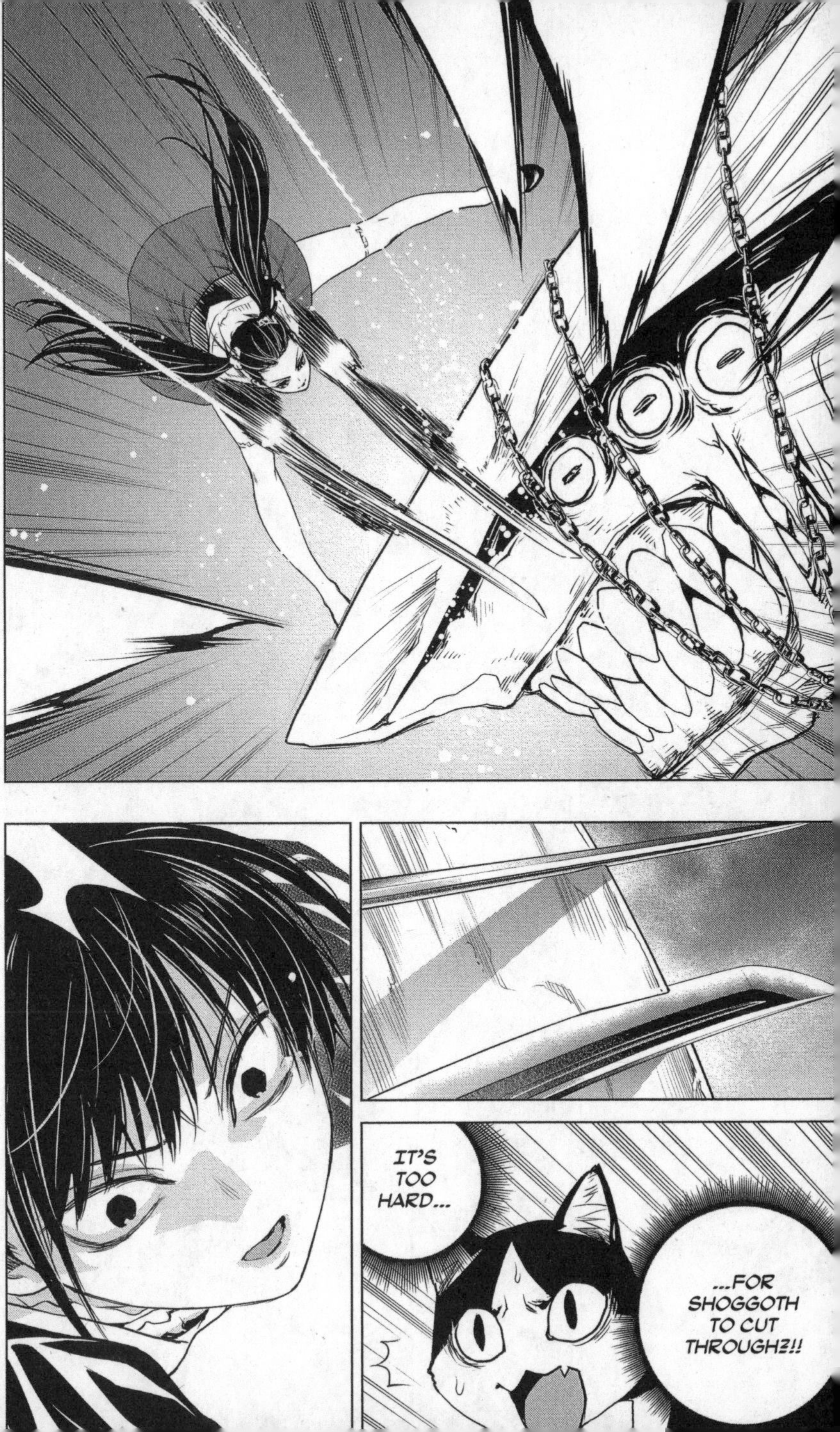
IT'S TOO HARD...
...FOR SHOGGOTH TO CUT THROUGH?!!

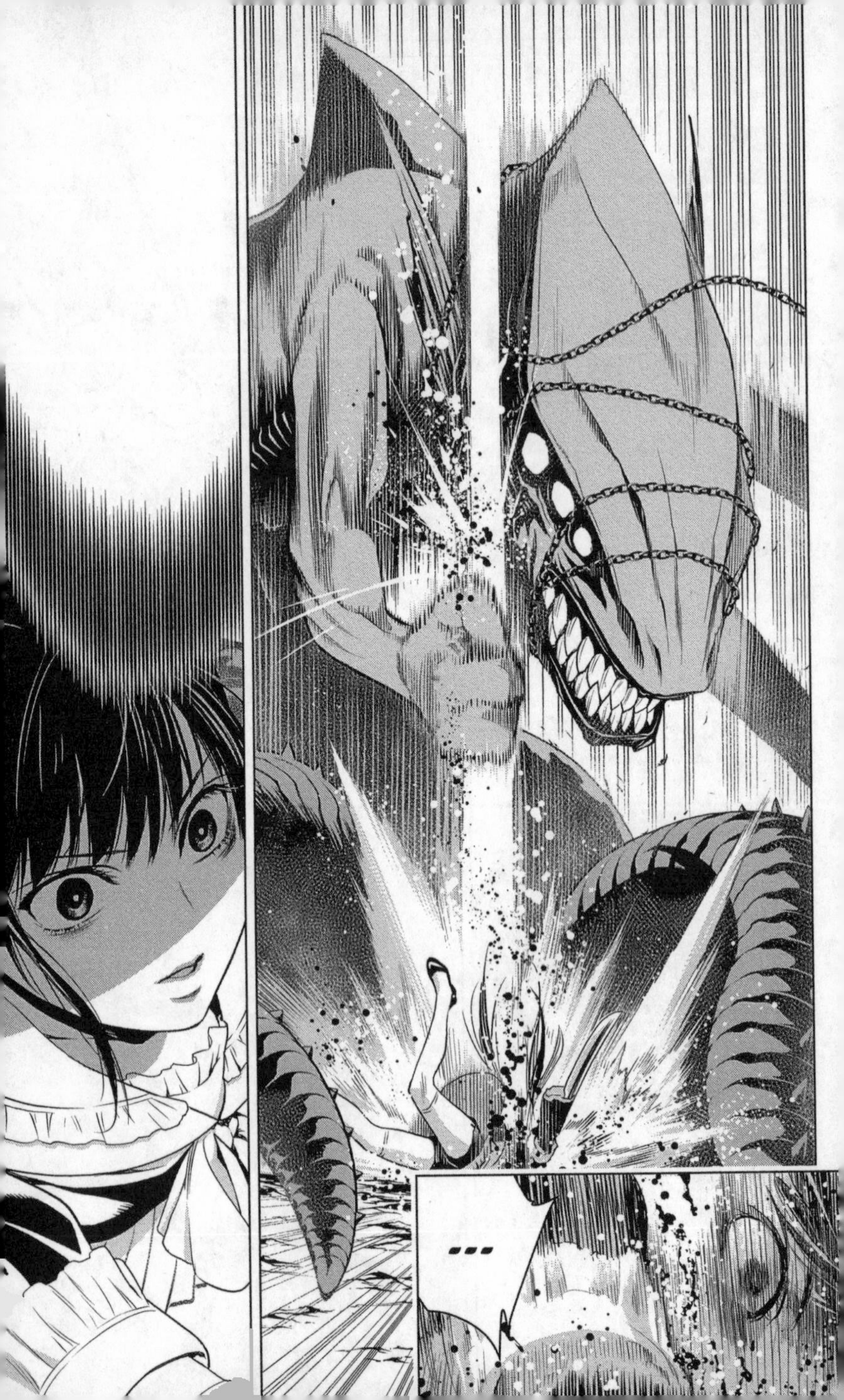
...

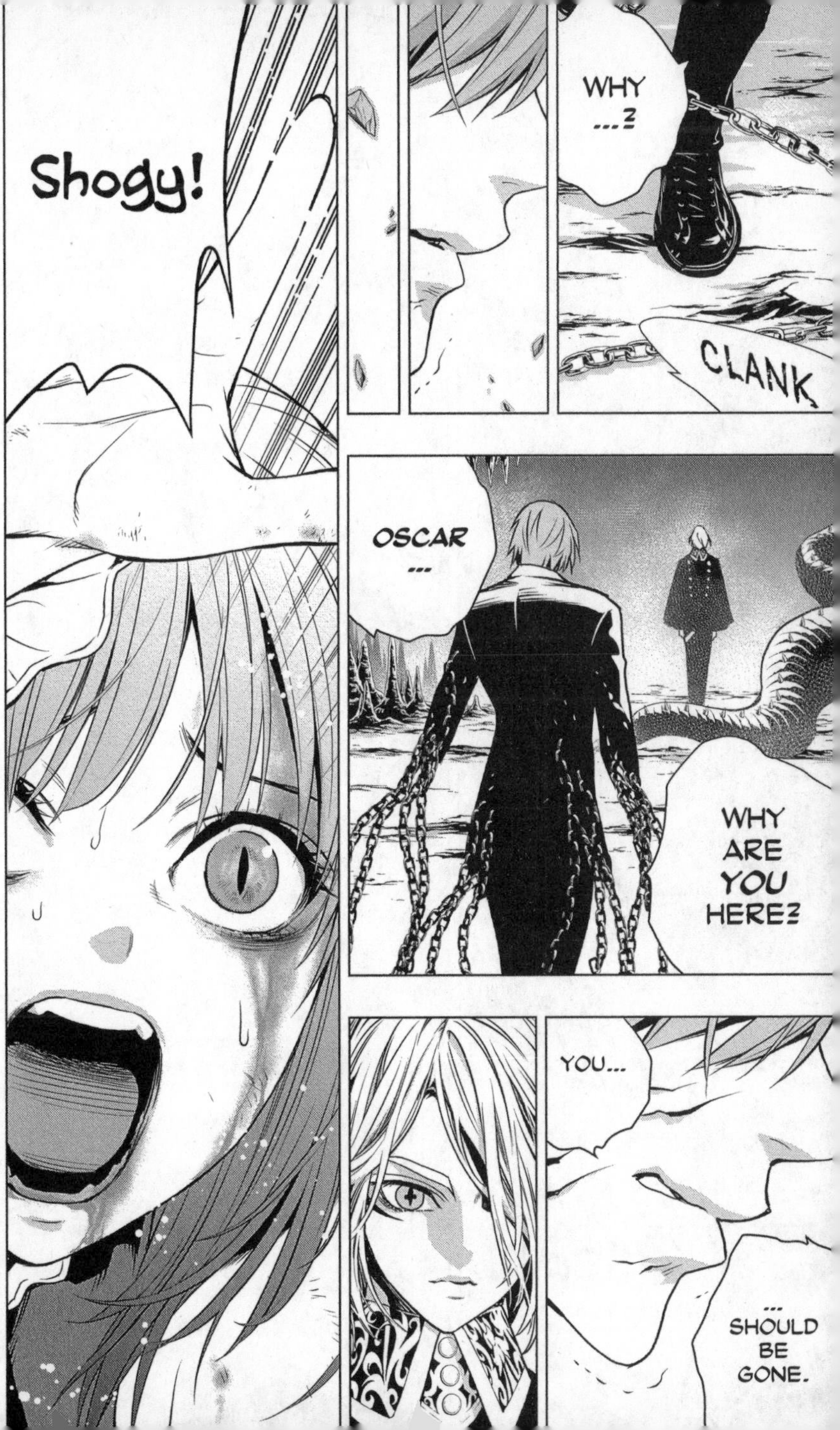
Shogy!
WHY ...?
CLANK
OSCAR ...
WHY ARE YOU HERE?
YOU...
... SHOULD BE GONE.

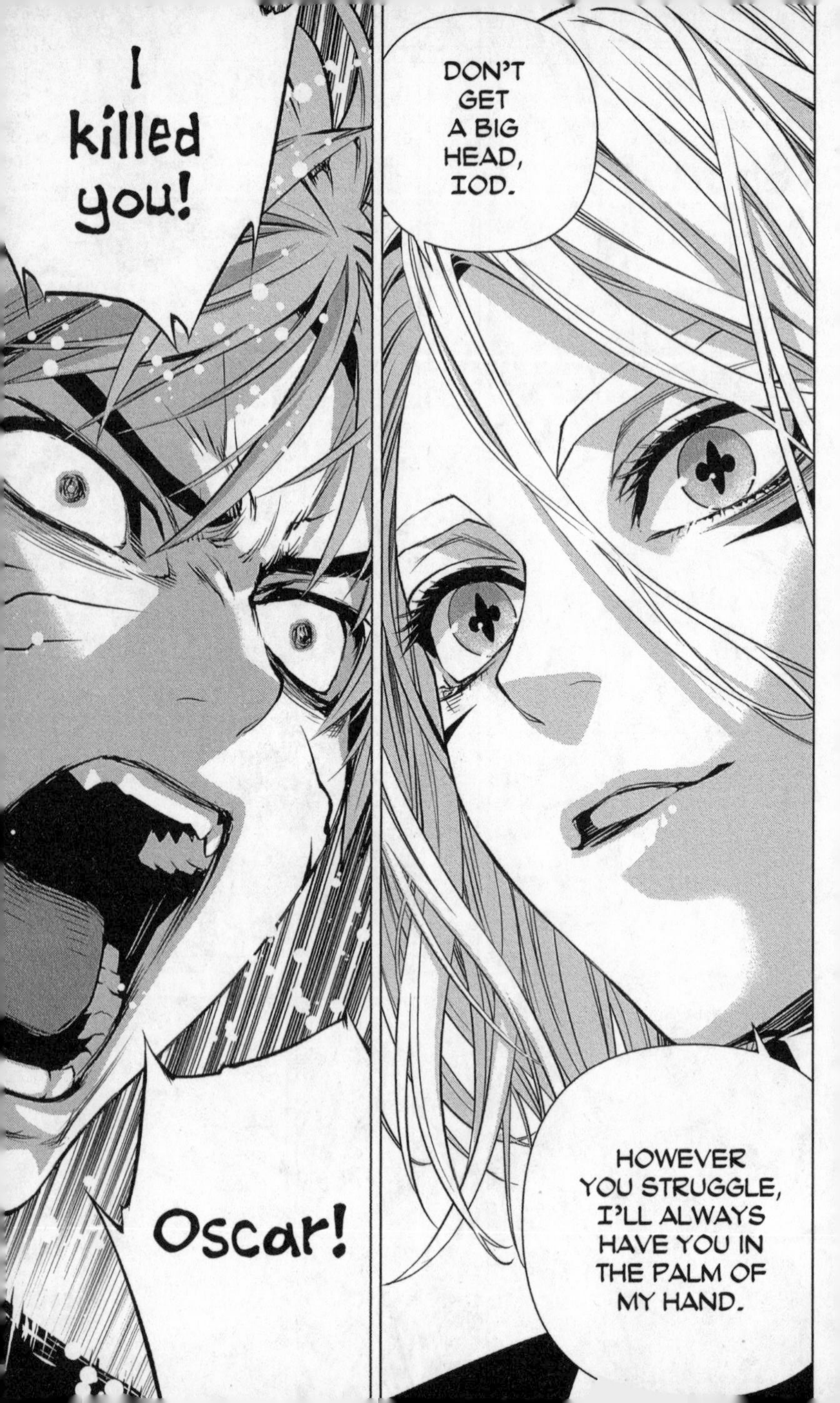
I killed you!
Oscar!
DON'T GET A BIG HEAD, IOD.
HOWEVER YOU STRUGGLE, I'LL ALWAYS HAVE YOU IN THE PALM OF MY HAND.

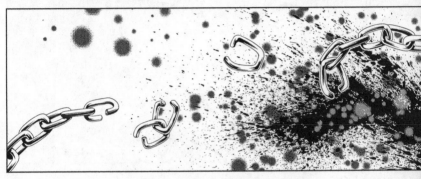

GOD...

ANY GOD...

PLEASE GIVE ME STRENGTH ...

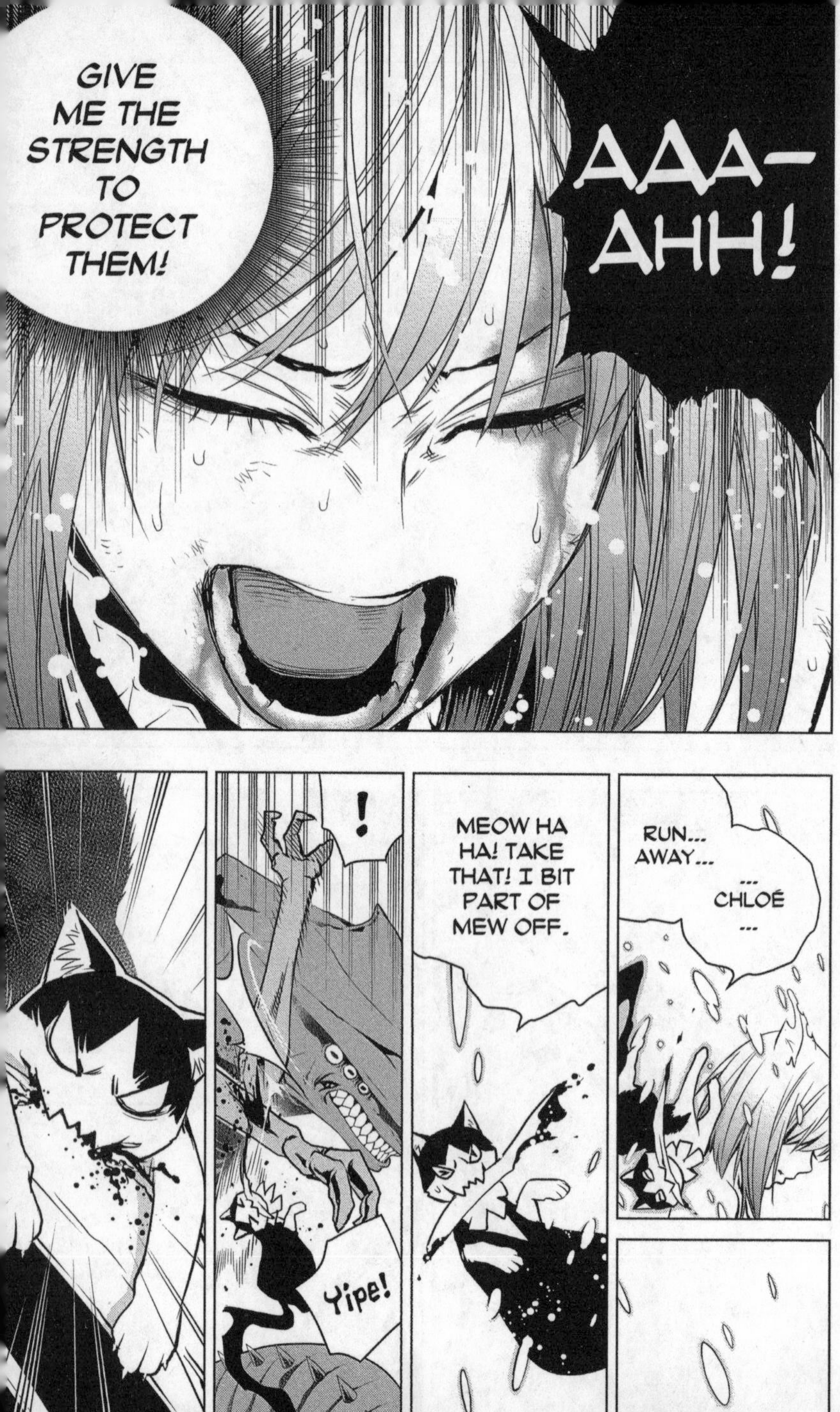

GIVE ME THE STRENGTH TO PROTECT THEM!
AAA-AHH!
!
Yipe!
MEOW HA HA! TAKE THAT! I BIT PART OF MEW OFF.
RUN... AWAY... ...CHLOE...

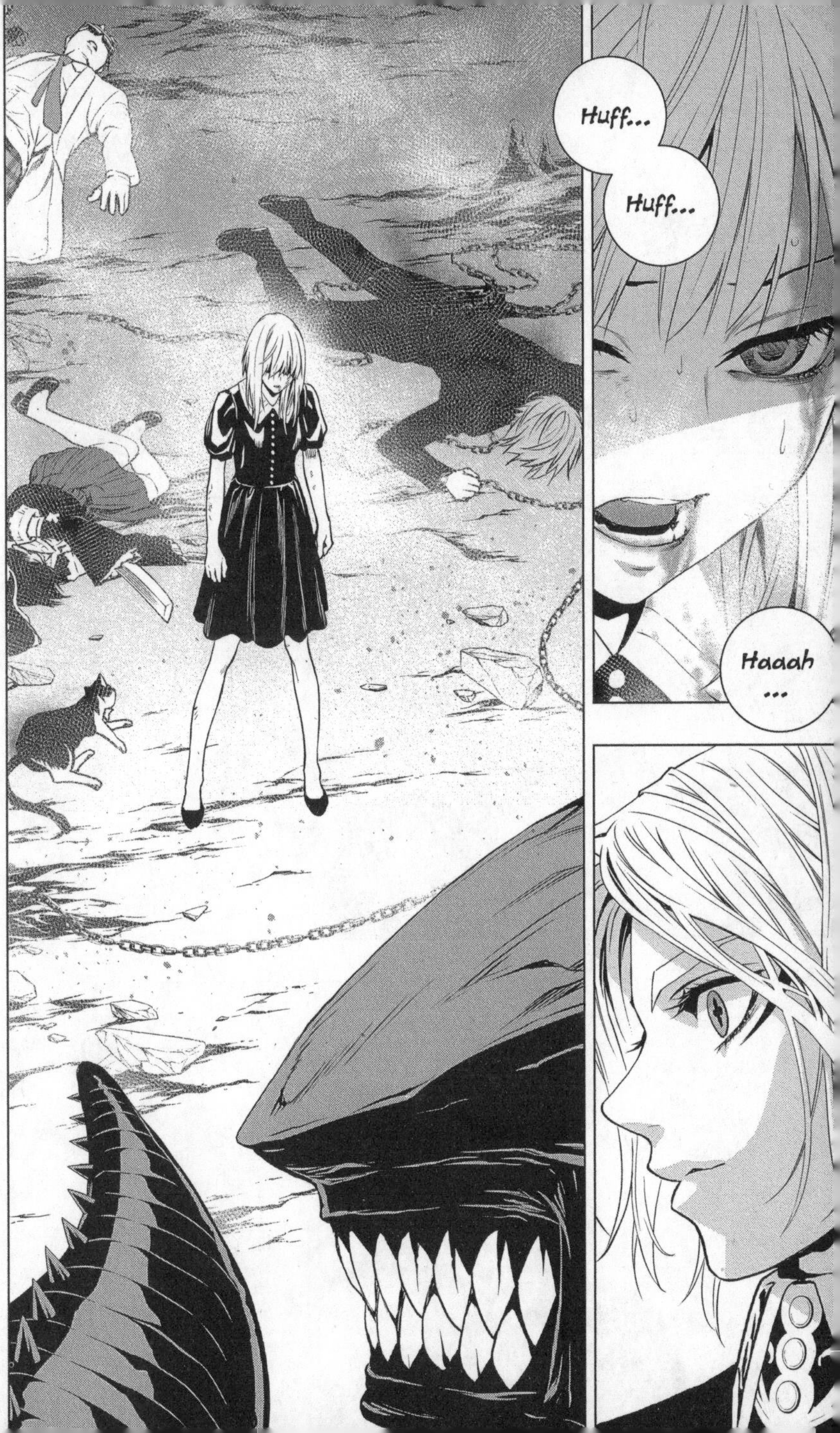
Huff...
Huff...
Haaah ...

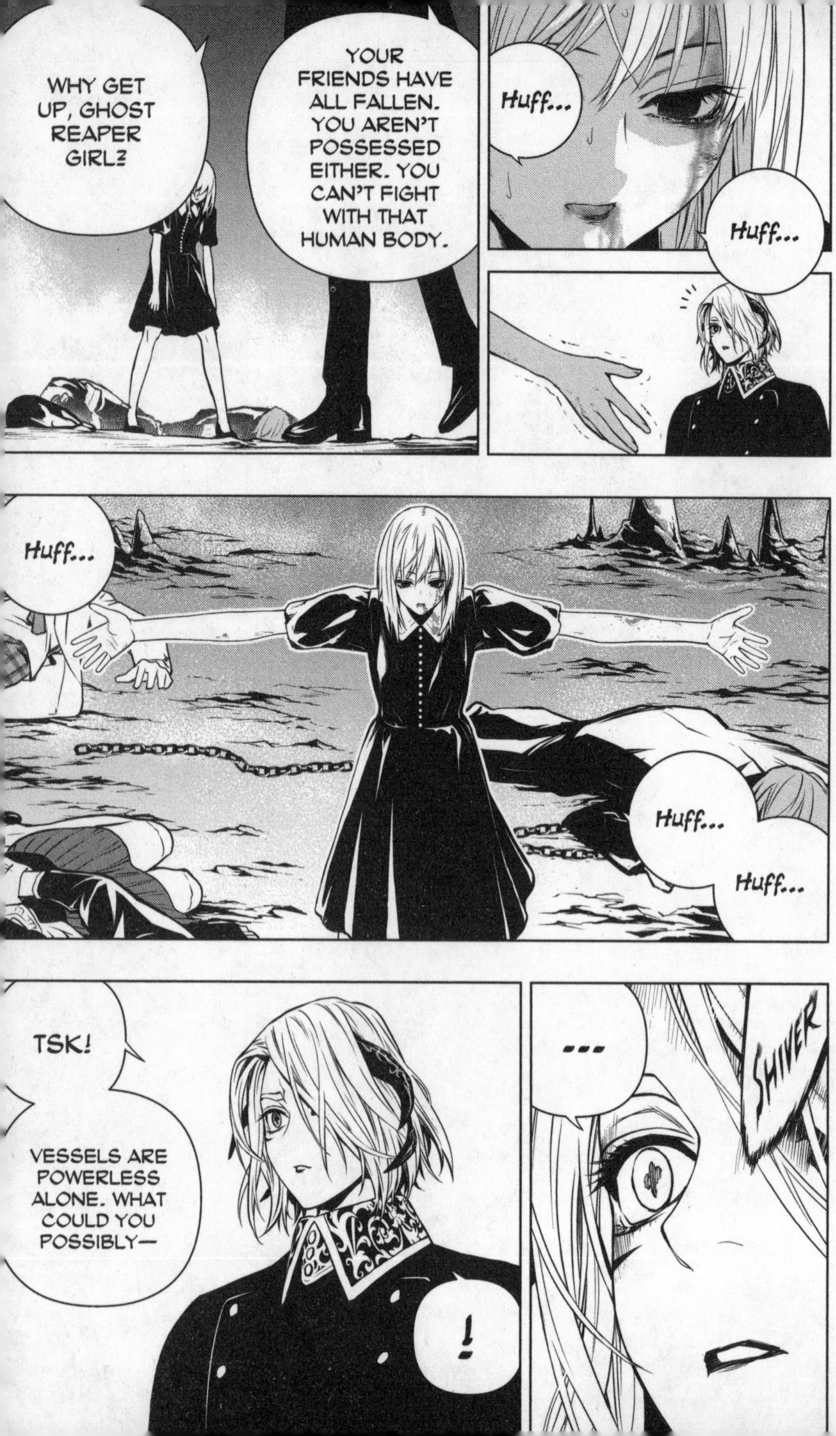
WHY GET UP, GHOST REAPER GIRL?
YOUR FRIENDS HAVE ALL FALLEN. YOU AREN'T POSSESSED EITHER. YOU CAN'T FIGHT WITH THAT HUMAN BODY.
Huff...
Huff...
Huff...
Huff...
Huff...
TSK!
VESSELS ARE POWERLESS ALONE. WHAT COULD YOU POSSIBLY—
!
...
SHIVER

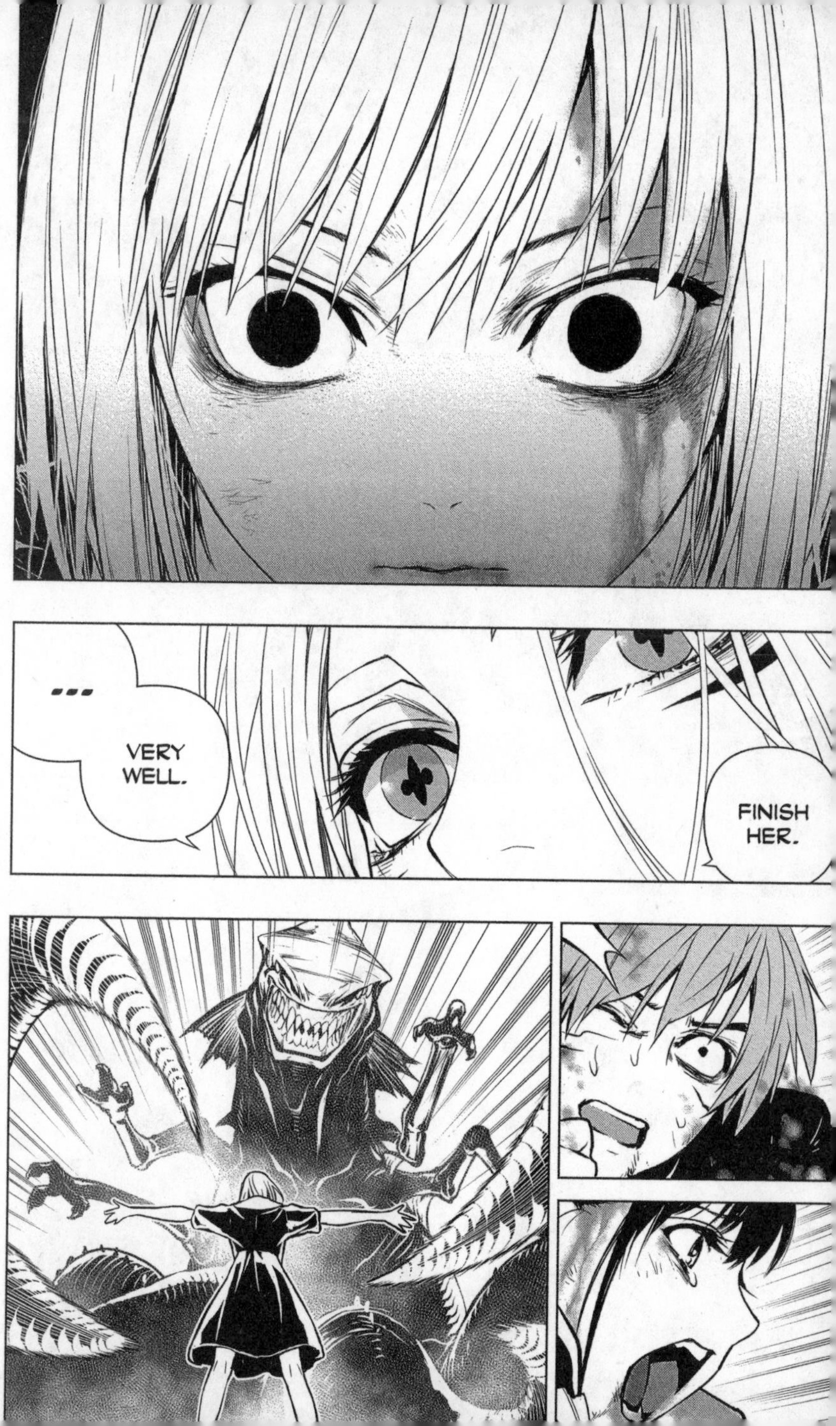
...
VERY WELL.
FINISH HER.

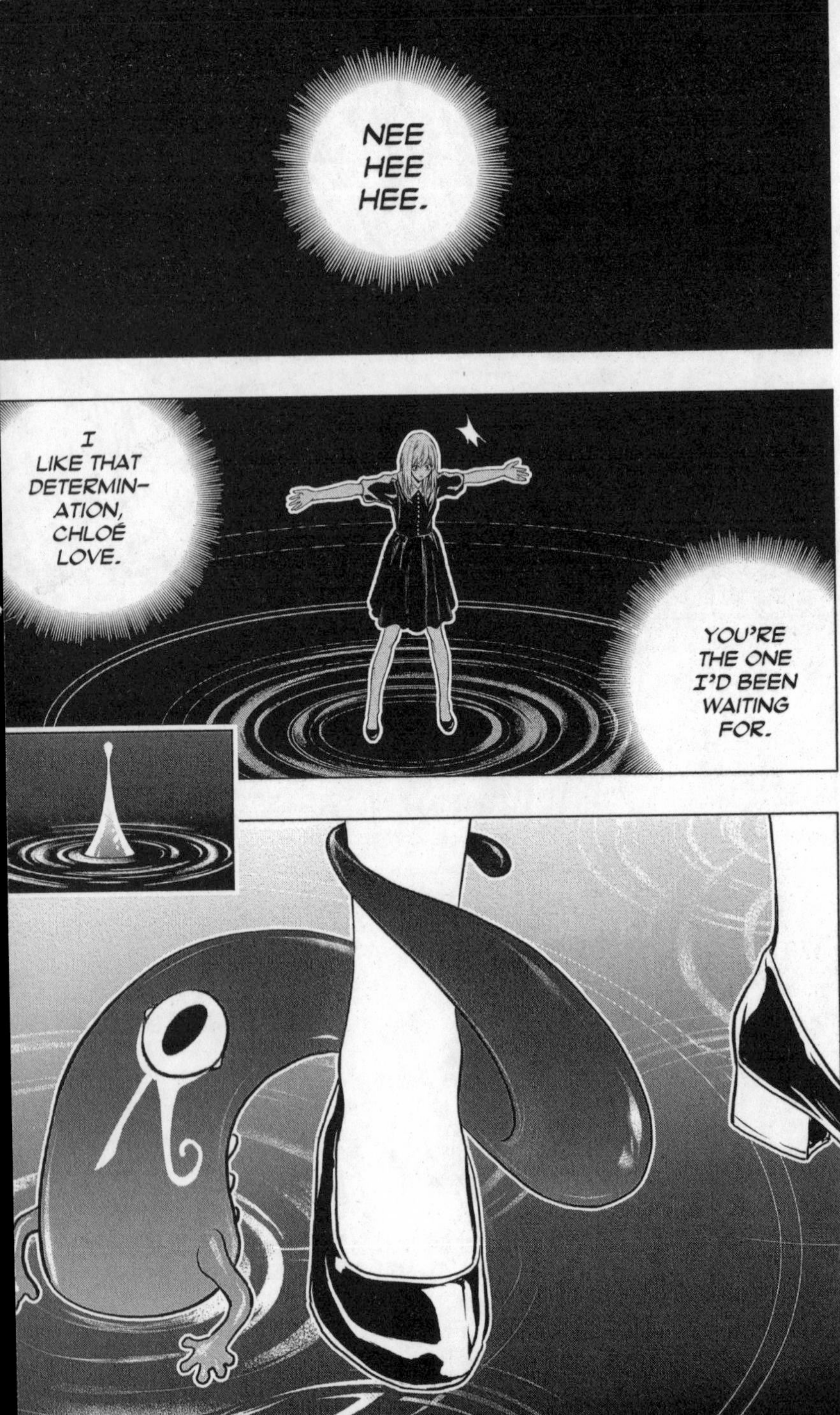
NEE HEE HEE.
I LIKE THAT DETERMINATION, CHLOÉ LOVE.
YOU'RE THE ONE I'D BEEN WAITING FOR.

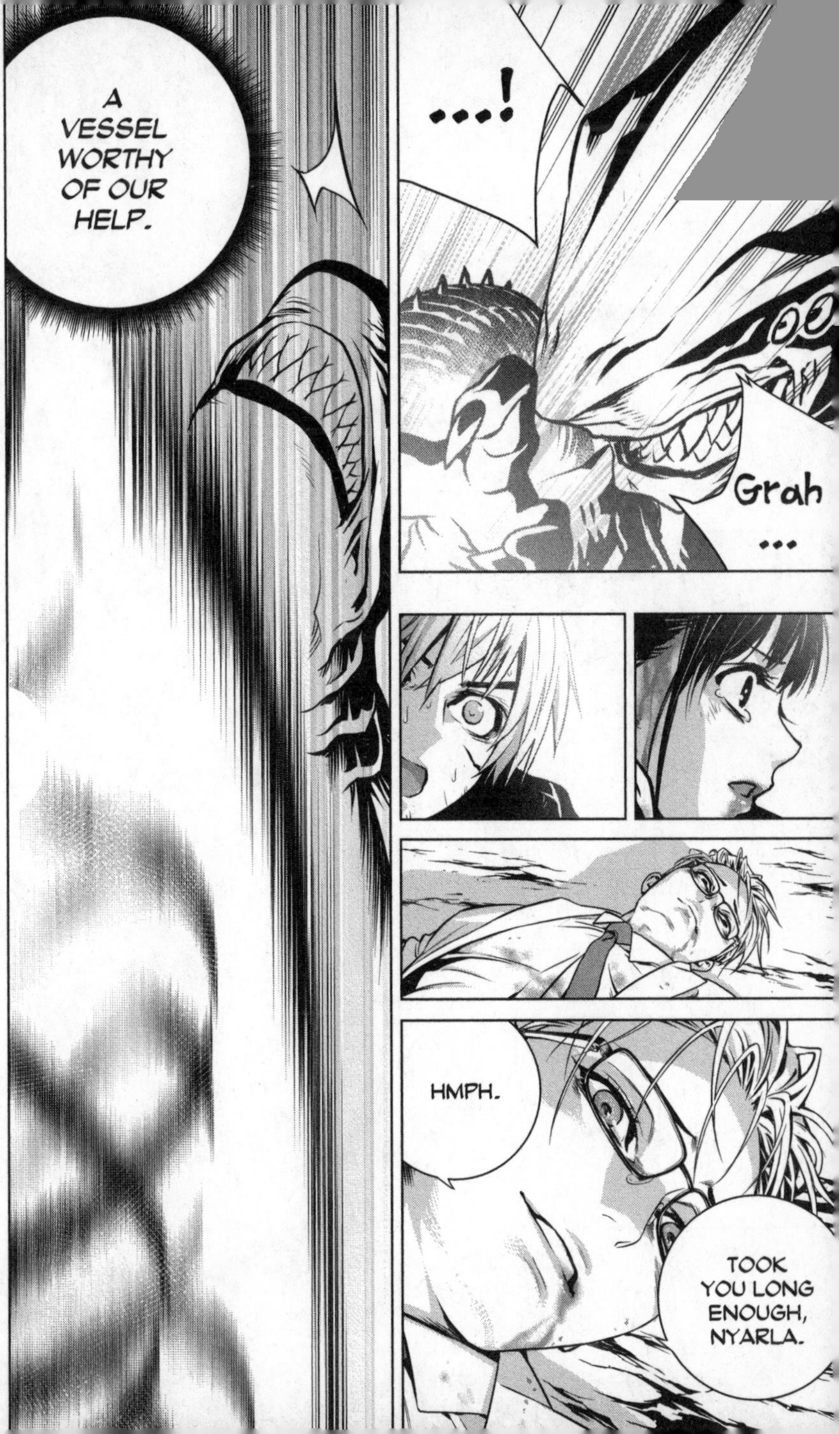
A VESSEL WORTHY OF OUR HELP.
...!
Grah ...
HMPH.
TOOK YOU LONG ENOUGH, NYARLA.

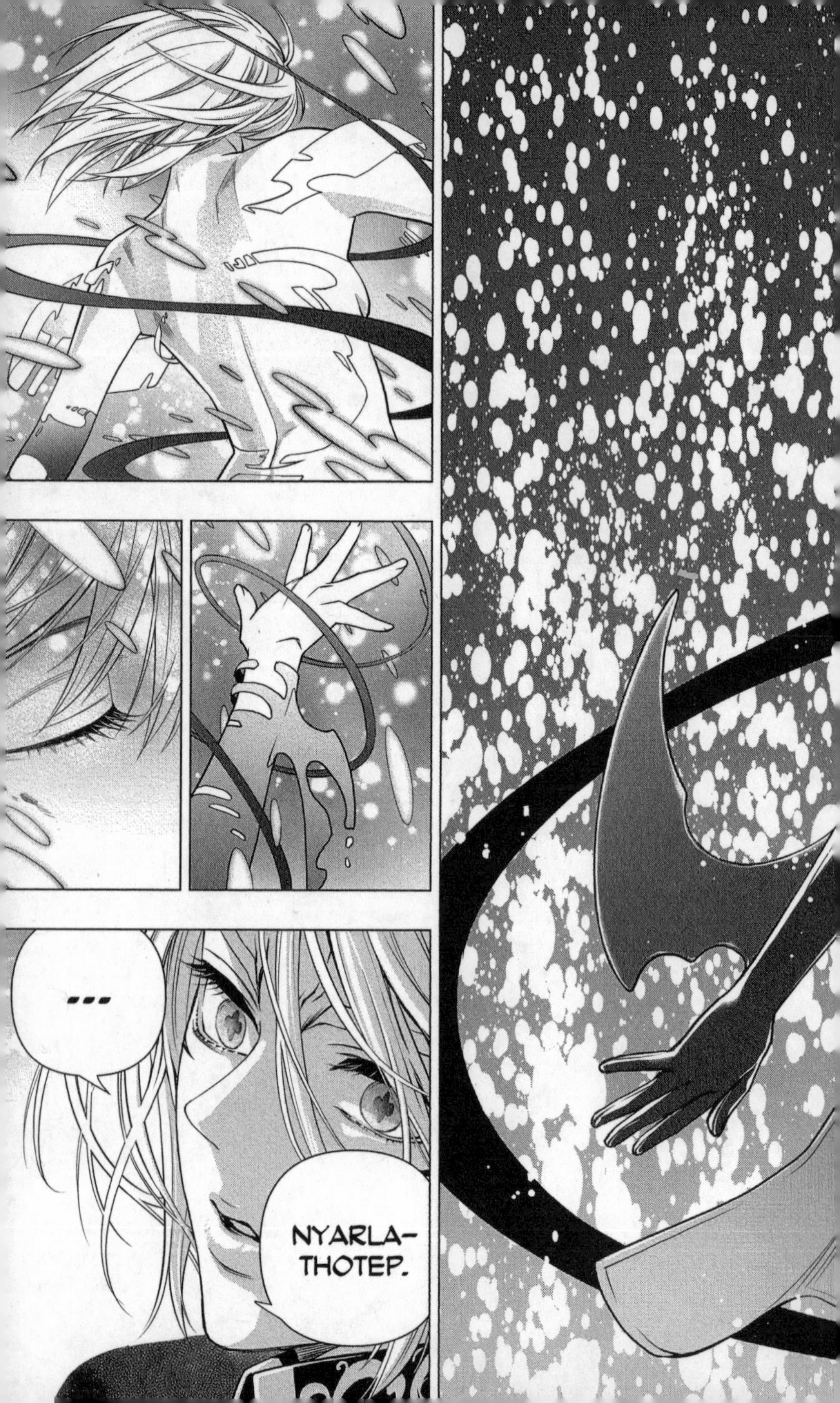
...
NYARLA-THOTEP.

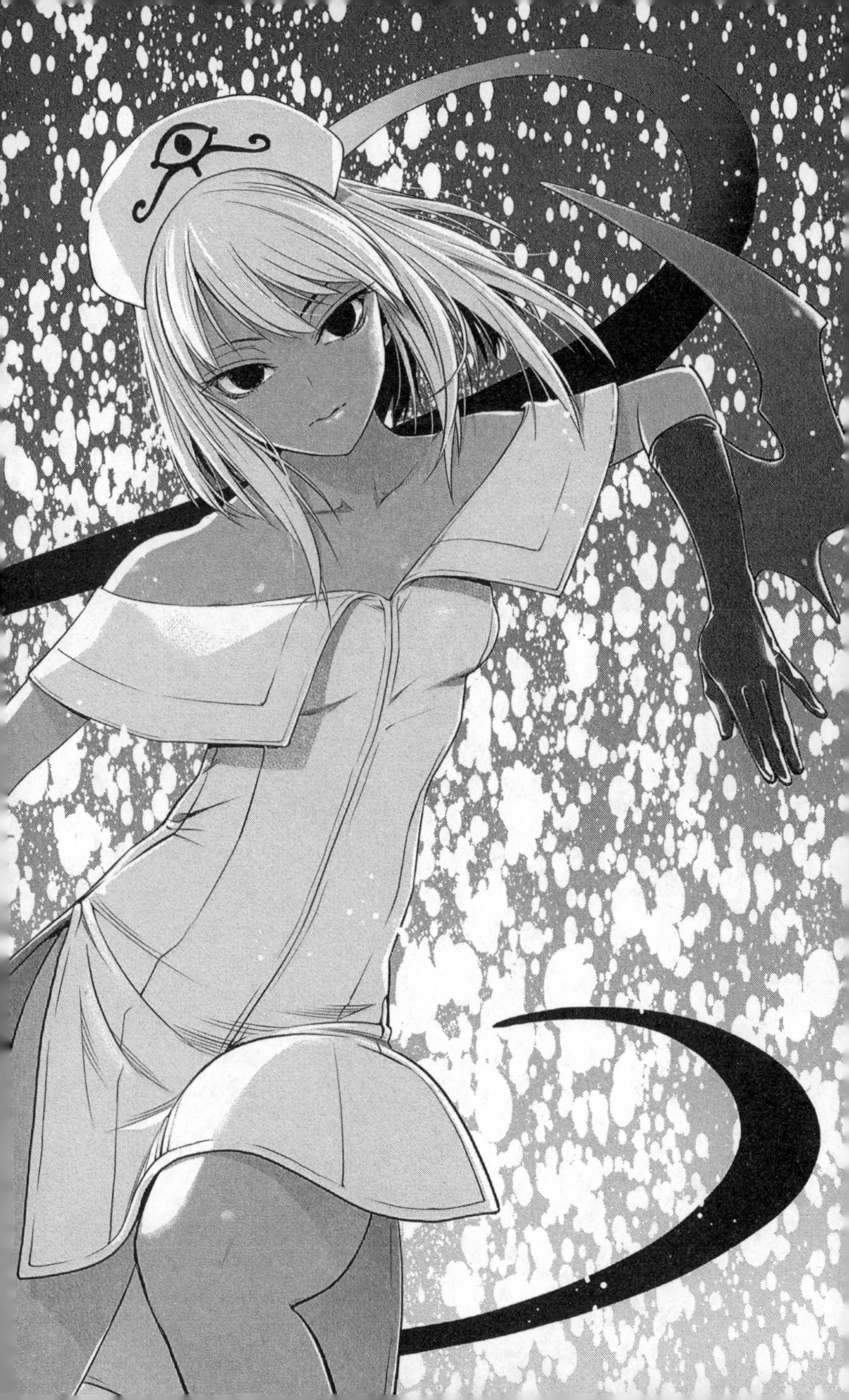

20: POWER GAME

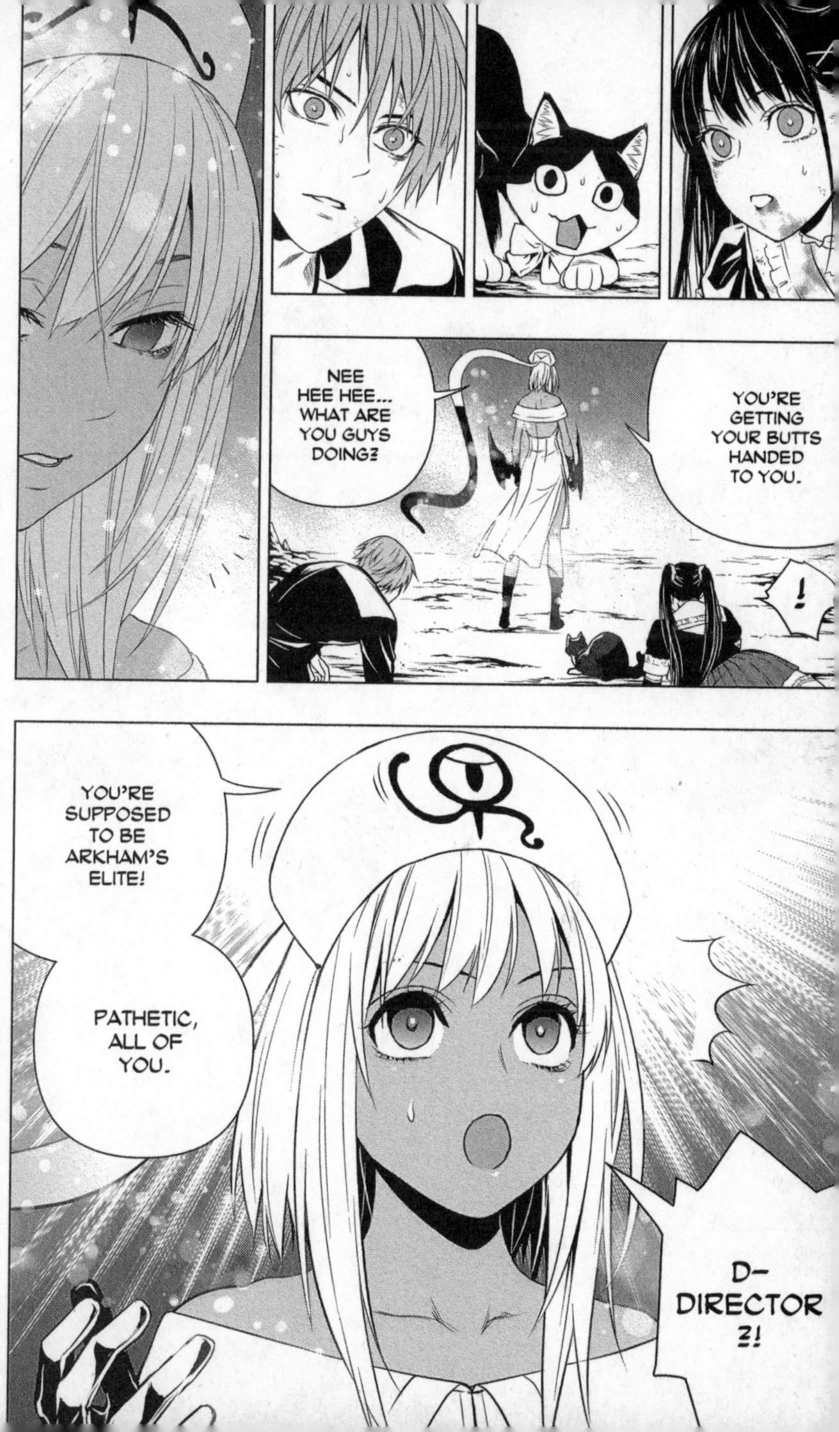
NEE HEE HEE... WHAT ARE YOU GUYS DOING?
YOU'RE GETTING YOUR BUTTS HANDED TO YOU.
!
YOU'RE SUPPOSED TO BE ARKHAM'S ELITE!
PATHETIC, ALL OF YOU.
D-DIRECTOR?!

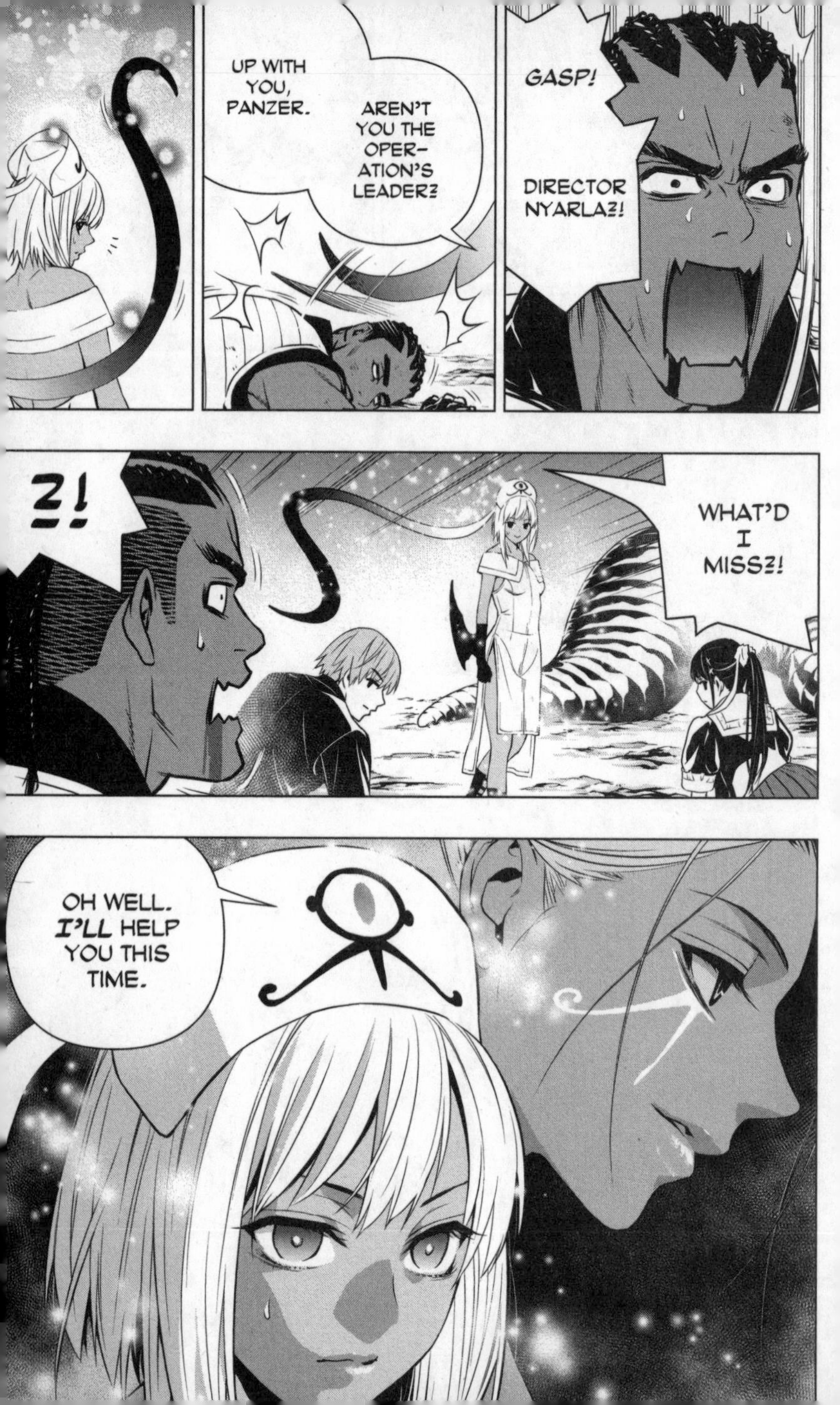
UP WITH YOU, PANZER.
AREN'T YOU THE OPER-ATION'S LEADER?
GASP!
DIRECTOR NYARLA?!
?!
WHAT'D I MISS?!
OH WELL. ***I'LL*** HELP YOU THIS TIME.

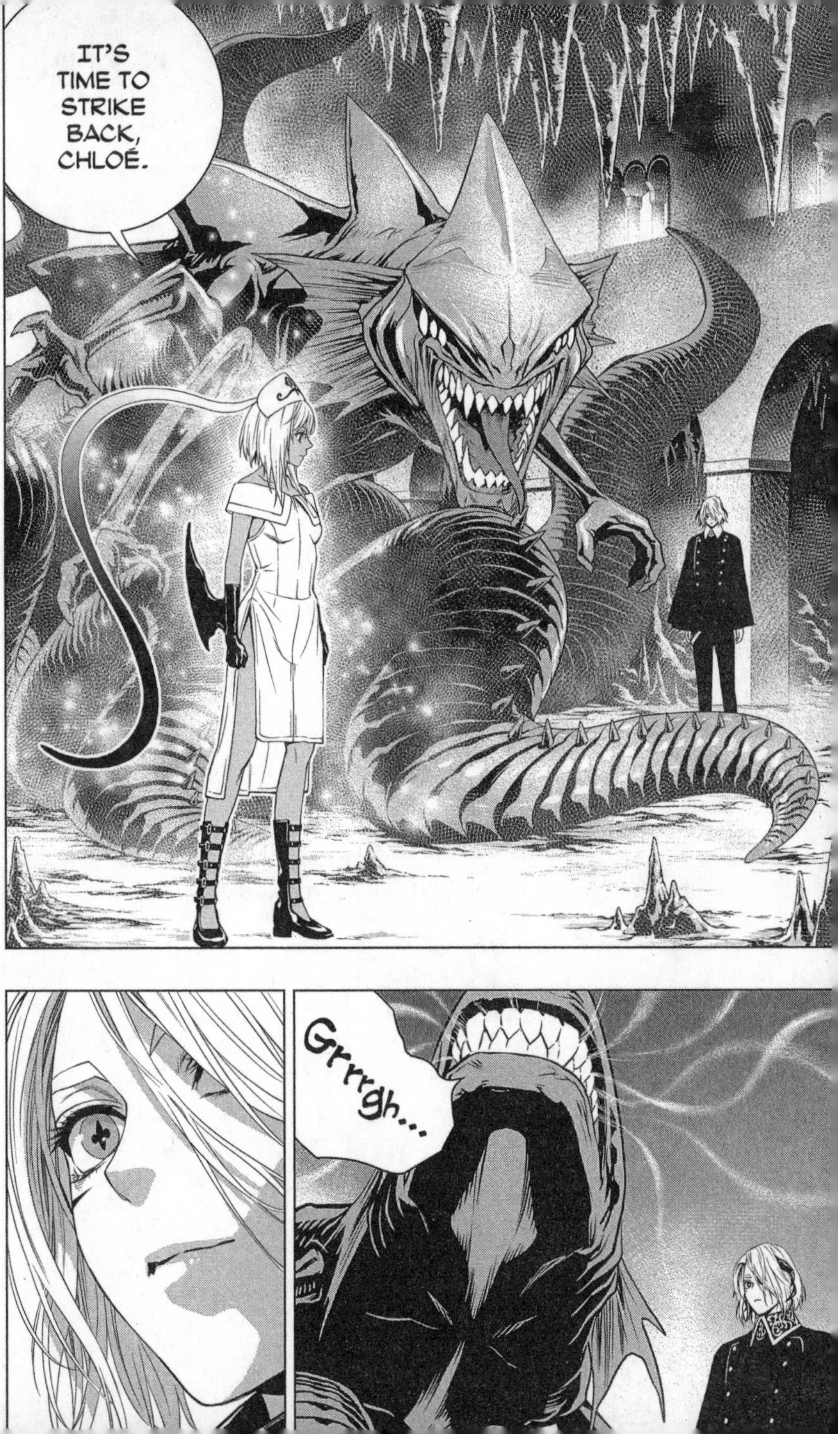
IT'S TIME TO STRIKE BACK, CHLOÉ.
Grrrgh...

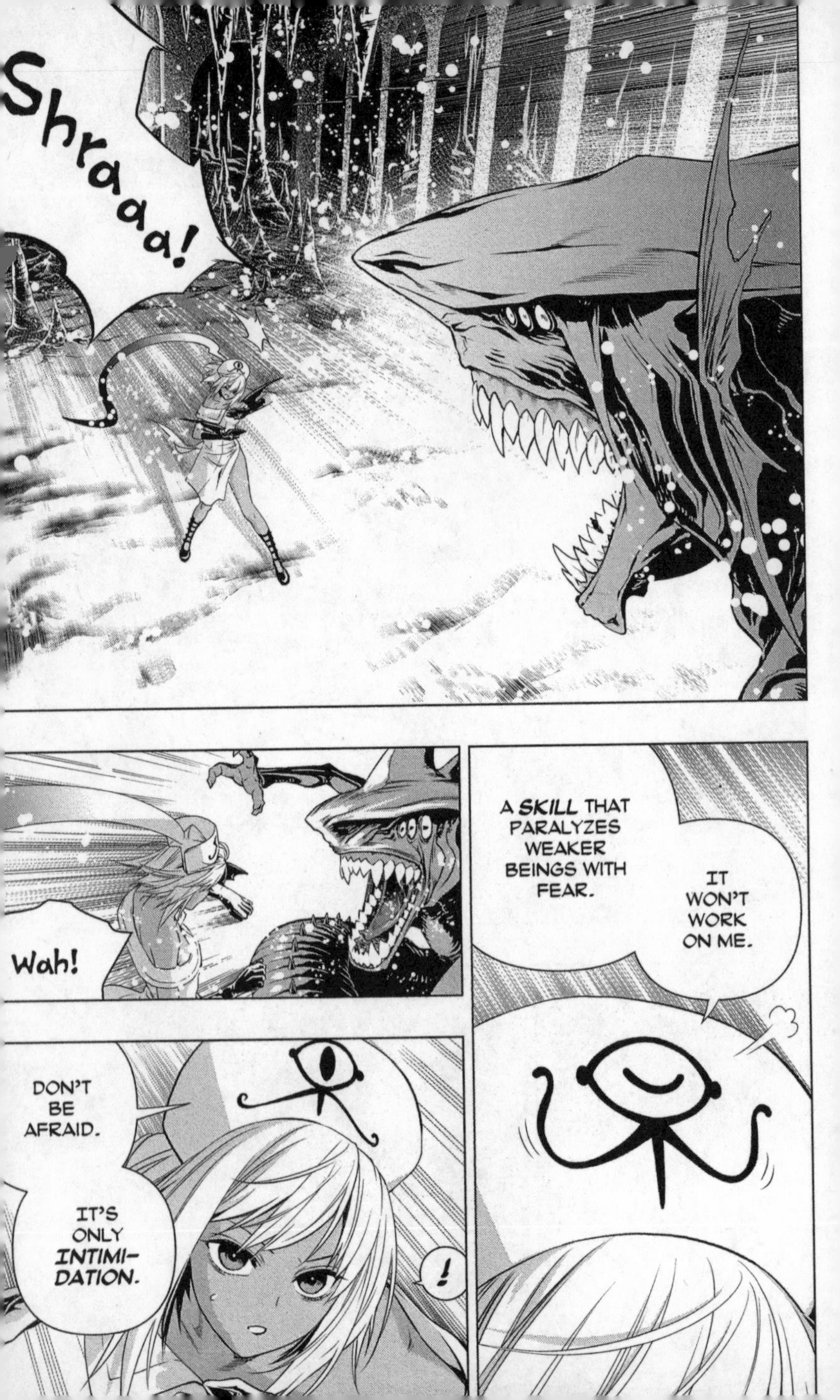
Shraaaa!
Wah!
DON'T BE AFRAID.
IT'S ONLY *INTIMIDATION*.
!
A *SKILL* THAT PARALYZES WEAKER BEINGS WITH FEAR.
IT WON'T WORK ON ME.

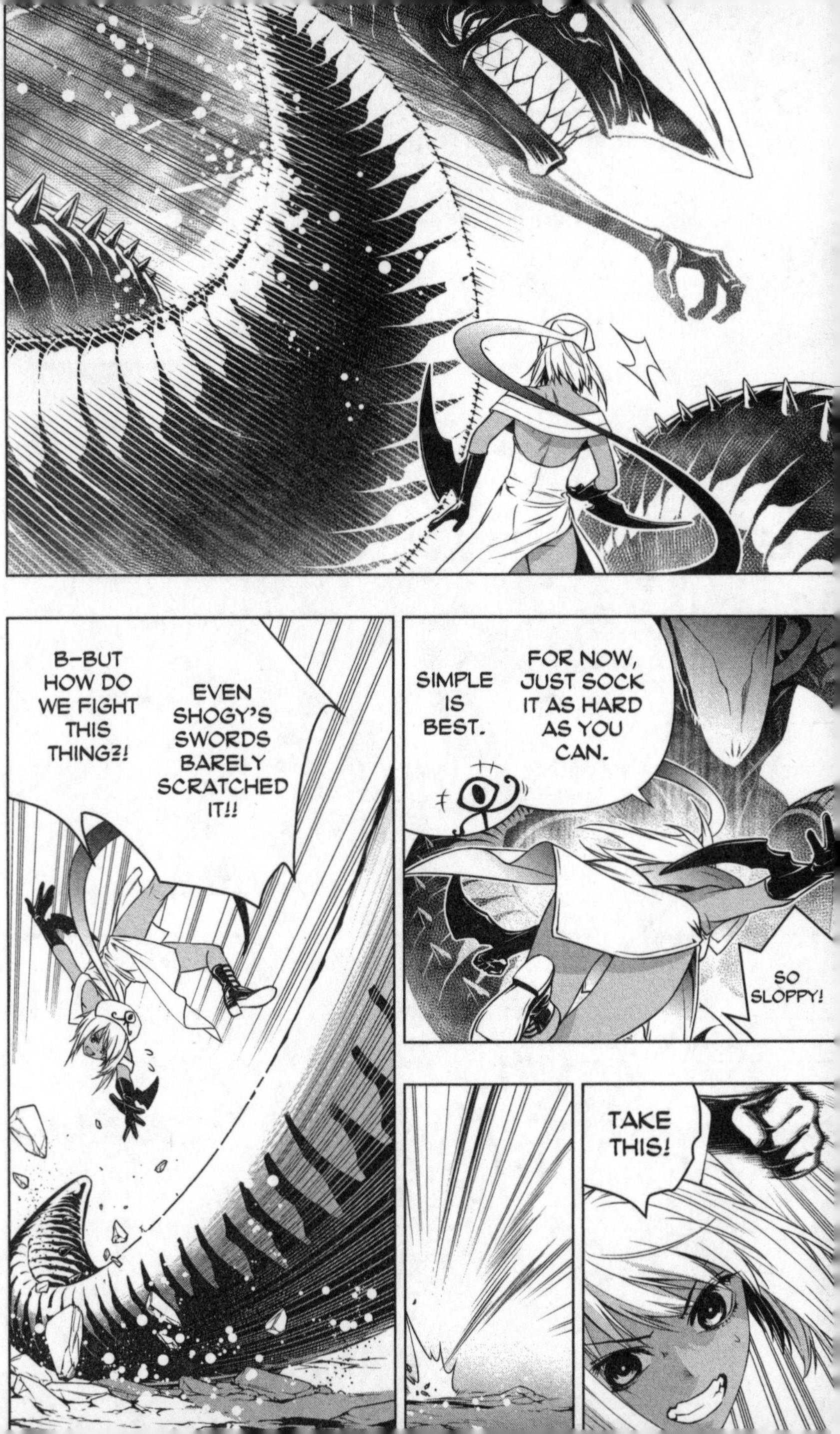
B-BUT HOW DO WE FIGHT THIS THING?!
EVEN SHOGY'S SWORDS BARELY SCRATCHED IT!!
SIMPLE IS BEST.
FOR NOW, JUST SOCK IT AS HARD AS YOU CAN.
SO SLOPPY!
TAKE THIS!

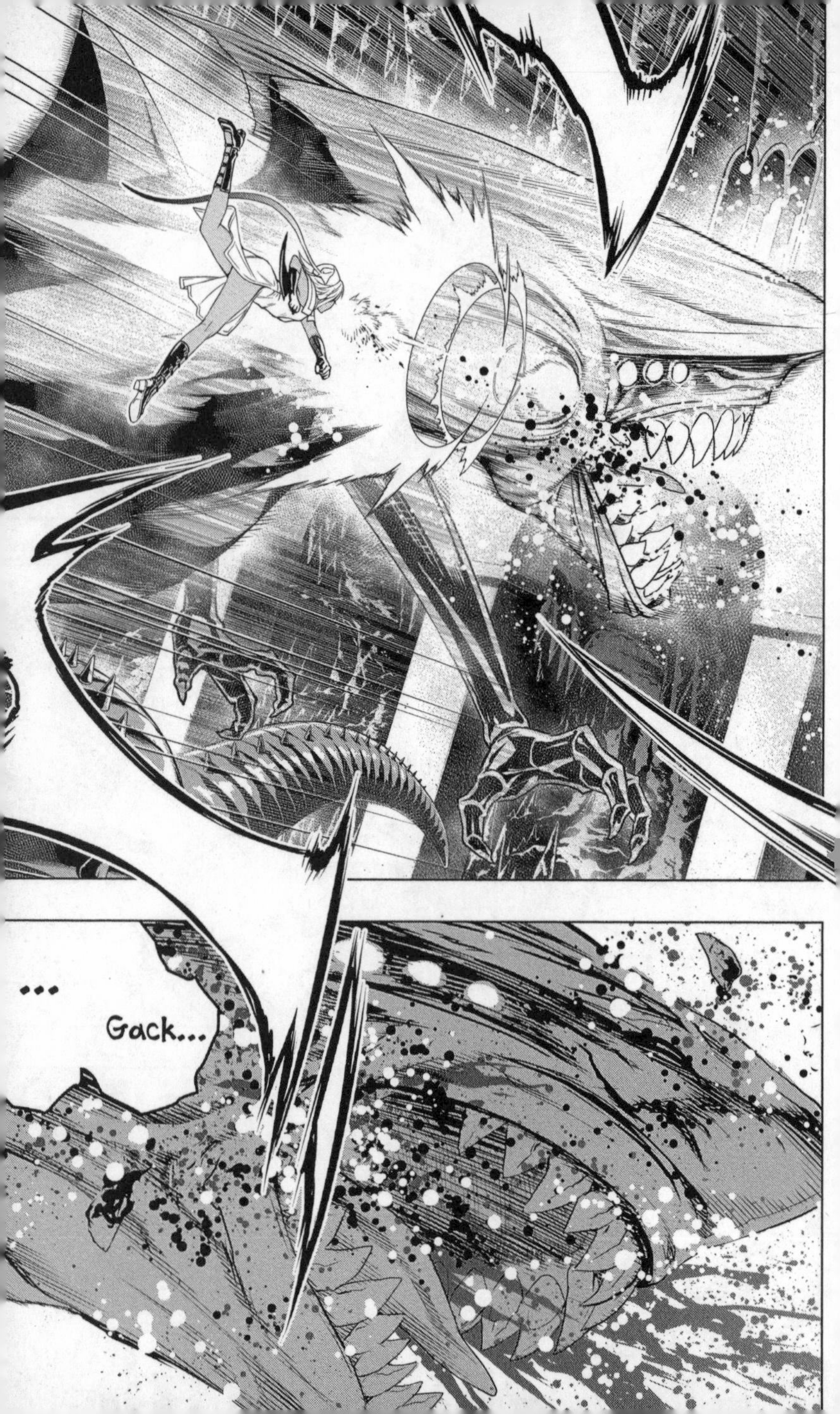
...
Gack...

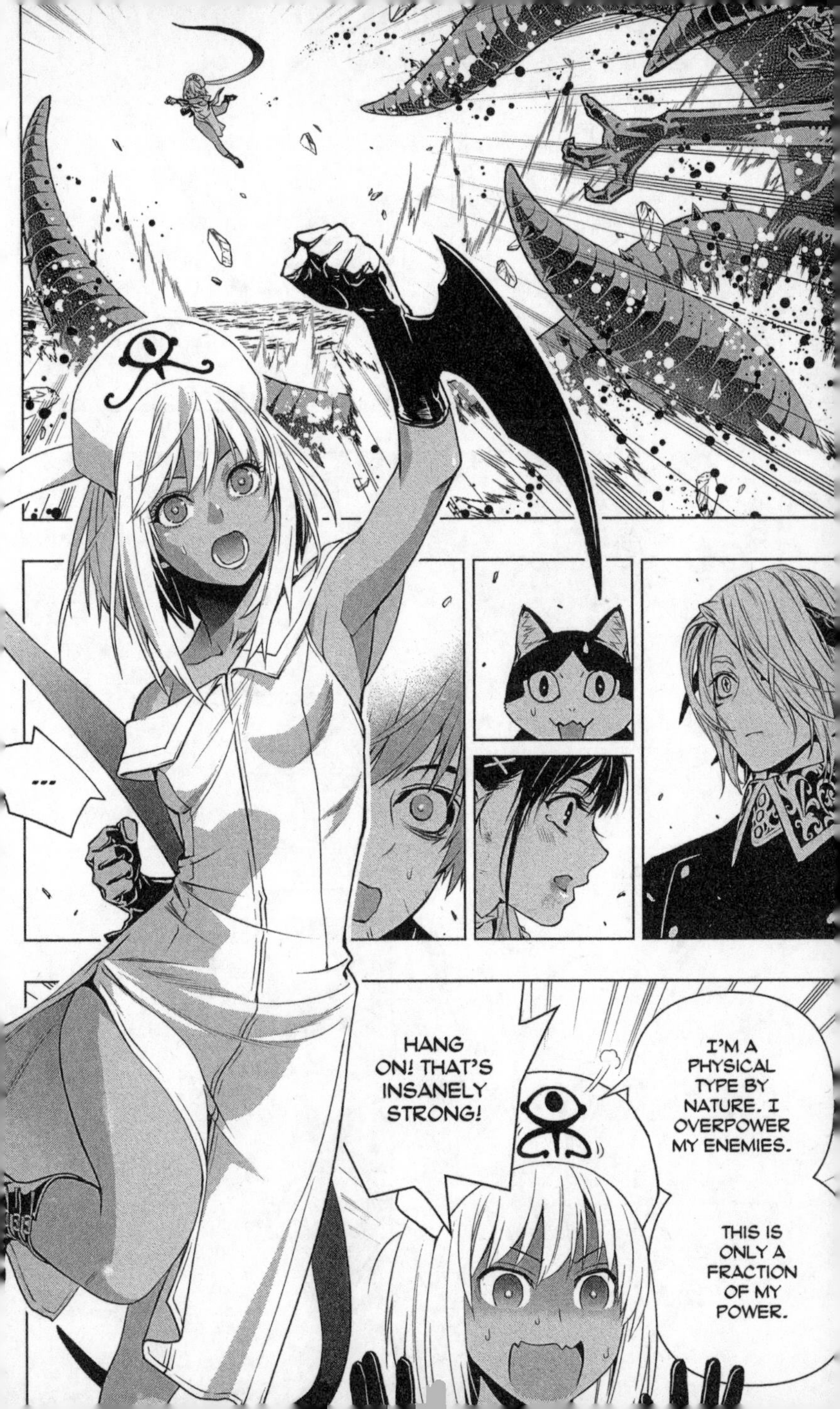
...
HANG ON! THAT'S INSANELY STRONG!
I'M A PHYSICAL TYPE BY NATURE. I OVERPOWER MY ENEMIES.
THIS IS ONLY A FRACTION OF MY POWER.

LOOK. EVEN ARMOR STRONG ENOUGH TO DEFLECT SWORDS...

...CAN'T STOP BLUNT FORCE TRAUMA.

Greh...

POWER IS PURE STRENGTH!!

GO ON, CHLOÉ! PULVERIZE IT!

NEVER TOOK YOU FOR A MEATHEAD!!

Grahh!

?!

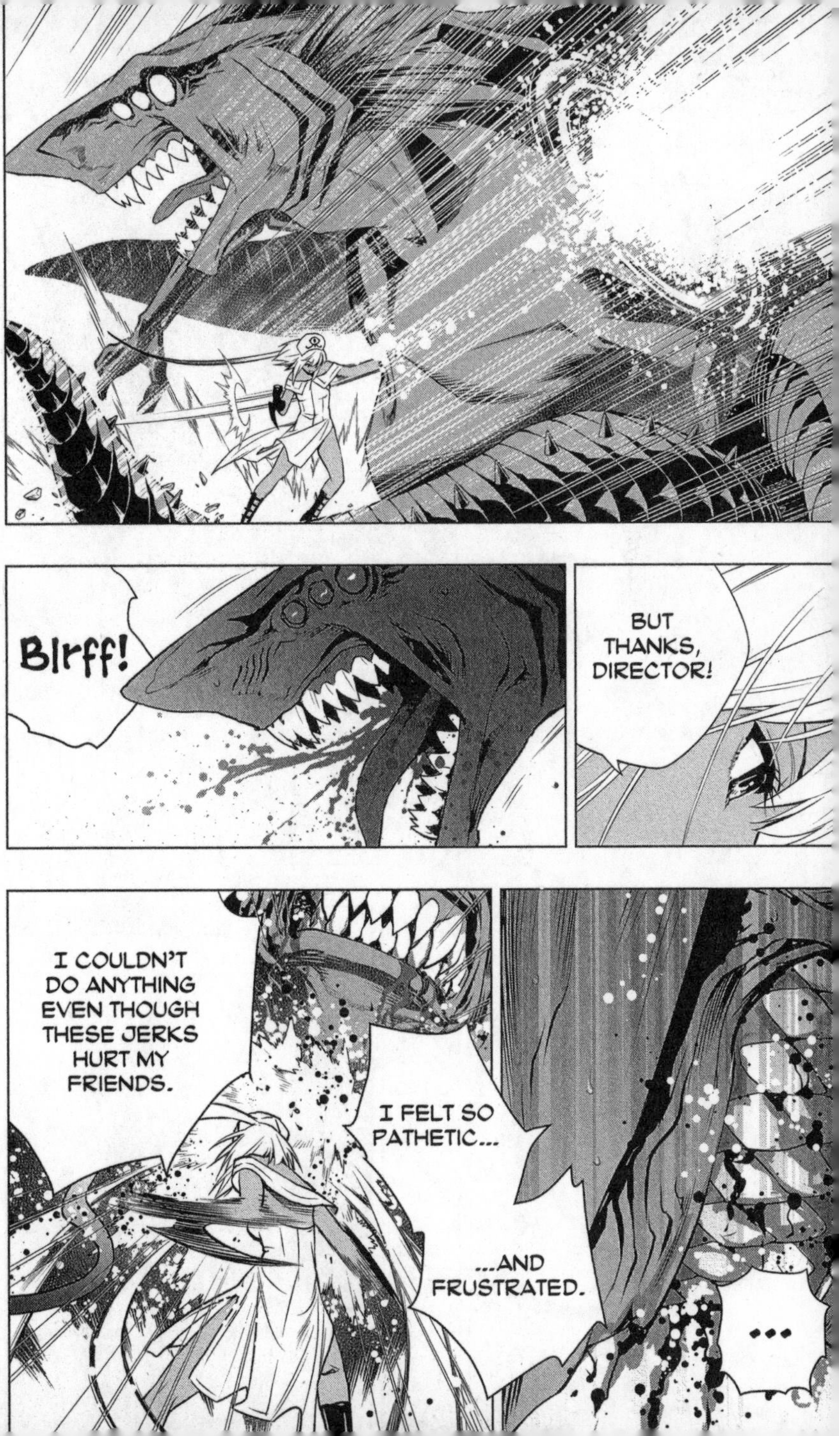
Blrff!
BUT THANKS, DIRECTOR!
I COULDN'T DO ANYTHING EVEN THOUGH THESE JERKS HURT MY FRIENDS.
I FELT SO PATHETIC...
...AND FRUSTRATED.
...

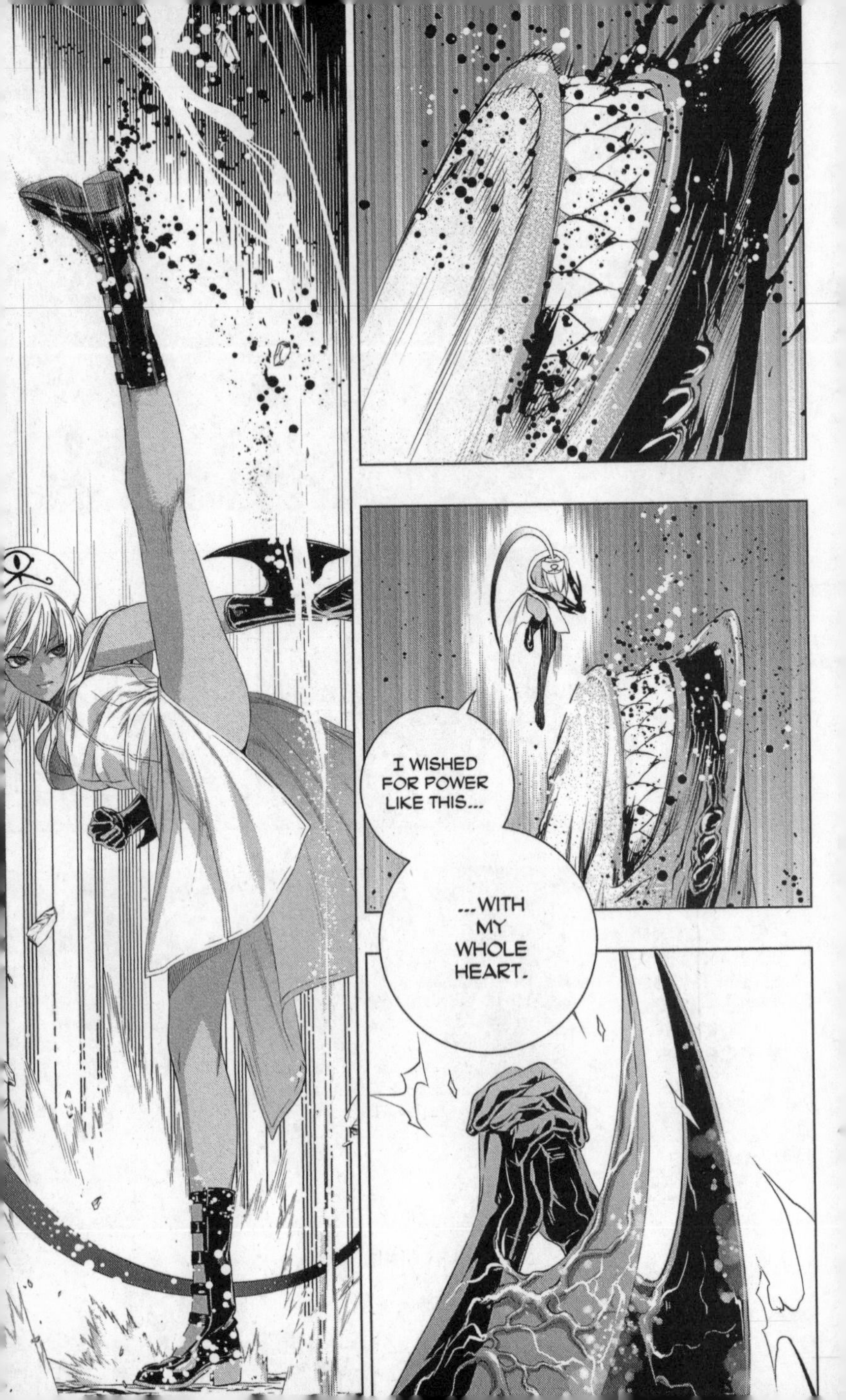
I WISHED FOR POWER LIKE THIS...
...WITH MY WHOLE HEART.

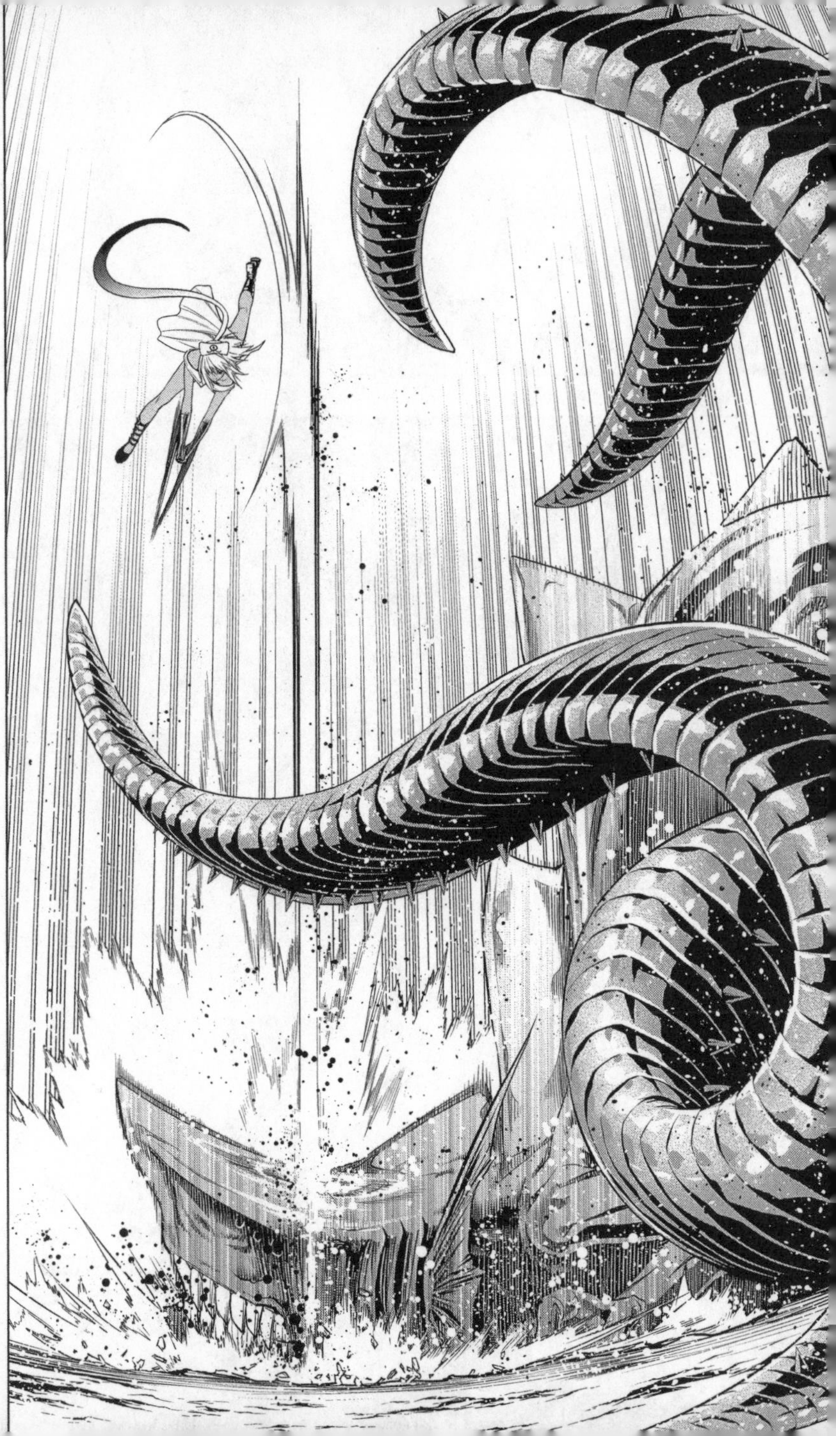

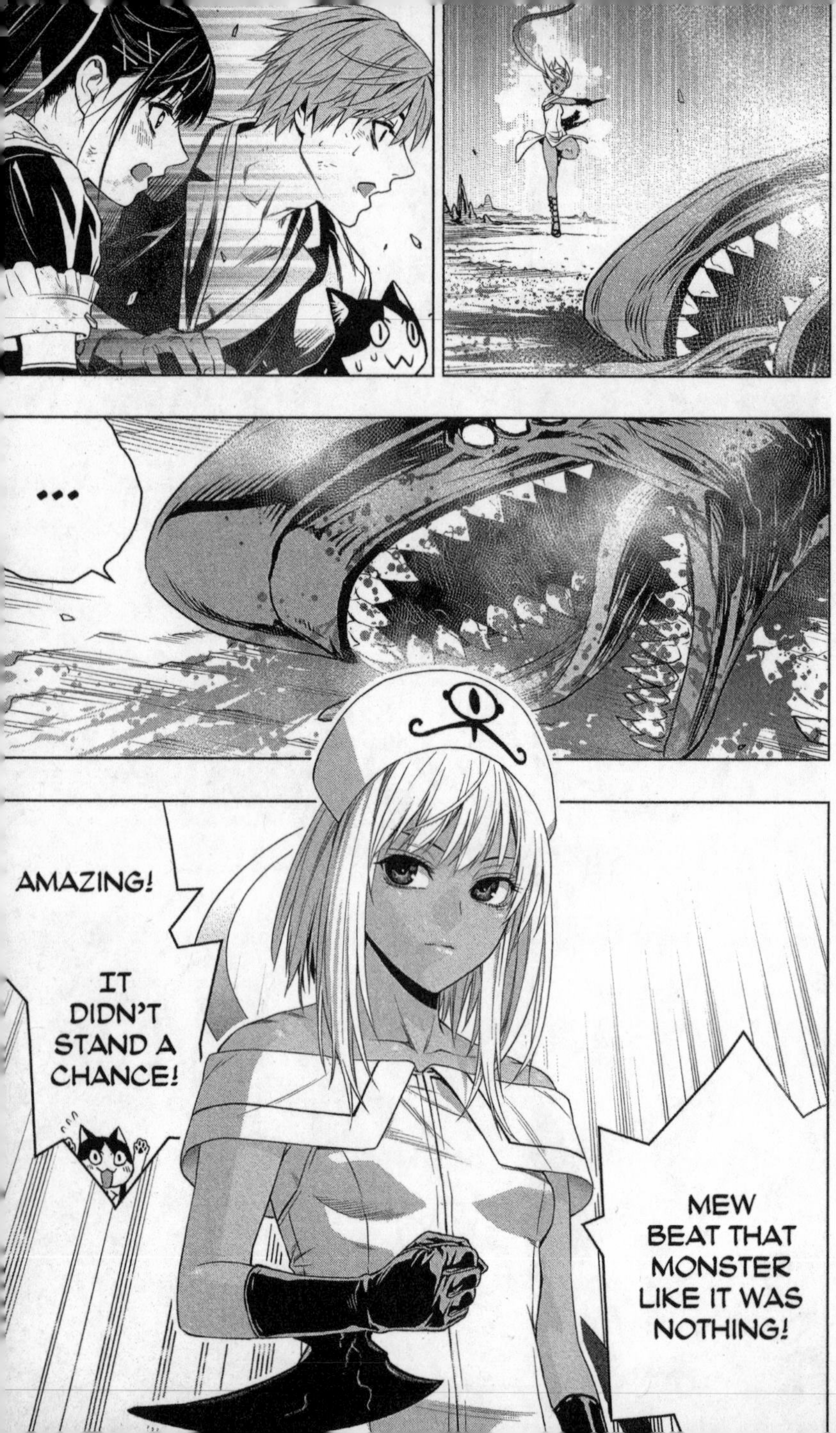
...
AMAZING!
IT DIDN'T STAND A CHANCE!
MEW BEAT THAT MONSTER LIKE IT WAS NOTHING!

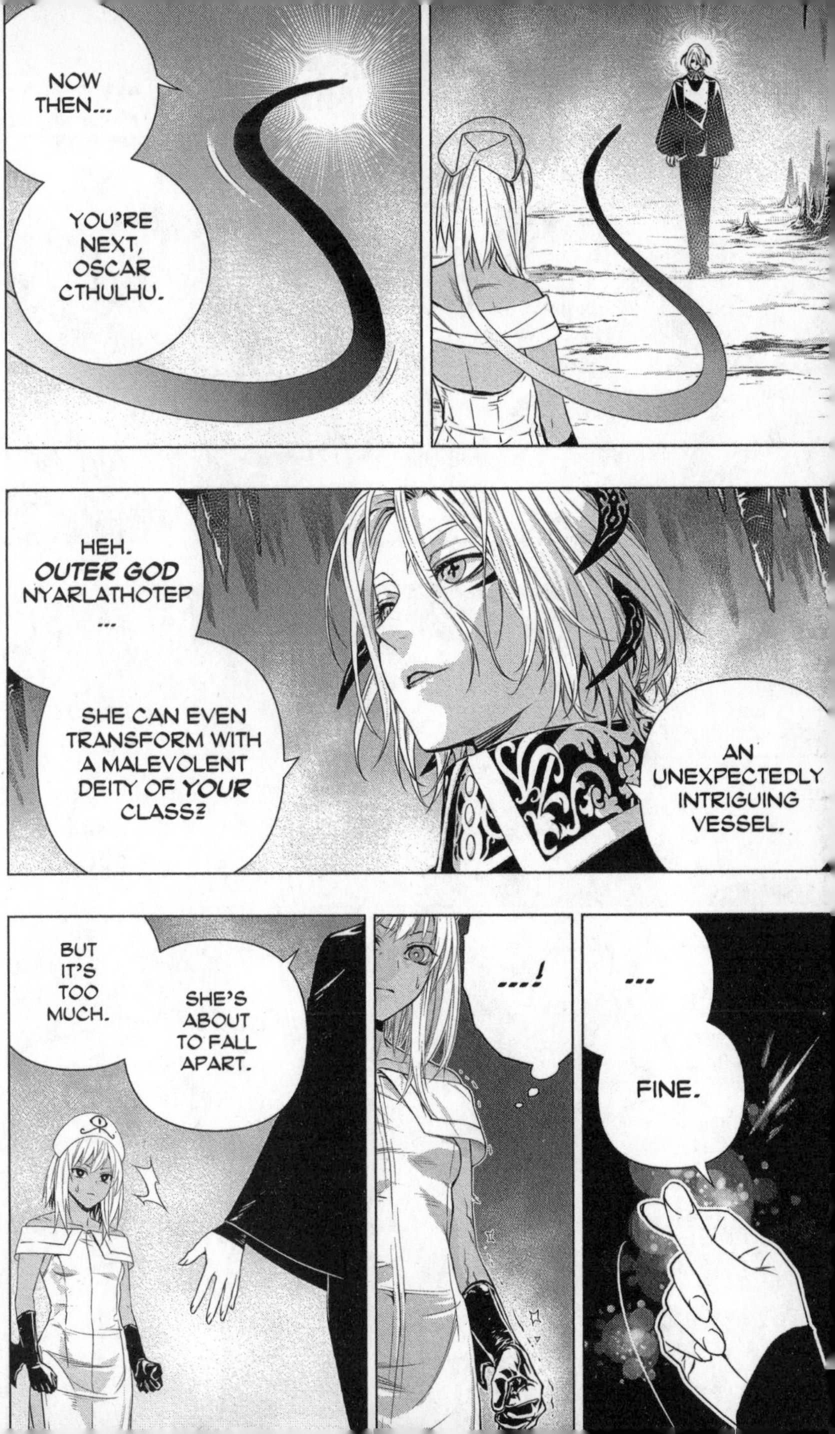
NOW THEN...
YOU'RE NEXT, OSCAR CTHULHU.
HEH. *OUTER GOD* NYARLATHOTEP ...
SHE CAN EVEN TRANSFORM WITH A MALEVOLENT DEITY OF *YOUR* CLASS?
AN UNEXPECTEDLY INTRIGUING VESSEL.
BUT IT'S TOO MUCH.
SHE'S ABOUT TO FALL APART.
...!
...
FINE.

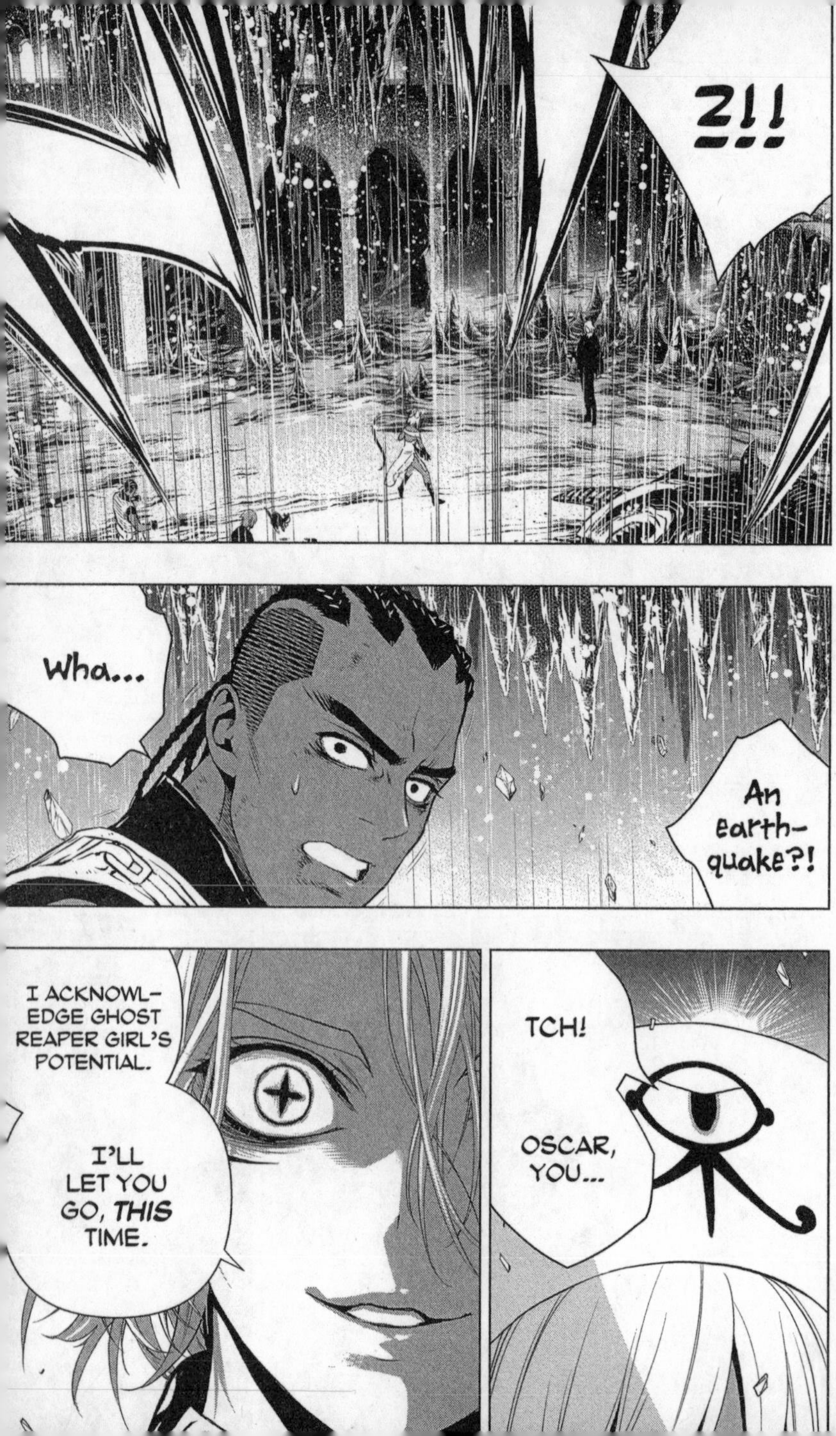
Z!!
Wha...
An earth-quake?!
I ACKNOWL-EDGE GHOST REAPER GIRL'S POTENTIAL.
I'LL LET YOU GO, *THIS* TIME.
TCH!
OSCAR, YOU...

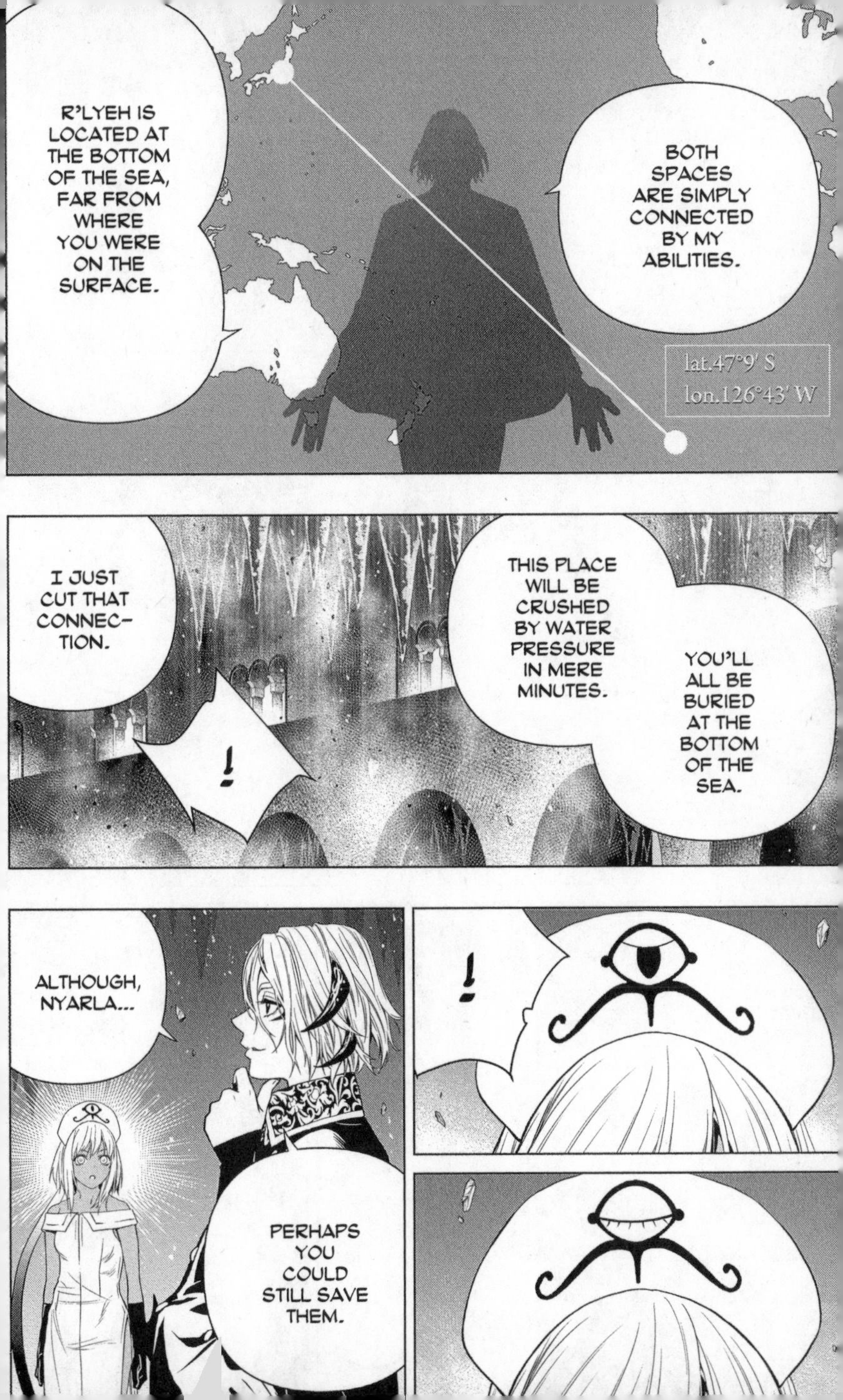
R'LYEH IS LOCATED AT THE BOTTOM OF THE SEA, FAR FROM WHERE YOU WERE ON THE SURFACE.
BOTH SPACES ARE SIMPLY CONNECTED BY MY ABILITIES.
lat.47°9' S
lon.126°43' W
I JUST CUT THAT CONNEC-TION.
!
THIS PLACE WILL BE CRUSHED BY WATER PRESSURE IN MERE MINUTES.
YOU'LL ALL BE BURIED AT THE BOTTOM OF THE SEA.
ALTHOUGH, NYARLA...
PERHAPS YOU COULD STILL SAVE THEM.
!

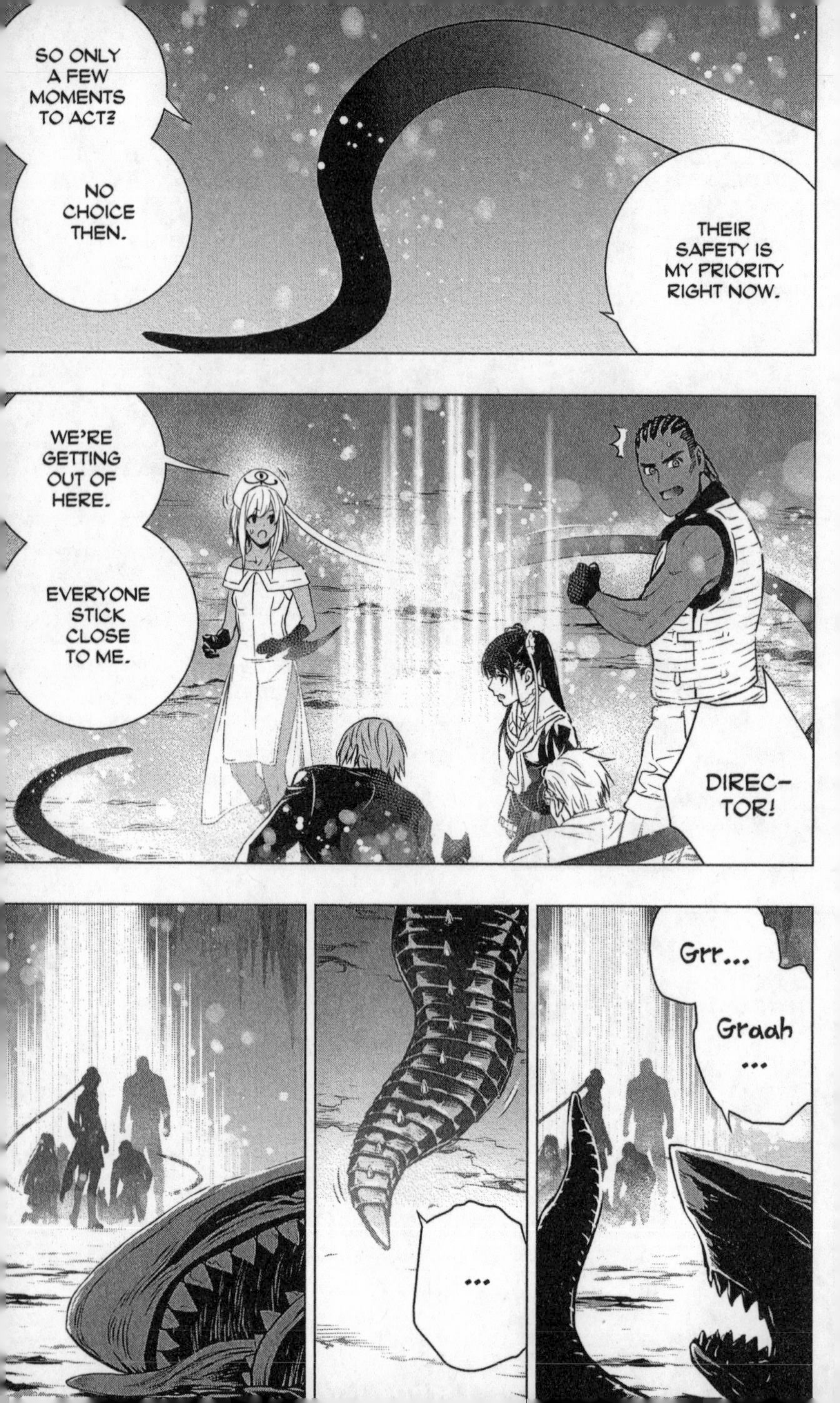
SO ONLY A FEW MOMENTS TO ACT?
NO CHOICE THEN.
THEIR SAFETY IS MY PRIORITY RIGHT NOW.
WE'RE GETTING OUT OF HERE.
EVERYONE STICK CLOSE TO ME.
DIREC-TOR!
...
Grr...
Graah ...

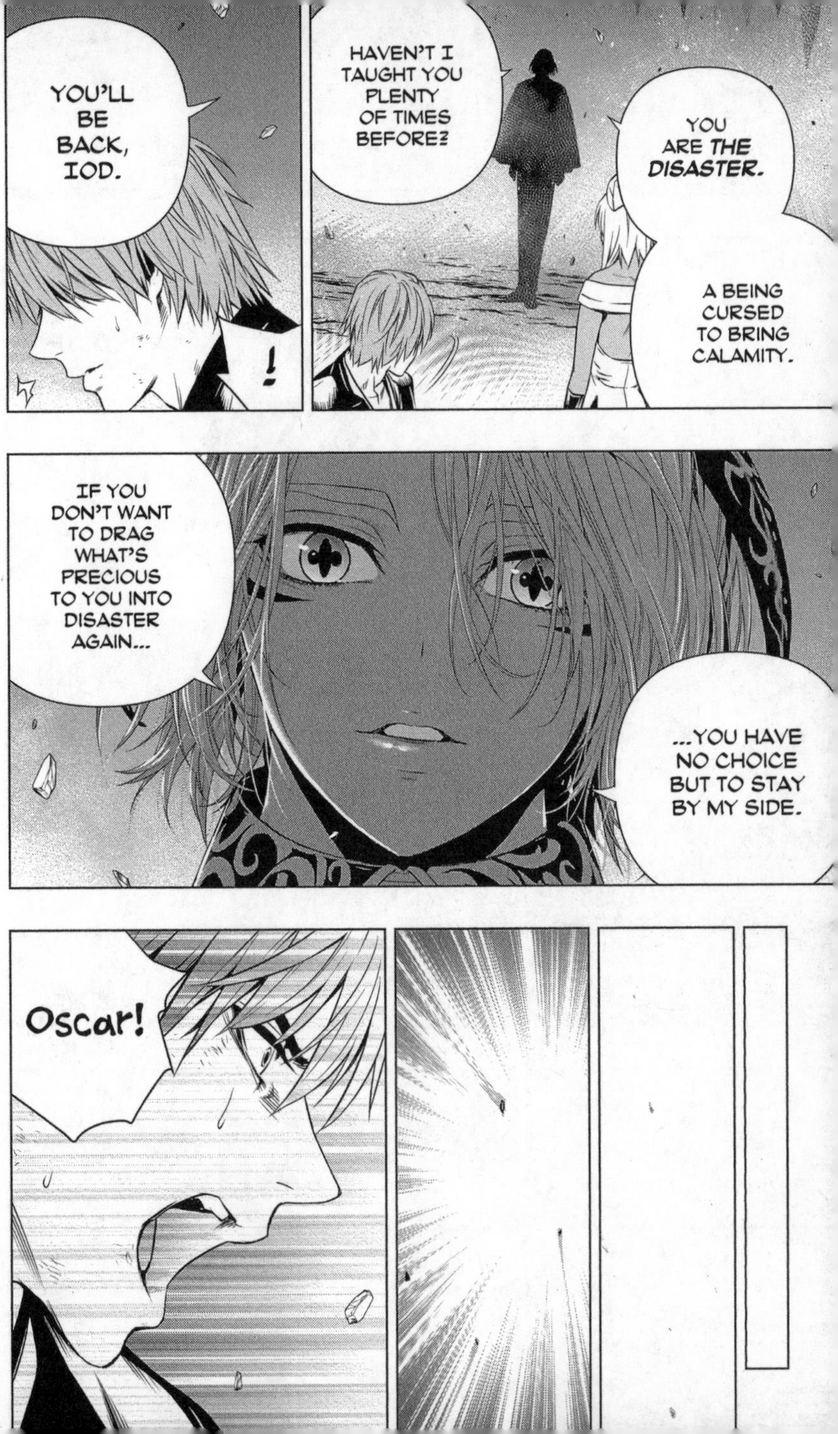
YOU'LL BE BACK, IOD.
!
HAVEN'T I TAUGHT YOU PLENTY OF TIMES BEFORE?
YOU ARE THE DISASTER.
A BEING CURSED TO BRING CALAMITY.
IF YOU DON'T WANT TO DRAG WHAT'S PRECIOUS TO YOU INTO DISASTER AGAIN...
...YOU HAVE NO CHOICE BUT TO STAY BY MY SIDE.
Oscar!

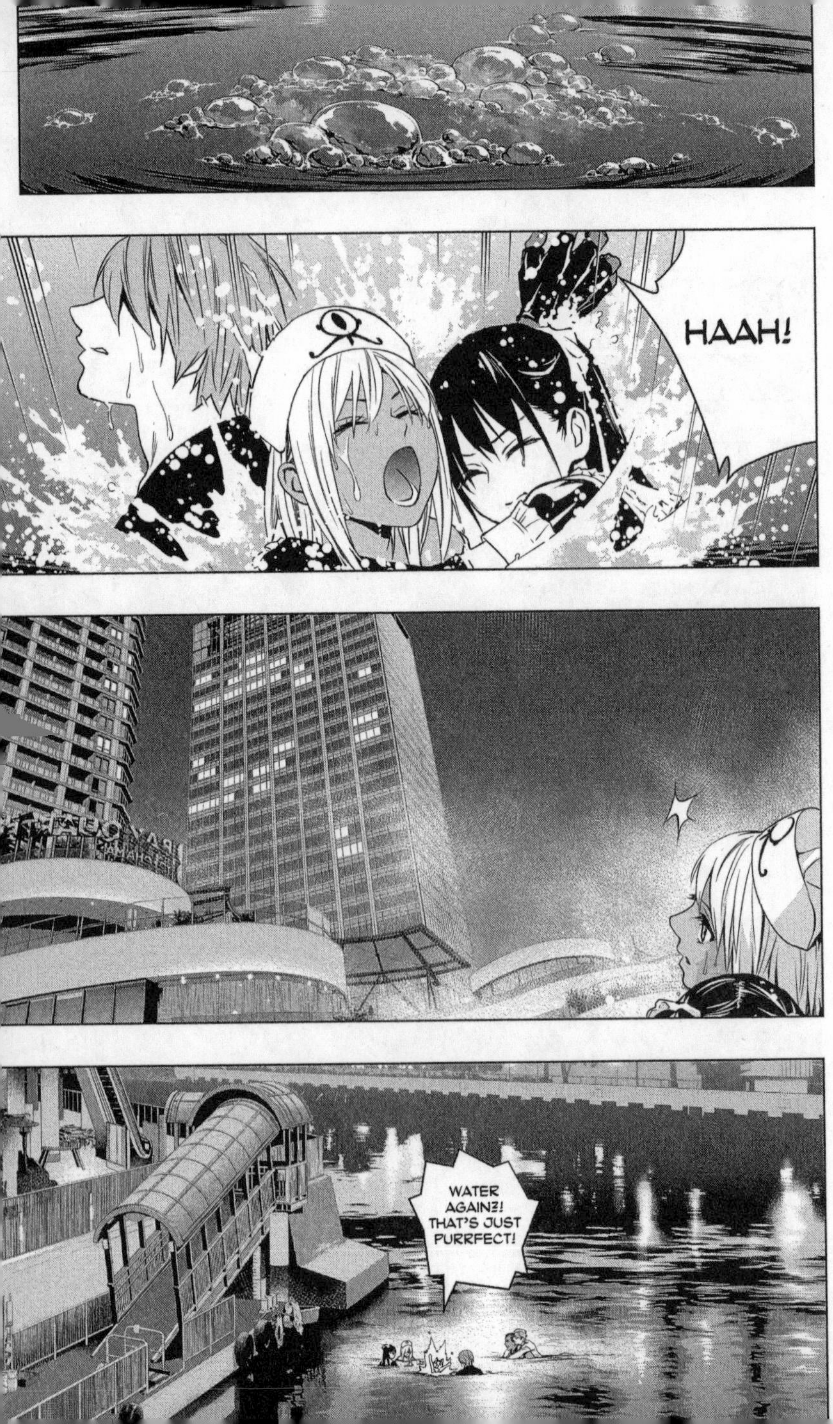
HAAH!
WATER AGAIN?! THAT'S JUST PURRFECT!

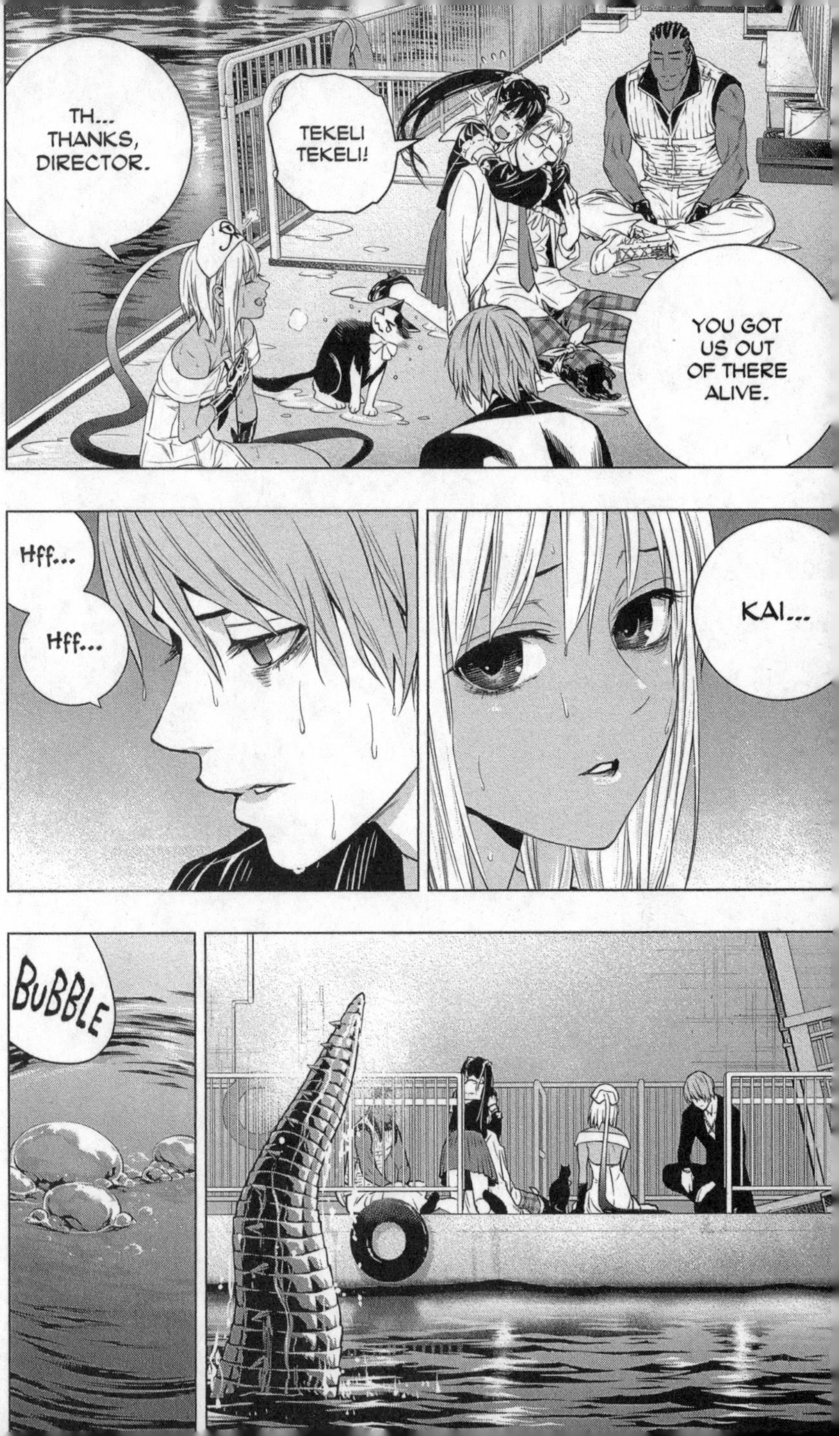
TH... THANKS, DIRECTOR.
TEKELI TEKELI!
YOU GOT US OUT OF THERE ALIVE.
Hff...
Hff...
KAI...
BUBBLE

21: THE PRICE

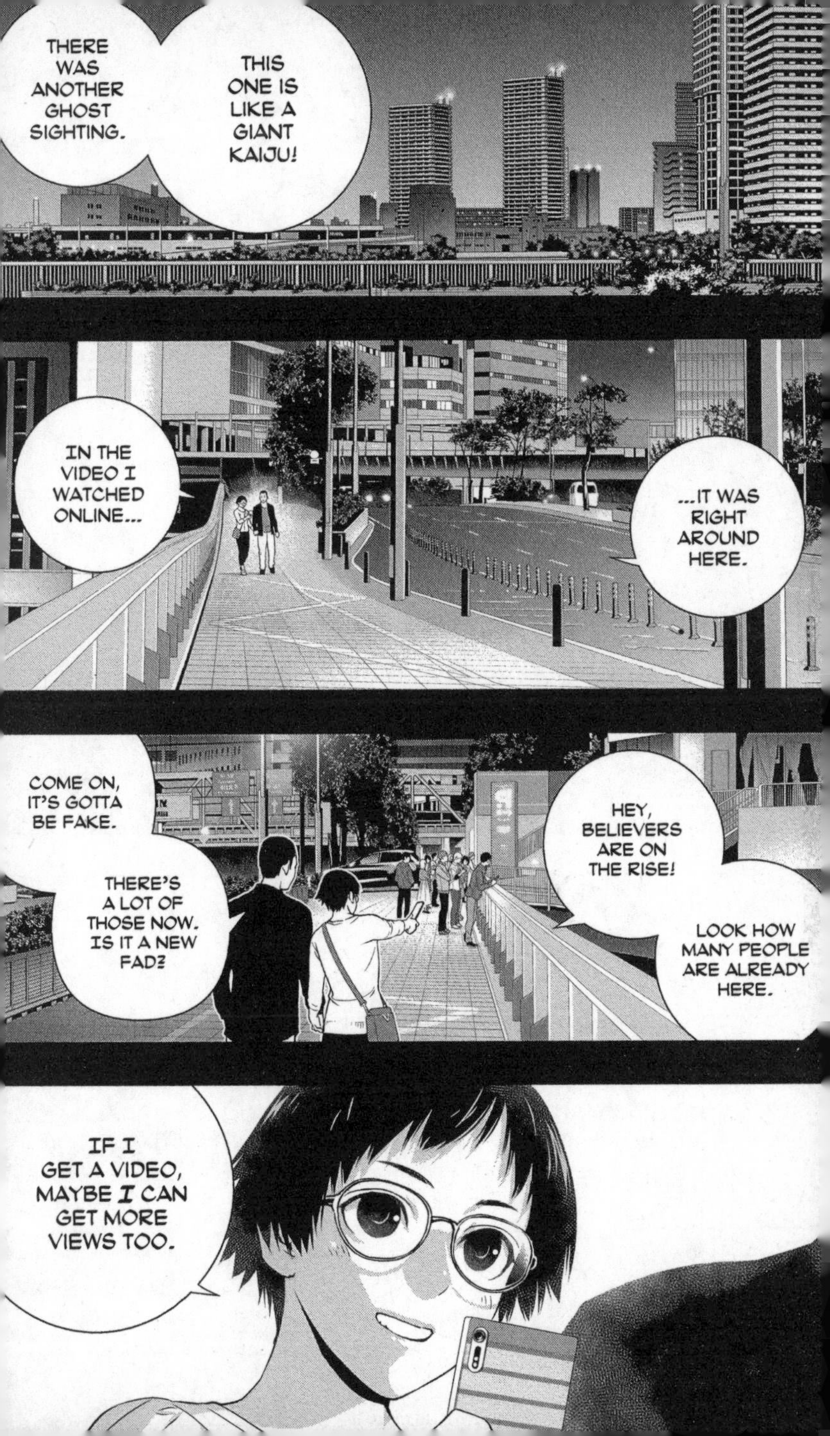
THERE WAS ANOTHER GHOST SIGHTING.
THIS ONE IS LIKE A GIANT KAIJU!
IN THE VIDEO I WATCHED ONLINE...
...IT WAS RIGHT AROUND HERE.
COME ON, IT'S GOTTA BE FAKE.
THERE'S A LOT OF THOSE NOW. IS IT A NEW FAD?
HEY, BELIEVERS ARE ON THE RISE!
LOOK HOW MANY PEOPLE ARE ALREADY HERE.
IF I GET A VIDEO, MAYBE *I* CAN GET MORE VIEWS TOO.

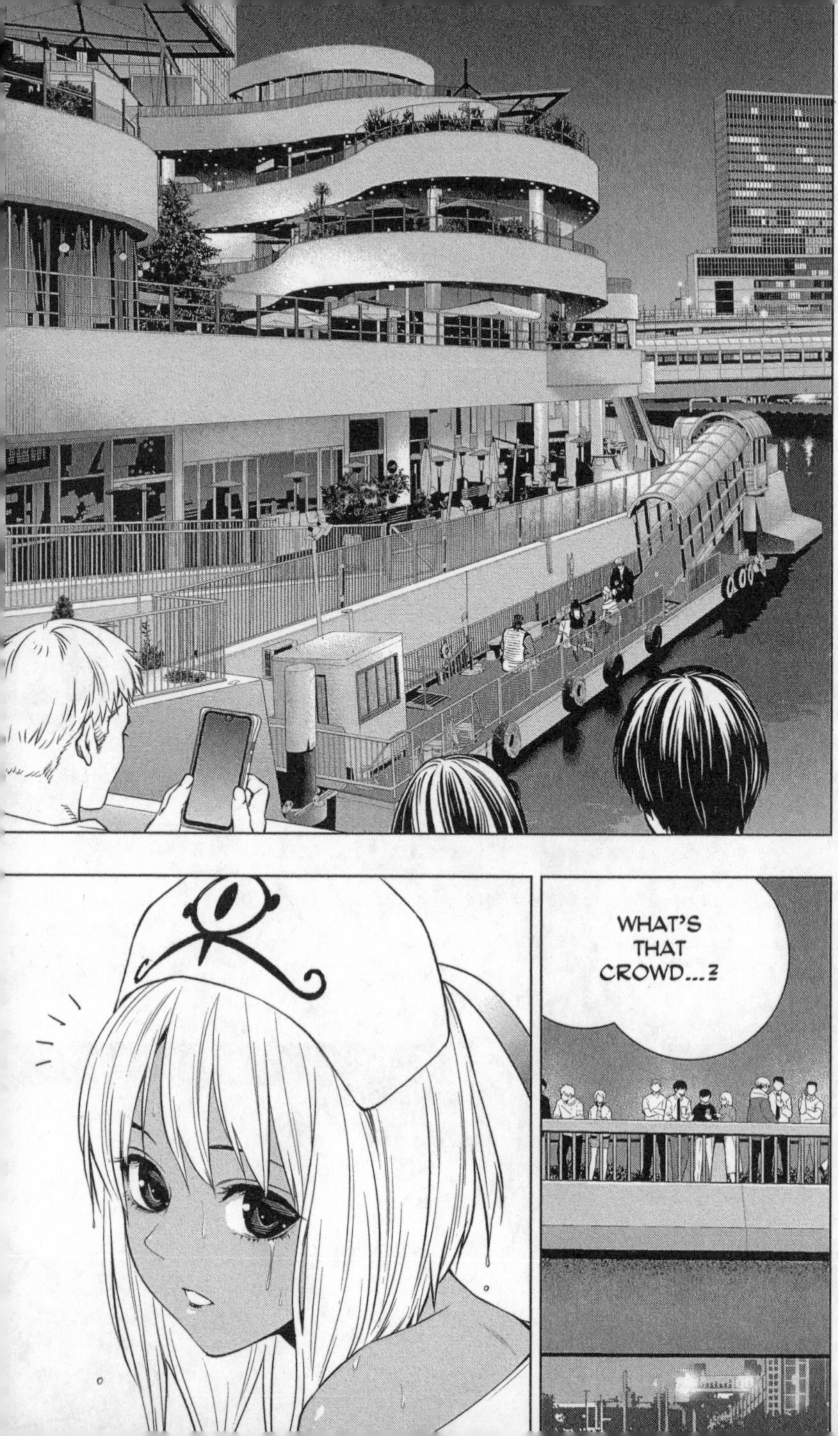
WHAT'S THAT CROWD...?

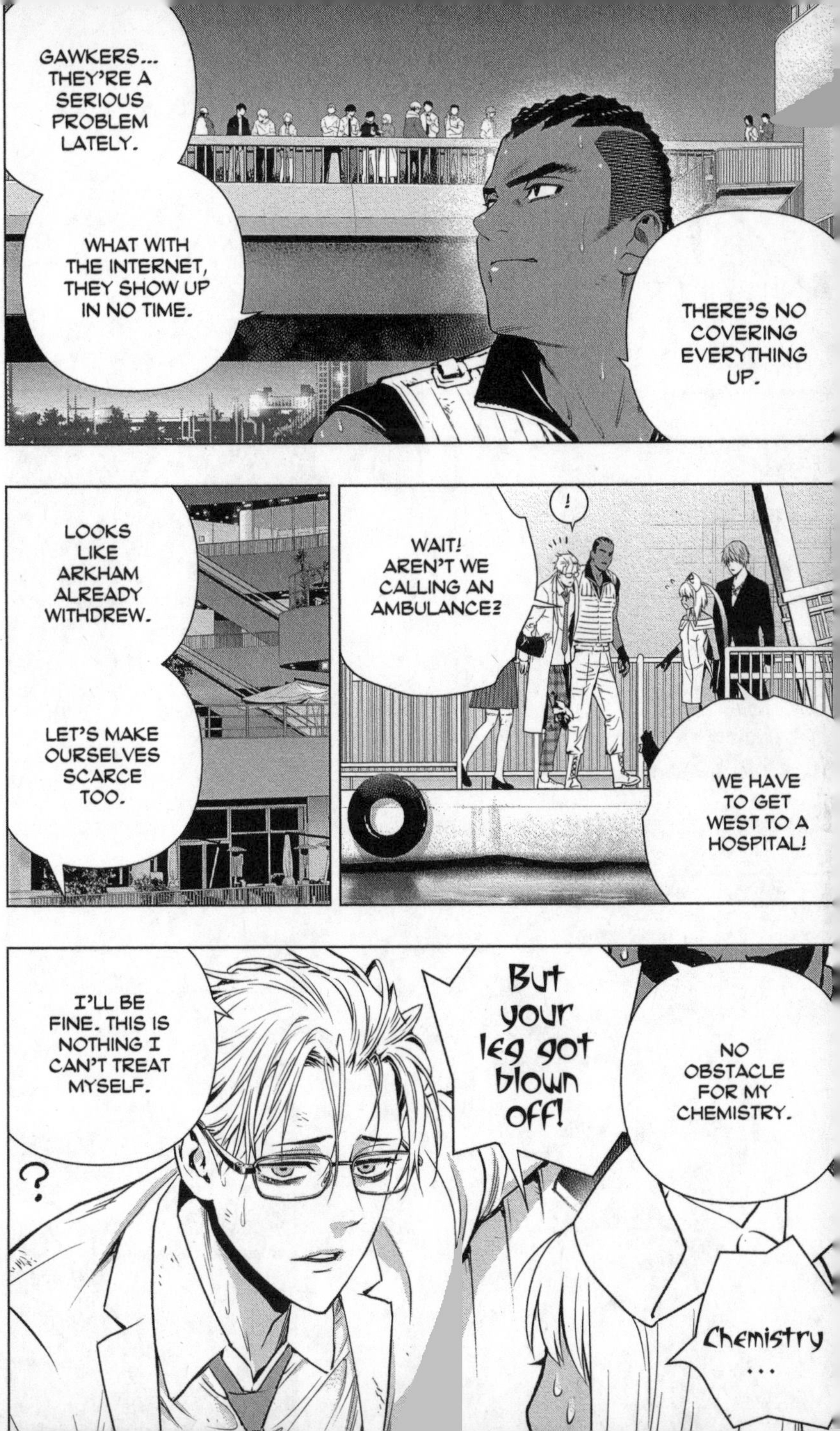
GAWKERS... THEY'RE A SERIOUS PROBLEM LATELY.
WHAT WITH THE INTERNET, THEY SHOW UP IN NO TIME.
THERE'S NO COVERING EVERYTHING UP.
LOOKS LIKE ARKHAM ALREADY WITHDREW.
LET'S MAKE OURSELVES SCARCE TOO.
!
WAIT! AREN'T WE CALLING AN AMBULANCE?
WE HAVE TO GET WEST TO A HOSPITAL!
I'LL BE FINE. THIS IS NOTHING I CAN'T TREAT MYSELF.
?
But your leg got blown off!
NO OBSTACLE FOR MY CHEMISTRY.
Chemistry...

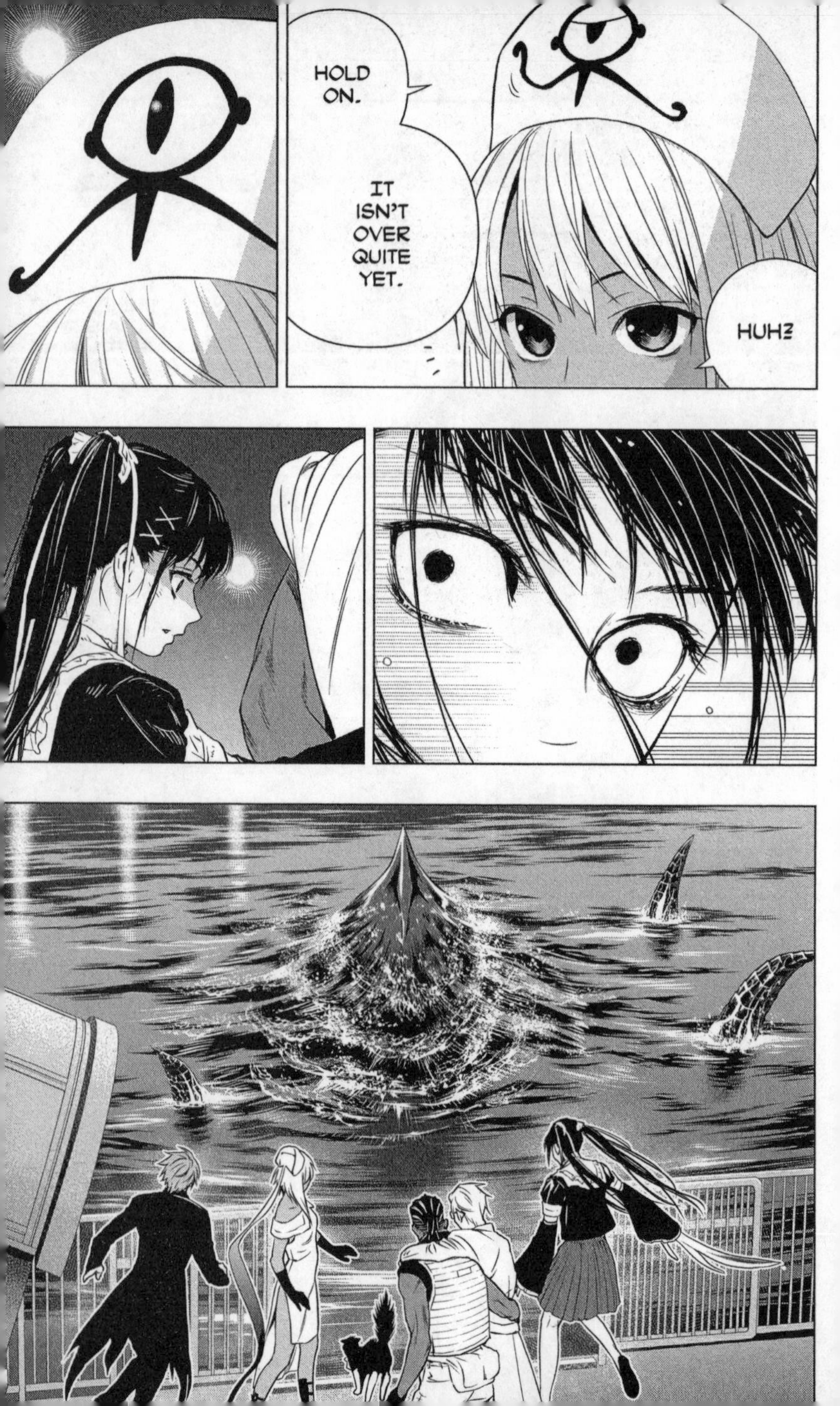
HOLD ON.
IT ISN'T OVER QUITE YET.
HUH?

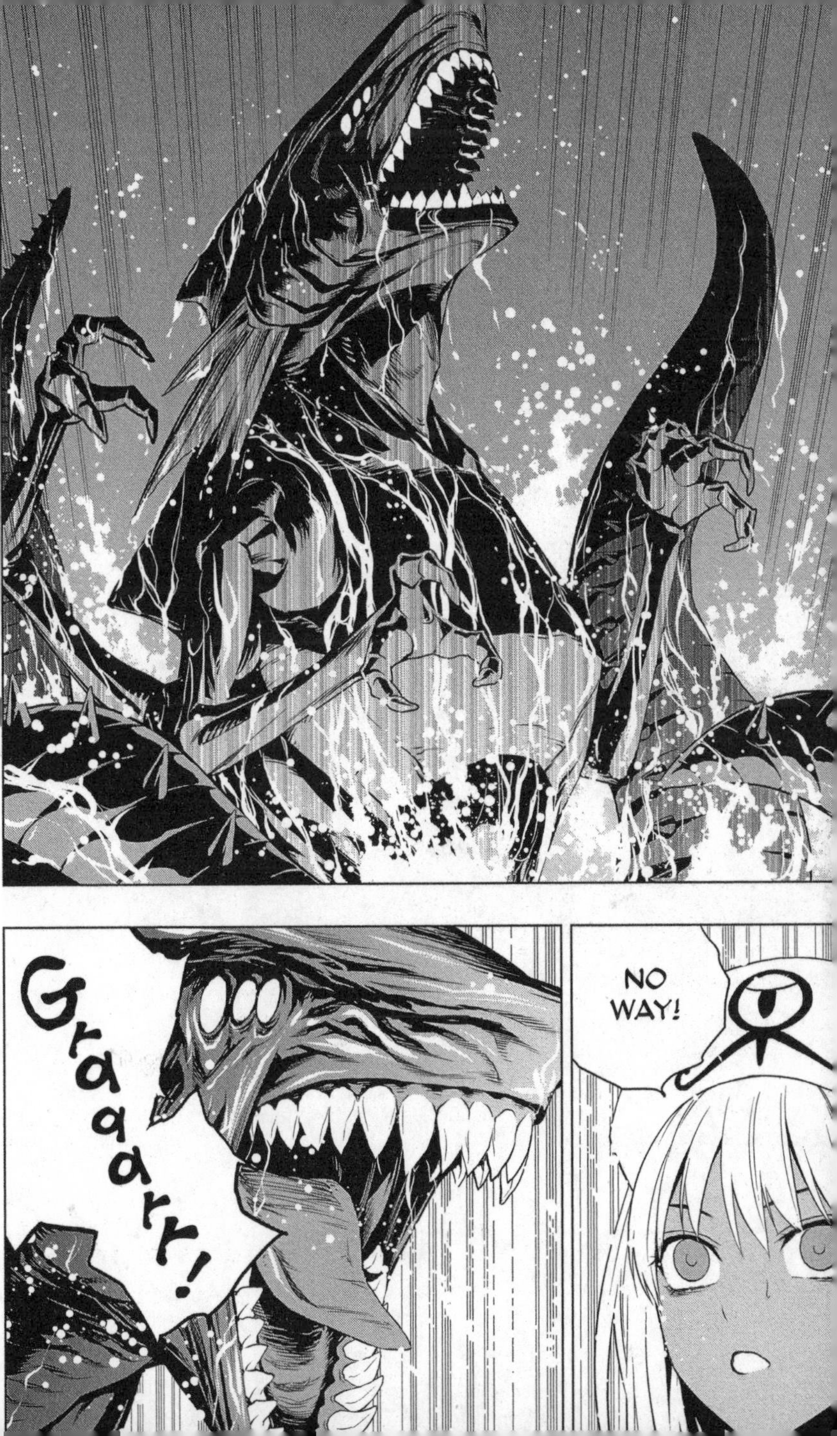
Graaarr!
NO WAY!

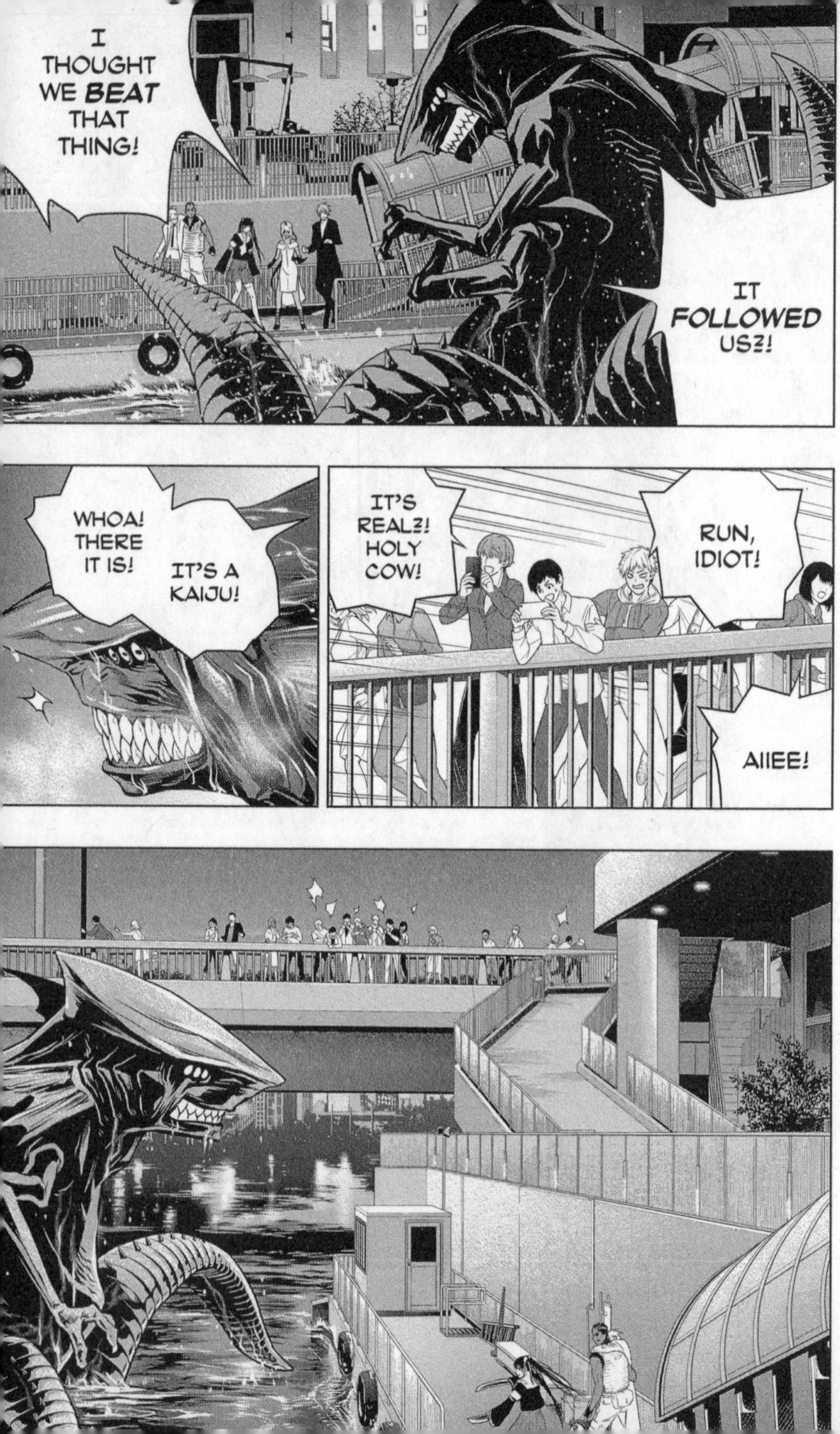
I THOUGHT WE BEAT THAT THING!
IT FOLLOWED US?!
WHOA! THERE IT IS!
IT'S A KAIJU!
IT'S REAL?! HOLY COW!
RUN, IDIOT!
AIIEE!

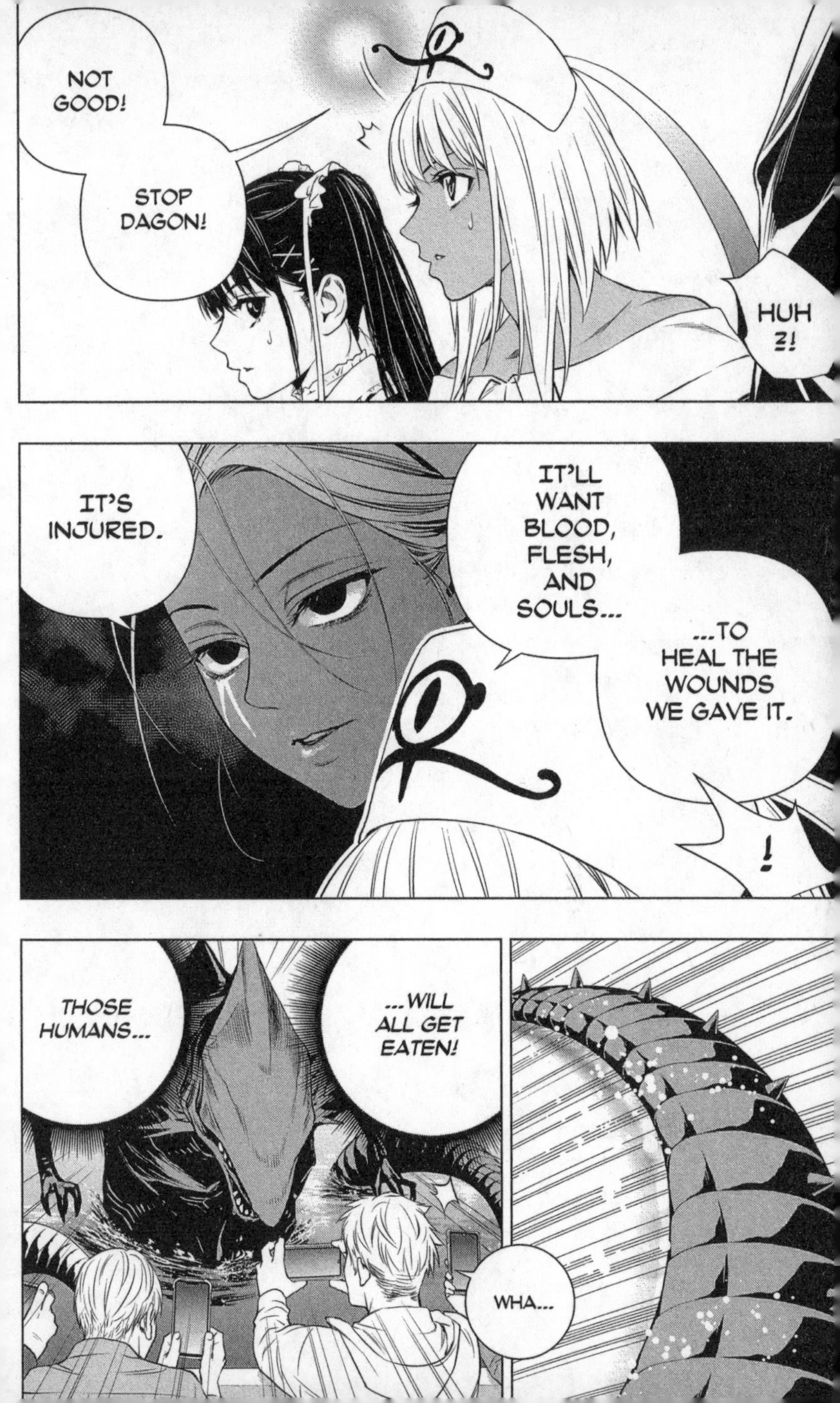
NOT GOOD!
STOP DAGON!
HUH ?!
IT'S INJURED.
IT'LL WANT BLOOD, FLESH, AND SOULS...
...TO HEAL THE WOUNDS WE GAVE IT.
!
THOSE HUMANS...
...WILL ALL GET EATEN!
WHA...

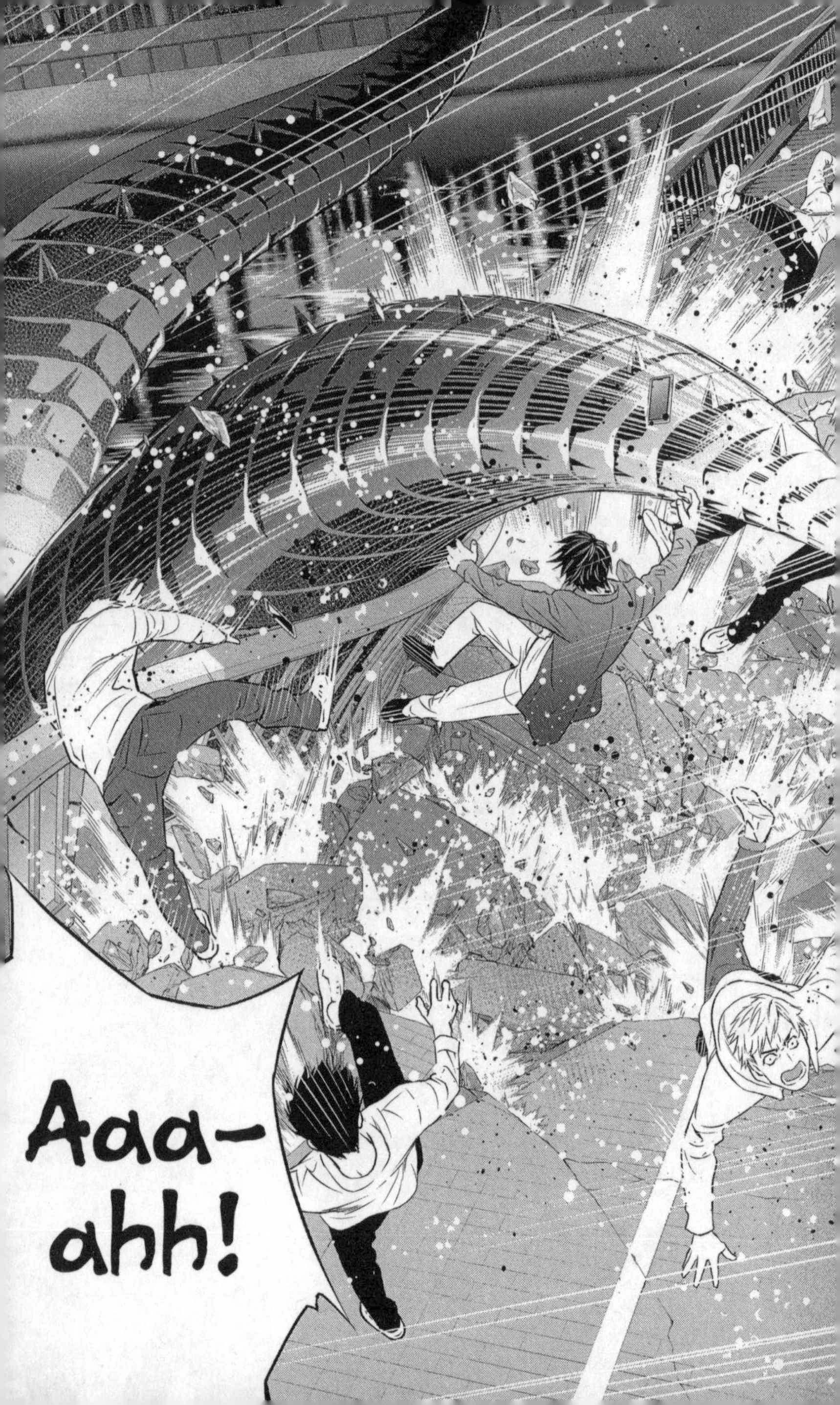
Aaa-ahh!

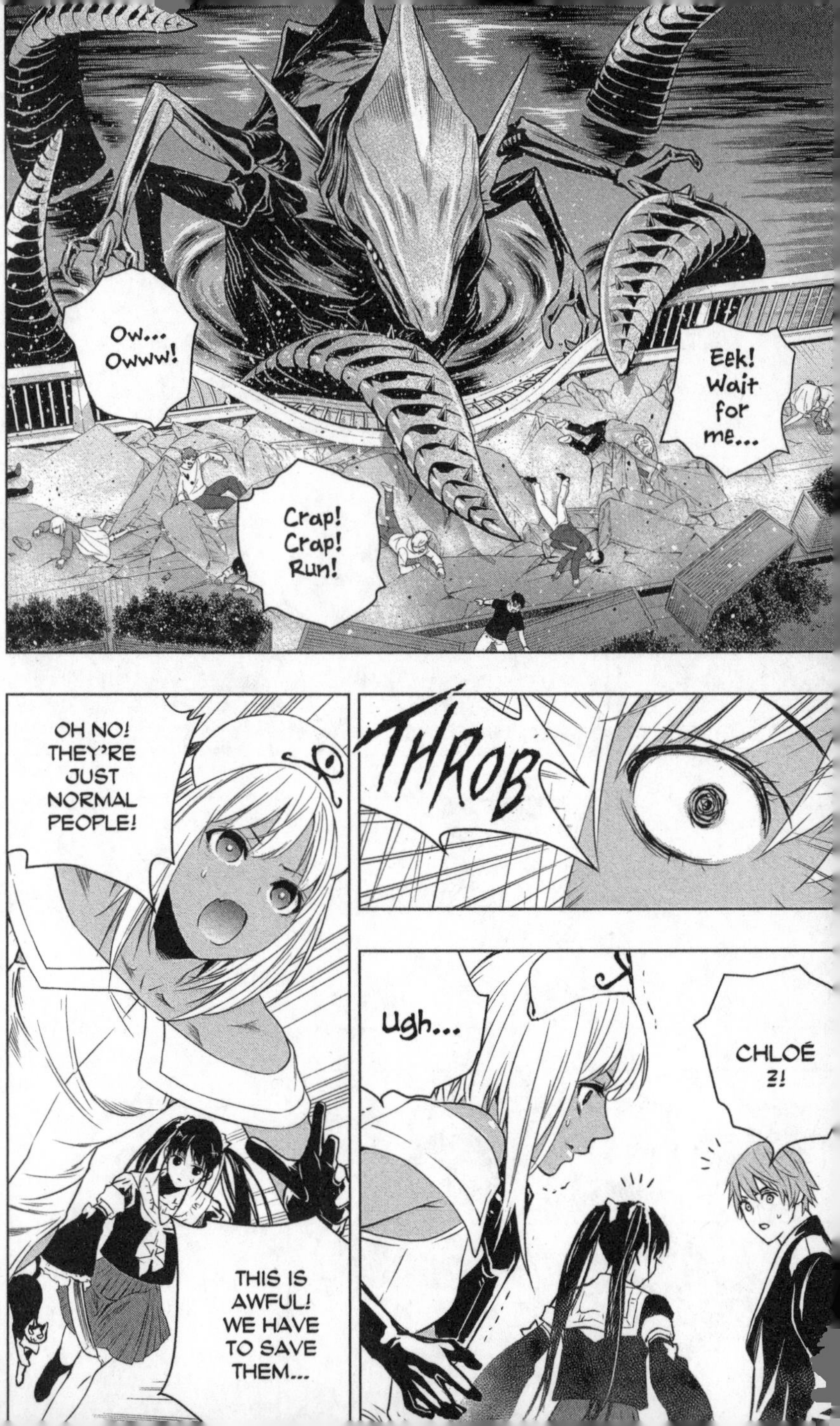
Ow...
Owww!
Crap!
Crap!
Run!
Eek!
Wait
for
me...
OH NO!
THEY'RE
JUST
NORMAL
PEOPLE!
THROB
THIS IS
AWFUL!
WE HAVE
TO SAVE
THEM...
Ugh...
CHLOÉ
?!

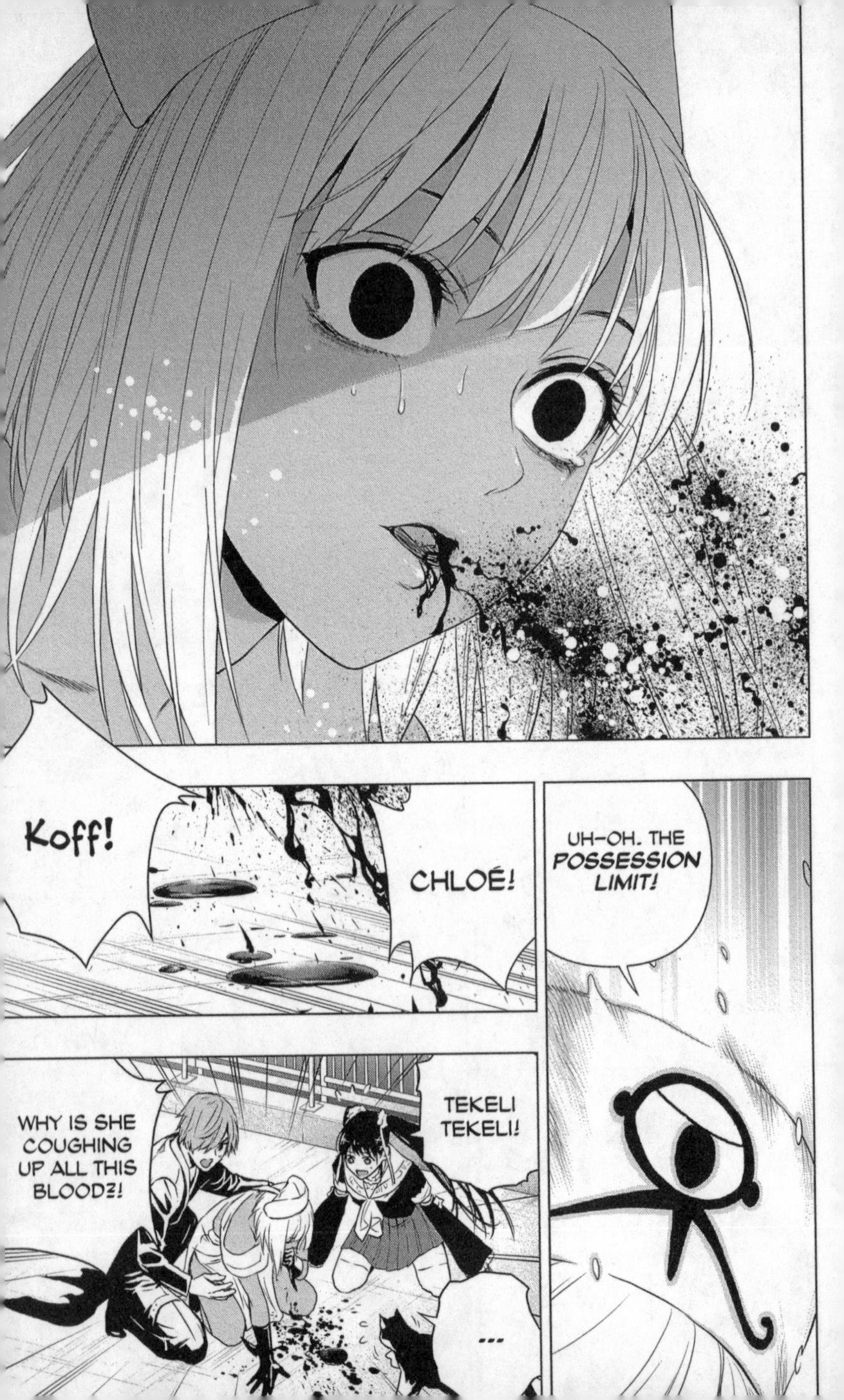
Koff!
CHLOÉ!
WHY IS SHE COUGHING UP ALL THIS BLOOD?!
TEKELI TEKELI!
...
UH-OH. THE POSSESSION LIMIT!

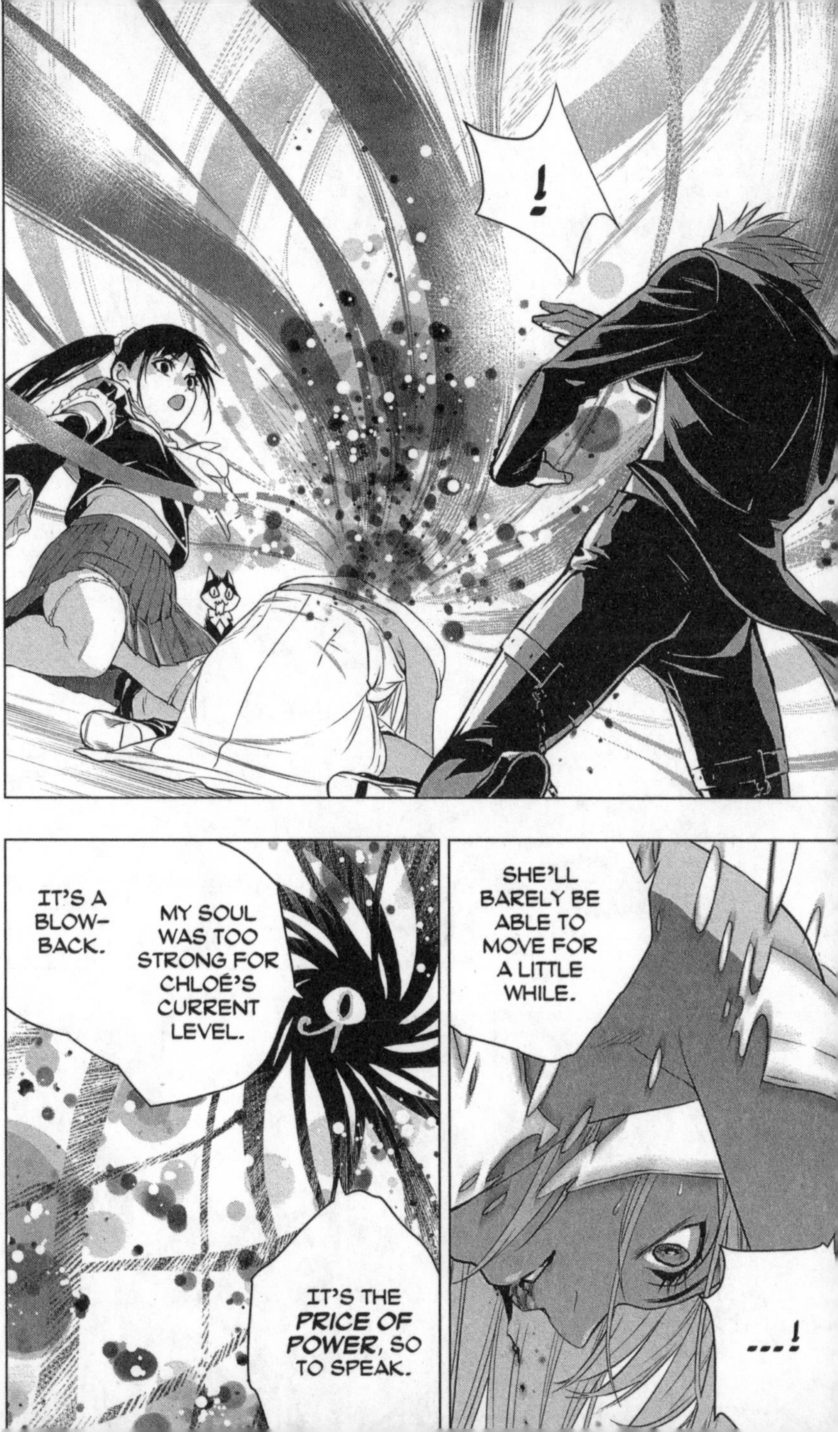
!
IT'S A BLOW-BACK.
MY SOUL WAS TOO STRONG FOR CHLOÉ'S CURRENT LEVEL.
IT'S THE *PRICE OF POWER*, SO TO SPEAK.
SHE'LL BARELY BE ABLE TO MOVE FOR A LITTLE WHILE.
...!

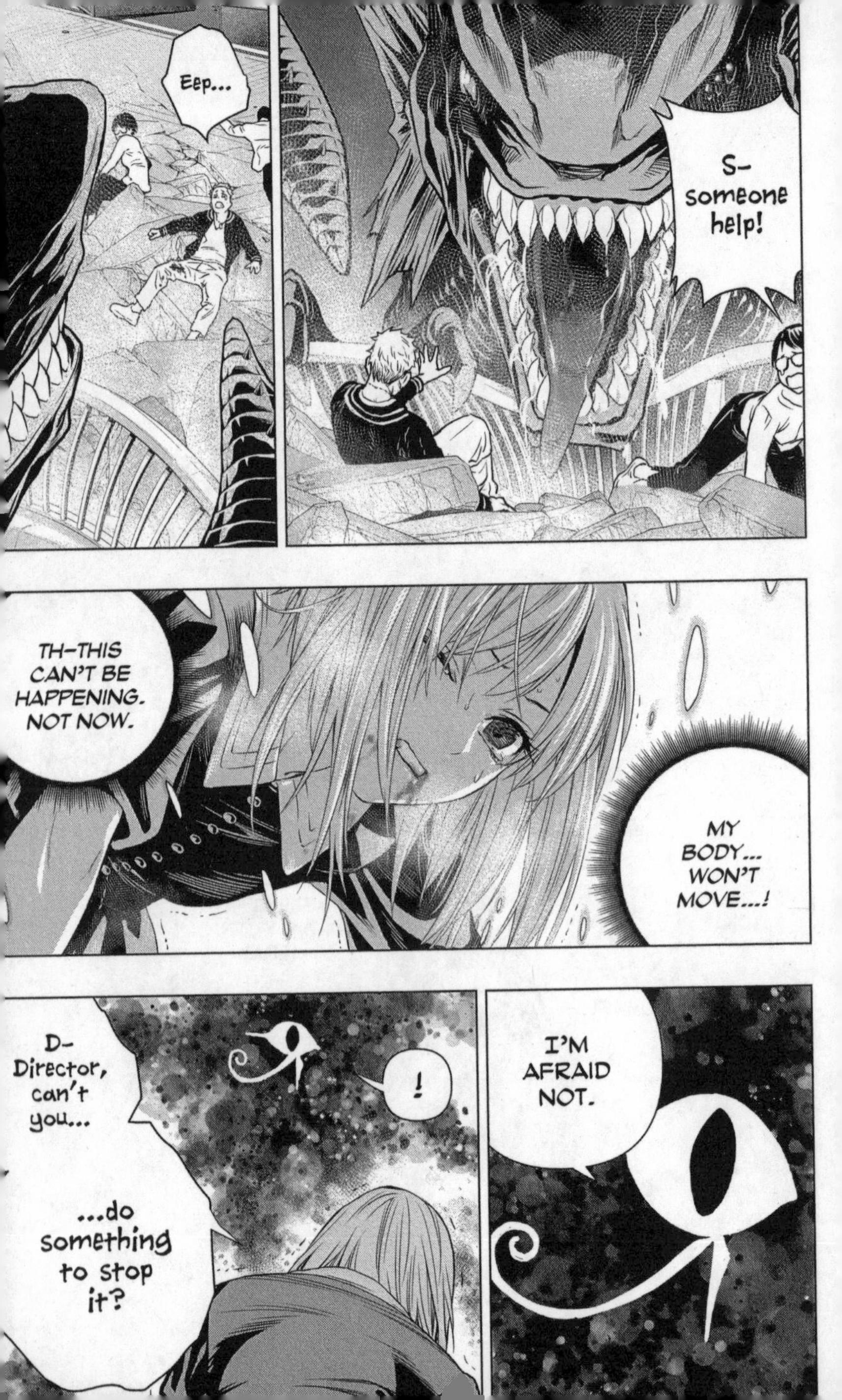
Eep...
S-someone help!
TH-THIS CAN'T BE HAPPENING. NOT NOW.
MY BODY... WON'T MOVE...!
D-Director, can't you...
...do something to stop it?
!
I'M AFRAID NOT.

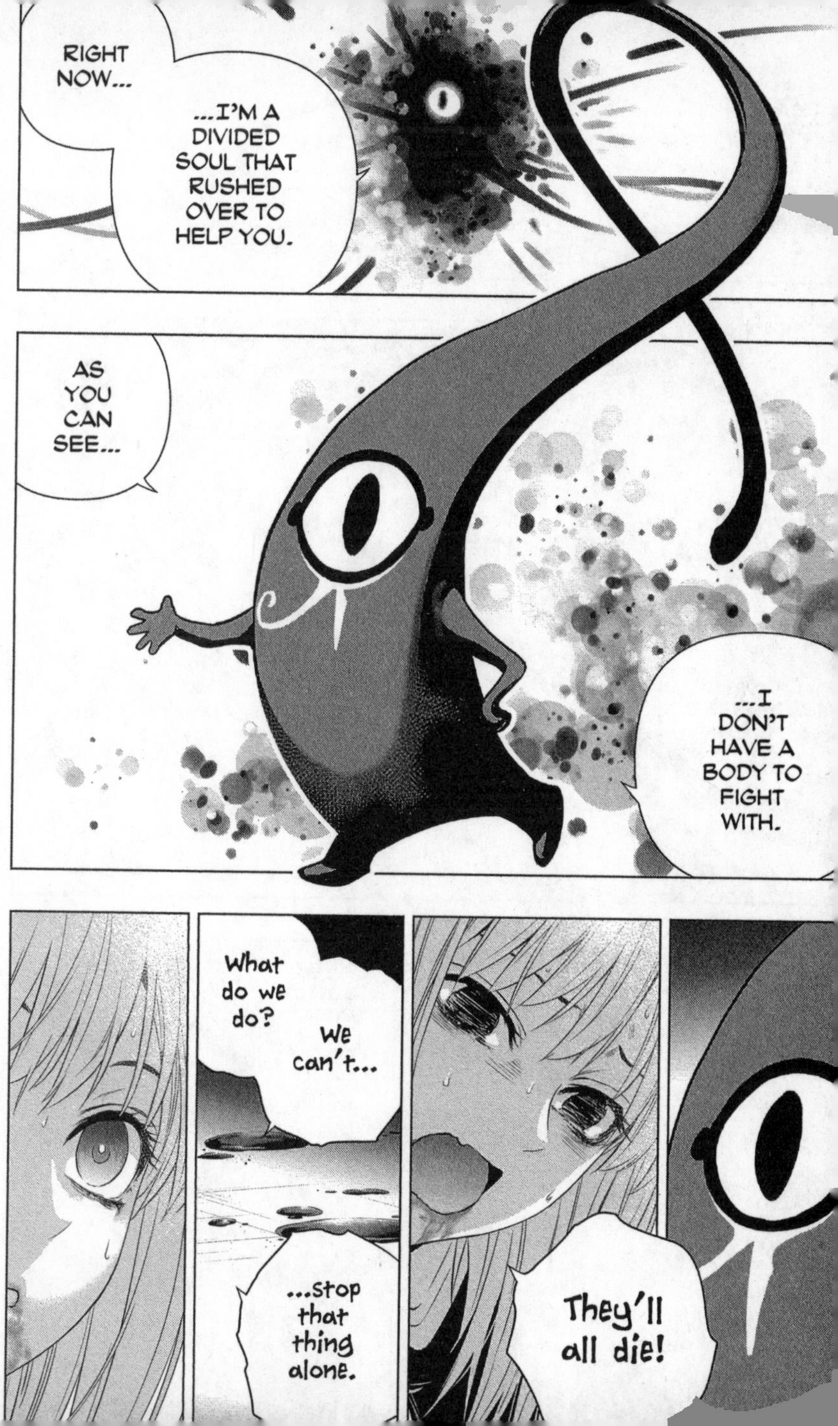
RIGHT NOW...
...I'M A DIVIDED SOUL THAT RUSHED OVER TO HELP YOU.
AS YOU CAN SEE...
...I DON'T HAVE A BODY TO FIGHT WITH.
What do we do?
We can't...
...stop that thing alone.
They'll all die!

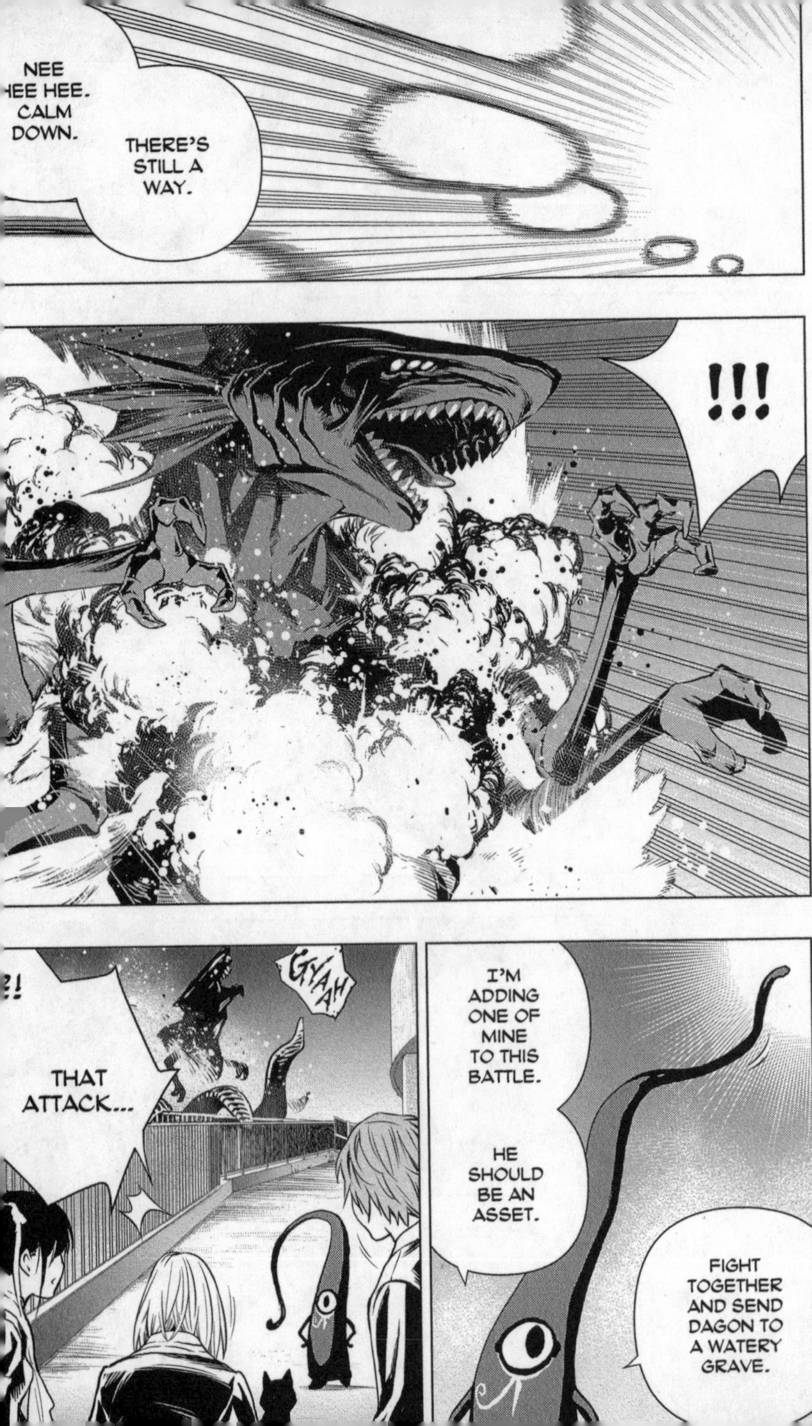
NEE HEE HEE. CALM DOWN.
THERE'S STILL A WAY.
!!!
GYAAH
THAT ATTACK...
I'M ADDING ONE OF MINE TO THIS BATTLE.
HE SHOULD BE AN ASSET.
FIGHT TOGETHER AND SEND DAGON TO A WATERY GRAVE.

22: I'M SORRY

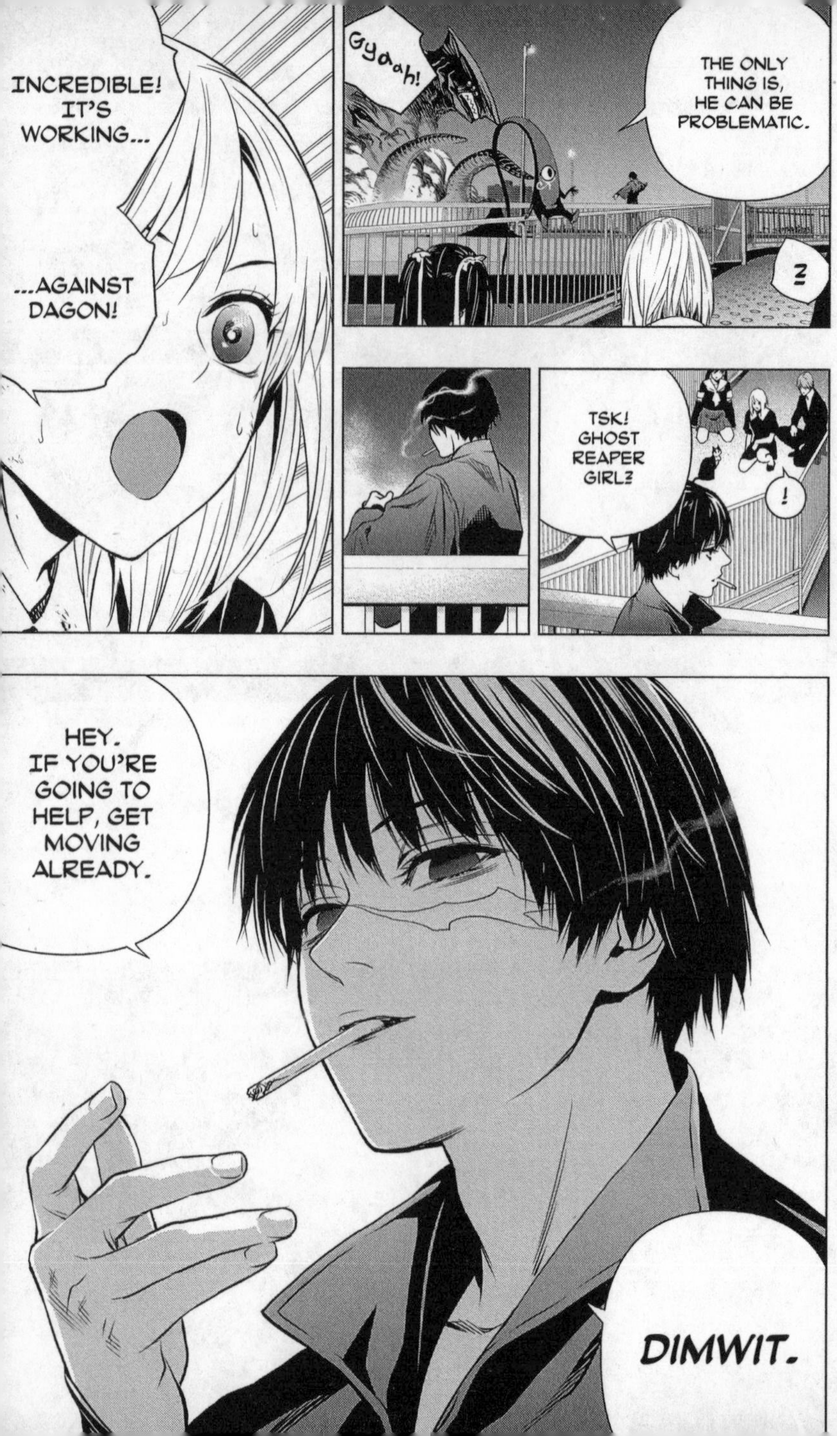
INCREDIBLE! IT'S WORKING...
...AGAINST DAGON!
Gyaah!
THE ONLY THING IS, HE CAN BE PROBLEMATIC.
?
TSK! GHOST REAPER GIRL?
!
HEY. IF YOU'RE GOING TO HELP, GET MOVING ALREADY.
DIMWIT.

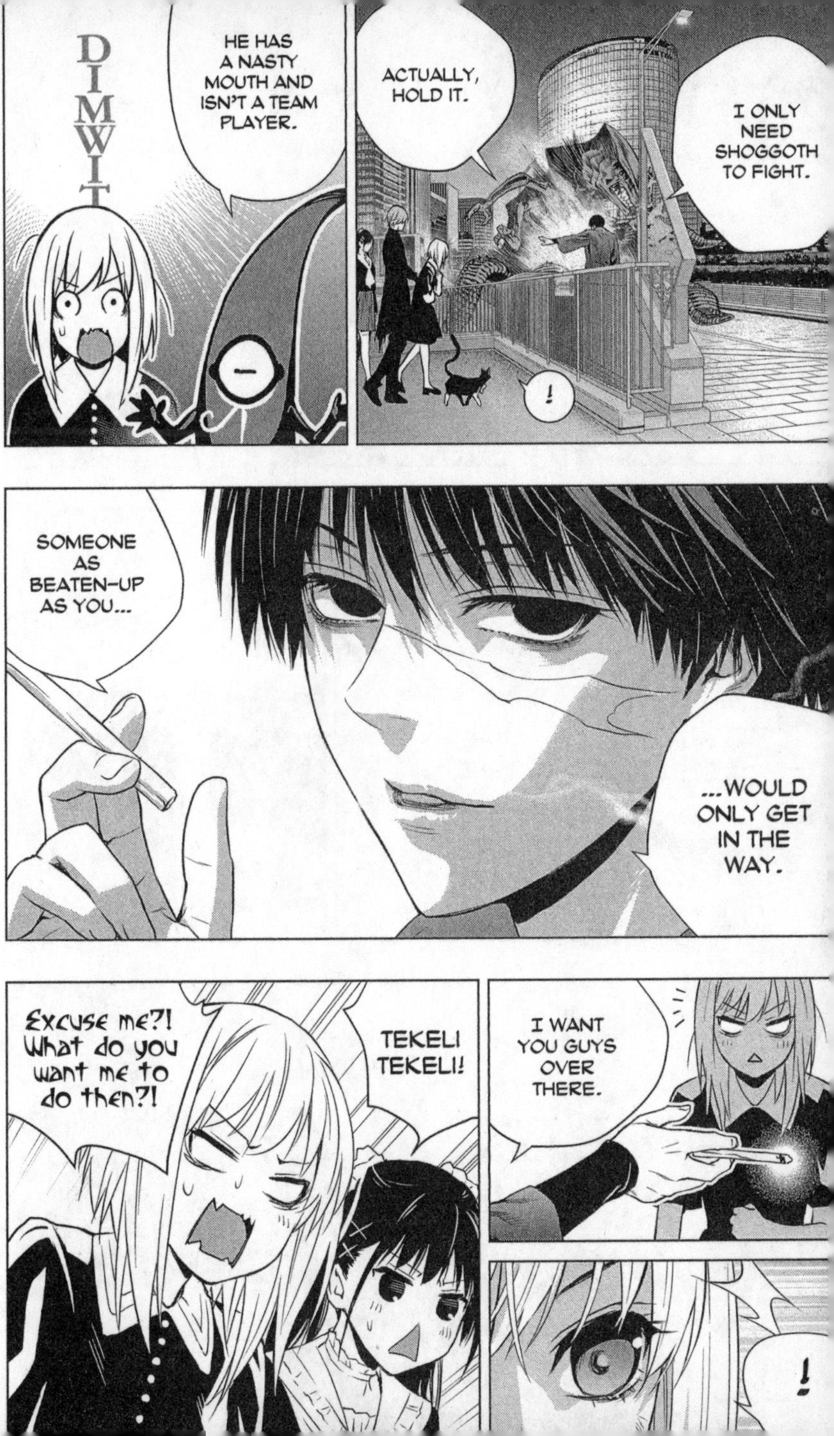
DIMWIT
HE HAS A NASTY MOUTH AND ISN'T A TEAM PLAYER.
–
ACTUALLY, HOLD IT.
I ONLY NEED SHOGGOTH TO FIGHT.
!
SOMEONE AS BEATEN-UP AS YOU...
...WOULD ONLY GET IN THE WAY.
Excuse me?! What do you want me to do then?!
TEKELI TEKELI!
I WANT YOU GUYS OVER THERE.
!

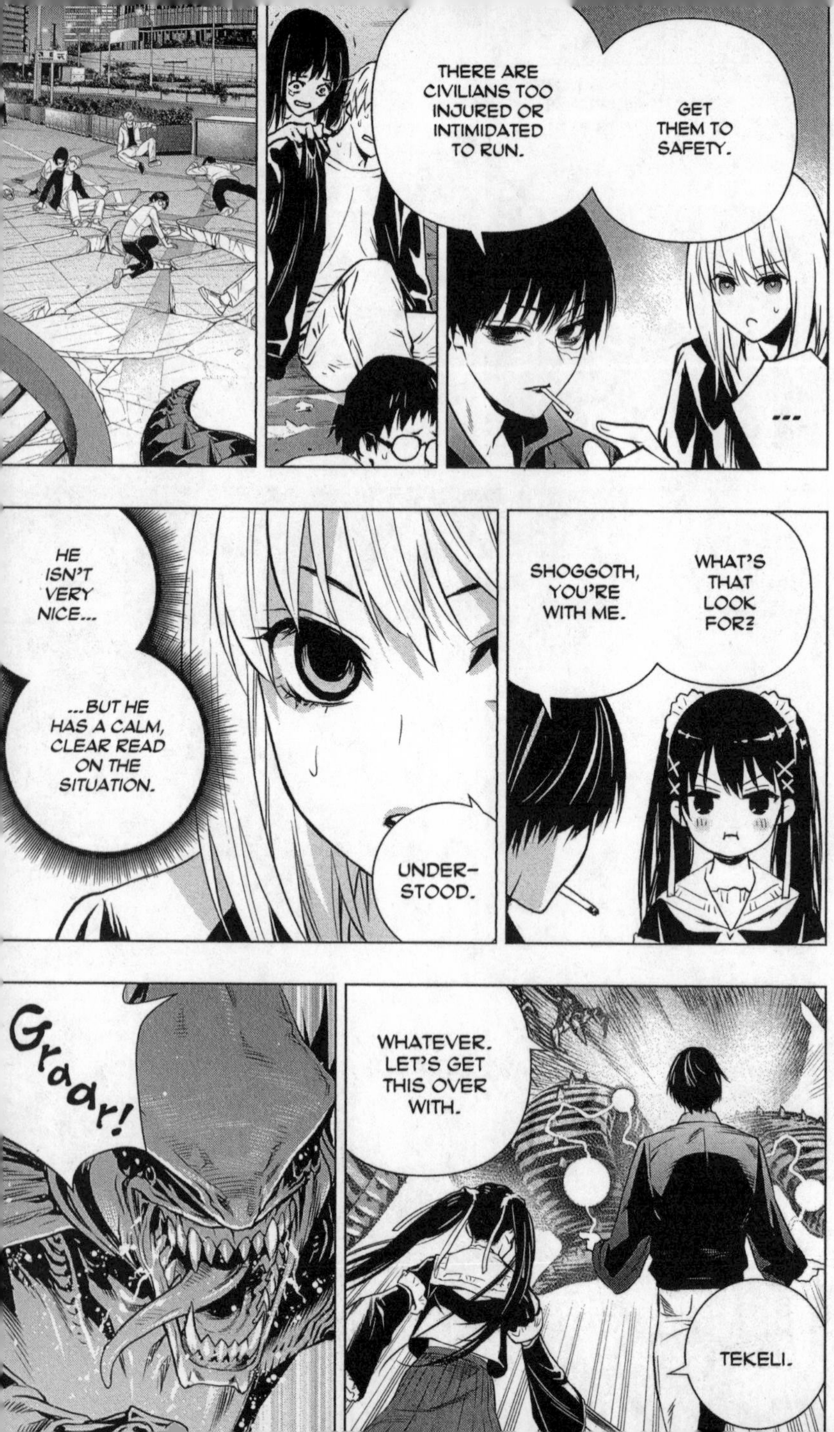
THERE ARE CIVILIANS TOO INJURED OR INTIMIDATED TO RUN.
GET THEM TO SAFETY.
...
HE ISN'T VERY NICE...
...BUT HE HAS A CALM, CLEAR READ ON THE SITUATION.
UNDER-STOOD.
SHOGGOTH, YOU'RE WITH ME.
WHAT'S THAT LOOK FOR?
Graar!
WHATEVER. LET'S GET THIS OVER WITH.
TEKELI.

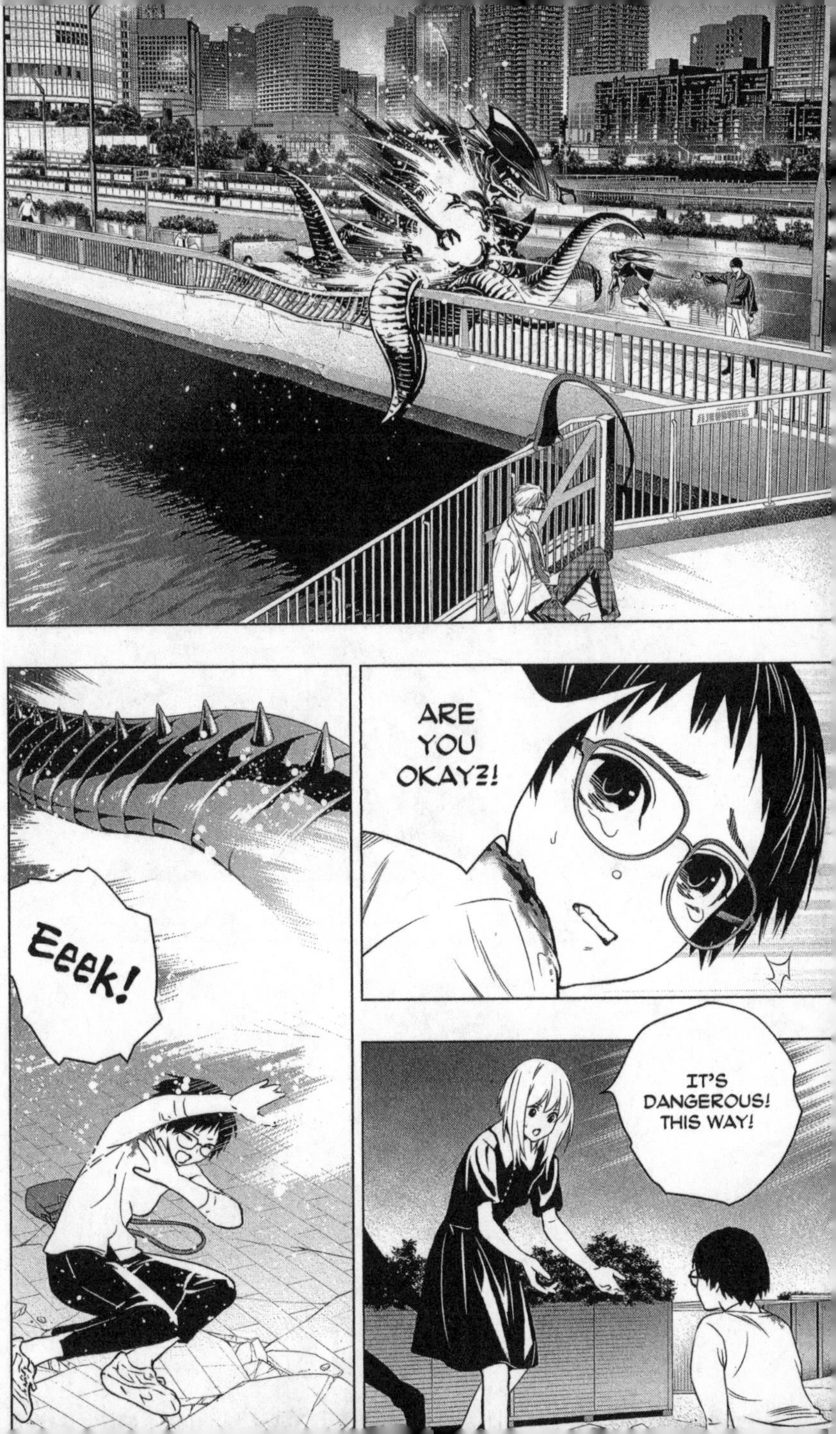
Eeek!
ARE YOU OKAY?!
IT'S DANGEROUS! THIS WAY!

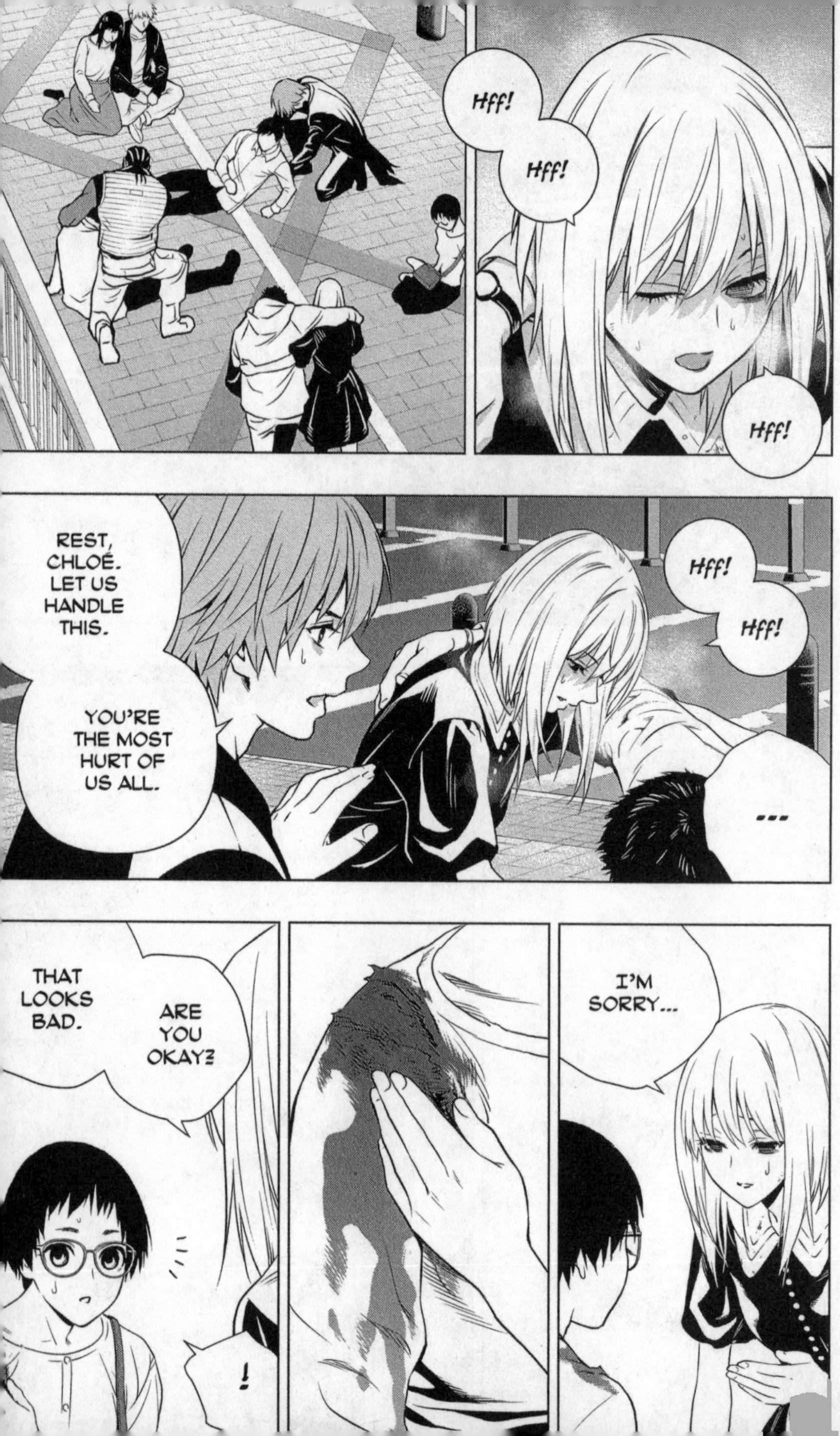
Hff!
Hff!
Hff!
Hff!
Hff!
REST, CHLOÉ. LET US HANDLE THIS.
YOU'RE THE MOST HURT OF US ALL.
...
I'M SORRY...
THAT LOOKS BAD.
ARE YOU OKAY?
!

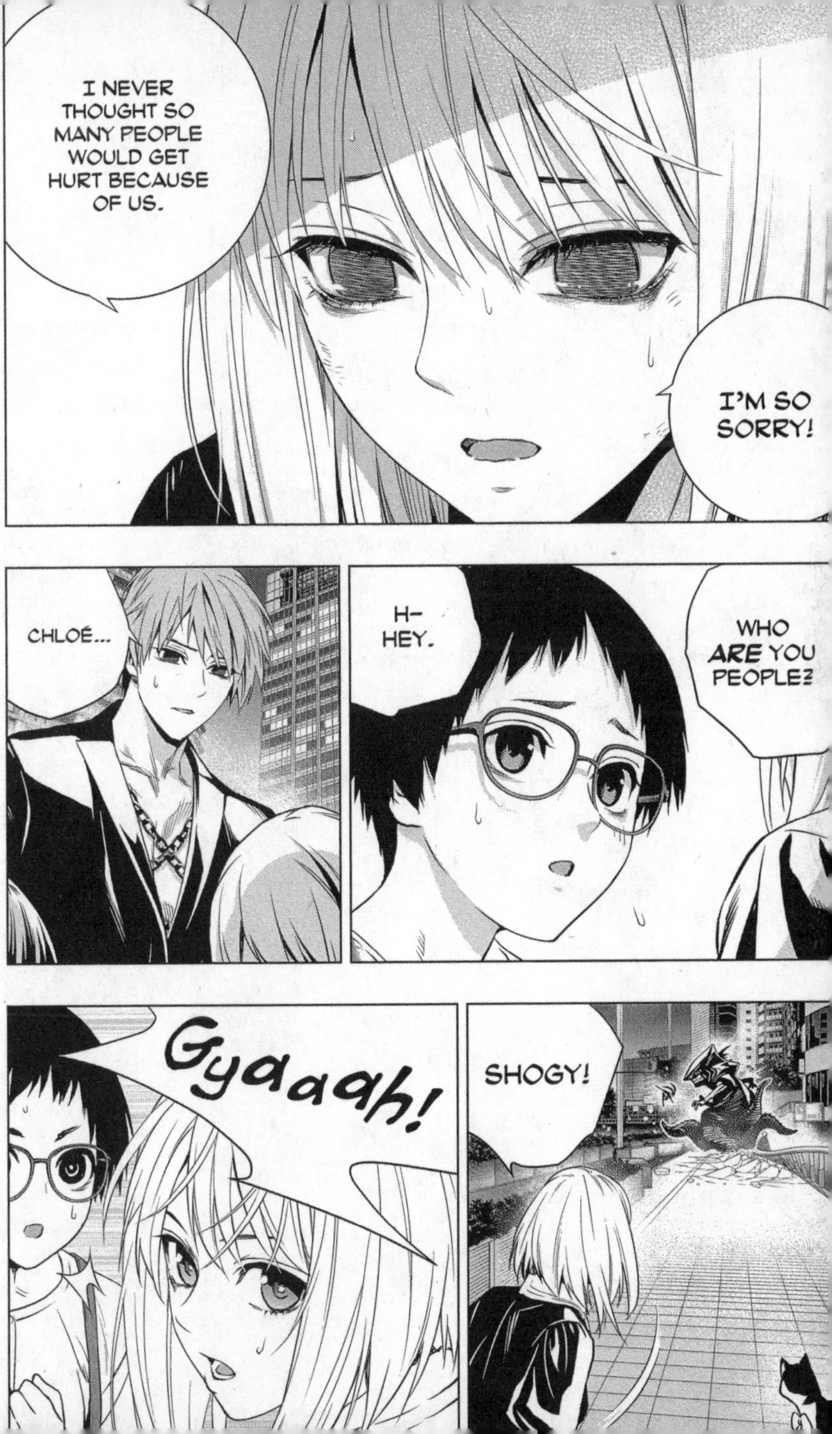
I'M SO SORRY!
I NEVER THOUGHT SO MANY PEOPLE WOULD GET HURT BECAUSE OF US.
WHO ARE YOU PEOPLE?
H-HEY.
CHLOÉ...
SHOGY!
Gyaaah!

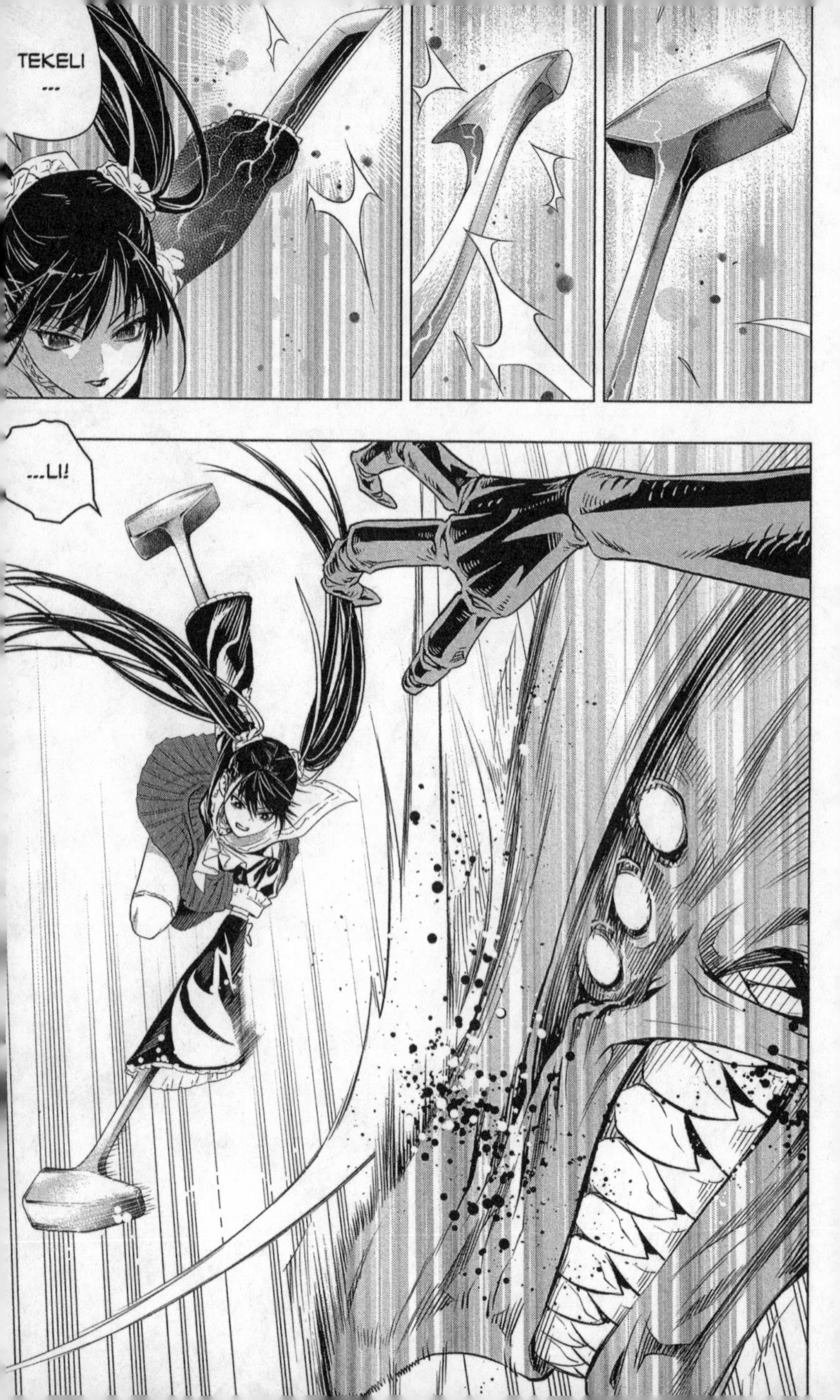
TEKELI
...
...LI!

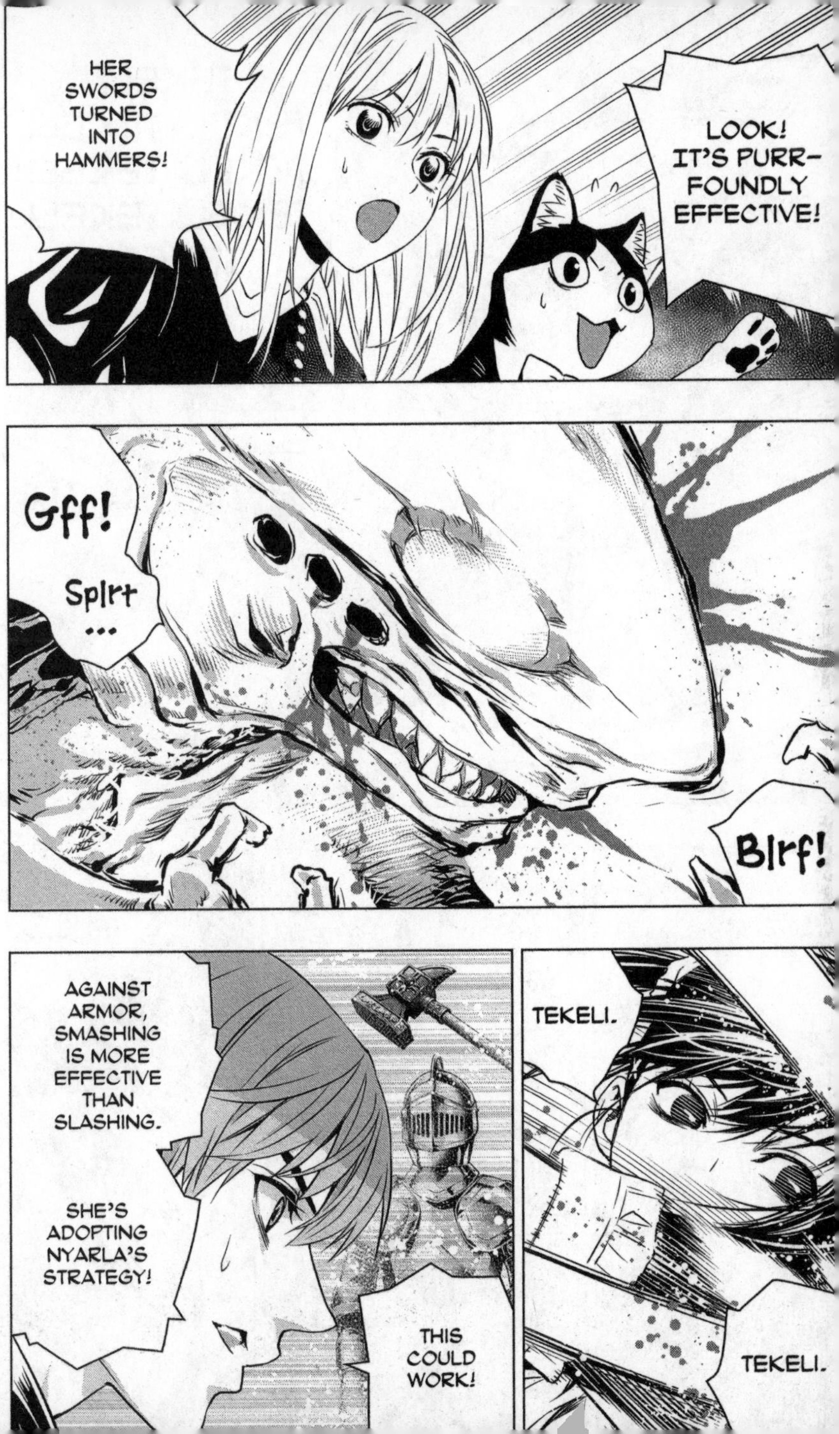
HER SWORDS TURNED INTO HAMMERS!
LOOK! IT'S PURR-FOUNDLY EFFECTIVE!
Gff!
Splrt ...
Blrf!
AGAINST ARMOR, SMASHING IS MORE EFFECTIVE THAN SLASHING.
SHE'S ADOPTING NYARLA'S STRATEGY!
THIS COULD WORK!
TEKELI.
TEKELI.

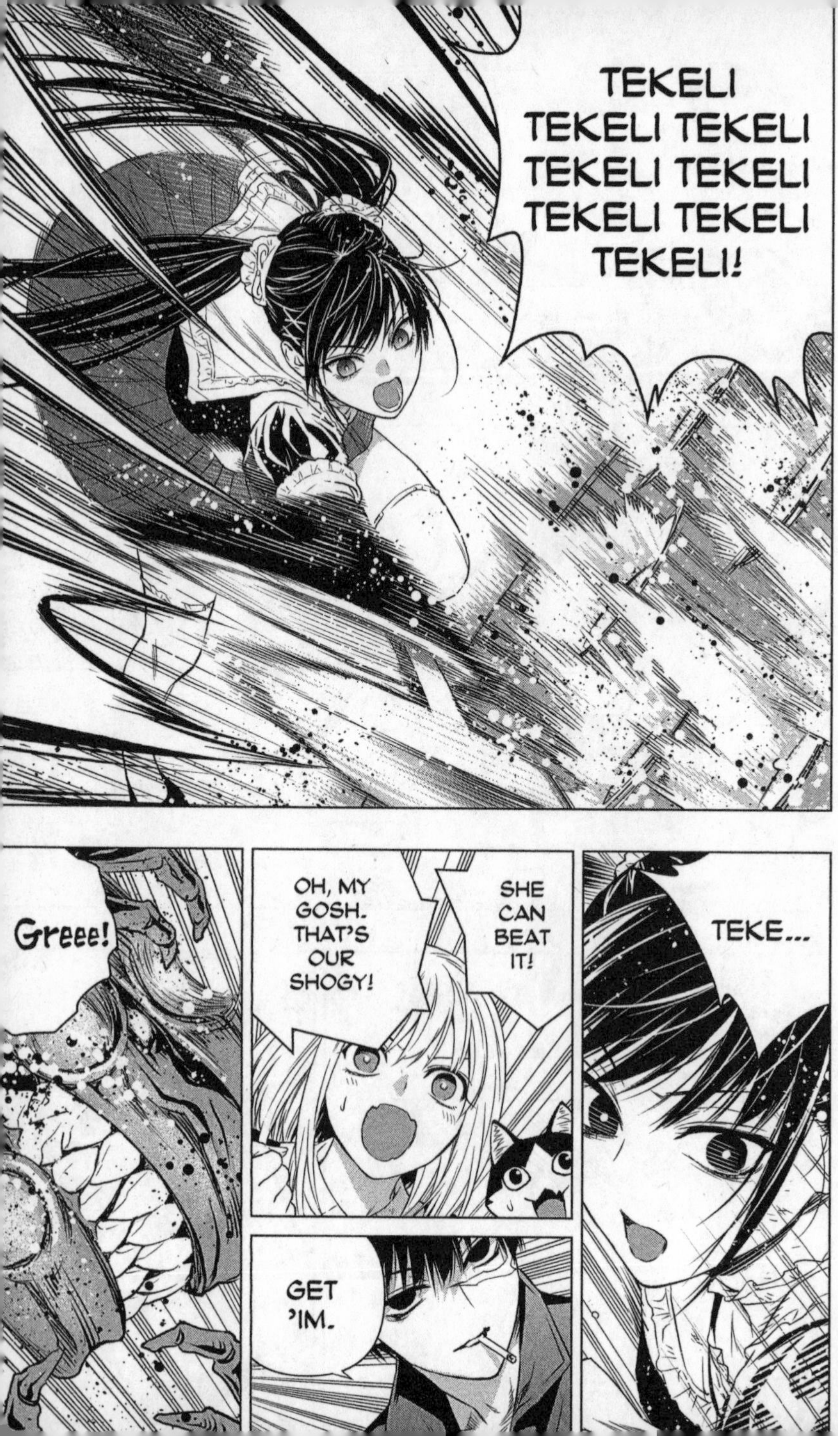
TEKELI TEKELI TEKELI TEKELI TEKELI TEKELI TEKELI TEKELI!
Greee!
OH, MY GOSH. THAT'S OUR SHOGY!
SHE CAN BEAT IT!
GET 'IM.
TEKE...

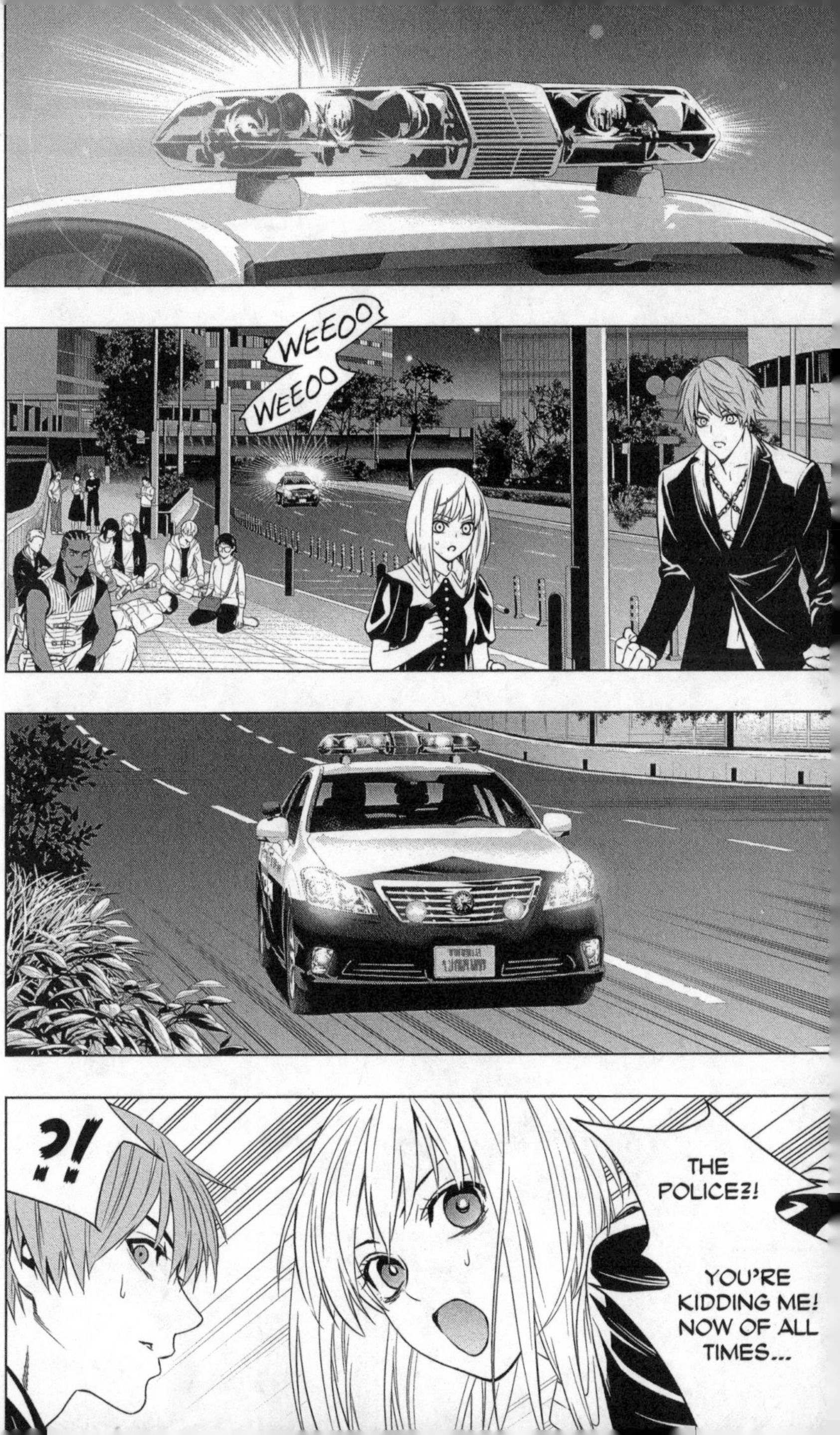
WEEOO
WEEOO
?!
THE POLICE?!
YOU'RE KIDDING ME! NOW OF ALL TIMES...

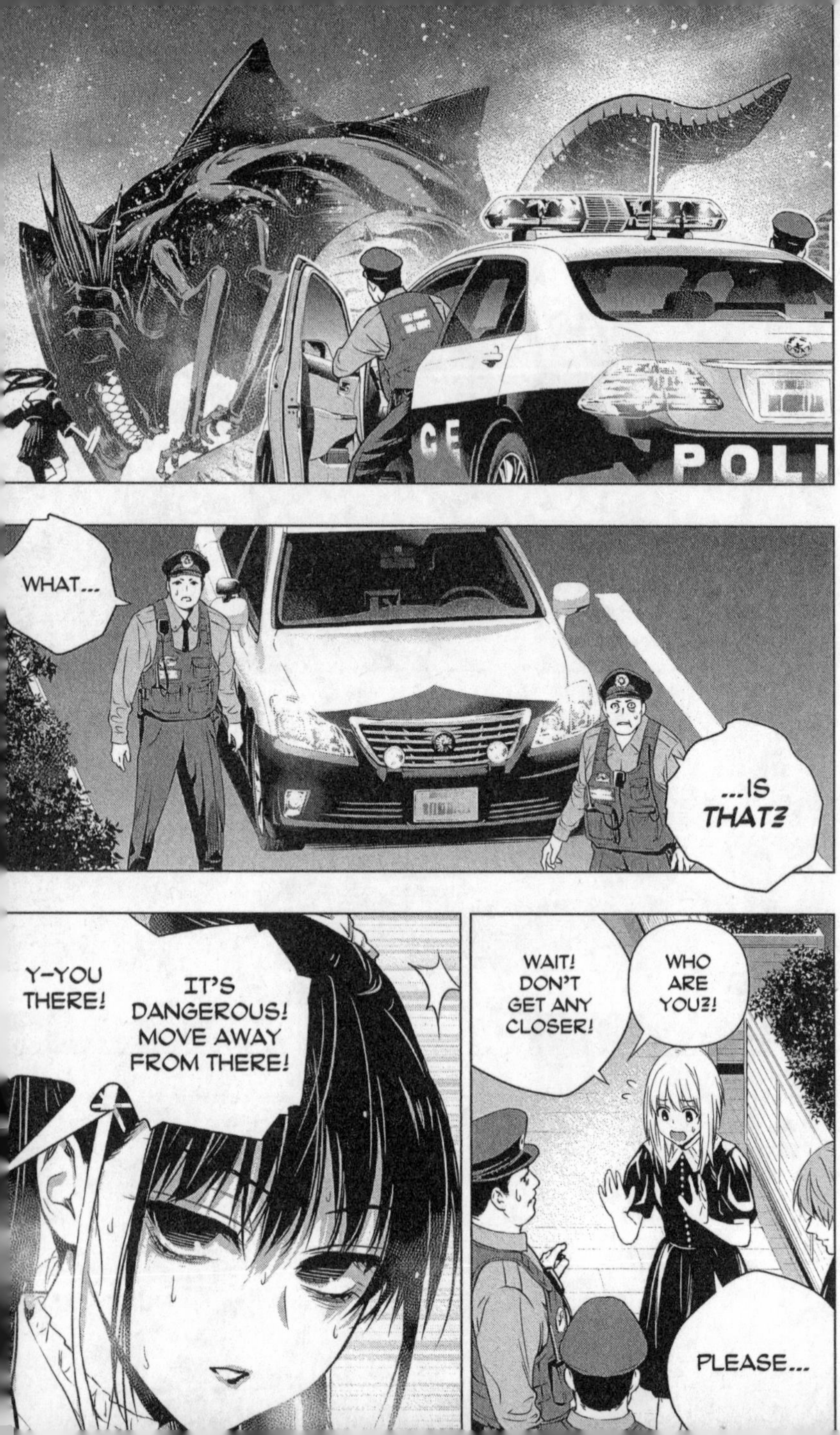
CE
POLI
WHAT...
...IS THAT?
Y-YOU THERE!
IT'S DANGEROUS! MOVE AWAY FROM THERE!
WAIT! DON'T GET ANY CLOSER!
WHO ARE YOU?!
PLEASE...

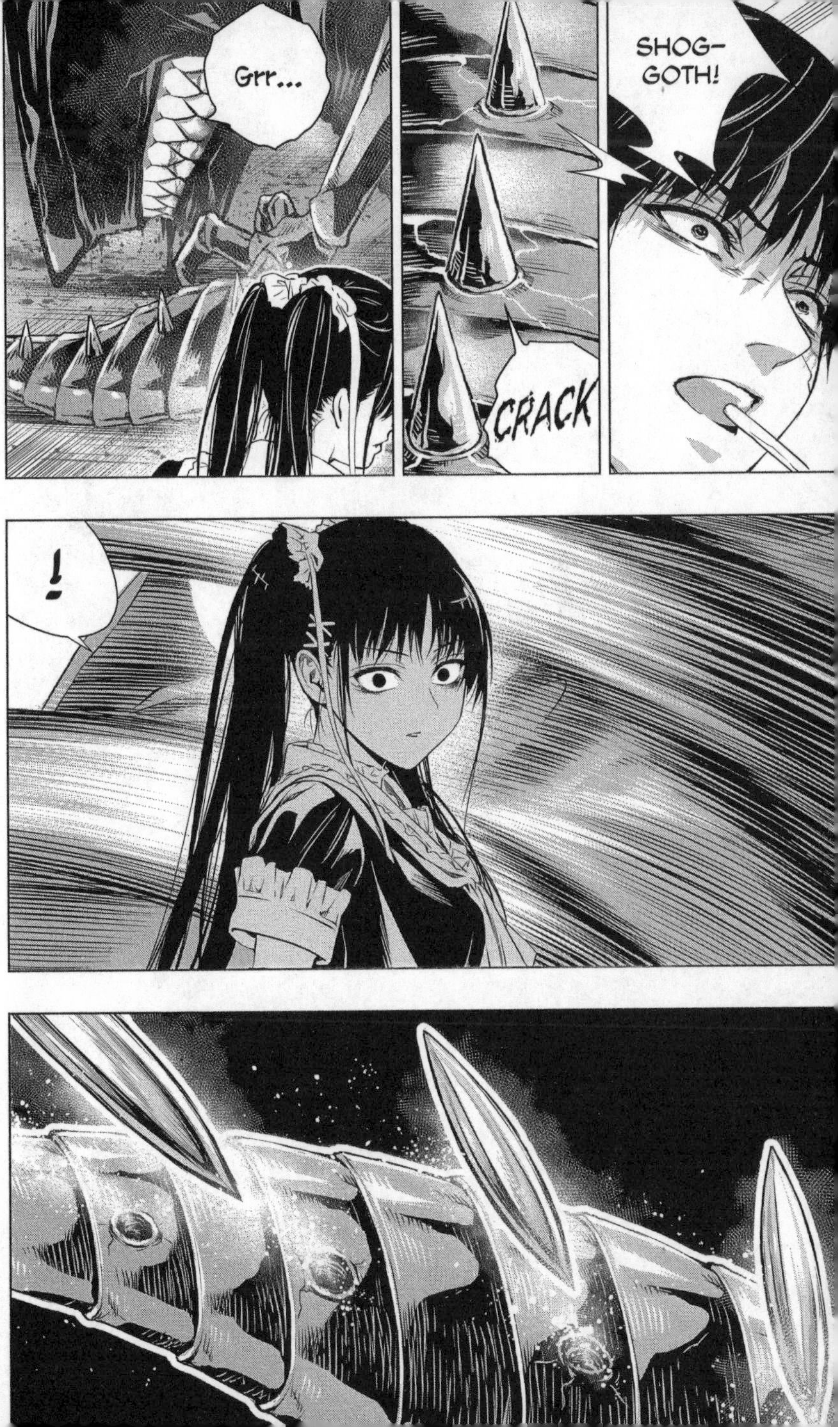
Grr...
CRACK
SHOG-
GOTH!
!

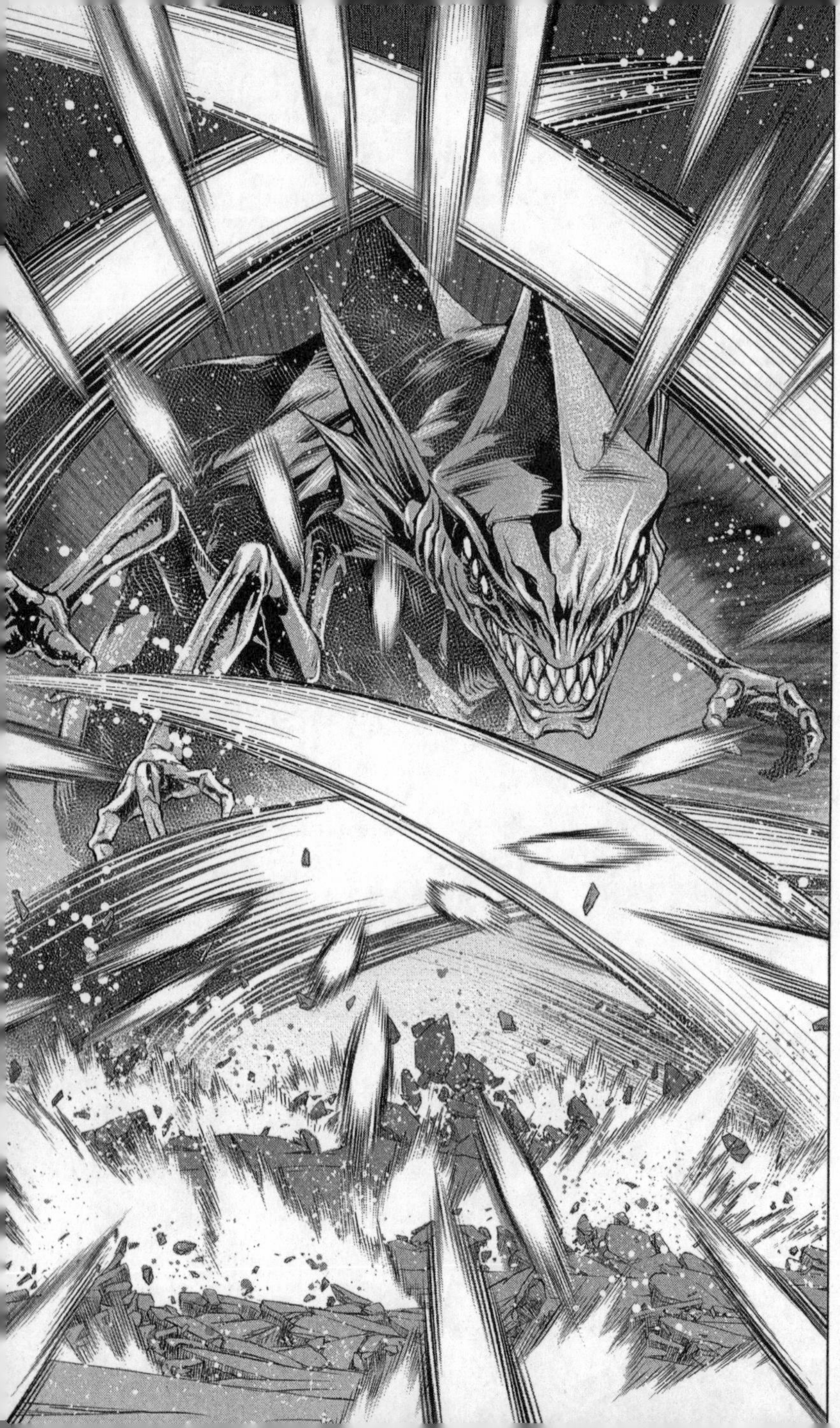

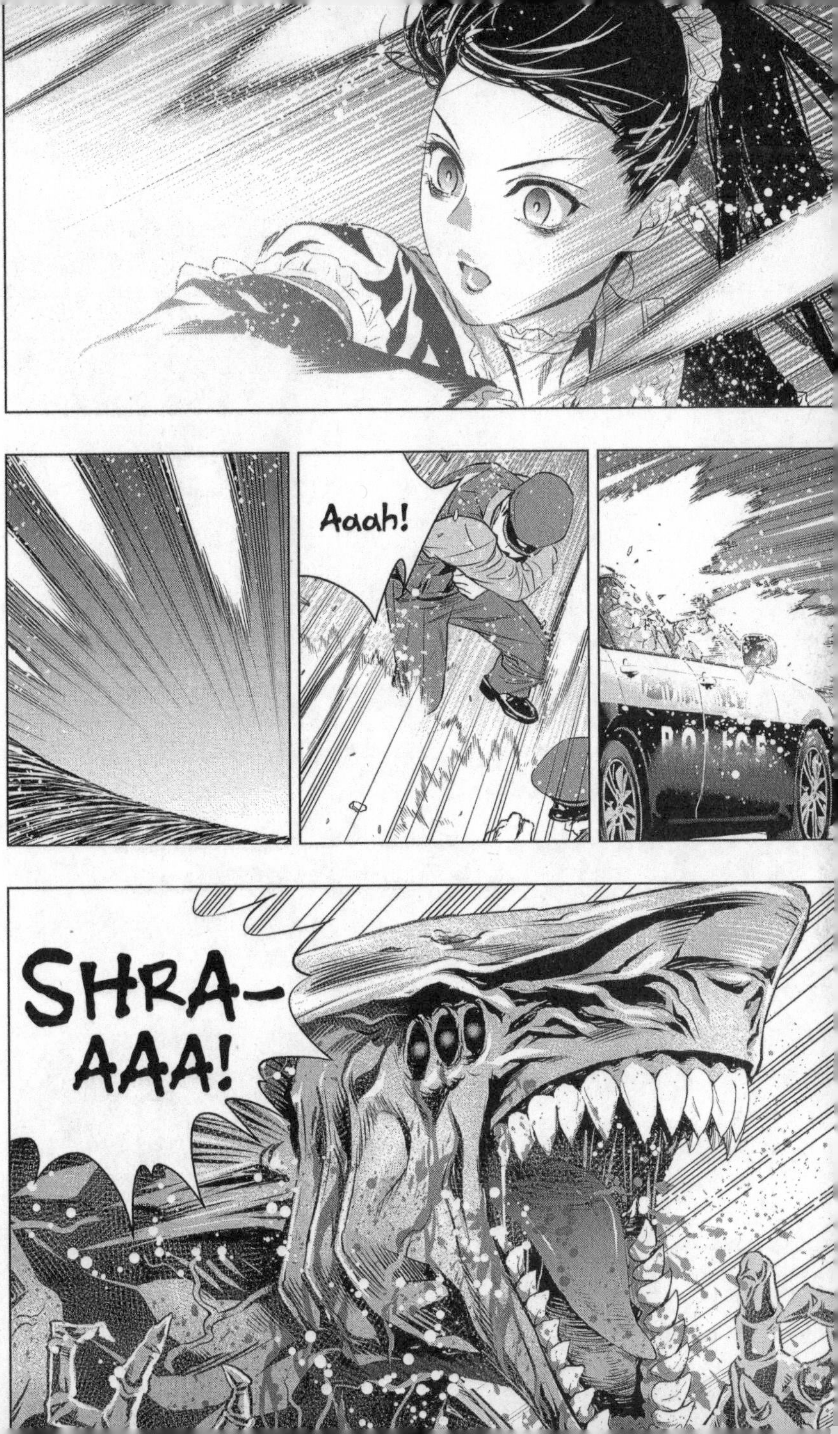
Aaah!
POLICE
SHRA-
AAA!

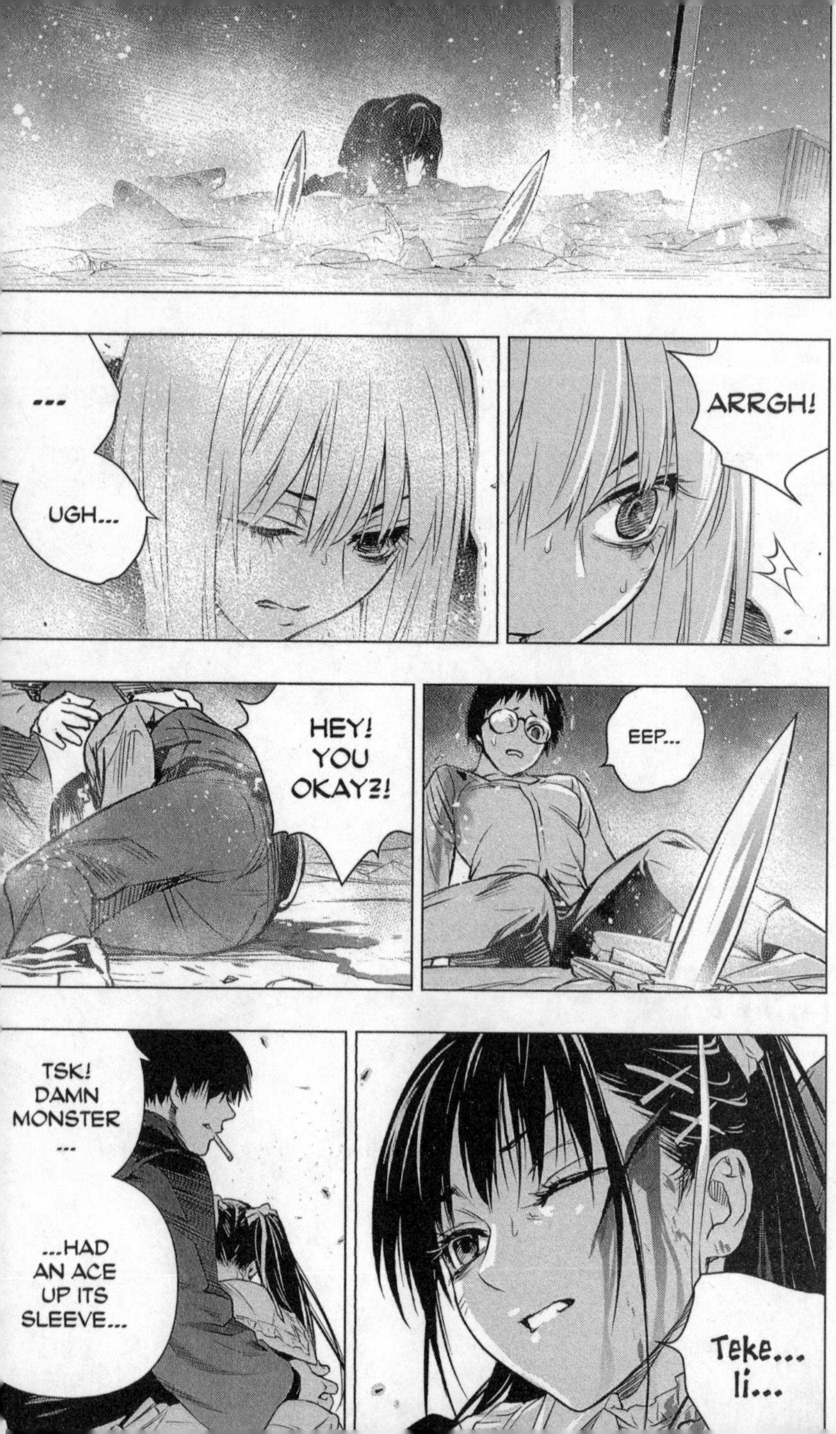

...
UGH...
ARRGH!
HEY! YOU OKAY?!
EEP...
TSK! DAMN MONSTER...
...HAD AN ACE UP ITS SLEEVE...
Teke... li...

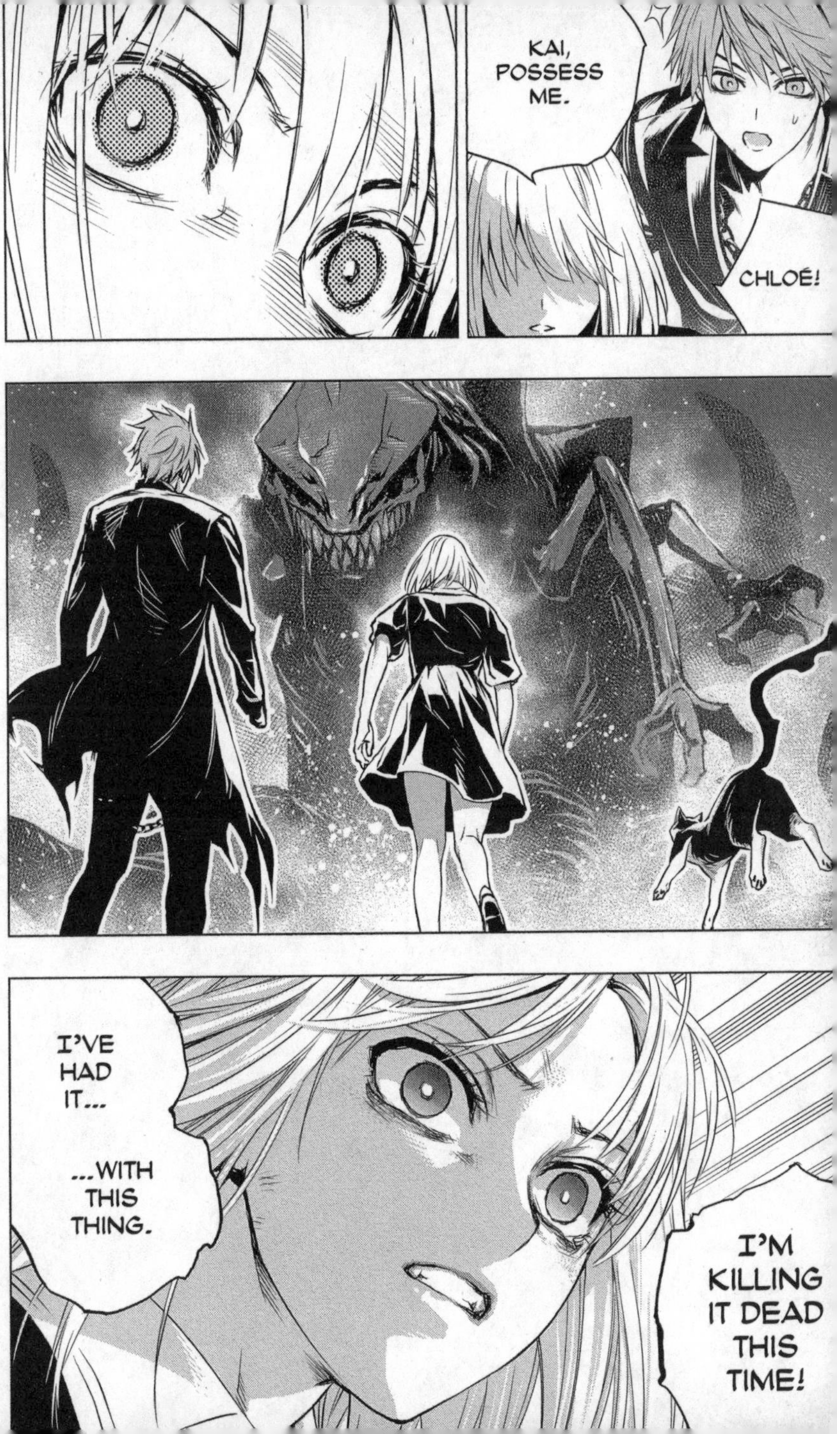
KAI, POSSESS ME.
CHLOÉ!
I'VE HAD IT...
...WITH THIS THING.
I'M KILLING IT DEAD THIS TIME!

23: THE DAY TO BECOME A HERO

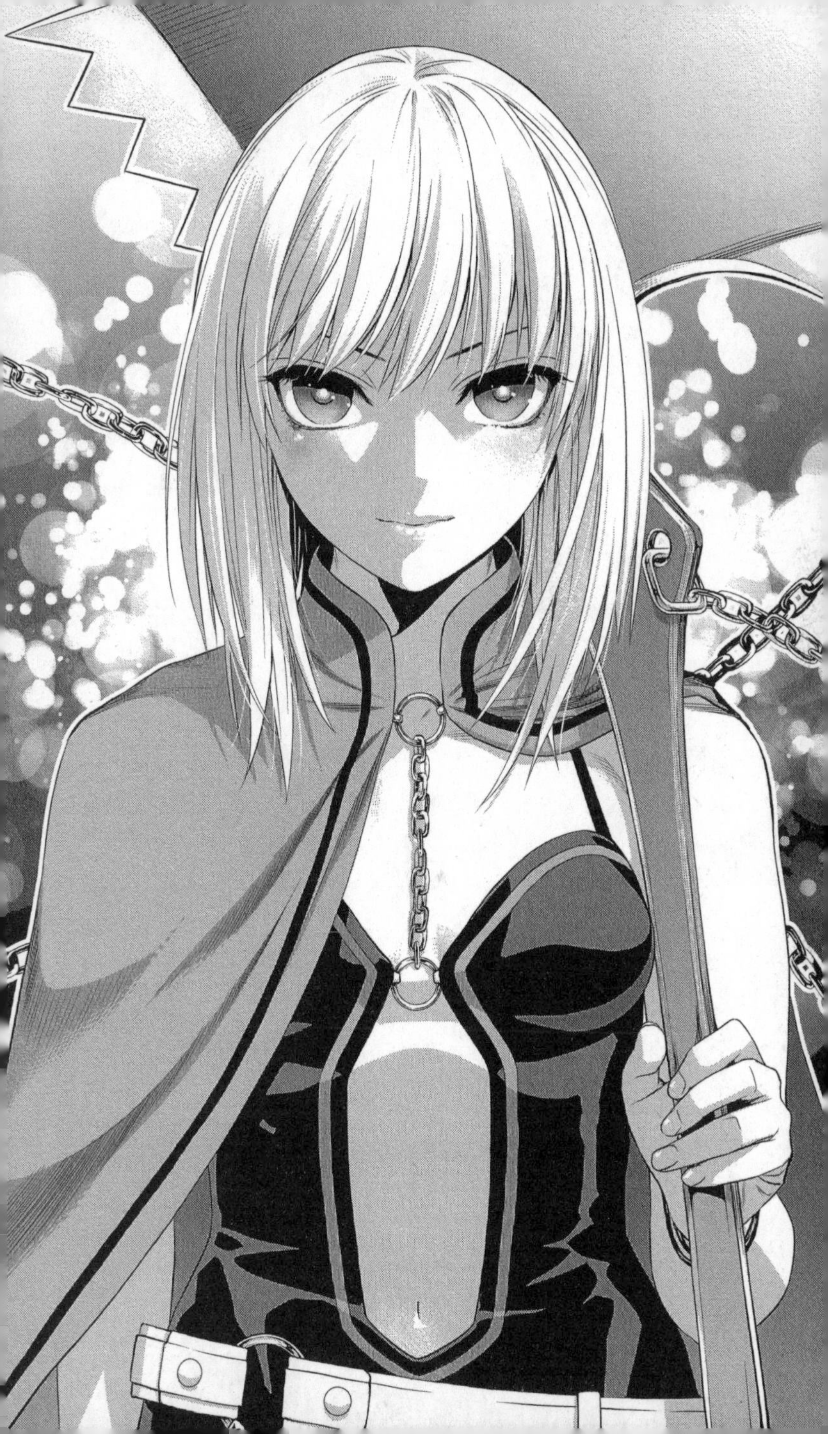

I'M THIS CLOSE TO PASSING OUT FROM THE PAIN.

MY BODY IS WAY PAST ITS LIMIT.

EVEN SO—

POSSESS ME, KAI!

WE'RE PUTTING DAGON DOWN RIGHT HERE, RIGHT NOW!

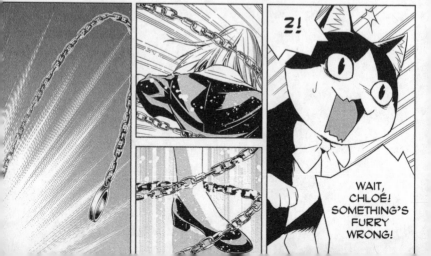

?!

WAIT, CHLOÉ! SOMETHING'S FURRY WRONG!

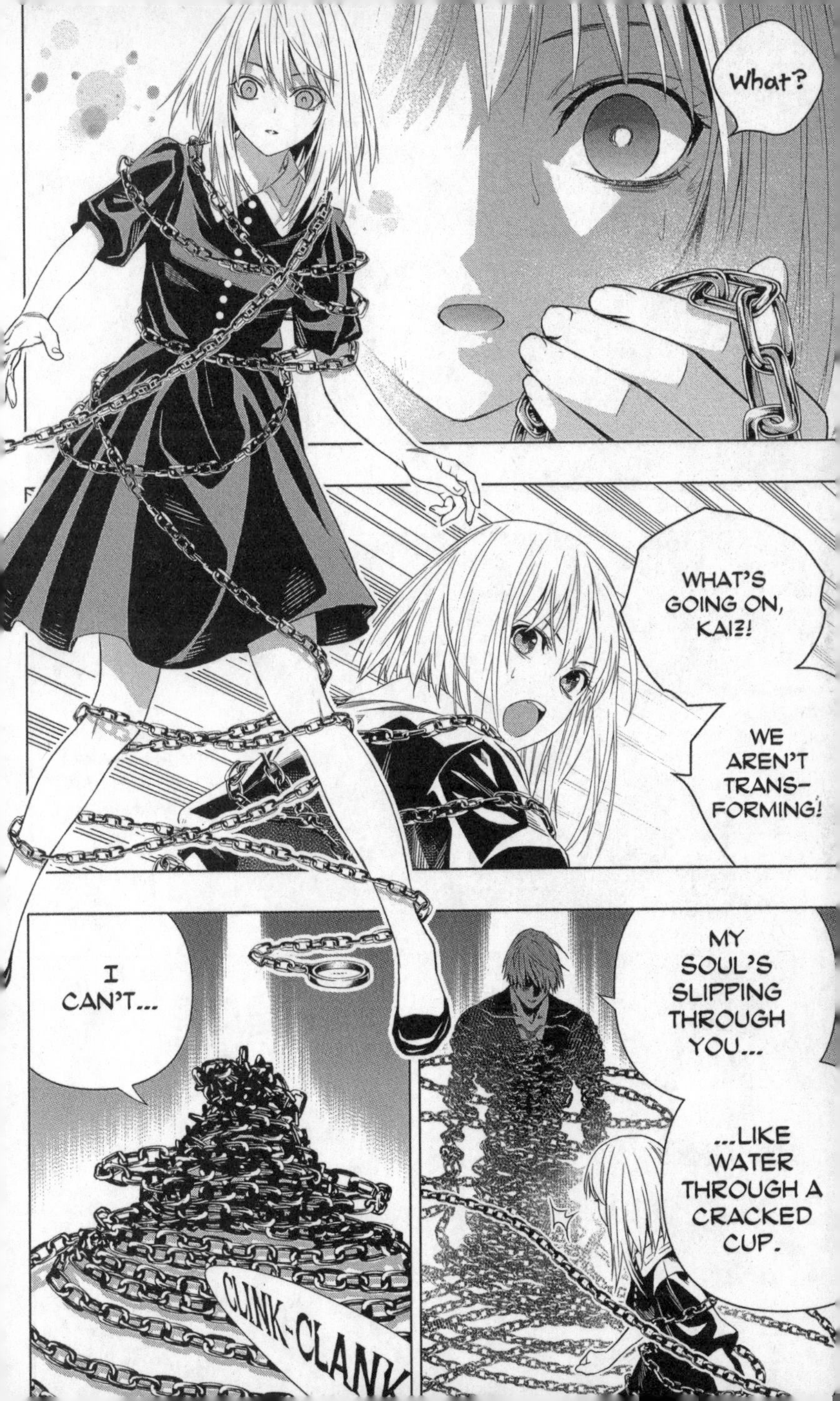

What?
WHAT'S GOING ON, KAI?!
WE AREN'T TRANS-FORMING!
I CAN'T...
CLINK-CLANK
MY SOUL'S SLIPPING THROUGH YOU...
...LIKE WATER THROUGH A CRACKED CUP.

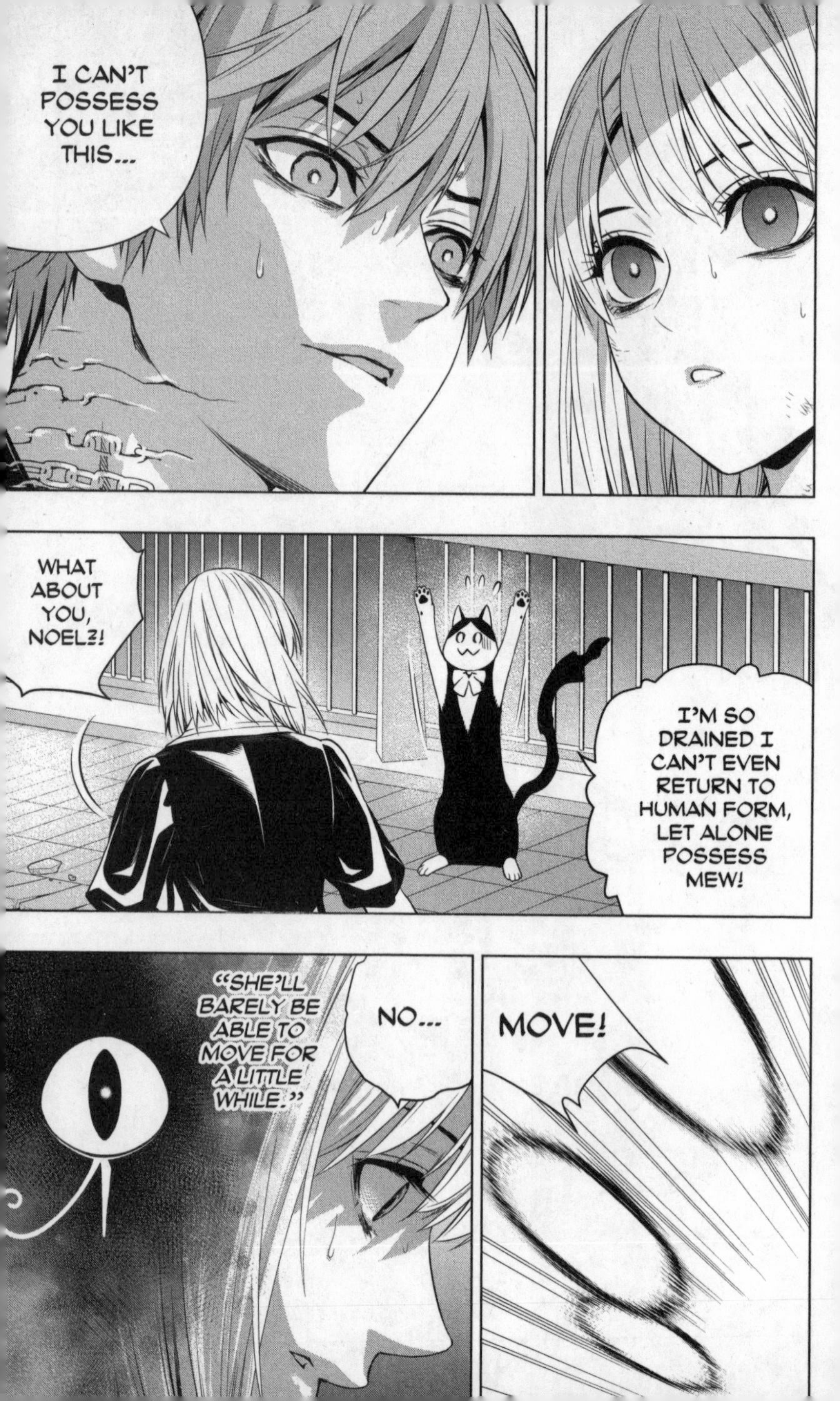
I CAN'T POSSESS YOU LIKE THIS...
WHAT ABOUT YOU, NOEL?!
I'M SO DRAINED I CAN'T EVEN RETURN TO HUMAN FORM, LET ALONE POSSESS MEW!
MOVE!
NO...
"SHE'LL BARELY BE ABLE TO MOVE FOR A LITTLE WHILE."

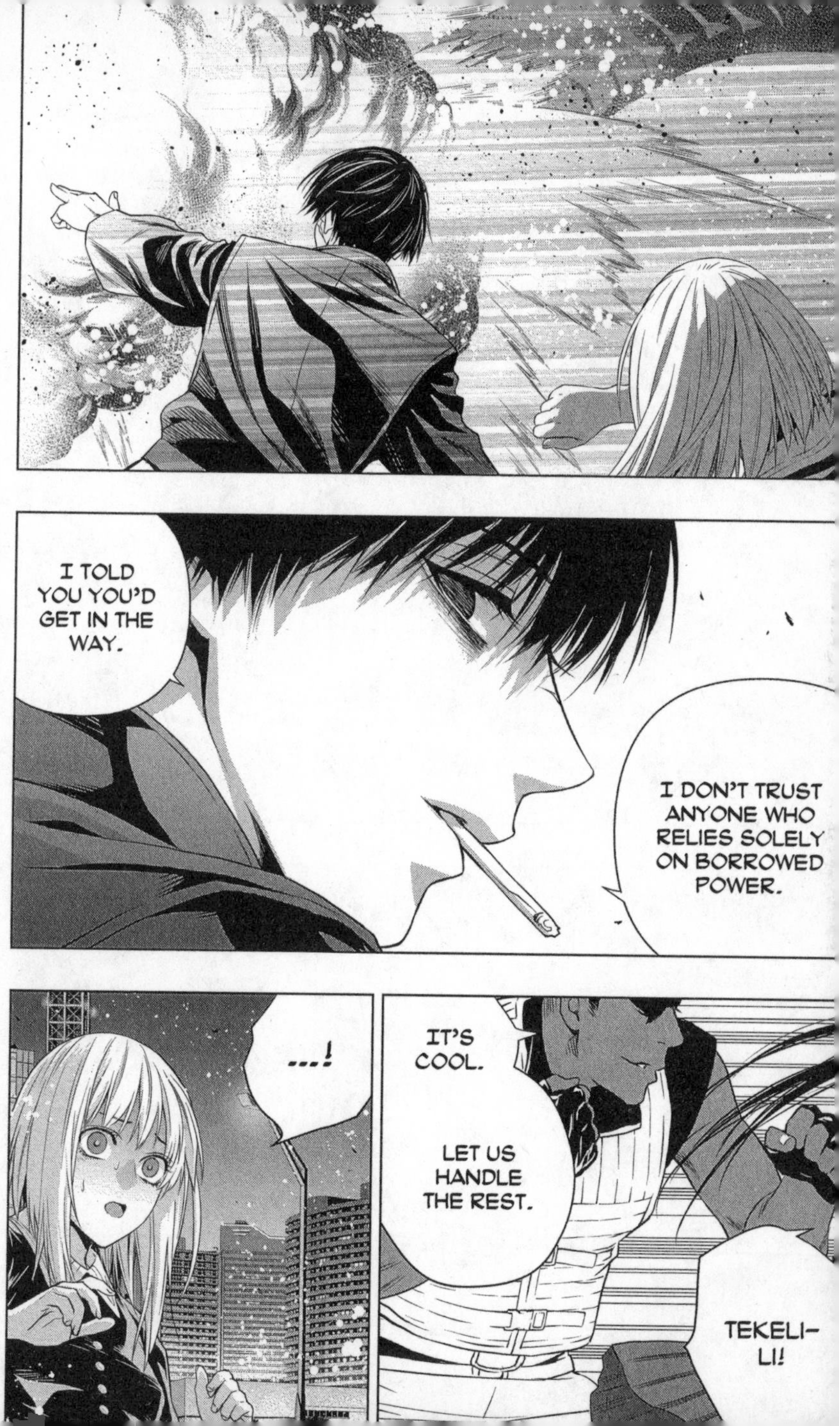
I TOLD YOU YOU'D GET IN THE WAY.
I DON'T TRUST ANYONE WHO RELIES SOLELY ON BORROWED POWER.
...!
IT'S COOL.
LET US HANDLE THE REST.
TEKELI-LI!

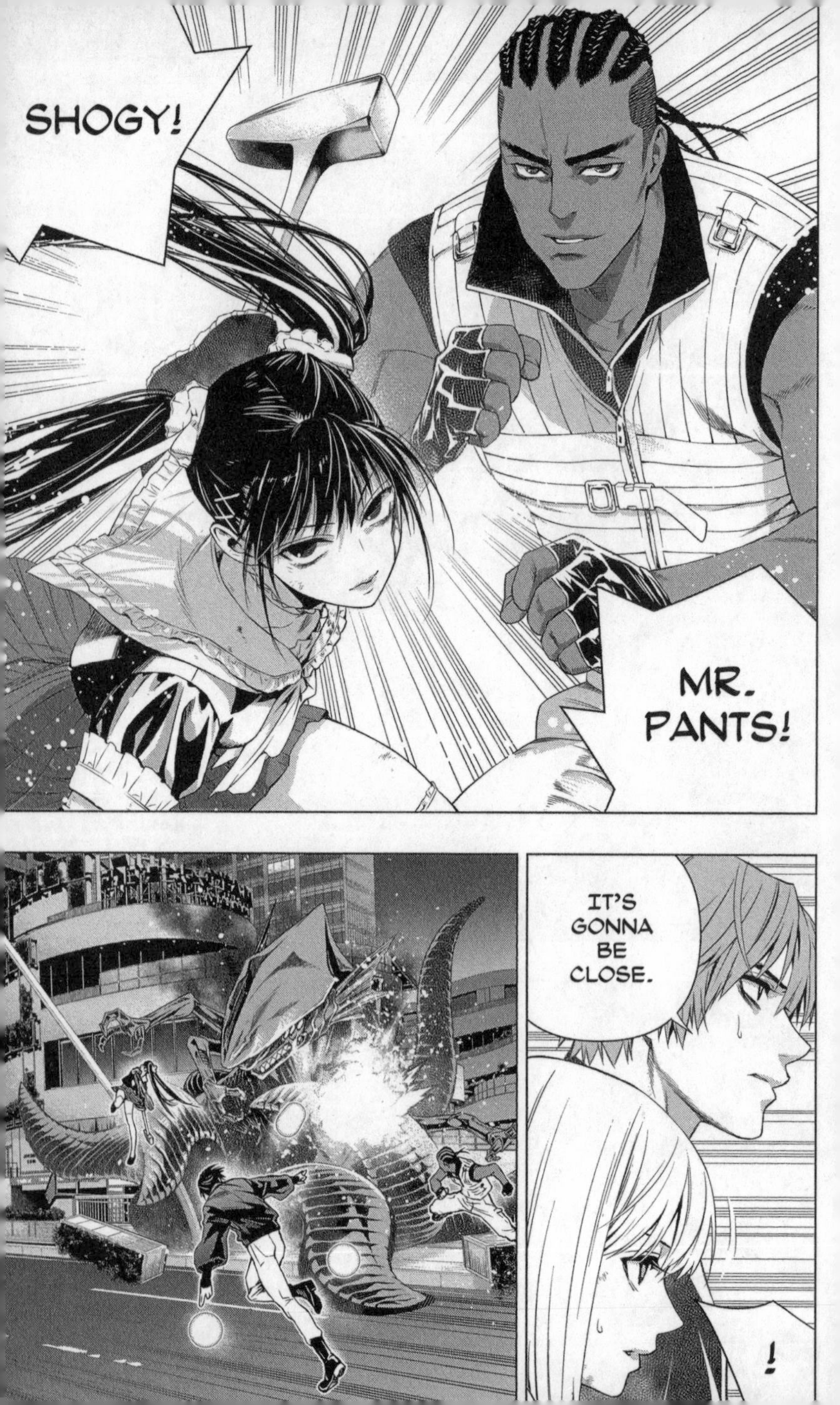
SHOGY!
MR. PANTS!
IT'S GONNA BE CLOSE.
!

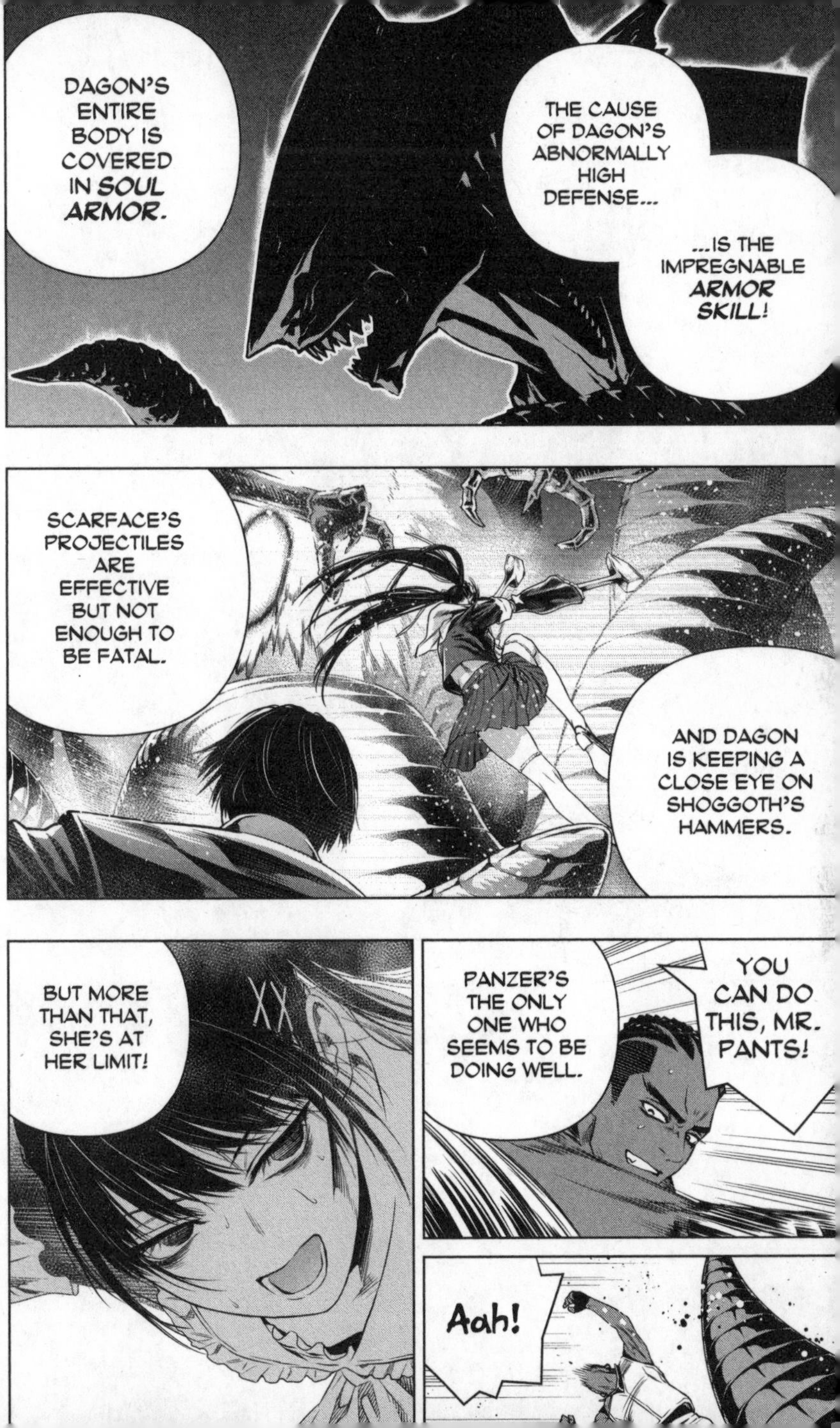

DAGON'S ENTIRE BODY IS COVERED IN SOUL ARMOR.
THE CAUSE OF DAGON'S ABNORMALLY HIGH DEFENSE...
...IS THE IMPREGNABLE ARMOR SKILL!
SCARFACE'S PROJECTILES ARE EFFECTIVE BUT NOT ENOUGH TO BE FATAL.
AND DAGON IS KEEPING A CLOSE EYE ON SHOGGOTH'S HAMMERS.
BUT MORE THAN THAT, SHE'S AT HER LIMIT!
PANZER'S THE ONLY ONE WHO SEEMS TO BE DOING WELL.
YOU CAN DO THIS, MR. PANTS!
Aah!

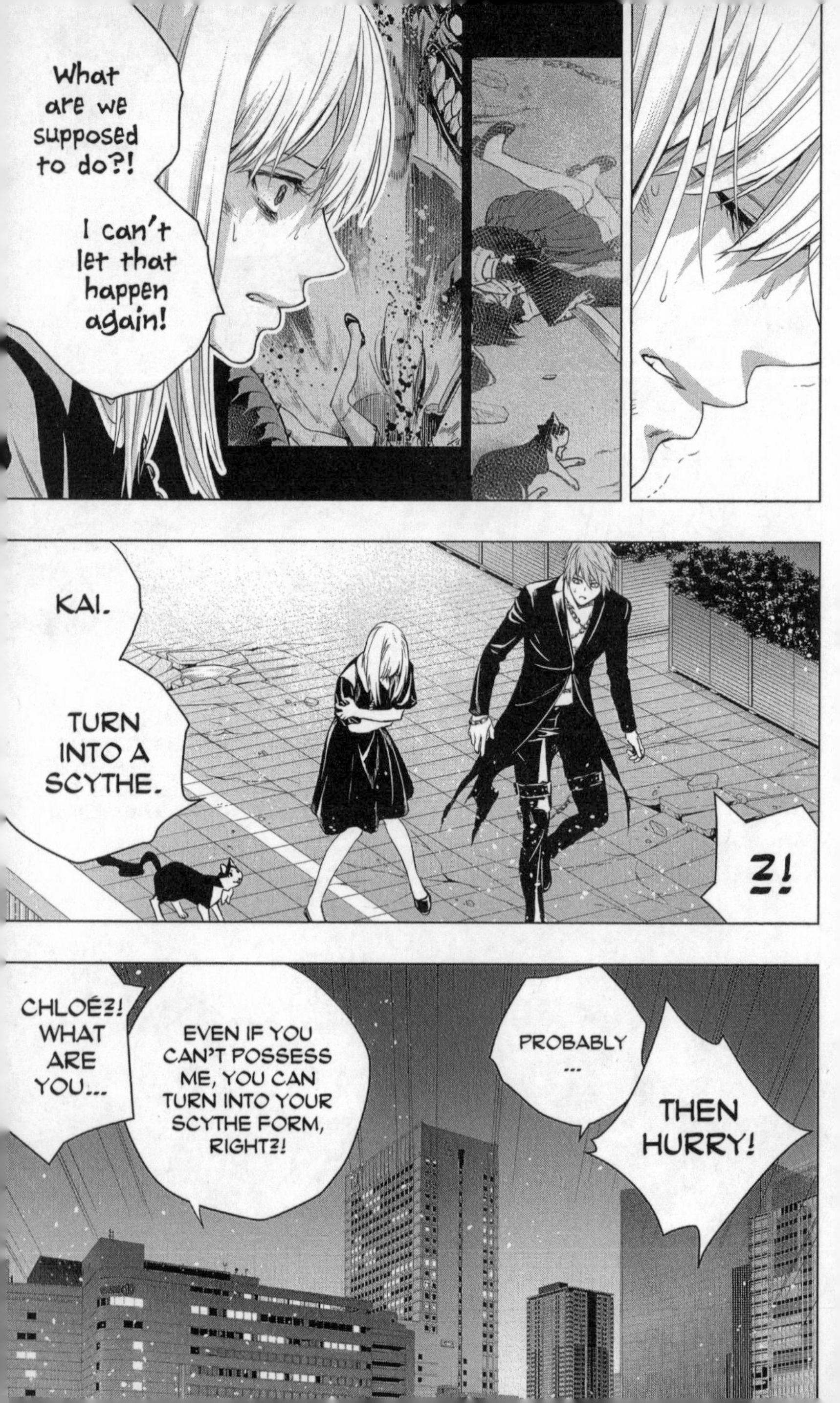
What are we supposed to do?!
I can't let that happen again!
KAI.
TURN INTO A SCYTHE.
?!
CHLOÉ?! WHAT ARE YOU...
EVEN IF YOU CAN'T POSSESS ME, YOU CAN TURN INTO YOUR SCYTHE FORM, RIGHT?!
PROBABLY...
THEN HURRY!

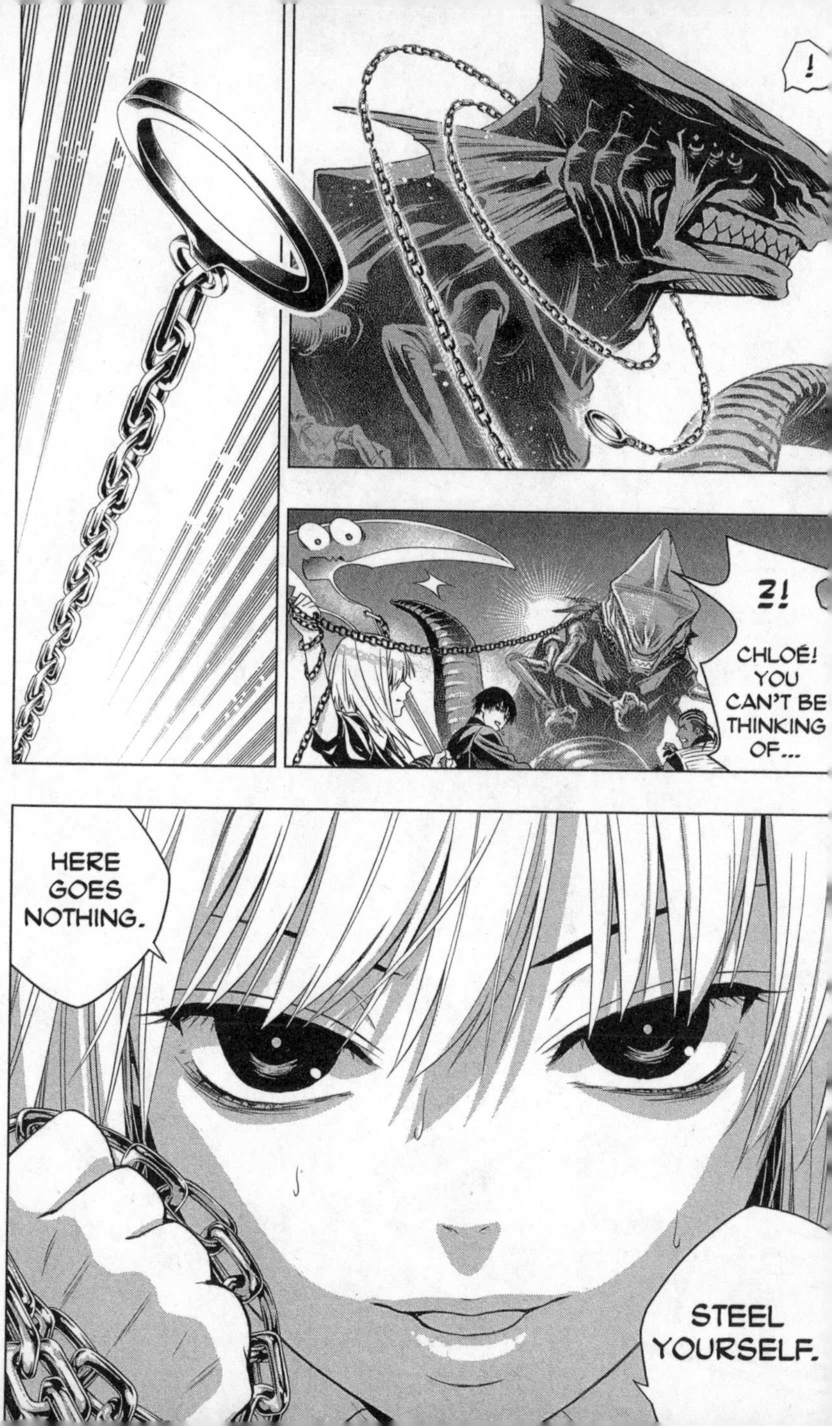
!
Z!
CHLOÉ! YOU CAN'T BE THINKING OF...
HERE GOES NOTHING.
STEEL YOURSELF.

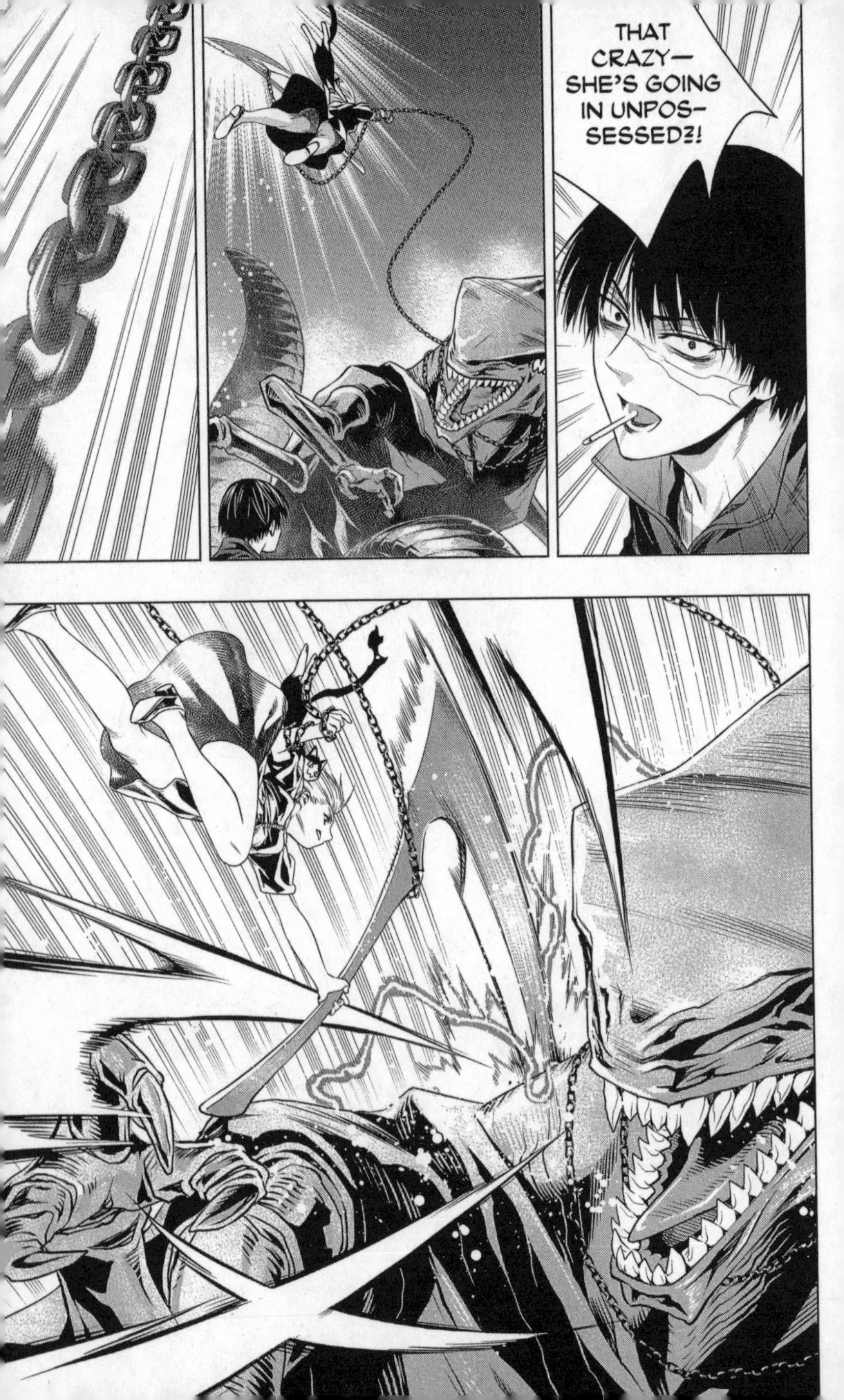
THAT CRAZY—SHE'S GOING IN UNPOSSESSED?!

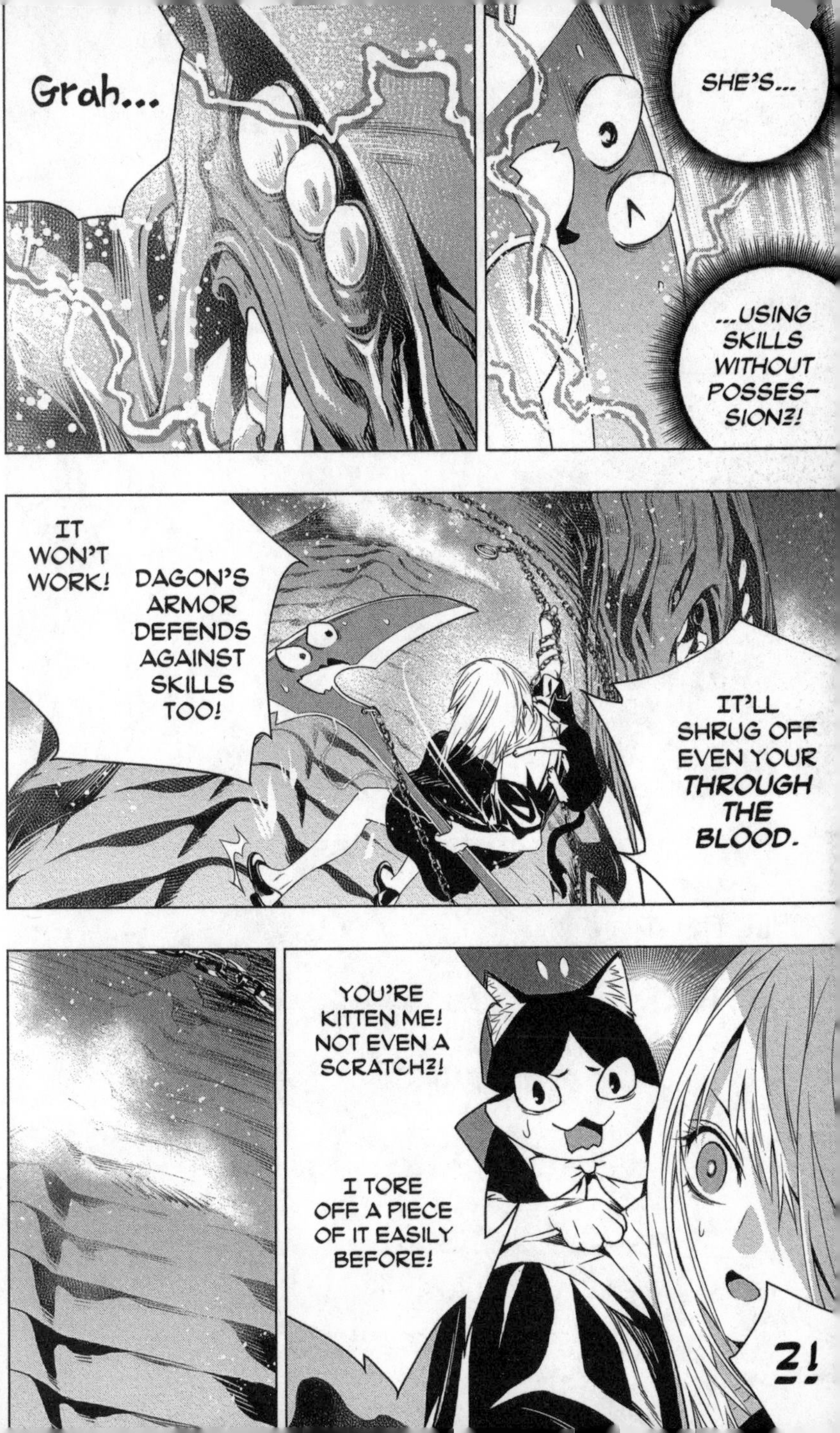

Grah...
SHE'S...
...USING SKILLS WITHOUT POSSESSION?!
IT WON'T WORK!
DAGON'S ARMOR DEFENDS AGAINST SKILLS TOO!
IT'LL SHRUG OFF EVEN YOUR THROUGH THE BLOOD.
YOU'RE KITTEN ME! NOT EVEN A SCRATCH?!
I TORE OFF A PIECE OF IT EASILY BEFORE!
?!

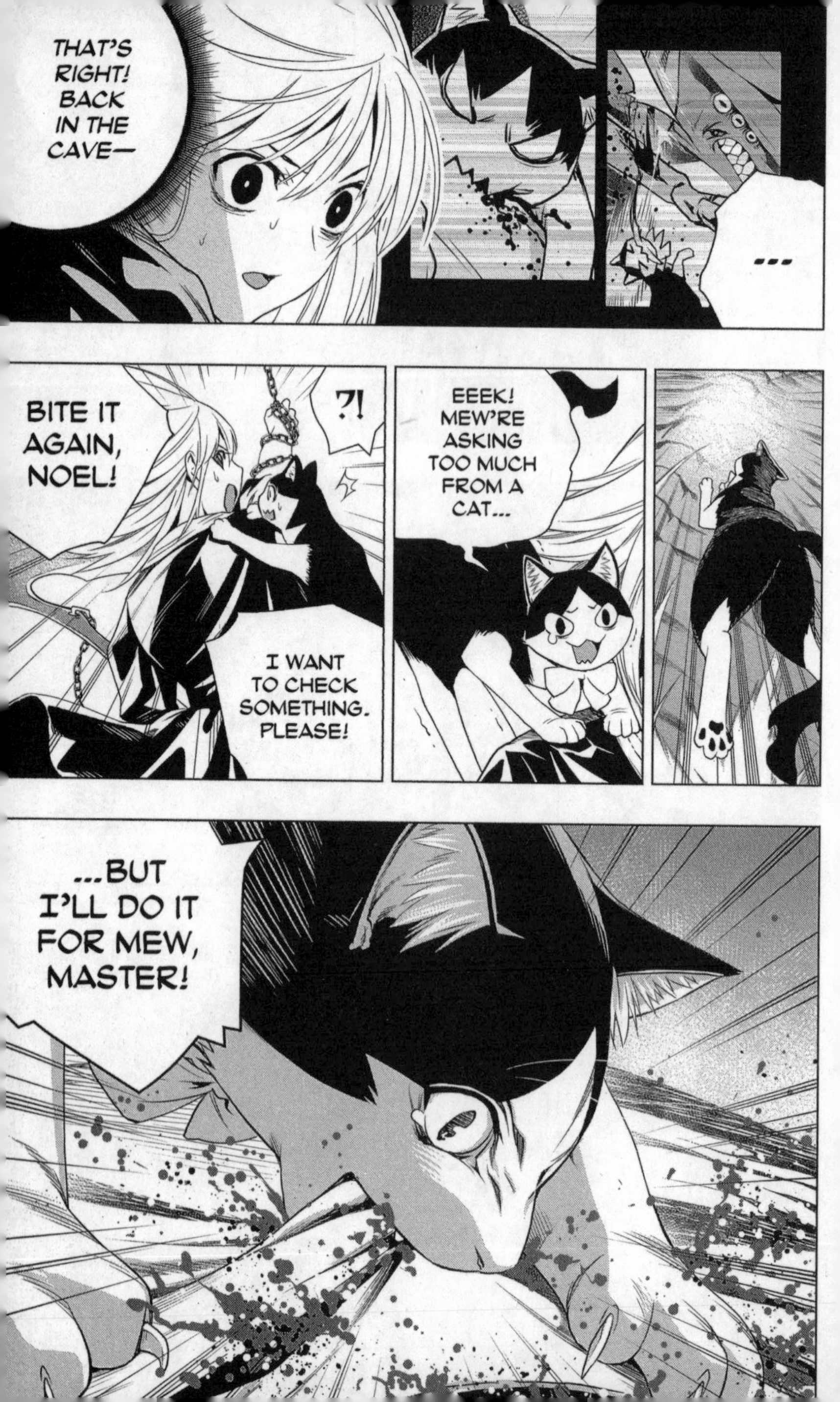
THAT'S RIGHT! BACK IN THE CAVE—
...
BITE IT AGAIN, NOEL!
?!
I WANT TO CHECK SOMETHING. PLEASE!
EEEK! MEW'RE ASKING TOO MUCH FROM A CAT...
...BUT I'LL DO IT FOR MEW, MASTER!

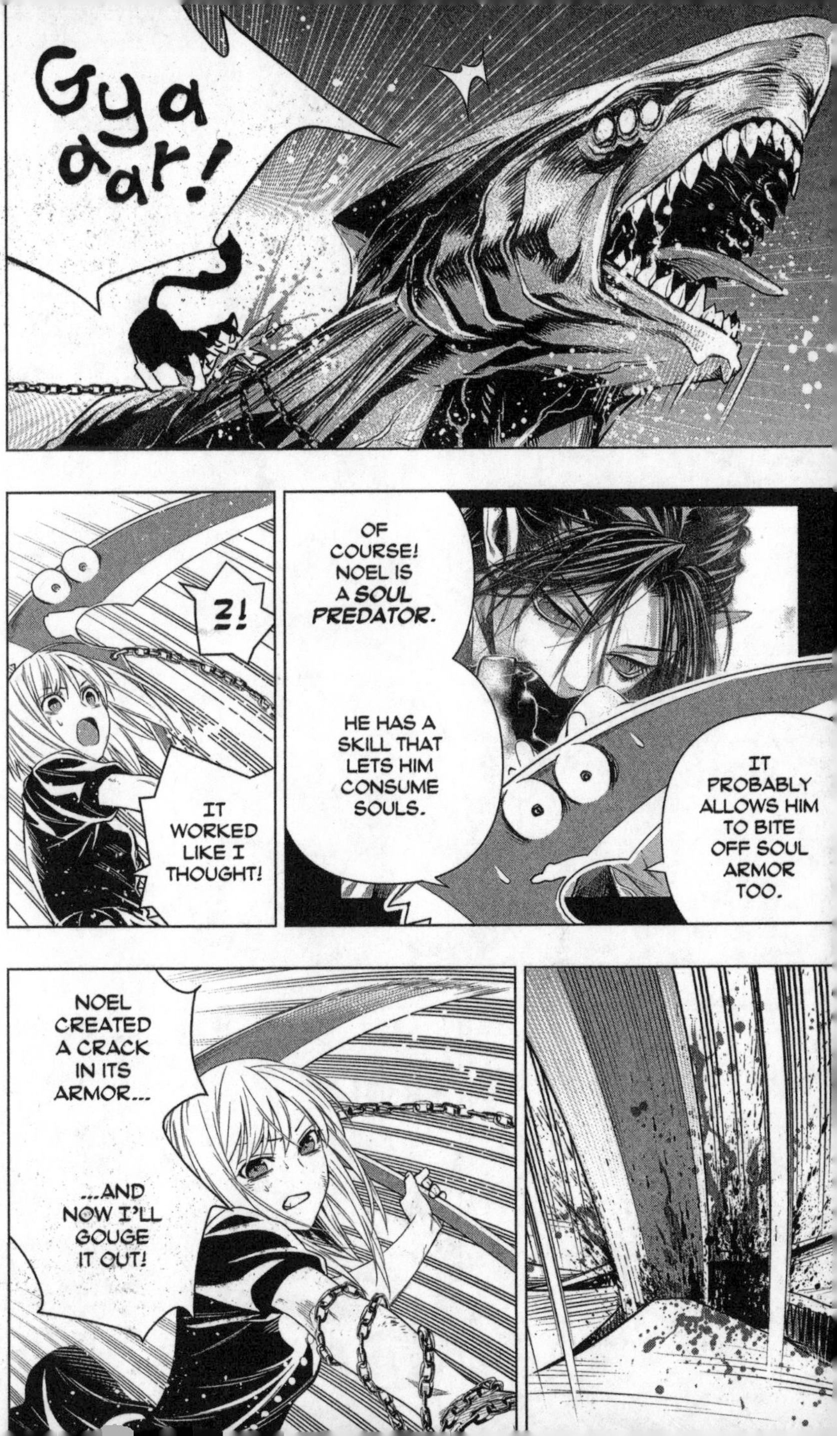
Gyaaar!
?!
IT WORKED LIKE I THOUGHT!
OF COURSE! NOEL IS A SOUL PREDATOR.
HE HAS A SKILL THAT LETS HIM CONSUME SOULS.
IT PROBABLY ALLOWS HIM TO BITE OFF SOUL ARMOR TOO.
NOEL CREATED A CRACK IN ITS ARMOR...
...AND NOW I'LL GOUGE IT OUT!

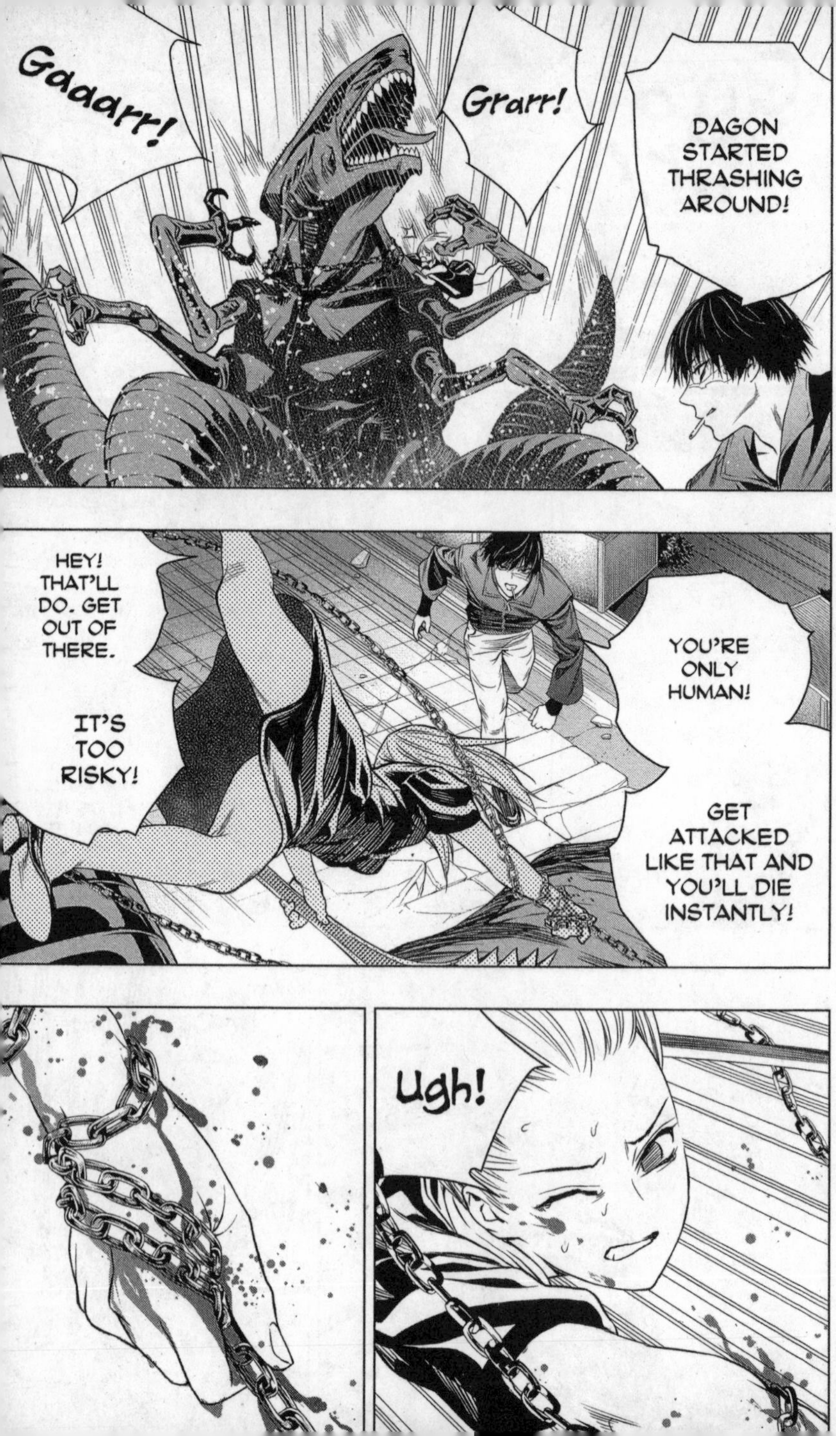
Gaaarr!
Grarr!
DAGON STARTED THRASHING AROUND!
HEY! THAT'LL DO. GET OUT OF THERE.
IT'S TOO RISKY!
YOU'RE ONLY HUMAN!
GET ATTACKED LIKE THAT AND YOU'LL DIE INSTANTLY!
Ugh!

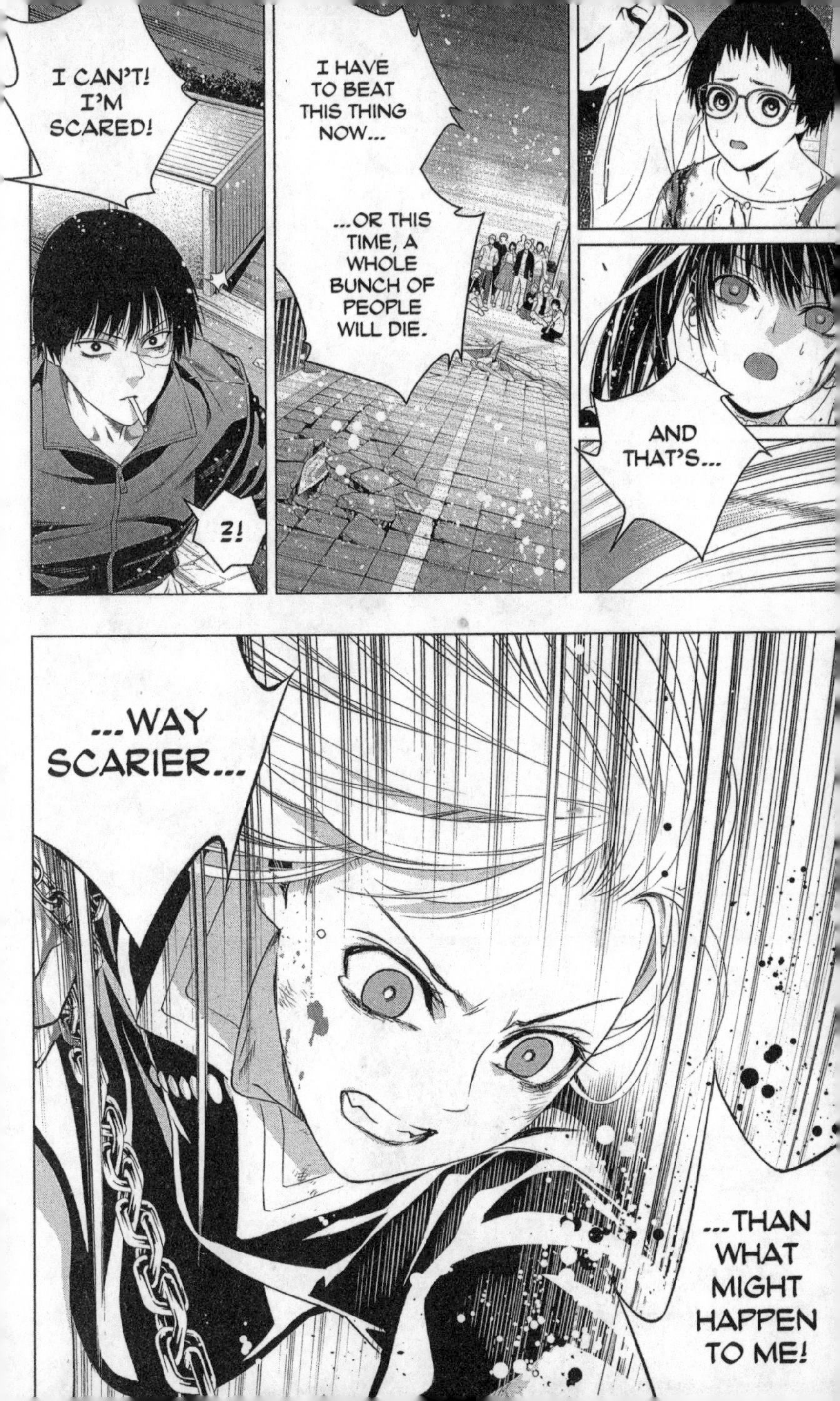
I CAN'T! I'M SCARED!
?!
I HAVE TO BEAT THIS THING NOW...
...OR THIS TIME, A WHOLE BUNCH OF PEOPLE WILL DIE.
AND THAT'S...
...WAY SCARIER...
...THAN WHAT MIGHT HAPPEN TO ME!

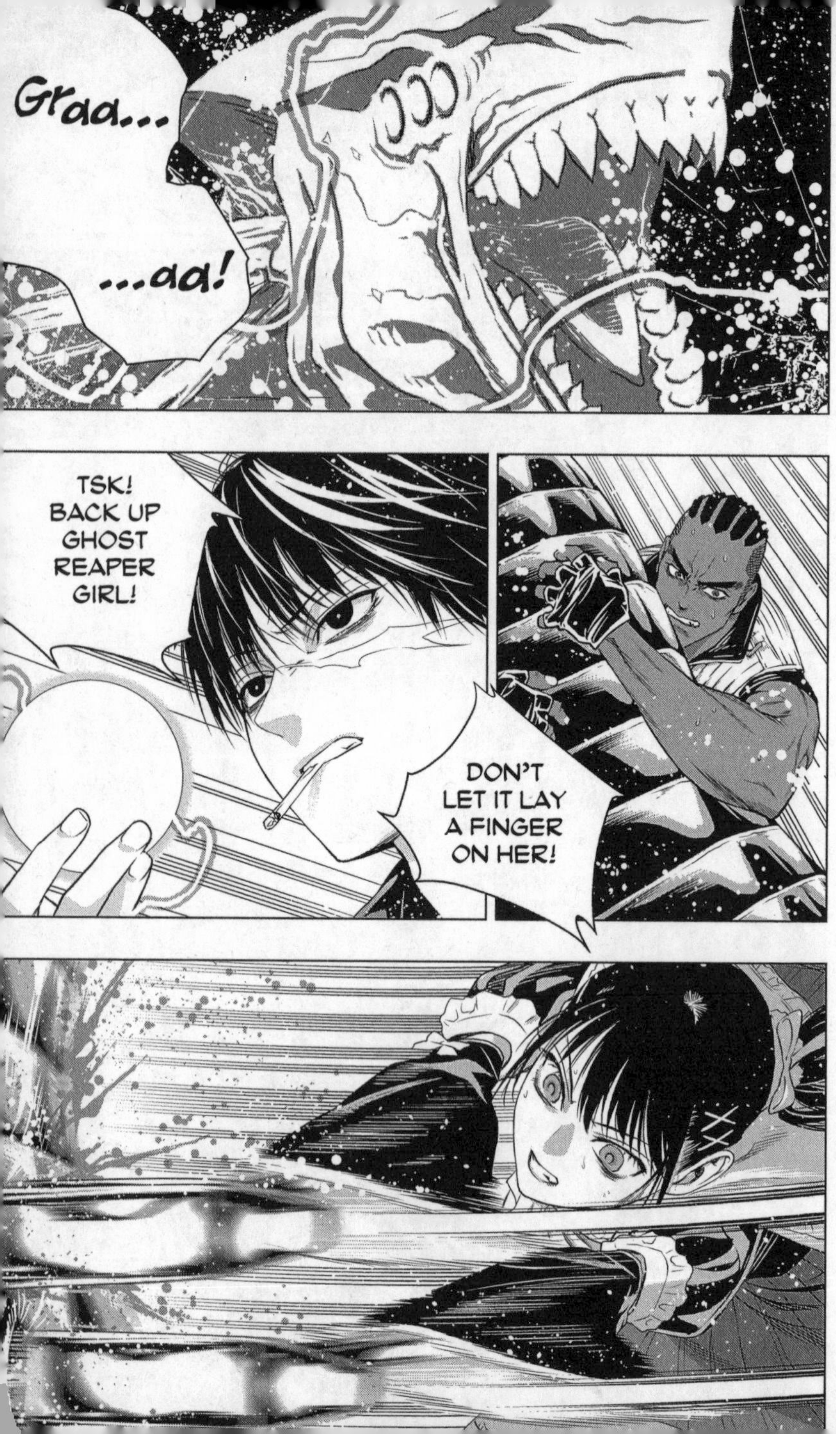
Graa...
...aa!
TSK! BACK UP GHOST REAPER GIRL!
DON'T LET IT LAY A FINGER ON HER!

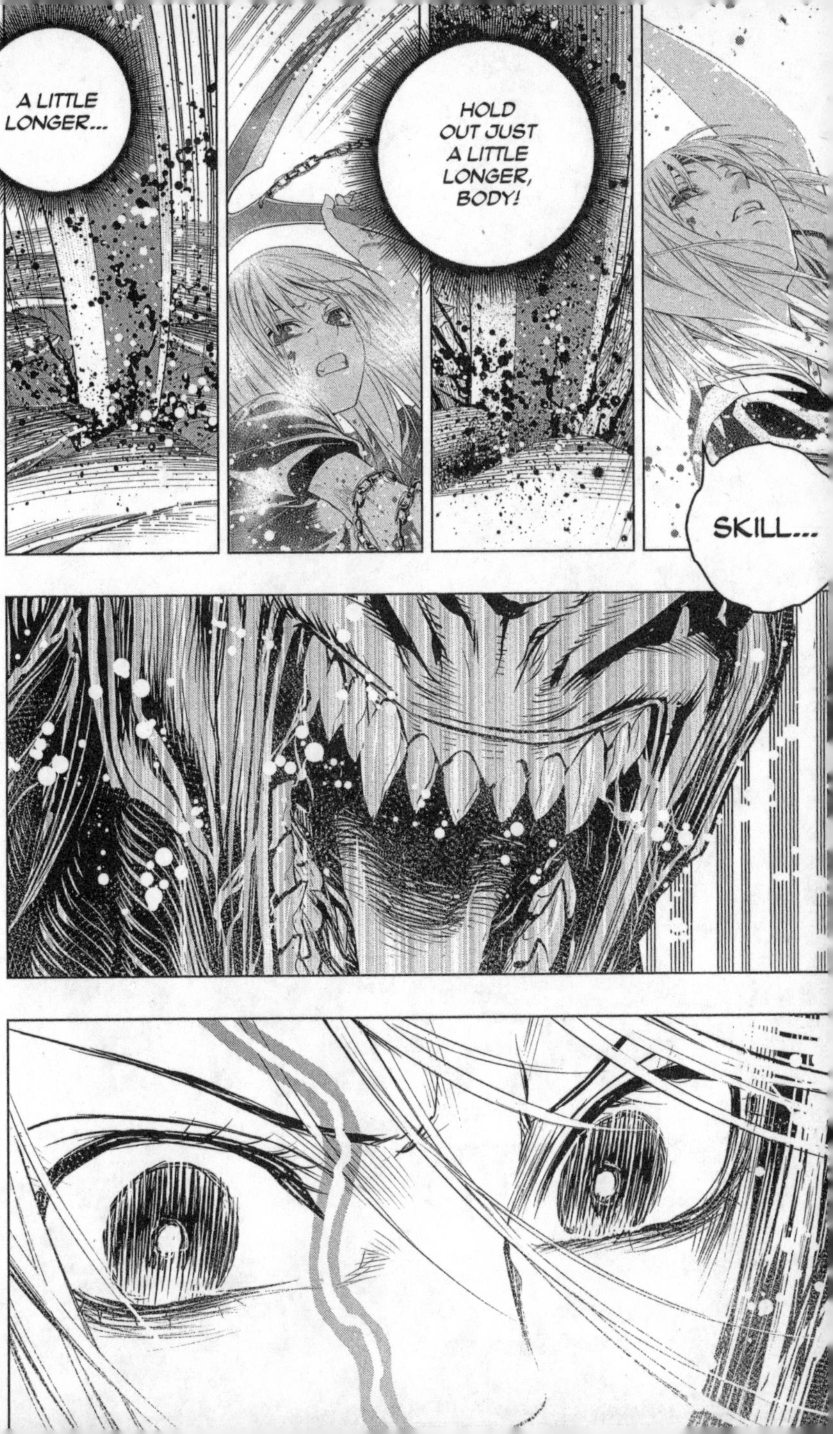
A LITTLE LONGER...
HOLD OUT JUST A LITTLE LONGER, BODY!
SKILL...

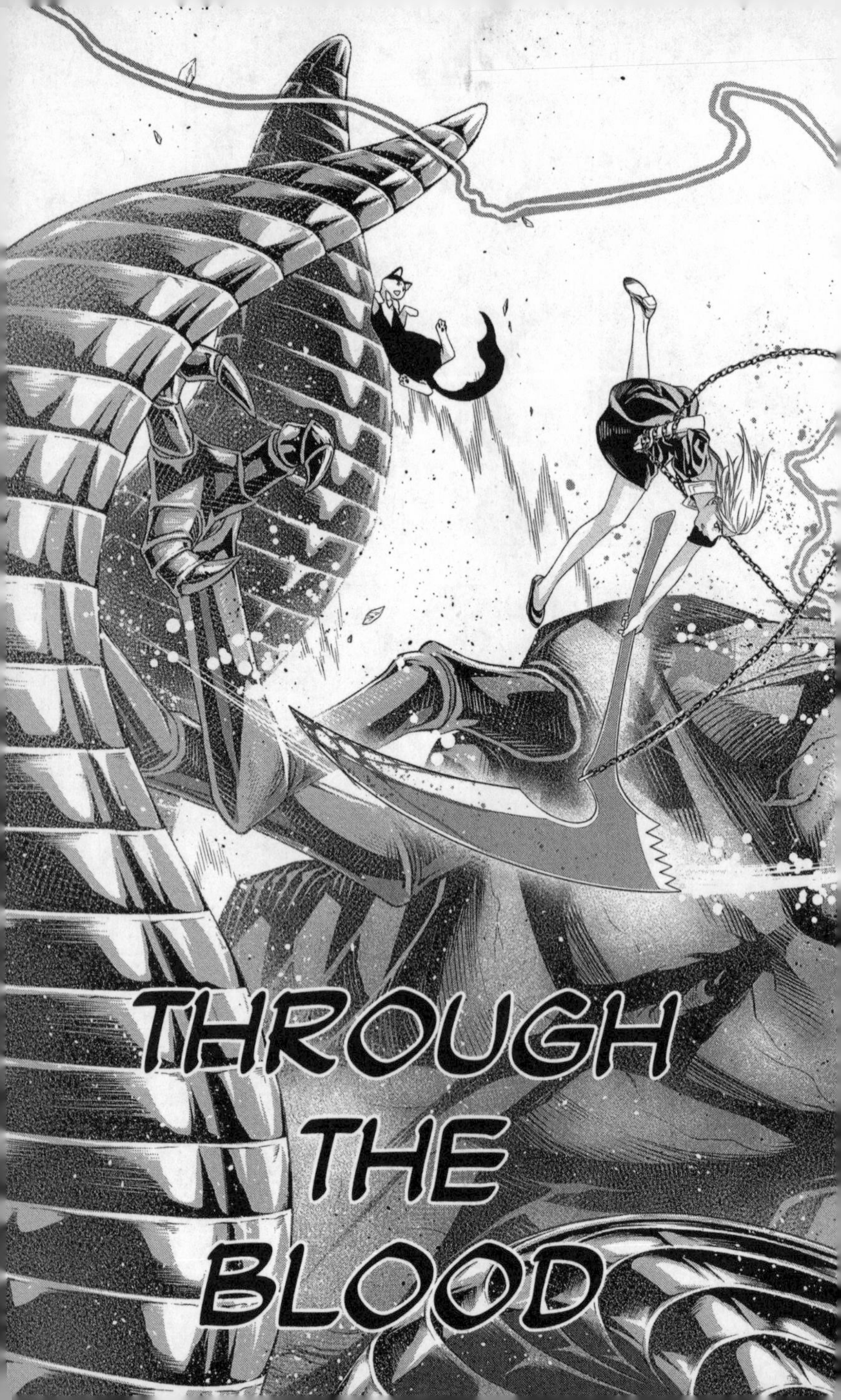
THROUGH
THE
BLOOD

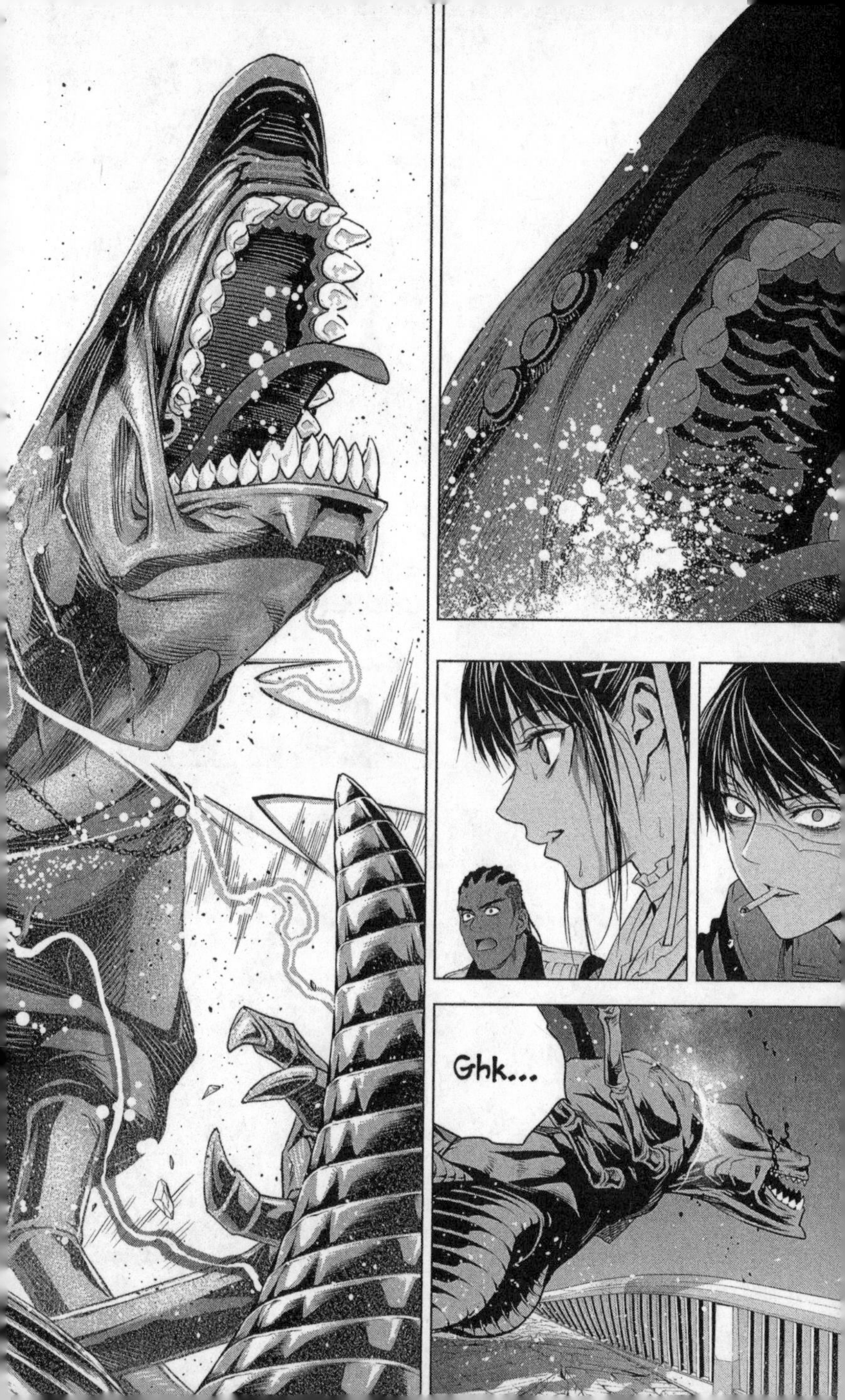
Ghk...

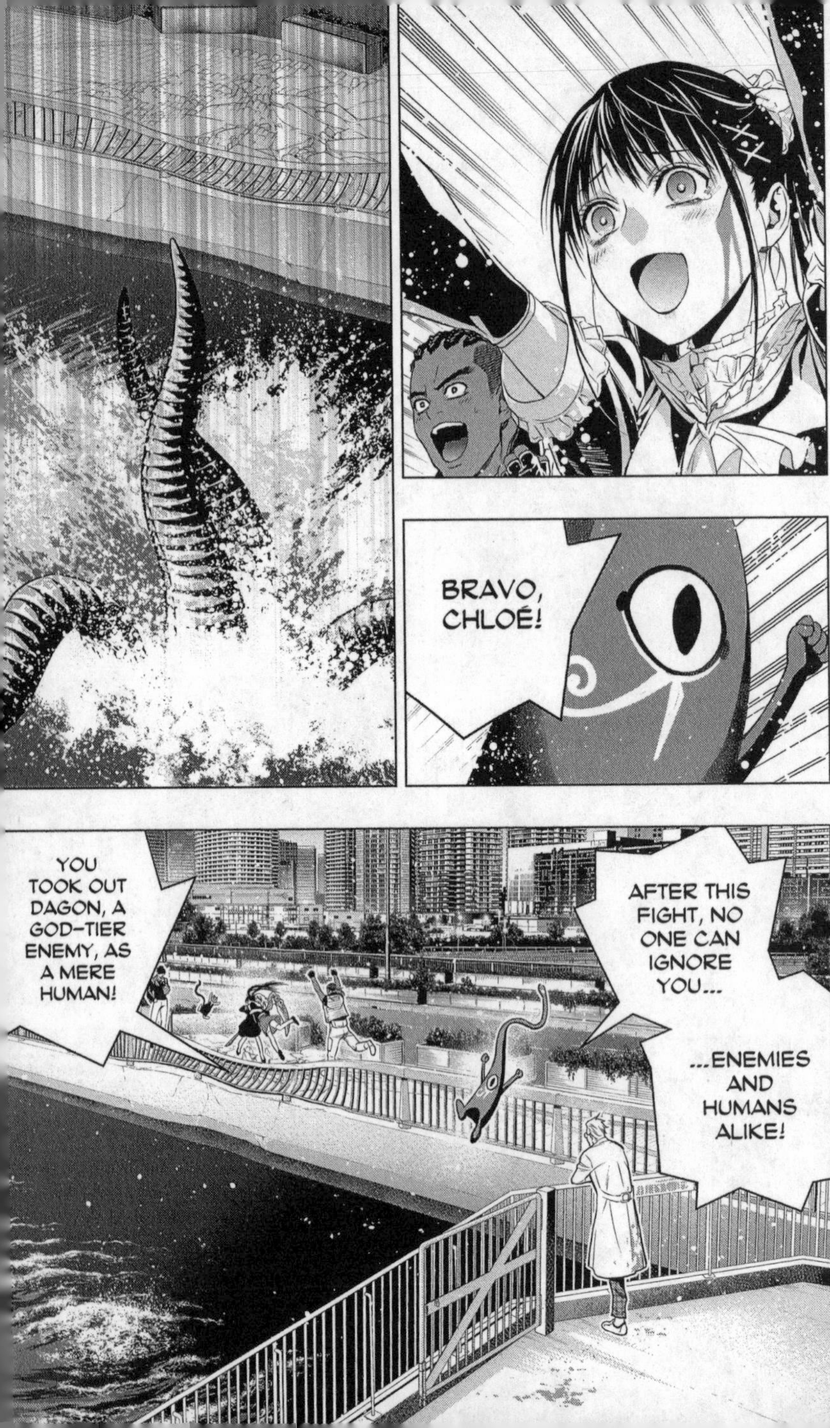
BRAVO, CHLOÉ!
YOU TOOK OUT DAGON, A GOD-TIER ENEMY, AS A MERE HUMAN!
AFTER THIS FIGHT, NO ONE CAN IGNORE YOU...
...ENEMIES AND HUMANS ALIKE!

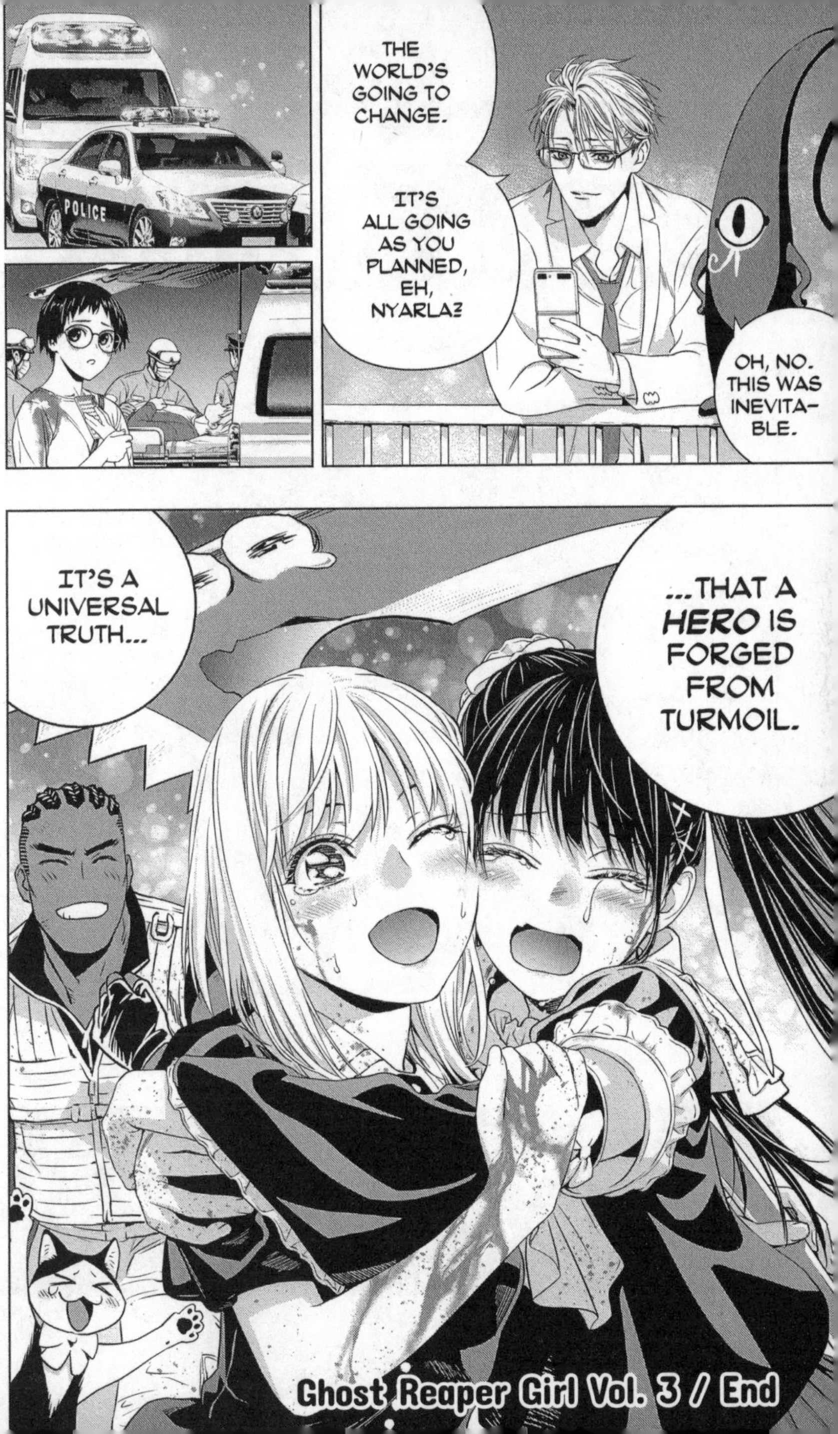
THE WORLD'S GOING TO CHANGE.
IT'S ALL GOING AS YOU PLANNED, EH, NYARLA?
OH, NO. THIS WAS INEVITABLE.
IT'S A UNIVERSAL TRUTH...
...THAT A HERO IS FORGED FROM TURMOIL.
Ghost Reaper Girl Vol. 3 / End

Carefree Bonus Theater

OH NO... DAGON CAME AFTER US AGAIN!

THE WINDOW! THE WINDOW!

CHLOÉ, I THINK YOU SHOULD GET SOME REST!

EXHAUSTION AND ALCOHOL ARE A GATEWAY TO MEOWDNESS.

Bonus Chapter 3: Reflections on the Battle

Was That Really a Cat?

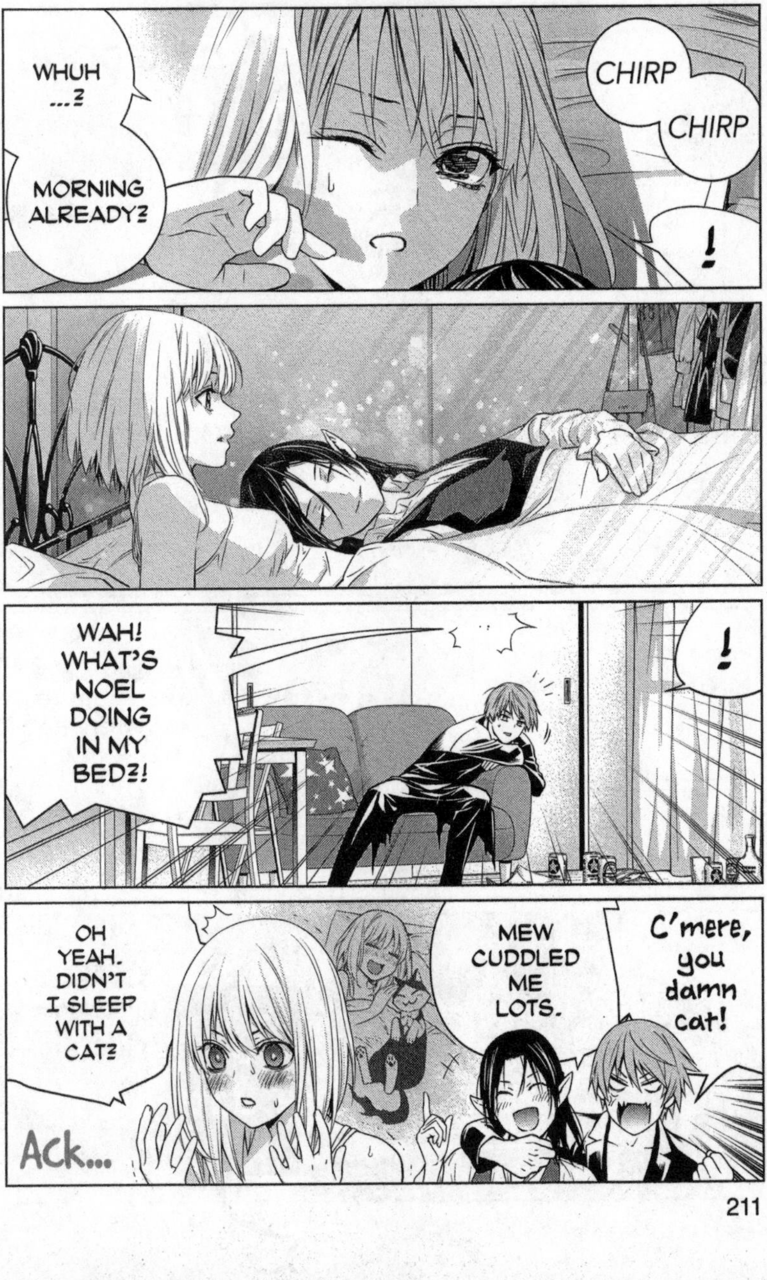
WHUH ...?
MORNING ALREADY?
CHIRP
CHIRP
!
WAH! WHAT'S NOEL DOING IN MY BED?!
!
OH YEAH. DIDN'T I SLEEP WITH A CAT?
MEW CUDDLED ME LOTS.
C'mere, you damn cat!
Ack...

Jealous and Homicidal

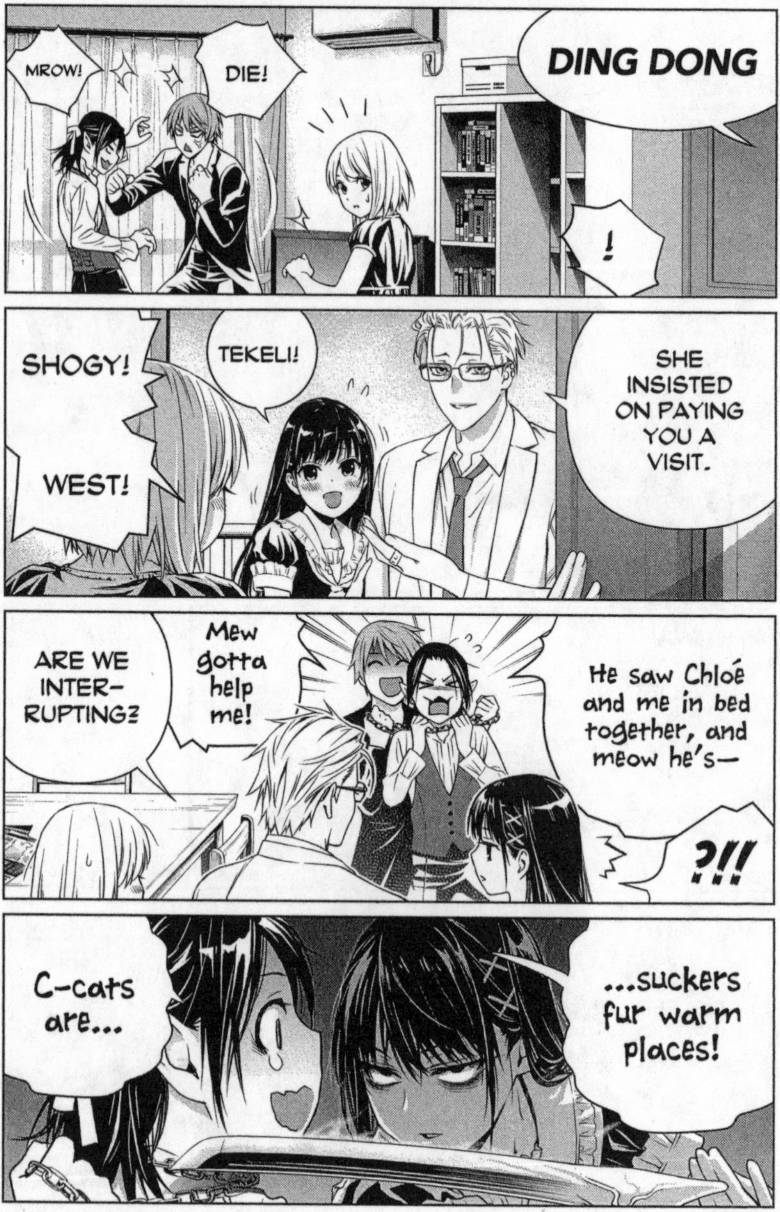

MROW!
DIE!
DING DONG
!
SHOGY!
WEST!
TEKELI!
SHE INSISTED ON PAYING YOU A VISIT.
ARE WE INTER-RUPTING?
Mew gotta help me!
He saw Chloé and me in bed together, and meow he's—
?!!
C-cats are...
...suckers fur warm places!

Chemistry

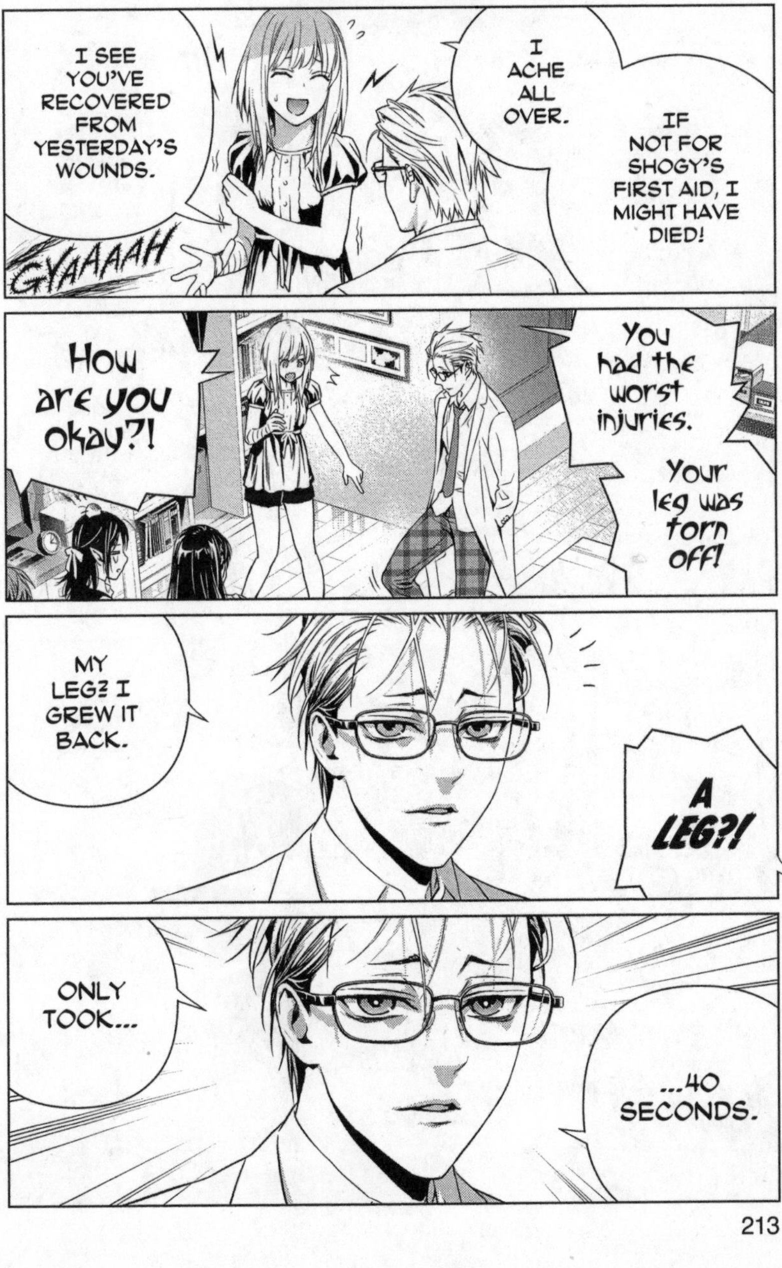
I SEE YOU'VE RECOVERED FROM YESTERDAY'S WOUNDS.
GYAAAAH
I ACHE ALL OVER.
IF NOT FOR SHOGY'S FIRST AID, I MIGHT HAVE DIED!
How are you okay?!
You had the worst injuries.
Your leg was torn off!
MY LEG? I GREW IT BACK.
A LEG?!
ONLY TOOK...
...40 SECONDS.

He Did Take Those

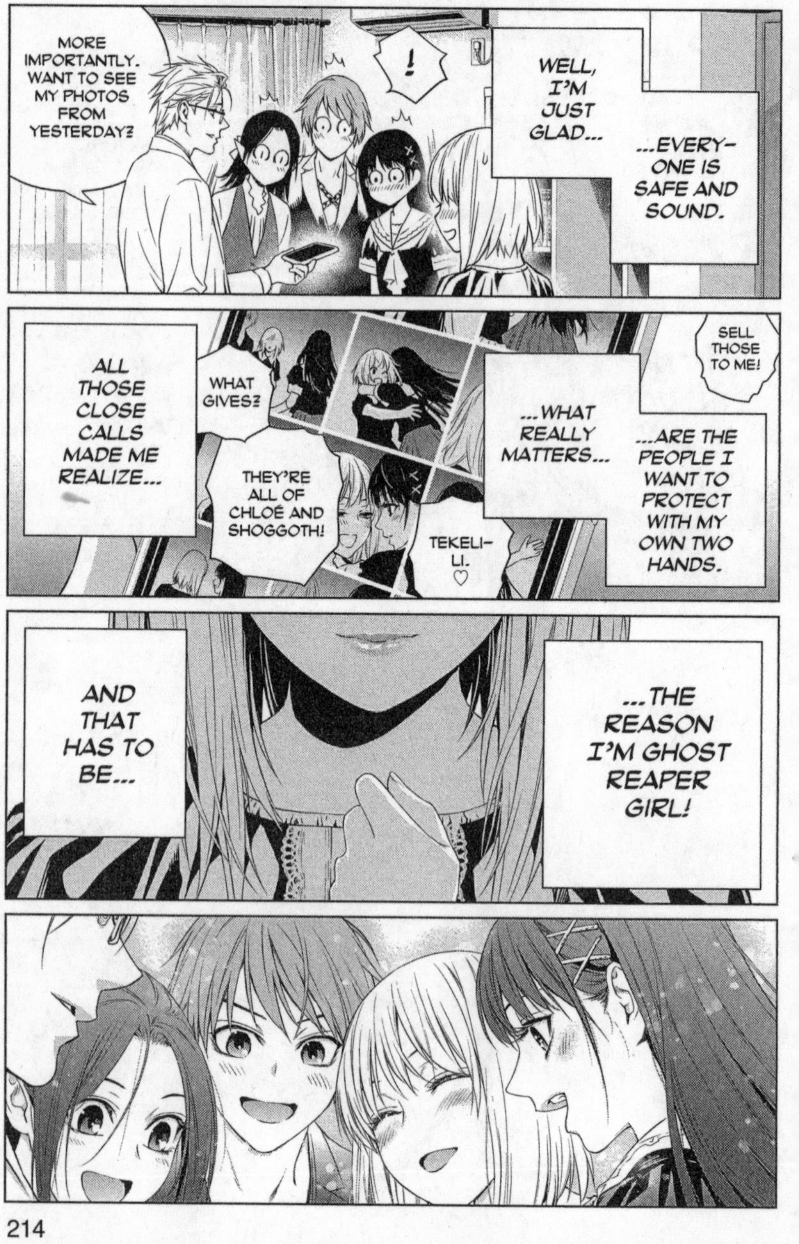
MORE IMPORTANTLY. WANT TO SEE MY PHOTOS FROM YESTERDAY?
!
WELL, I'M JUST GLAD...
...EVERYONE IS SAFE AND SOUND.
ALL THOSE CLOSE CALLS MADE ME REALIZE...
WHAT GIVES?
THEY'RE ALL OF CHLOÉ AND SHOGGOTH!
TEKELI-LI. ♡
...WHAT REALLY MATTERS...
...ARE THE PEOPLE I WANT TO PROTECT WITH MY OWN TWO HANDS.
SELL THOSE TO ME!
AND THAT HAS TO BE...
...THE REASON I'M GHOST REAPER GIRL!

Why?

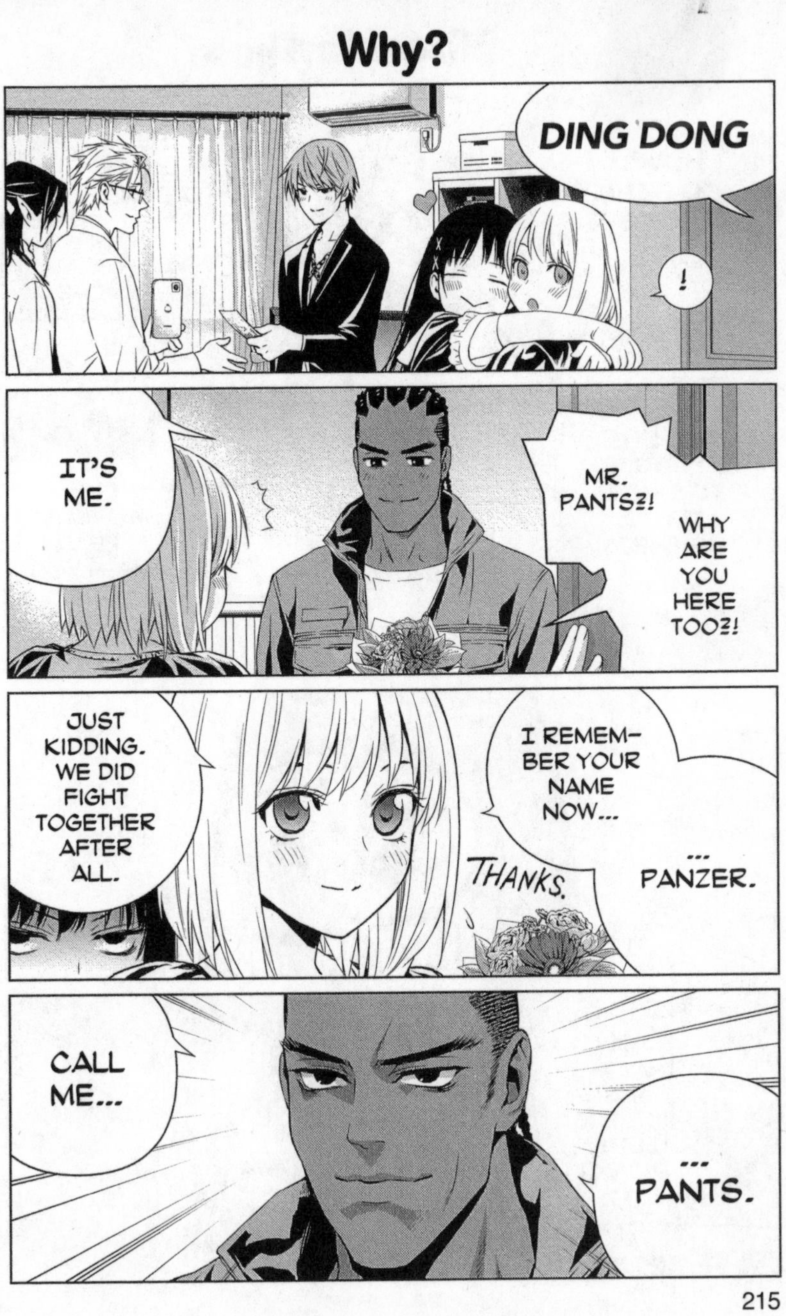
DING DONG
!
IT'S ME.
MR. PANTS?!
WHY ARE YOU HERE TOO?!
JUST KIDDING. WE DID FIGHT TOGETHER AFTER ALL.
I REMEM-BER YOUR NAME NOW...
THANKS.
... PANZER.
CALL ME...
... PANTS.

Creeping

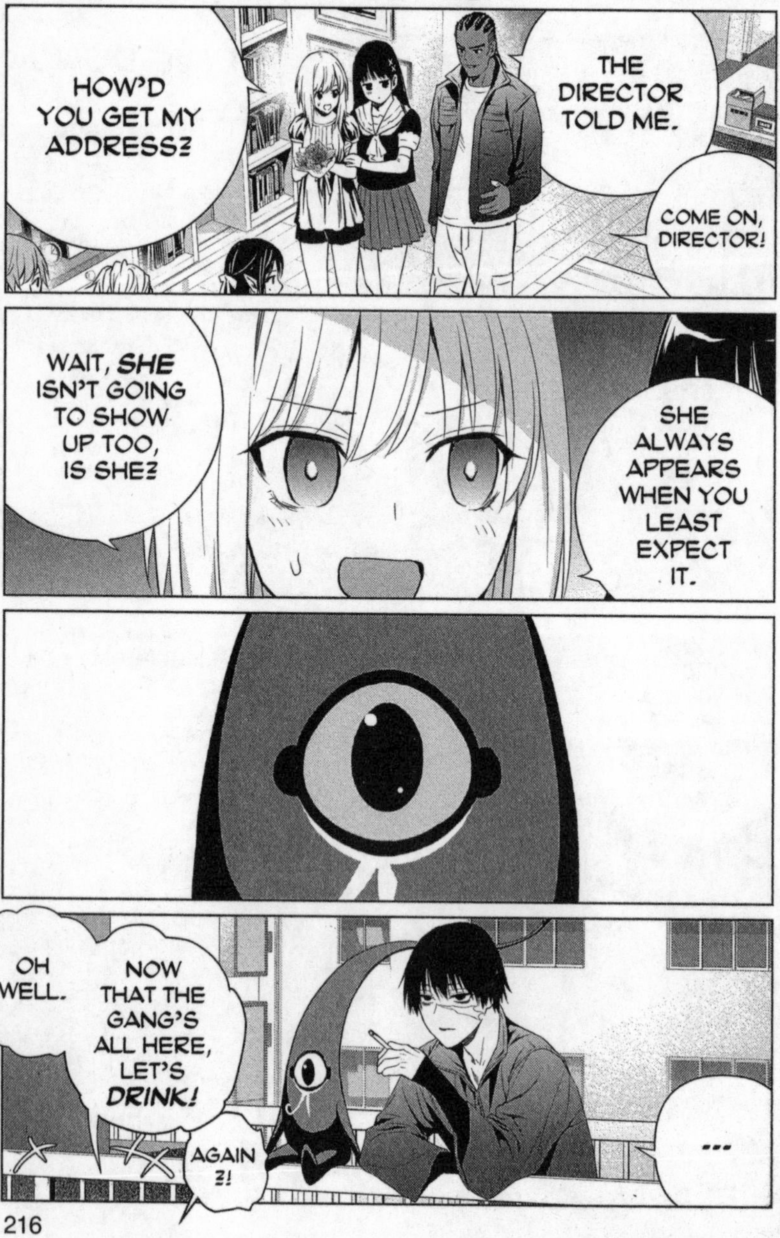

HOW'D YOU GET MY ADDRESS?
THE DIRECTOR TOLD ME.
COME ON, DIRECTOR!
WAIT, *SHE* ISN'T GOING TO SHOW UP TOO, IS SHE?
SHE ALWAYS APPEARS WHEN YOU LEAST EXPECT IT.
OH WELL.
NOW THAT THE GANG'S ALL HERE, LET'S *DRINK!*
AGAIN?!
...

Teasing

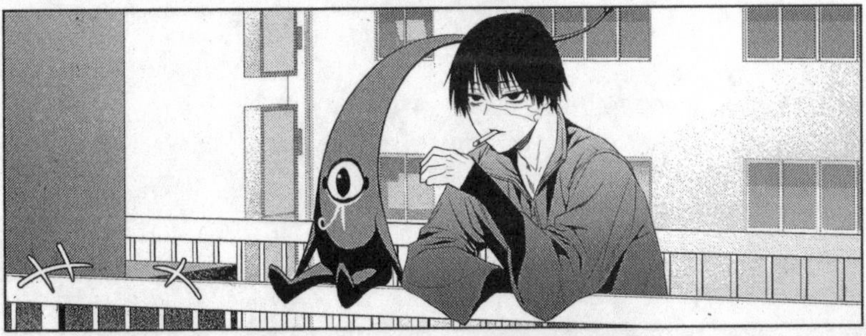

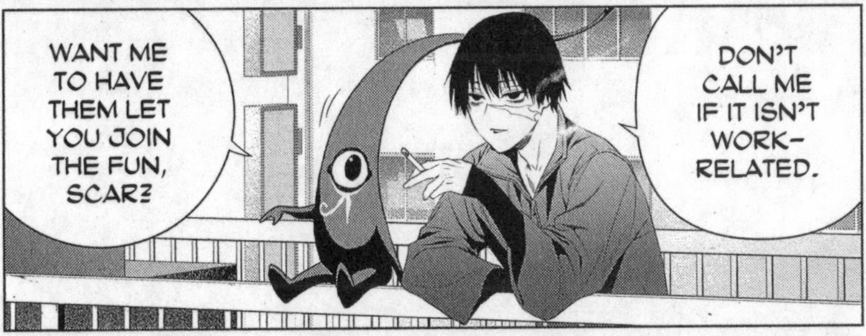
WANT ME TO HAVE THEM LET YOU JOIN THE FUN, SCAR?
DON'T CALL ME IF IT ISN'T WORK-RELATED.

GHOST REAPER GIRL

Staff

Akissa Saiké Rika Shirota Hashimoto Daisuke Nogishi

Editors

Harukata Kasai Satoshi Watanabe

Designer

Daiju Asami

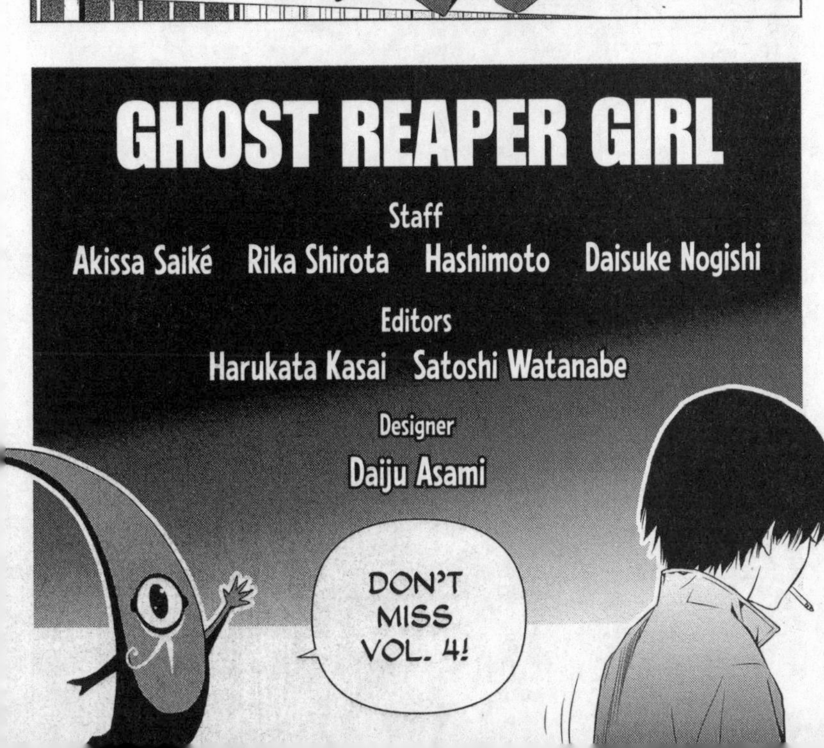
DON'T MISS VOL. 4!

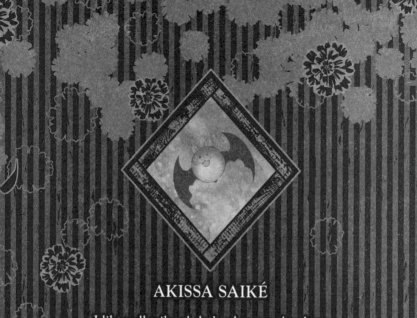

AKISSA SAIKÉ

I like well-tailored clothes because they have
good cost performance.

Good cost performance isn't about cheap prices. It shouldn't be
about saving time either, like only listening to a song's chorus
or watching movie summary videos rather than the full movies.
Shoddily made things won't develop my senses. In terms of
input, nothing could have worse cost performance.

That's why I like well-tailored clothes. Even if they're expensive,
I feel invigorated when I wear them, and since they're long-
lasting they save you money in the long run.

It's my hope that *Ghost Reaper Girl* will be a creation with good
cost performance for you!

Akissa Saiké began working professionally as a manga
artist with the four-volume magical-warrior fantasy series
Kiruto in 2002, which was serialized in *Monthly Shonen
Jump*. *Rosario+Vampire* began serialization in *Monthly
Shonen Jump* in March of 2004 and continued in *Jump SQ*
as *Rosario+Vampire: Season II*. In 2020, he changed his pen
name from Akihisa Ikeda and launched *Ghost Reaper Girl* on
the Jump+ platform.

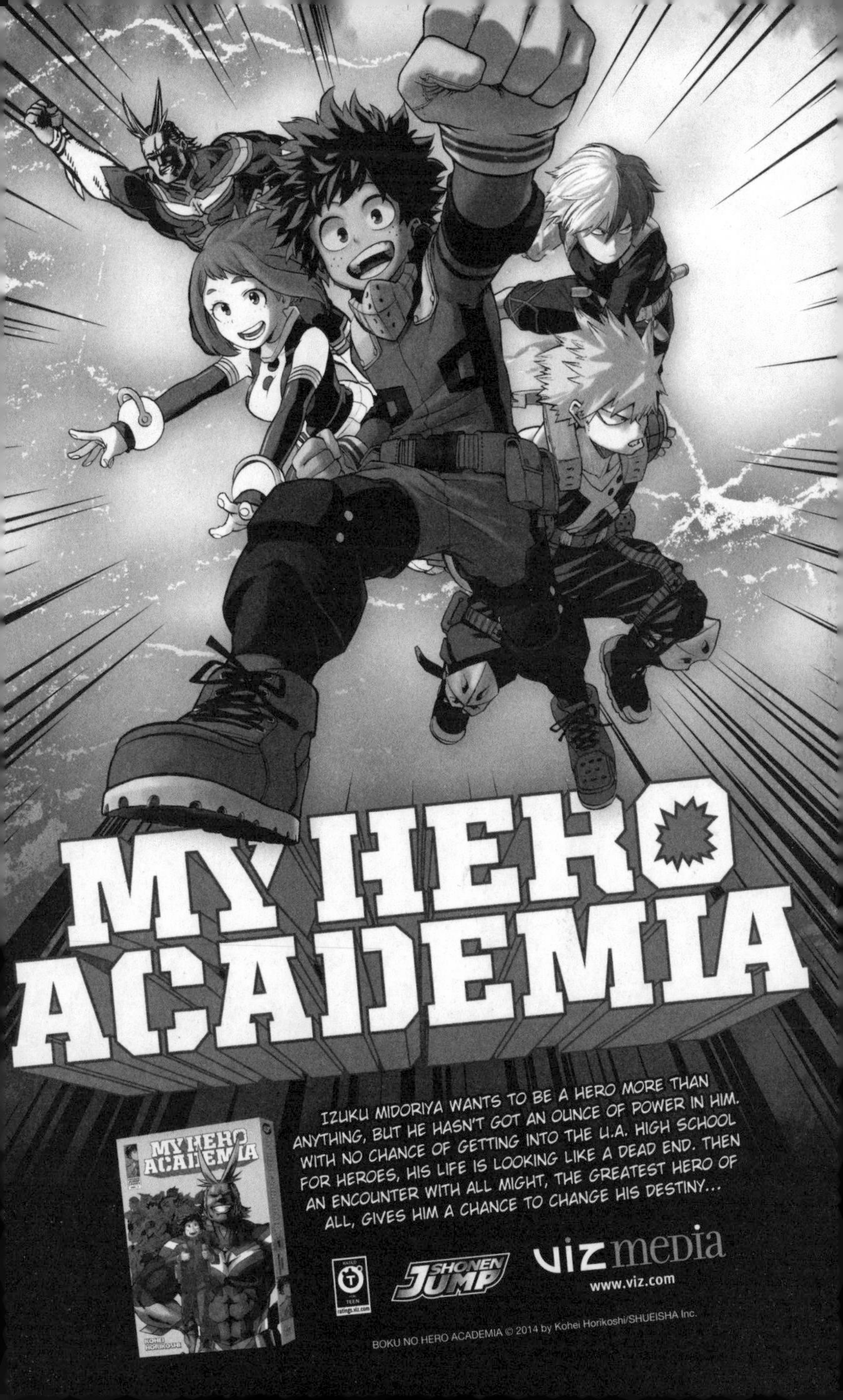
MY HERO ACADEMIA
IZUKU MIDORIYA WANTS TO BE A HERO MORE THAN ANYTHING, BUT HE HASN'T GOT AN OUNCE OF POWER IN HIM. WITH NO CHANCE OF GETTING INTO THE U.A. HIGH SCHOOL FOR HEROES, HIS LIFE IS LOOKING LIKE A DEAD END. THEN AN ENCOUNTER WITH ALL MIGHT, THE GREATEST HERO OF ALL, GIVES HIM A CHANCE TO CHANGE HIS DESTINY...
SHONEN JUMP
viz media
www.viz.com
BOKU NO HERO ACADEMIA © 2014 by Kohei Horikoshi/SHUEISHA Inc.

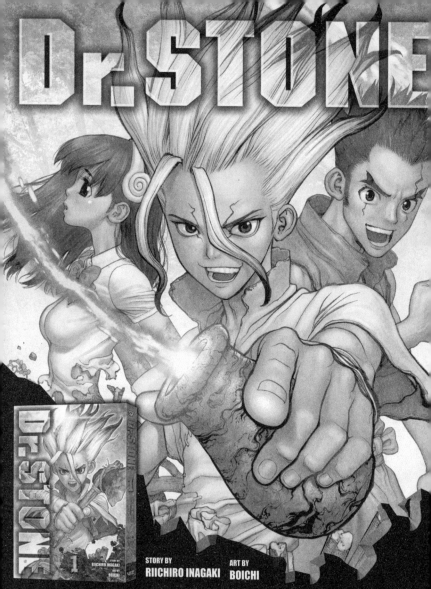

Dr.STONE

STORY BY
RIICHIRO INAGAKI

ART BY
BOICHI

One fateful day, all of humanity turned to stone. Many millennia later, Taiju frees himself from petrification and finds himself surrounded by statues. The situation looks grim—until he runs into his science-loving friend Senku! Together they plan to restart

Story and Art by
KOYOHARU GOTOUGE

In Taisho-era Japan, kindhearted Tanjiro Kamado makes a living selling charcoal. But his peaceful life is shattered when a demon slaughters his entire family. His little sister Nezuko is the only survivor, but she has been transformed into a demon herself! Tanjiro sets out on a dangerous journey to find a way to return his sister to normal and destroy the demon who ruined his life.

Black ✤ Clover

STORY & ART BY YŪKI TABATA

Asta is a young boy who dreams of becoming the greatest mage in the kingdom. Only one problem—he can't use any magic! Luckily for Asta, he receives the incredibly rare five-leaf clover grimoire that gives him the power of anti-magic. Can someone who can't use magic really become the Wizard King? One thing's for sure—Asta will never give up!

www.viz.com

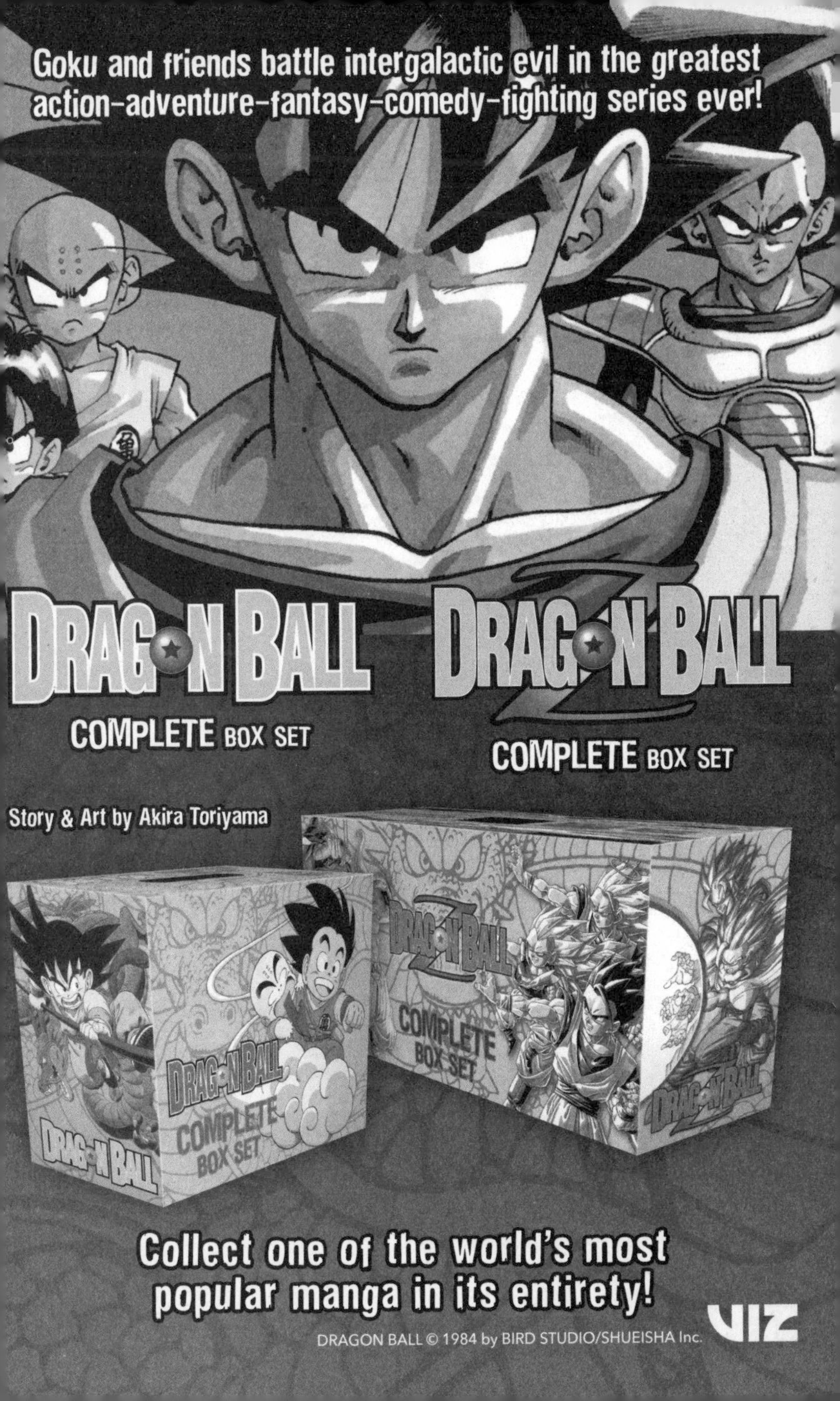

YOU'RE READING
THE
WRONG WAY!

Have evil spirits taken over this manga?!
How can this be the wrong way?

Unlike most manga, *Ghost Reaper Girl*
reads left to right in traditional English
order, as requested by Akissa Saiké,
creator of the series.